John Stott (NT)
Derek Tidball (Bible Themes)

The Message of
Jeremiah

To the memory of

Derek Kidner
(1913 – 2008)

All the royalties from this book have been irrevocably assigned to **Langham Literature**.

Langham Literature is one of the three programmes of **Langham Partnership**, founded by John Stott. Chris Wright is the International Ministries Director.

Langham Literature distributes evangelical books to pastors, theological students and seminary libraries in the Majority World, and fosters the writing and publishing of Christian literature in many regional languages. *Langham Preaching* establishes movements for biblical preaching in many countries, training people in how to study and preach the Bible in their own contexts, with continuous learning in local preachers' networks. *Langham Scholars* provides funding for gifted leaders to study for doctorates in Bible and Theology, and return to their home countries to teach future pastors in seminaries.

For further information, visit www.langham.org

THE BIBLE SPEAKS TODAY

The Message of Jeremiah

Against Wind and Tide

CHRISTOPHER J. H. WRIGHT

IVP Academic

An imprint of InterVarsity Press
Downers Grove, Illinois

InterVarsity Press
P.O. Box 1400, Downers Grove, IL 60515-1426
ivpress.com
email@ivpress.com

Cover design: Cindy Kiple
Image: Marilee Whitehouse-Holm/Getty Images

ISBN 978-0-8308-2439-7 (print)
ISBN 978-0-8308-9636-3 (digital)

Printed in the United States of America ♾

green press *As a member of the Green Press Initiative, InterVarsity Press is committed to protecting*
INITIATIVE *the environment and to the responsible use of natural resources. To learn more, visit*
greenpressinitiative.org.

Library of Congress Cataloging-in-Publication Data
A catalog record for this book is available from the Library of Congress.

P	24	23	22	21	20	19	18	17	16	15	14	13	12	11	10	9	8	7	6	5	4	3
Y	36	35	34	33	32	31	30	29	28	27	26	25	24	23	22	21	20	19	18	17		

Contents

BST | The Bible Speaks Today

GENERAL PREFACE

THE BIBLE SPEAKS TODAY describes three series of expositions, based on the books of the Old and New Testaments, and on Bible themes that run through the whole of Scripture. Each series is characterized by a threefold ideal:

- to expound the biblical text with accuracy
- to relate it to contemporary life, and
- to be readable.

These books are, therefore, not 'commentaries', for the commentary seeks rather to elucidate the text than to apply it, and tends to be a work rather of reference than of literature. Nor, on the other hand, do they contain the kinds of 'sermons' that attempt to be contemporary and readable without taking Scripture seriously enough. The contributors to *The Bible Speaks Today* series are all united in their convictions that God still speaks through what he has spoken, and that nothing is more necessary for the life, health and growth of Christians than that they should hear what the Spirit is saying to them through his ancient – yet ever modern – Word.

ALEC MOTYER
JOHN STOTT
DEREK TIDBALL
Series editors

Author's preface

1984, says the date at the top of some rather shabby and much scribbled-on lecture notes beside the title: *Jeremiah*. That was the year I first taught a full course on the book of Jeremiah, at the Union Biblical Seminary, Pune, India. For several years, successive classes of Indian students worked through the book (or at least selections of it) with me, and marvelled at its breadth, depth, and scale – and at the relevance of Jeremiah's life, struggles, preaching and theology to the contemporary world at all sorts of levels.

Later, as well as writing some notes on its central chapters for Scripture Union, I took an annual 'Speakers Class' of students at All Nations Christian College in which we wrestled with how to preach (again selectively) from the book. More learning and insights enriched my thinking from these men and women who were relating the biblical text to their calling and contexts in Christian mission.

And behind all these efforts over the years has been a personal desire to do for the book of Jeremiah what John Hercus had done for me when I myself was a student – bring the prophet to life. John Hercus published *More Pages from God's Case-book* in 1965. Using the technique of imaginary conversations with Isaiah, Jeremiah and Ezekiel, he vividly brought the world of the biblical characters into direct engagement with the modern world. As I said in the Preface to my BST exposition of Ezekiel, we need not accept all the imaginative reconstruction that Hercus creates (nor did he expect us to), but we can learn from his creative gift of letting the prophets speak for themselves. In some ways, his books were an early form of 'the Bible speaks today', without being directly expository.

Lectures, essays and notes – they all have their place in a teacher's life. But sitting down to write a full-scale exposition of the whole book was a different challenge that has accompanied me now for nearly seven years. I am grateful to all who helped along the way, including all those from whose writings and seminars I have gained more than can ever find its way into a single exposition. I am also

9

grateful to the Langham Partnership for building writing time into my working contract, and to the late John Stott for the use of the Hookses, his writing retreat in Wales where a lot of the work on this book has been done over the years. I owe the subtitle of the book, 'Grace in the end', to Gordon McConville, who gave that title to his fine book on the theology of the Deuteronomic history. It applies with equal if not even greater appropriateness to the whole book of Jeremiah.

While the BST series has a wide range of readers, I have had in mind particularly pastors and preachers whose awesome responsibility it is to feed God's people with God's word regularly. They need, in John Stott's words, to exercise the faculty of 'double-listening' – listening to the word, and listening to the world. We listen to the word of God (from Jeremiah, who more than any other prophet uses that phrase) in order to receive, believe, learn and submit to it. We listen the world in order to understand it and know the contexts into which God still speaks today through his word. Bringing word and world together, bridging the historical and cultural gap, by explaining the first and engaging the second – that is the task of all biblical interpretation and preaching. My hope is that the expositions of the text that follow do enough of the first to help readers understand the text of that word as clearly as possible in the world it was first spoken, and just enough of the second to suggest (rather than dogmatically prescribe) ways in which the word can address issues in today's world (realizing they vary enormously from culture to culture). For that reason, each chapter ends with a few short notes for expository and theological reflection.

The text of the Bible used throughout (unless otherwise specified) is the NIV 2011 version and all proper names follow the spellings used there. Of recent commentaries, Lundbom is among the grandest in sheer scale and depth, while I have consistently found those by Fretheim and Stulman to be the most stimulating and insightful.

This book is a replacement volume, at the request of IVP and Alec Motyer, for the original exposition of Jeremiah in the BST series by the late Derek Kidner. First published in 1987, it was one of the early volumes in the series and space restrictions were perhaps not really adequate for the second longest book in the Bible. Thankfully I have been given greater liberty to try to do it justice in this exposition (remembering that the BST series aims at careful exposition rather than the detailed exegesis that is found in scholarly critical commentaries).

Derek Kidner was a beloved gentle giant of British Old Testament scholarship. He was Warden of Tyndale House when I was a mere theology undergraduate, and my doctoral studies on the Old

10

Testament were pursued there at Tyndale House in the 1970s under his avuncular pastoral care and mischievous sense of humour. I remember driving with him to a seminar at which John Goldingay gave a lecture, and hearing him describe John as 'a bright young thing'. Many of us once-upon-a-time 'bright young things' owe an enormous amount to the example of faithful, winsome, evangelical biblical scholarship that Derek Kidner modelled for us. I dedicate this book respectfully to his memory, hoping he might have considered it a moderately worthy successor for his original volume.

CHRIS WRIGHT
June 2013

11

Abbreviations

ESV	English Standard Version
KJV	King James Version
LXX	Septuagint
MT	Masoretic Text
NAB	New American Bible
NASB	New American Standard Bible
NIV	New International Version
NRSV	New Revised Standard Version
REB	Revised English Bible
TNIV	Today's New International Version

Select bibliography

In the notes, commentaries are referred to by author surname (and date if necessary) only. Other works listed below are referred to by author name and short title.

Commentaries

Allen, L. C., *Jeremiah: A Commentary*, Old Testament Library (Louisville: Westminster John Knox, 2008).

Bright, J., *Jeremiah*, Anchor Bible (Garden City: Doubleday, 1965).

Brueggemann, W., *To Pluck up, To Tear Down: A Commentary on Jeremiah 1-25*, International Theological Commentary (Grand Rapids: Eerdmans, 1988).

——, *To Build, To Plant: A Commentary on Jeremiah 26-52*, International Theological Commentary (Grand Rapids: Eerdmans, 1991).

Carroll, R. P., *Jeremiah: A Commentary*, Old Testament Library (London: SCM, 1986).

Clements, R. E., *Jeremiah*, Interpretation (Atlanta: John Knox, 1988).

Craigie, P. C., Kelley, P. H. and Drinkard, J. F., *Jeremiah 1-25*, Word Biblical Commentary 26 (Dallas: Word, 1991).

Coulibaly, I., 'Jeremiah', in Adeyemo, T. (ed.), *Africa Bible Commentary* (Nairobi: Word Alive and Grand Rapids: Zondervan, 2006).

Dearman, J. A., *Jeremiah and Lamentations*, NIV Application Commentary (Grand Rapids: Zondervan, 2002).

Fretheim, T. E., *Jeremiah*, Smyth and Helwys Bible Commentary (Macon: Smyth and Helwys, 2002).

Harrison, R. K., *Jeremiah and Lamentations*, Tyndale Old Testament Commentaries (Leicester: IVP, 1973).

Holladay, W. L., *Jeremiah 1: A Commentary on the Book of the Prophet Jeremiah Chapters 1-25*, Hermeneia (Philadelphia: Fortress, 1986).

———, *Jeremiah 2: A Commentary on the Book of the Prophet Jeremiah Chapters 26-52*, Hermeneia (Philadelphia: Fortress, 1989).

Keown, G. L., Scalise, P. J. and Smothers, T. G., *Jeremiah 26-52*, Word Biblical Commentary 27 (Dallas: Word, 1995).

Kidner, D., *The Message of Jeremiah: Against Wind and Tide*, The Bible Speaks Today (Leicester: IVP, 1987).

Lalleman, H., *Jeremiah and Lamentations*, Tyndale Old Testament Commentaries (Nottingham: IVP, 2013).

Longman III, T., *Jeremiah, Lamentations*, New International Biblical Commentary (Peabody: Hendrickson, 2008).

Lundbom, J. R., *Jeremiah 1-20: A New Translation with Introduction and Commentary*, Anchor Bible (New York: Doubleday, 1999).

———, *Jeremiah 21-36: A New Translation with Introduction and Commentary*, Anchor Bible (New York: Doubleday, 2004).

———, *Jeremiah 37-52: A New Translation with Introduction and Commentary*, Anchor Bible (New York: Doubleday, 2004).

Martens, E. A., *Jeremiah*, Believers Church Bible Commentary (Scottdale: Herald, 1986).

McKane, W., *A Critical and Exegetical Commentary on Jeremiah*, vol. 1, International Critical Commentary (Edinburgh: T&T Clark, 1986).

———, *A Critical and Exegetical Commentary on Jeremiah*, vol. 2, International Critical Commentary (Edinburgh: T&T Clark, 1996).

Stulman, L., *Jeremiah*, Abingdon Old Testament Commentaries (Nashville: Abingdon, 2005).

Thompson, J. A., *The Book of Jeremiah*, New International Commentary on the Old Testament (Grand Rapids: Eerdmans, 1980).

Other works

Aitken, K. T., 'The oracles against Babylon in Jeremiah 50–51: Structures and perspectives', *Tyndale Bulletin* 35 (1984), pp. 25–63.

Berrigan, D., *Jeremiah: The World, The Wound of God* (Minneapolis: Fortress, 1999).

Bozak, B., *Life 'Anew': A Literary-Theological Study of Jer. 30-31*, Analecta Biblica 122 (Rome: Pontifical Bible Institute, 1991). Referenced in Keown, Scalise and Smothers, pp. 86–87.

Fretheim, T. E., *The Suffering of God: An Old Testament Perspective* (Philadelphia: Fortress, 1984).

Hercus, J., *More Pages from God's Case-Book* (London: IVP, 1965).

Heschel, A. J., *The Prophets* (New York: Harper and Row, 1962).

Holladay, W. L., *Jeremiah: Reading the Prophet in His Time – And Ours* (Minneapolis: Fortress, 1990).

Hunsberger, G., 'Proposals for a Missional Hermeneutic: Mapping the Conversation', available at <http://www.gocn.org/resources/articles/proposals-missional-hermeneutic-mapping-conversation>, 28 January 2009 (accessed 7 June 2013).

McConville, J. G., *Judgment and Promise: An Interpretation of the Book of Jeremiah* (Leicester: Apollos, 1993).

Meadors, E. P., *Idolatry and the Hardening of the Heart: A Study in Biblical Theology* (London and New York: T&T Clark, 2006).

Moberly, R. W. L., *Prophecy and Discernment* (Cambridge: Cambridge University Press, 2006).

Nicholson, E. W., *Preaching to the Exiles: A Study of the Prose Tradition in the Book of Jeremiah* (Oxford: Blackwell, 1970).

Overhold, T. W., *The Threat of Falsehood: A Study in the Theology of the Book of Jeremiah*, Series in Biblical Theology 16 (London: SCM-Canterbury Press, 1970).

Shead, A. G., *A Mouth Full of Fire: The Word of God in the Words of Jeremiah* (Nottingham: Apollos, 2012).

Skinner, J., *Prophecy and Religion: Studies in the Life of Jeremiah* (Cambridge: Cambridge University Press, 1936).

Stott, J. R. W., *The Cross of Christ* (Leicester: IVP, 1986).

Wright, C. J. H., *God's People in God's Land* (Grand Rapids: Eerdmans and Carlisle: Paternoster, 1990).

——, *Deuteronomy*, New International Biblical Commentary Old Testament Series (Peabody: Hendrikson and Carlisle: Paternoster, 1996).

——, *The Message of Ezekiel*, The Bible Speaks Today (Leicester and Downers Grove: IVP, 2001).

——, *Old Testament Ethics for the People of God* (Leicester and Downers Grove: IVP, 2004).

——, *The Mission of God: Unlocking the Bible's Grand Narrative* (Downers Grove: IVP, 2006).

——, *Knowing the Holy Spirit through the Old Testament* (Downers Grove: IVP, 2006).

——, *Knowing God the Father through the Old Testament* (Downers Grove: IVP, 2007).

——, *The God I Don't Understand: Reflections on Tough Questions of Faith* (Grand Rapids: Zondervan, 2008).

——, *The Mission of God's People: A Biblical Theology of the Church's Mission* (Grand Rapids: Zondervan, 2010).

———, '"Prophet to the Nations": Missional Reflections on the Book of Jeremiah', in Grant, J. A., Lo, A. and Wenham, G. J. (eds.), *A God of Faithfulness: Essays in Honour of J. Gordon McConville on his 60th Birthday* (New York and London: T&T Clark, 2011), pp. 112–129.

Introduction

Welcome to the book of the prophet Jeremiah! The book and the man are, of course, inseparably bound together, but it is important to recognize the difference between them.

Jeremiah the prophet addressed the people of Judah and Jerusalem over a forty-year period leading up to the destruction of Jerusalem in 587 BC (and for a few years after that). Jeremiah the book addressed the exiles in the years after the catastrophe, especially the exiles in Babylon where it seems most likely that the present edited form of the book was preserved. And of course, Jeremiah the book has continued to speak to all subsequent generations of God's people, including readers who share the conviction of this series that the Bible speaks today.

First of all, then, we must encounter Jeremiah, man and boy – the prophet who, from his youth to old age, delivered the word of God to the people of Israel at the most terrifying time in all their troubled history. Understanding the times he lived in is essential to understanding his life and message. Then we must strive to grasp the scale of editorial accomplishment that this enormous book represents (it is the second longest book in the Bible, after Psalms). How has it come to us and is there any order and reason in the way it has been put together? And finally, if Jeremiah the man spoke in his day, and if Jeremiah the book still speaks today, in both cases it is because of the God who called the man to speak and commanded the book to be written. So we must encounter the God of Jeremiah, an encounter that should be both profoundly disturbing and ultimately reassuring, as it was for him.

1. Jeremiah and the times he spoke into

a. The era before his call

About one hundred years before Jeremiah was born,[1] Assyria rose to dominate the whole region and its empire lasted until half way through

---

[1] It is widely agreed that the date in Jer. 1:2 (the thirteenth year of Josiah, i.e. 627 BC), was the year of Jeremiah's call (not his birth). We do not know exactly what age he was at the time, other than he called himself 'a youth'. If that means he was between late teens and twenty, then his birth would have been around 645 BC.

his lifetime. The world of Jeremiah's youth was Assyrian. By the time he died, the world was Babylonian. Here's the story in brief.

In 745 BC Tiglath Pileser III became king of Assyria. With abundant ambition and energy he expanded Assyrian power by ruthless force of arms to the west, impacting the whole network of small states in Palestine, including Israel and Judah.

In 735 BC a coalition of Syria and the northern kingdom of Israel was formed to resist Assyria. When Judah refused to join in, the coalition attacked Judah, leading to great panic in Jerusalem.[2] The king of Judah, Ahaz, declined Isaiah's instruction to trust in God for protection and turned instead to Assyria itself for assistance. The result of this disastrous decision was that as soon as the Assyrians had trounced both Syria and Israel, they imposed vassal status on Judah. Judah was subservient to Assyria for decades to come, forced to pay heavy tribute and to pay homage to Assyrian gods.

In 722/1 BC the northern kingdom of Israel rebelled again. The Assyrians attacked once more, destroyed their capital city, Samaria, deported the population and put an end to Israel as an independent state. The region became simply a province of the Assyrian empire.[3]

In 715 BC, Hezekiah came to the throne of Judah. He reversed the policies of Ahaz and introduced radical reforms that were both religious (removing idolatrous shrines and cleansing the temple) and also political (moving to a more anti-Assyrian stance; seeking the re-unification of the northern and southern parts of fractured Israel and Judah).[4]

In 705 BC, Sennacherib became ruler of Assyria, sparking widespread revolt around the west of the empire. Hezekiah, against the advice of Isaiah, joined the revolt in alliance with Egypt. When Sennacherib marched west to put down the rebellion in 701 BC, he invaded and ravaged Judah fiercely[5] and then besieged Jerusalem itself. Panic once again in Jerusalem. This time Isaiah's counsel prevailed, Hezekiah sought the Lord, and the city was spared with a miraculous deliverance (though Hezekiah did in fact submit to heavy tribute).[6]

At the time, it must have seemed like a triumph of Isaiah's wisdom, Hezekiah's faith, and the Lord's protection. And it was all of those things. But it seems to have left a less glorious long-term legacy. Isaiah himself did not seem very impressed with any change in the lives of the people who had experienced God's deliverance. And by

[2] Isa. 7:1 – 8:18.
[3] 2 Kgs 17.
[4] 2 Kgs 18; 2 Chr. 29 – 31.
[5] Possibly reflected in Isa. 1:7–9.
[6] 2 Kgs 18:13 – 19:36.

Jeremiah's time, it seems from his sermon in the temple in Jeremiah 7 that the people had come to believe that God would always preserve and protect his city and temple, no matter what. A complacent faith that the temple was inviolable had become a national self-deception, a falsehood that Jeremiah exposed and denounced almost at the cost of his own life.

In 687 BC, Manasseh came to the throne of Judah. He utterly reversed Hezekiah's policies, submitted fully to Assyrian sovereignty (though he may have had little choice), and enthusiastically embraced Assyrian religion. His long reign (almost half a century) led Judah into its worst period of religious corruption, apostasy and syncretism. Along with that went social oppression, injustice, violence and bloodshed. The biblical historians regarded Manasseh as the most evil king that ever sat on Judah's throne. Indeed, they saw the sins of his reign as justification in themselves for the judgment that later fell on the nation.[7] He was followed by his son Amon, whose reign was even worse but mercifully shorter.

Jeremiah was born some time during the last years of Manasseh's reign, so his childhood was spent in the midst of this advanced state of religious and social evil. Light dawned, however, with the next king, a boy who was probably just a few years older than Jeremiah.

In 640 BC, Josiah became king at the age of 8.[8] At the age of sixteen 'he began to seek the God of his father David',[9] which may mean some kind of personal commitment to the true faith of Israel, but could also indicate a change of national policy towards greater independence for the kingdom David had founded. At the age of twenty-one, in 629 BC, he launched a programme of sweeping reforms that brought about massive religious and social change to his nation. He purged all the non-Yahwistic cults and shrines and all Assyrian idolatrous and occult practices. And he sought to extend his kingdom's boundaries into the former territories of Israel, which of course was a challenge to Assyria, since that land was now a province of Assyria's empire.

Two years later, in 627 BC, when Josiah's reformation was gathering pace, God called Jeremiah to be his prophet. And in 622 BC, when Josiah had been king for eighteen years and Jeremiah a prophet for five, the Book of the Law was discovered in the temple – most likely a version of the book of Deuteronomy – which intensified and accelerated Josiah's reforms.

In 627 BC, the year of Jeremiah's call, another ominous event had happened. Ashurbanipal, the last really strong Assyrian king, died.

---

[7] 2 Kgs 21.
[8] The account of his remarkable reign is in 2 Kgs 22 – 23 and 2 Chr. 34 – 35.
[9] 2 Chr. 34:3.

After that, Assyria weakened on many fronts. Egypt was resurgent in the west. To the north were unpredictable tribes of Cimmerians and Scythians and the rising force of the Medes. And to the south lay the rising ambitions of Babylon under Nabopolassar (father of Nebuchadnezzar), who drove the Assyrians out of Babylon the year after Ashurbanipal died.

What, then, was the state of the world into which Jeremiah was called to speak for God in the year 627 BC? For people who had lived through the previous decades it must have seemed like an enormous transition. Nationally, they were in the throes of a royal reformation that seemed to turn upside down the practices of half a century. The changes would have impacted the priestly family of Jeremiah in his home village of Anathoth, and were probably not popular. Politically, there was a resurgence of nationalism and drive for independence from Assyria – reminiscent of the heyday of Hezekiah but perhaps with greater hope of success now that Assyria was beginning to crumble. And internationally, that very crumbling of the empire that had ruled the region for 150 years must have produced anxieties as to what re-configuration of nations, alliances and empires might emerge from the rubble. It was the end of an era, with some hopes for Judah and considerable unease about the rest of the world.

And God's answer? A nervous youth who thought he couldn't speak. God is good at that kind of surprise. Centuries earlier God's answer had been a nervous octogenarian who also thought he couldn't speak. Yet both of them ended up with God's words in their mouths.[10] And centuries later God's final answer, in a world creaking under a far greater empire than Assyria or Babylon, would be a baby, God's Word become flesh.

b. The years of his ministry

We shall follow the history along with the text, so only a short summary is needed here.[11] As the introduction to the book tells us (1:1–3), Jeremiah's ministry as a prophet spanned the reigns of three major kings, Josiah, Jehoiakim and Zedekiah, along with two others whose reigns were too short to mention (a matter of a few weeks in each case), Jehoahaz and Jehoiachin, both of whom were deposed and exiled by Egypt and Babylon respectively.

Josiah's attempt to assert Judah's independence was fleeting. In the year 609 BC he tried to stop an Egyptian army under Pharaoh Necho II coming to the help of the Assyrians against Babylon. Josiah

[10] Deut. 18:18; Jer. 1:9.
[11] The story can be read in a few well-spent minutes in 2 Kgs 22 – 25.

was defeated and killed in battle with the Egyptians at Megiddo, and for a short time Egypt took control of Judah. They carried off to Egypt the rightful king, Josiah's son and heir Jehoahaz, and placed Jehoiakim on the throne in Jerusalem. During Jehoiakim's reign, the rise of Babylon became unstoppable. Having already defeated Assyria's armies at the battle of Nineveh in 612 BC, the Babylonians under their new leader (soon to become king), Nebuchadnezzar, thrashed the Egyptians at the decisive battle of Carchemish in 605 BC. From that date Babylon was the undisputed imperial power in the region for almost seventy years. And from that date Judah's politics was entirely governed by the question of what stance they should take towards Babylon – submission or rebellion. Jeremiah's answer was unambiguous, unwelcome, and unheeded.

In 597 Jehoiakim chose rebellion. Nebuchadnezzar launched retribution. Jehoiakim died (or was murdered), and his son Jehoiachin became king. Wisely, Jehoiachin surrendered the city, which spared it the ravages it would suffer ten years later, but at the cost of his own throne and freedom. Nebuchadnezzar took Jehoiachin captive to Babylon, along with a whole batch of the ruling classes – the First Deportation, as it is called. Nebuchadnezzar installed another son of Josiah, Zedekiah, as a puppet king in Jerusalem.

The puppet, however, allowed his strings to be pulled in every direction by factions at court during his tumultuous ten-year reign. In the end, in spite of all the pleas and warnings of Jeremiah, Zedekiah too chose the path of rebellion in 589 BC. This time Nebuchadnezzar finished the job. Jerusalem was surrounded and after an eighteen-month siege, the city fell to the Babylonian armies in 587 BC. The Judean army fled. The king was captured, blinded after watching his sons executed in front of him, and carried off in chains to die in Babylon. Many of the people were rounded up and taken off similarly to captivity in exile – the Second Deportation. The unthinkable had happened: the city and temple were destroyed and burnt; the people were driven out of the land.

Jeremiah, who had spent the months of the siege in prison for his allegedly traitorous preaching, was released by the Babylonian officer in charge, and joined a group of poorer people whom the Babylonians allowed to remain in the land. However, after some horrendous post-traumatic violence and further bloodshed, that group left the land and fled to Egypt, taking Jeremiah with them, against his advice and against his will. And there, as far as we know, he died.

In the early years of his ministry Jeremiah probably supported the reforming agenda of Josiah, but he saw little change in the hearts of the people beneath all the outward upheavals. Idolatry reigned.

Cheating and dishonesty were rife. The culture was rotten from top to bottom. He called for genuine repentance, authenticated by actual change of behaviour, and he seems to have done so with some hope that it might avert the calamity he saw coming. But as his appeals were systematically rejected, he set about the task God had given him, to 'uproot and tear down, to destroy and overthrow' (1:10). One after another Jeremiah dismantled and demolished in his preaching the great pillars of Israel's historical faith: election, land, law, covenant, temple and monarchy. The people had betrayed all of these in their rebellion and perversity, to such an extent that putting faith in them was simply self-deception. They had become 'falsehood' – one of the most damning words Jeremiah hurls at the whole religious and political establishment. The future for an unrepentant people trusting in falsehood was bleak beyond what people could believe or bear to hear.

In 605 BC, at the mid-point of his ministry, two pivotal things happened. After the battle of Carchemish, Babylon became the imperial power. From then on the 'foe from the north' that Jeremiah had spoken of became a constant looming threat on the horizon. In that same year, King Jehoiakim chose to listen to all the words of the Lord that Jeremiah had spoken for twenty-three years, written down on a scroll and read aloud in his presence – and then burned them in a fire, slice by slice. His blatant defiance set his kingdom on a course that led inexorably to its final destruction in the fires of 587 BC.

As portrayed by Jeremiah, it was a disaster that was 'nothing less than the collapse of the world, cosmic crumbling, and the end of a culture . . . Long standing institutions associated with God's blessing, cherished belief systems, and social structures that appeared invincible had come to a cataclysmic end'.[12]

It was into that collapsing and collapsed world that Jeremiah was called to speak the words that God would put in his mouth, to weep the tears that flowed from God's own heart, and to bring the gospel of the inexplicable grace and love with which God would create a very different future.

2. Jeremiah and the book he speaks through

a. The scrolls begin

We ought to marvel more than we do at the amazing story of how we got our Bible. The words of Jeremiah in English (or whatever

---

[12] Stulman, p. 1.

language in which you are reading this book and your Bible), printed in ink on the pages of a book or digitally projected on the screen of a tablet or phone, originated in the ancient Hebrew language in the brain cells of a man who lived more than 600 years before Jesus walked the earth, a man who most probably died at a ripe old age in Egypt. His words would have disappeared like his body into the sands of Egypt, but for two things. First, the words he thought and spoke constituted the word of God, and secondly God told him to get them written down. What we read on our page or screen started out (looking very different) as Hebrew words written on a scroll of papyrus by a diligent and courageous secretary as they were dictated by a prophet who was in hiding from political enemies. Twenty-three years of spoken prophecy, committed to the fragile vessel of a papyrus scroll – so fragile indeed that at its third reading on a single day it was sliced and burned by a king who defied and rejected every word it contained. Jehoiakim could defy the word of God, but he could not destroy it. In the end, it would destroy him. The scroll was re-written and began its life-journey through history.

In Jeremiah 36, in fact, we have a most illuminating insight into the Bible in the making. Of course it only describes the origin of one book in the Bible (even if it is almost the longest!), but it may well be illustrative of how other books came into being over the centuries. Our exposition of that chapter explores a number of questions about the event described. It is generally agreed that the scroll written by Baruch in Jeremiah 36 would have contained much of what we now know as Jeremiah 1 – 25; that is, the record of Jeremiah's preaching during the first half of his ministry. The date given for chapter 25 and chapter 36 is the same – the fourth year of Jehoiakim, i.e. 605 BC. As mentioned above, it was a pivotal year, a point of no return in Judah's headlong rush to destruction at the hands of Babylon. It was, therefore, the point at which the word of God which had been *heard* through the words of Jeremiah up to time, was given the *written* format that would endure beyond the living memories of those who first heard the message as words spoken or proclaimed.

In 25:13 we read a reference to 'all the things . . . that are written in this book'. That may be a reference to the scroll produced in chapter 36, but since it specifically refers to what God had said against Babylon, it may perhaps more probably refer to another scroll containing what we now call chapters 46 – 51, the oracles against the foreign nations, including Babylon. In the LXX version of the book of Jeremiah (see below), those oracles are found exactly here – after 25:13a.

After the burning of the original scroll by Jehoiakim, we are told that 'Jeremiah took another scroll and gave it to the scribe Baruch, son of Neriah'. Jeremiah dictated and Baruch laboriously wrote out all those original words – words of Jeremiah, words of God. Then comes a little postscript, the scribe's weary footnote: 'And many similar words were added to them' (36:32). This may imply that the second scroll was even longer than the first, or it may mean that Baruch continued faithfully recording the spoken words of Jeremiah for years to come in additional or longer scrolls. We really don't know. Jeremiah 36 is a fascinating insight and hugely informative, but also tantalizing. However, there is at least a strong likelihood that Baruch continued to write, collect and arrange the words of Jeremiah, and may be responsible for the edited form of the Hebrew book that is preserved in the Masoretic Text (MT).

b. The scrolls diverge

But that version that underlies the MT was not the only scroll. The Septuagint (LXX) edition of Jeremiah in Greek clearly is a translation of an original Hebrew scroll that has some marked divergence from the version preserved in the MT. Fragments of the book of Jeremiah that have been found among the Dead Sea Scrolls show evidence of coming from both traditions – the one we have in the MT, and the one translated into the LXX. So both Hebrew editions of the book must have survived for several centuries, probably preserved in different locations, most likely Babylon and Egypt respectively.

Among many small differences between the MT and the LXX, two major ones stand out. Firstly, the LXX is a lot shorter – approximately one seventh shorter – than the MT. That suggests it was a translation of a Hebrew text that was created and preserved at an early stage, prior to a more lengthy edition of Jeremiah's prophecies being compiled. Secondly, there is a difference in the placement and the order of the oracles against the nations. In the LXX, chapters 46 – 51 (as we have them) come immediately after chapter 25:13a – that is, in the middle of the book, not at the end (as is the case with the books of Isaiah and Ezekiel).[13] Furthermore, the order of the foreign nations is different. In the LXX, Egypt and Babylon come second and third in the list. But in the MT, Egypt comes first (perhaps because that is where Jeremiah's voice is last heard), and significantly Babylon comes in a climactic final position. The finality of God's judgment against Babylon (by the end of the book) thus counter-balances

---

[13] This arrangement also means that the LXX version ends with ch. 45, Jeremiah's word to Baruch. This may be further indication that behind the LXX translation lies an early Hebrew scroll that was first compiled by Baruch, with this ending constituting a kind of 'signature'.

God's use of Babylon as the agent of his judgment against Judah (throughout the book), and concludes the whole book with the hope of deliverance and restoration after judgment.[14]

How can we account for these different versions? A huge amount of text-critical study has been done on this question and the major commentaries provide surveys of the complex issues and proposed solutions. Andrew Shead proposes a simple but plausible reconstruction of the process as follows:

> After Jeremiah went with Baruch to Egypt (Jer. 43:4–7) an edition of the book of Jeremiah was produced for local circulation, assembled and carefully edited from the written records Baruch had been collecting over the years [since the scroll of ch. 36]. This edition was preserved and transmitted, and eventually became the source of the Greek translation of Jeremiah known as the Septuagint. It remains the canonical version of the book in the Eastern Church to this day.
>
> . . .
>
> That was not the final version of the book, however. A new, revised and expanded edition – about one seventh longer than the LXX – was created from the same source material (plus one or two new sources such as Jer. 33:14–26). The name of Seraiah, Baruch's brother, has been linked to this edition by some scholars.[15] Its intended audience seems not to have been the local Egyptian community, but the exilic community in Babylon. After the Babylonian exiles returned and the biblical canon began to take final shape, it was this edition of Jeremiah that was included in the Prophets, and that eventually became part of the Masoretic Hebrew text (MT) that forms the basis of every English Bible version in common use today.[16]

Shead goes on to reflect on this fact that there were two early editions of the scroll of Jeremiah, both expressing the word of God through the words of the prophet:

---

[14] In this respect the present form of the book finds an echo in Revelation where the description of the final destruction of Babylon (using imagery drawn from Jeremiah along with prophetic oracles against Babylon) comes immediately before the description of the final redemption of God's people and all creation.

[15] We know that Seraiah, Baruch's brother, took the scroll containing the oracle against Babylon (Jer. 50 – 51) to Babylon (51:59–64). If there was communication between Jeremiah and Baruch in Egypt and Seraiah and the exiles in Babylon, it is possible that the revised and longer edition reached Babylon by that connection and became the starting point of the Babylonian transmission of the text.

[16] Shead, *A Mouth Full of Fire*, p. 49.

Jews and Christians in the New Testament period and before do not seem to have been troubled by this question and their attitude seems to have been to accept as Scripture whatever version they had to hand, or whatever version best lent itself to their purpose in citing it. If we follow the example of the New Testament authors, we ought to be happy to receive and read the Greek version of Jeremiah as the word of God. Yet at the same time I would suggest that the Masoretic version has a special place as Jeremiah's word *to us*. Not only was it his last and final version, but its target audience, the exilic community in Babylon, was in Jeremiah's eyes the one group of people with a future in the divine plan of salvation. The seeds of the church were planted in Babylonian soil.[17]

c. The final structure

If, as seems very likely, the fuller MT form of the text (which of course is the text translated in our Bibles and used in this BST exposition) was produced as a carefully edited, expanded and somewhat rearranged version of an earlier scroll that underlies the LXX, then we should assume that the person or persons responsible for that newer scroll had reasons for the way they ordered and structured the material. Unfortunately much modern scholarship has assumed the opposite – that the book is a rather chaotic assembly of texts with no apparent chronological or thematic order. Certainly, compared to the book of Ezekiel, with its carefully dated oracles marching along in almost completely consistent chronological order, the book of Jeremiah seems to skip backwards and forwards in time, from one king's reign to another and back again, in a manner guaranteed to confuse the casual reader. But chronology is not the only way to organize a text and casual is not the best way to read one.

The most noticeable change between the LXX and the MT is the placing of the oracles against the nations. This seems to have been done with deliberate intent and theological significance. At whatever point they were delivered in Jeremiah's ministry (chronologically), by gathering them all at the end (editorially), and climaxing with the destruction of Babylon, the book ends on a note of hope for the restoration and future of God's people. And in view of the pre-dominant message of judgment in the bulk of the book, that is no minor point. It is a deliberate theological statement consistent with that portion of Jeremiah's commission that was 'to build and to

[17] Shead, ibid, p. 51.

plant', and with the message of hope placed earlier in the book in the Book of Consolation (chs. 30 – 33).

More recent scholars are far more prepared to discern structural connections between groups of chapters, thematic links in otherwise disparate oracles, and plausible reasons for the kind of 'circling back' that happens especially between chapters 25 and 39.[18] Even though the broad storyline of the book progresses inexorably towards the final collapse of Judah under Zedekiah, we keep 'starting again' with events or sayings that go back to the early reign of Jehoiakim. The temple sermon (so prominently placed early in ch. 7) happened then (ch. 26). The halfway-point warning was given then (ch. 24). The burning of the scroll happened shortly after (ch. 36). It is as if we are being told that every downward slip on the slope to ruin was an unfolding of the course that Jehoiakim set when he led his people in determined rejection of God's word. This is not just random mixing of dates. This is a message reinforced by repetition and by revisiting the place where it all went so horribly wrong.

The most obvious structuring of the whole book can be seen in the two halves that are balanced on either side of chapter 25. Chapter 25 is clearly a 'hinge' chapter that first looks back to all that has gone before in chapters 1 – 24 (25:1–7). Then it effectively 'programmes' the rest of the book by looking forward to the inevitable judgment on Judah that God will bring through the agency of Nebuchadnezzar and Babylon (25:8–11), followed by God's promised judgment on Babylon itself and indeed on all the earth (25:12–38).

God's words to Jeremiah at his call in chapter 1 also provide a structural and thematic framework for the book. He was commissioned 'to uproot and tear down, to destroy and overthrow, to build and to plant' (1:10). These phrases are repeated throughout the book, and reflect the balance of material – twice as much judgment as restoration, as we might put it. But they also reflect the order of the book. In chapters 1 – 24 the message of Jeremiah is almost entirely one of relentless tearing down. The prophet systematically dismantles all the main pillars of the edifice of Israel's faith. By their persistent rebellion and unrepentant wickedness, the people have nullified the things they trusted in. The terrible and terrifying reality was that they had turned the great truths of their faith into deception and lies. Over these chapters Jeremiah effectively undermines all the old foundations of their security: their redemption from Egypt and the gift of land; the temple; the Sinai covenant and law; their election from among the

---

[18] I found the work of Stulman and Shead particularly helpful in seeing coherent blocks of material, thematic structuring and plausible reasons for the shaping of certain texts, where previous study has often seen only haphazard stitching of collections and additions.

nations; the king on David's throne. All of these are 'attacked' – not because they were not 'true', but because they had become the false security of a people determined to defy the very reason for them and the spiritual, ethical and social implications of them.

But in the second half of the book, although the voice of judgment is by no means muted, the word of grace beyond judgment is heard. The hammer of Babylon must fall, but Babylon's tyranny will be limited to seventy years, and then Israel's fortunes would change. But the future would not simply be a return to the *status quo ante*. God would do a new thing. The note of newness is sounded or implied: a new exodus, a new wilderness journey, a new entry into the land, a new king of righteousness, above all a new covenant.

Other than these macro-structural features, we will point out smaller thematic and structural connections as we work through the sections of the book in our exposition. The point to make here is: we may not always be able to say with certainty what reasons the compiler(s) of the scroll of Jeremiah had in mind in putting one thing alongside another and arranging the whole in the way we now have it, but we should at least respect their intelligence and integrity by making some effort to discern those reasons where we can by careful, not casual, attention to the text.

3. Jeremiah and the God he spoke for

a. The passion of God[19]

Not for nothing has Jeremiah been known down the centuries as 'the weeping prophet'. His book is drenched in tears. But whose tears? Naturally when we read texts that speak in the first person of weeping, mourning and crying out, we imagine the prophet himself giving vent to his grief in those ways. And we can be sure that he did. But as we shall see, in many of those texts the words of the prophet and the words of God blend together so closely that it is difficult to be sure who the weeping speaker is. It is not merely that Jeremiah speaks God's words; he also feels God's feelings. The prophet embodies the message to such an extent that his whole person and being – thoughts, feelings, words, actions – vibrate with the whole range of its emotional pitch and tone. And grief is only one of those emotions.

The most obvious and sustained emotion that we will encounter is anger. Open the book at random and the chances are you'll land

---

[19] The classic study of divine pathos in the prophets, and especially in Jeremiah, is Heschel, *The Prophets*.

on a passage in which God is giving voice to his anger against the people of Israel and his judgment on them, declaring that they will reap the consequences of the evil they have sown. Such language, and the passion that surges through it, is unmissable and as unpalatable to us in reading it as it must have been to the Israelites on first hearing it.

But what kind of anger is this? Is it the rage of someone simply lashing out vengefully at anyone who gets in the way? Is it the hot temper of a cosmic bully? Not at all, and it is very important to get this point clear. Read the text with care and sensitivity and see that the anger of God is the anger of suffering love. It is anger within a deep relationship that he passionately cares for. It is the anger, sodden with grief and pain, that wrestles with profound love in the heart of a betrayed husband or a rejected father. Jeremiah portrays the relationship between God and Israel using both of those images: husband-wife and father-son. Both relationships have the capacity to generate the deepest and most fulfilling love we can enjoy at human level. Both likewise have the capacity to generate the deepest and most agonizing experience of grief and anger when they are abused and betrayed. When love is betrayed, there is a perfectly appropriate response of jealousy and anger – not blind rage but open-eyed rejection and repulsion of whatever or whoever has invaded the relationship and threatened its peace and joy.

It is strange that some theologians and preachers see something incompatible or irreconcilable in the Bible's portrayal of God's anger and God's love. Anger and love can co-exist simultaneously in a human heart; why not in God's? I recall listening, with my wife, to a distraught woman telling us about the inexplicably hurtful actions of her husband. She was clearly angry against him for his behaviour. But through her tears she cried, 'But I love him so much and I just want him back.' Her anger and love in a way protected and validated each other. If she had not been angry at his behaviour, it would have shown she did not love him enough to care anyway. If she had not loved him as she did, she would not have felt anger at his betrayal of their relationship. If God were *not* angry at the evil that destroys human life, could he be said to love us? If God did *not* love us so much, why would he get angry against all that threatens to destroy us, including our own sinful rebellion and folly?

Again and again you will notice as we work through the challenging chapters to follow that outbursts of anger dissolve quickly into sobbing tears, or the wistfulness of longing love. God pleads with the people again and again to turn and change, so that the judgment that he and Jeremiah could foresee need not fall. As the people steadily stiffen their hearts to reject and resist all such appeals, the response of Jeremiah and God shifts from angry exposure of the people's evil and self-deception, to horror and grief in contemplating the awful fate that lay ahead of them – the traumas of invasion, siege, starvation, disease, slaughter, captivity, exile. God and his prophet suffer together in the anticipation and the actuality of the disaster.

It is Ezekiel, not Jeremiah, who tells us that God takes no pleasure in the death of anyone, not even the wicked,[20] but Jeremiah would have agreed. The outworking of God's judgment through the human agency of a Nebuchadnezzar would be the outworking of the consequences of Israel's rebellious, wicked and ultimately foolish persistence in doing evil. And when that judgment fell, God could scarcely bear to watch (see the section on Jer. 39). And it is Isaiah, not Jeremiah, who tells us that during the Egyptian oppression, 'in all their distress [God] too was distressed',[21] but again Jeremiah would have agreed. God suffered in and with his people, even though their suffering (in the exile, unlike in Egypt) was caused by their own evil bringing God's judgment upon them.

Reflecting like this on the suffering of God may cause difficulty for some who would raise questions about the *impassibility* of God. This classic ancient doctrine affirms that God cannot 'suffer' in the form that our sufferings take – often imposed upon us against our will, often connected to emotions and passions that rapidly change and easily get out of control. God is not the passive victim of suffering that we could inflict upon him nor is God subject to uncontrollable or transient fits of emotion in any one direction or another. He is, in that sense, 'without passions' just as much as he is without parts or body, to quote the Westminster Confession of Faith.

However, rightly understood, 'impassibility' does not mean (though it is often misrepresented to mean) that God has no feelings or affections, that he is as unfeeling as an iceberg. Such an unbiblical view would rule out God's love, compassion, mercy and delight, as much as God's suffering or God's anger. And very clearly the Bible teaches that all of these words speak of something true and real in the being and character of God.

We easily understand that when the Bible uses *anthropomorphic* language (e.g. about God's mouth, or hand, or eyes and ears, etc.) we need to do two things. On the one hand we know that we cannot take such language with simple literalism (God does not have those body parts as we humans do). Yet on the other we know that we cannot just dismiss them as mere metaphors or figures, lacking any

---

[20] Ezek. 18:23, 32; 33:11.
[21] Isa. 63:9.

actual reality in God as God truly is. They do communicate capacities and actions of God that are real and true of God, but do so in terms of human capacities and actions (the only way we can begin to grasp their meaning).

In the same way, when the Bible uses *anthropopathic* language (e.g. God feeling joyful, angry, regretful, disappointed, frustrated, delighted, compassionate, grieved, nostalgic, longing, etc.), as Jeremiah does so abundantly, we have to do the same two things. On the one hand we do not imagine that God is *subject* to emotional highs and lows, hurricanes and doldrums, in just the same way that we are in our psychological, neurological and temperamental humanity, reacting to the ever-changing circumstances that impinge upon us from day to day. And yet on the other hand we cannot dismiss this rich and pervasive biblical language as mere rhetorical emotionalism. Such language speaks truth (it is after all the language of the Bible). We are made in the image of God, and while God may not experience the 'passions' that we call emotions in the same way we do within our created, fallen world, nevertheless the emotions we experience and name do reflect truth about what goes on within the being of God. God truly and really *feels* ('without passions'), just as much as God truly and really thinks (without a brain) and truly and really sees (without eyes). The traditional doctrine of impassibility did not mean that God is aloof, uncaring, unfeeling, unaffected by what happens in his world. Such a view simply could not be compatible with the massive biblical teaching that God cares at the deepest affective level about his creation. Nor could such a view stand for one second at the foot of the cross of Christ. And the Bible affirms that included among what God feels is the suffering and pain of rejected love, anger against evil, compassion and love for his creatures.[22] We have to put human words to these things. That is what scriptures are for. And the Scriptures were God's idea.

So in the book of Jeremiah (as in so many other places in the Bible) our own emotions are assailed in multiple directions by the sheer passion of the poetry and prose with which Jeremiah spoke *God's* words to his people. If *we* know what it feels like to experience such things, if *we* can identify at a human level with such passion, pain, grief, anger, longing, hope and joy, then we can be confident that the words we (and Jeremiah) use to describe such feelings are true in some infinitely deeper or higher dimension of God's 'Godness'. We feel such things in the transient turmoil of our created human emotions. God feels them – and feels them even more really than we

---

[22] See, for example, Rob Lister, *God is Impassible and Impassioned: Toward a Theology of Divine Emotion* (Wheaton: Crossway and Leicester: Apollos, 2012).

do – in the infinite and eternal consciousness of God's own being and character.

b. The word of God

'Then the whole remnant of Judah . . . will know whose word will stand – mine or theirs' (44:28). These are almost the very last words God spoke through Jeremiah, in Egypt. In a sense they sum up the battle of the whole book between the word and will of God and the words and will of the people. And at the end of the day (and of the book) we know which word did indeed prevail: 'the word of the LORD that came to Jeremiah . . .'

It would be easy to skip over that last phrase since it occurs so often and fail to appreciate how much prominence the book of Jeremiah gives to the word and the words of God. Indeed, it is forcefully argued by Andrew Shead that the word of God is not only the major 'character' in the whole book, but fulfils a structural and thematic role in the arrangement of its content. Shead traces major sections of the book of Jeremiah around the themes of 'Word and speaker' (Jeremiah), 'Word and hearers' (the people), 'Word and power' (in the transforming message of future hope and restoration), and 'Word and permanence' (the transition from spoken word to written Scripture).

Even if Shead's proposal possibly exaggerates the extent to which the book of Jeremiah intentionally traces the 'mission' of the word of God through those years of Israel's history, his analysis of how the word of God functioned, how it was delivered by (even embodied in) Jeremiah, the response it received, the effect it accomplished, is rich and convincing. And the statistics certainly strengthen his case that this is a massively important element in the theology of the book as a whole. Consider, for example: [23]

- The *dbr* terms in noun and verb form (word, words, speak) occur more frequently in Jeremiah than any other book in the Old Testament – even more than Deuteronomy, where 'word' vocabulary is also prominent and clearly influential on Jeremiah.
- 'Word' (singular) occurs three times more often in Jeremiah than in Isaiah, and 'words' (plural) five times more often.
- Jeremiah uses 'word' formulas more often than any other prophet, in three forms: the Messenger Formula ('thus says the LORD'); the Narrative Formula ('the word of the LORD came to Jeremiah saying . . .'); and what Shead calls the Disjunctive

---

[23] Shead, *A Mouth Full of Fire*, pp. 44–46.

Formula (not a sentence, but a heading that is used to mark major structural breaks in the narrative and sections of the book, e.g. at 1:1; 7:1; 11:1; 18:1; 21:1; 25:1; 30:1; 35:1; 40:1; 44:1).

• The small phrase, 'oracle of the LORD' (sometimes translated: 'declares the LORD') occurs 167 times in Jeremiah, which accounts for sixty per cent of its use in the whole Old Testament.

A repeated accusation levelled at the people is that for generation after generation they simply would not *listen* to the word of God. And a major source of conflict in the book is around the question of whether Jeremiah or the other prophets in Jerusalem had heard and were speaking the true word of God. Likewise a major source of anxiety for Jeremiah was whether and when God would vindicate his own word – even though it caused Jeremiah unbearable pain when he contemplated what that would actually mean for his people. And conversely a major source of comfort to Jeremiah in such times was the reassurance given at his commissioning, and repeated at key points afterwards, that God was 'watching' over his word to fulfil it (1:12). Kings could lock up the prophet, but God's word still soared free (ch. 32). Kings could burn a scroll, but the word lived on (ch. 36). The people could be a thousand miles away, but God's word could reach them (ch. 29). Babylon might rule the world, but God's word would sink it (51:62–64).

The book begins and ends (apart from the appendix of ch. 52) with the *inclusio*, 'the words of Jeremiah' (1:1; 51:64), and the first of these identifies the words of Jeremiah as being at one and the same time 'the word of the LORD'. Since the phrase embraces the whole book in between those 'bookends', the implication is that we hear the word of God not only in those parts of the text where we hear/read the spoken words of Jeremiah the prophet, but in all the rest of the material in Jeremiah the book – narrative, dialogue, actions, arguments, etc. All that Jeremiah said, thought, felt, did and suffered, as recorded in the book of Jeremiah, constitute 'the words of Jeremiah', and thereby, the word of God. We receive the book as a whole as both. That's what it means to call it Scripture. And that is why, as such, 'the Bible Speaks Today'.

c. The sovereignty of God

The book of Jeremiah presents not only a battle of words but also a battle of wills. From the very first chapter Jeremiah and the readers of his book are warned that this will be the case. God will state his purpose, and the people will resist it. Jeremiah will need to be 'a fortified city, an iron pillar, a bronze wall' (1:18) in order faithfully to declare the sovereign will of God in the face of relentless opposition. The sovereignty of God drives the book forward at various levels.

(i) God is sovereign over Israel

Though the imagery of the betrayed husband and rejected father might suggest God was the impotent victim of the sins of his people, the reality was very different. Such images could portray the suffering love of God because of his passionate commitment to the relationship between God and Israel, the relationship they were so determined to trample on. But God was not imprisoned or paralyzed by the sin of the people. His ultimate purpose would prevail *over* them in judgment, *for* them in restoring grace, and *through* them for the sake of the nations. Even though he could change his plans according to their response (in 'responsive sovereignty' – see the section on ch. 18), as the divine Potter it would be his sovereign intention that would ultimately be realized.

(ii) God is sovereign over the nations

The lesson of the potter applied to 'any nation' (18:7–10), and indeed, Jeremiah was appointed as 'a prophet to the nations' (1:5). In the course of the book God has words for all the surrounding nations; not only in the oracles against the nations collected in chapters 46 – 51, but elsewhere, whether in condemnation (e.g. 25:15–26), or in the offer of restoration (e.g. 12:14–17). But above all, God's sovereignty is seen most vividly in relation to Babylon and Nebuchadnezzar. Just as Isaiah had portrayed Assyria as a stick in the hand of God that he was using to punish Israel, so Jeremiah portrays Nebuchadnezzar as God's agent of judgment. The Babylonians would come, but it was the God of Israel who would summon them. Nebuchadnezzar would follow his own arrogant imperial ambitions, but he would do so as 'my servant' – the one who would carry out the will of the God of Israel at that moment of history (chs. 25 and 27). So whereas, in the worldview of nations like Babylon, YHWH was the god of a small territory defeated, destroyed and digested by the world's most powerful empire of the day, in reality YHWH was the God who was directing the whole drama.

(iii) God is sovereign over all creation

The God who rules the nations also rules creation (ch. 10), and cares for it. References to the natural order are frequent in Jeremiah. He laments the suffering and destruction of creation that accompanies human evil and he rejoices in the abundance of creation that will accompany God's redeeming and restoring grace. Creation bears witness to the unnaturalness of human perversity, and to the consistency and eternity of God's faithfulness.

(iv) God is sovereign over all time

God sovereignly interprets Israel's past – exposing how Israel's covenant-breaking rebellion had turned the great truths of their historical faith into falsehood and deception. God sovereignly interprets Israel's present. When they thought all was well God warned them of the disaster to come. When they saw themselves as victims of Nebuchadnezzar's ethnic cleansing, God told them '*I* carried you into exile'. When they saw Babylon only as the place of weeping and vengeance (Ps. 137), God told them to see it as a place of prayer and welfare-seeking – for Babylon itself (29:7). And God sovereignly interprets Israel's future, as one of hope beyond judgment, of grace beyond logic, of blessing to the nations beyond their own borders.

d. The mission of God

To say that the Lord God of Israel is sovereign over Israel, all nations, all creation and all time, is to contemplate the contours of God's mission. The Bible as a whole presents the grand narrative that runs from creation to new creation. God's plan and purpose (or God's mission) is to bring the whole of creation, spoiled and broken by human and satanic evil, into unity in Christ, through whom he has accomplished its reconciliation by the blood of the cross.[24] And that new creation will be populated by people from every tribe and nation and language and people, who will have been redeemed through the Lord Jesus Christ, in fulfilment of God's promise to Abraham that through him and his descendants all nations on earth would enter into God's blessing.[25] We can read the whole Bible from this missional perspective, seeing all the Scriptures as the witness to, and deposit of, the great saving mission of God, spanning the whole of creation, directing the whole of history, and centred on the whole gospel of Jesus Christ.[26]

[24] Eph. 1:9–10; Col. 1:20.
[25] Rev. 7:9–10; Gen. 12:1–3; 18:18; 22:15–18.
[26] I have explored this missional hermeneutic of the whole Bible extensively in Wright, *The Mission of God*. In 2008 George Hunsberger surveyed the way the phrase 'missional hermeneutic of scripture' is being used in contemporary scholarship, and identified four distinct usages: the missional direction or framework of the biblical narrative; the missional purpose of the biblical texts; the missional locatedness of readers of the Bible; and the missional engagement of the gospel with cultures. I made use of these categories in an essay on missional reflections on the book of Jeremiah (see Wright, 'Prophet to the Nations'). The following paragraphs are an extract from that more extensive survey of the topic.

The mission of God is what fills the gap between, on the one hand, the spoiled creation and the nations scattered in rebellion of Genesis 3–11, and on the other hand, the nations gathered in worship and the new creation of Revelation 21–22.

Thus, God's election of Abraham and gift of a land is instrumental in God's plan for the blessing of all nations and the whole earth. The sequence of election, redemption, covenant and land-gift is thus paradigmatic for the wider story of God's multinational people, redeemed to inhabit the earth.

But the failure of Old Testament Israel, and the broken covenant, led to both *judgment* (in the immediate history of Old Testament Israel – exile), and also to *future hope* (the eschatology of restoration for Israel and ingathering of the nations). This is a theme that is found in poetic anticipation in Deuteronomy 32, but gathers clarity and emphasis in the prophets, especially during and after the exile itself. All this prepares the way for the New Testament proclamation of the embodiment and fulfilment of God's mission through Israel in the person and accomplishment of Jesus of Nazareth, and the New Testament mission of the church in the power of the Spirit to accomplish the ingathering of the nations by going to them with the message of the gospel.

Where does the book of Jeremiah fit into this great matrix? Although no single passage expresses the whole sweep of the scenario sketched above, it is clear that Jeremiah endorses its broad contours in at least four ways. He sees the wider purpose of Israel's election; he exposes the reality of failure and judgment; he holds out hope for restoration; and he envisages blessing for the nations alongside the hope of Israel.[27]

In 13:1–11 Jeremiah shows that God's purpose in binding Israel to himself in covenant relationship was like wearing an attractive piece of clothing that is for God's own 'renown and praise and honour' – a triplet that is found in Deuteronomy 26:19 (and again at Jer. 33:8–9) to describe Israel's position among the nations. The reality of Israel's failure and God's judgment is everywhere apparent in the book. Israel was failing to fulfil the purpose of their election and thus frustrating God's wider mission in the world. However, when God would act in restoration and renewal of Israel, the impact would be felt among the nations. In fact, the same offer of restoration on the basis of repentance is made to the other nations as well as to Israel. YHWH's sovereignty over the nations can be experienced redemptively, not only through historical judgments (12:14–17).

---

[27] Wright, 'Prophet to the Nations', pp. 114–115.

Though it is nowhere as prominent in Jeremiah as in the soaring vision of Isaiah, the universal dimension of God's dealings with Israel for the sake of the nations is certainly expressed. In 4:1–2, Jeremiah sees that Israel's repentance would have implications, not merely in sparing them God's judgment, but in furthering God's agenda for the nations in fulfilment of his promise to Abraham. The same note (the nations coming to worship YHWH) is buried in 3:17 in the midst of prolonged appeals to Israel to repent. The nations and the earth itself, who were summoned to witness God's covenant wrath against Israel in action (6:18–19), are summoned again in the same terms to witness God's covenant love redeeming them once more (31:10). And when that time of cleansing and forgiveness comes, then God's 'renown, joy, praise and honour' will be known to the ends of the earth (33:8–9). For YHWH is assuredly not the God of Israel only, but of all nations on earth (10:6–7, 10).

So, as one might say, Jeremiah knew the story he was in. Even in his dismantling of the people's false security in what that story told them, even in the midst of the climactic calamity of 587 BC, and especially in his vision of a future filled with hope and blessing for Israel, Jeremiah was aware of the universality of the God of Israel, and the scope of his global mission. His twin call to Israel, on the one hand to abandon their idolatry and return to the radical monotheism of their covenant faith, and on the other hand to change their ways and be shaped by the covenant ethic, both served this missional agenda that flows through the whole Bible. The mission of the one true, living, creator and redeemer God calls God's people to be committed exclusively to know him and make him known, and to live in this world in ethical distinctiveness. This is as much at the heart of what it means, in faith and life, to declare that Jesus is Lord, as it was for Israel to declare that YHWH is God in heaven above and the earth beneath and there is no other and to love him with all their heart, and soul and strength by walking in his ways.[28] Jeremiah is a sustained summons to missional monotheism and missional ethics.

So while Jeremiah tackles Israel's idolatry head on, with only sidelong glances at the nations around, those glances are signifi-cant. The need for Israel to return to the radical monotheism of their covenant faith was not just a matter of getting them to believe in the right God. It was an essential part of their very reason for existence – to serve the mission of God to make himself known to the nations.

[28] Deut. 4:39; 6:4–9.

Recalling Israel to their covenant monotheism was thus profoundly missional in its *shaping* function. Those who refuse to worship the one living God are simply mis-shapen. They cannot fittingly participate in God's mission to be known to the nations if they themselves participate in the futile idolatry of the nations.

. . .

The missional purpose of the text of Jeremiah, then, was to bring Israel back to their covenant shape. But the longer-distant purpose of *that* was to enable them to fulfil their mission of bringing blessing to the nations. In other words, here as in so many places in the Old Testament, there is a fundamental, inextricable connection between the ethical quality of life of the people of God and their mission to the nations. There is no biblical mission without biblical ethics, and Jeremiah would agree.[29]

Another important dimension of any missional reading of biblical texts must be to consider what has been called the 'missional locatedness' of the readers. In the exposition to follow we shall notice that the edited scroll of Jeremiah addressed the exiles and challenged them to respond to God's word there and see the missional potential of their location (even if it was not permanent; see especially ch. 29). But modern Christian readers have their own missional location and this calls us to engage the text with our contexts. Throughout our exposition, and particularly in the notes at the end of each chapter, we shall encourage such reflection. But in brief:

There are many ways in which the world into which Jeremiah spoke is reflected in today's international world, and the message that Jeremiah brought has continuing sharpness. So our missional reading of Jeremiah engages the text from the perspective of the many concerns of our own context, which find matching concerns in the text. All of the list below could be teased out in fruitful discussion, relating text to modern context in richly suggestive and challenging ways. We can do no more than mention them here, rather than explore them in depth. That should be the task of biblical preaching and teaching in the community of the church.

Here then are some features of the book of Jeremiah that deserve missiological reflection in our world.

- The international scene: collapse of an old world order, fear over new threats to world stability.

[29] Wright, 'Prophet to the Nations', pp. 122–124.

- Religious confusion among God's own people: Josiah's reformation had produced enormous social and religious change and stress, but there was continuing idolatry, and misplaced nationalism posturing as patriotism.
- Social evils abounded: inequality, cheating, injustice, immorality.
- Political abuse of power to stifle dissent: prophets who spoke the truth were silenced; Jeremiah, for opposing the official position of the political and religious establishment, was treated with hostility, ostracism, false accusation, physical abuse and even death threats.
- Abuse of religious power: false prophets and corrupt priests cushioned the government from the voice of God or conscience, and colluded in social evils and immorality.
- The message of God's sovereignty in history: in the midst of all the confusion, Jeremiah affirmed that God was ultimately in control, including contemporary events, and saw his hand even in the attack upon the homeland; the moral inevitability of judgment is an uncomfortable theme.
- The mission of God's people even in exile: even after the collapse of their whole world and culture under God's judgment, God had a mission for his scattered people – to carry on with the Abrahamic mandate of being a blessing among the nations, seeking their welfare and praying for them.
- Grace in the end: as with other prophetic books, Jeremiah is finally a hopeful book, for it sees restoration after judgment, and, in the promise of a new covenant, sets the scene for the unquenchable hope that undergirds Christian mission to the ends of the earth and the end of the world.

So, yes, in our own missional locatedness in the 21st century, we can read the words and themes of Jeremiah against the background of his day and discern multiple messages of power and relevance to our own. Such reading gives biblical missiology a sharp prophetic cutting edge that is vital to all our engagement with our world for God's sake and in Christ's name.[30]

e. The victory of God

'Finally a hopeful book.' Is it? After all, in a book so full of conflict, of warring words and a battle of wills, who wins in the end?

[30] Wright, 'Prophet to the Nations', pp. 125–126.

Nebuchadnezzar wins, in a sense. Successive kings of Israel thrust their puny rebellious fists in his face and he smashed them in a final orgy of violence and destruction (chs. 39, 52). The book ends with a clear winner. Babylon rules and Nebuchadnezzar is the head of gold on its statue. But Nebuchadnezzar's victory was (a) God's doing, and (b) short-lived (in the grand scheme of things). His empire was one of the shortest in the long history of human empires. Babylon was God's immediate agent, but not God's long-term agenda.

Jeremiah wins, in a sense. After a lifetime of rejection and apparent failure, his word is ultimately vindicated and his status as a faithful and true prophet of the Lord is confirmed. The opening and closing chapters of the book show that beyond doubt. But it was a costly winning and one he could hardly be said to have 'enjoyed'. His life of lonely suffering – social, spiritual and physical – ended in exile, and not even among the exiles in Babylon who had the future he foresaw as 'good figs', but among the terminally rejected exiles in Egypt. Nevertheless, in the battle between truth and falsehood, Jeremiah (prophet and book) are the winners, by divine and canonical affirmation.

But above all, God wins. At one level, God wins in a way that gave him no joy and came at great cost. In the battle of words and wills, the people relentlessly pursue their self-chosen course of continuing idolatry and social evil. Through the prophet's appeals, God sought to warn and wean and win them away from that, to achieve a different kind of winning – of hearts and minds and wills – bringing people through repentance and change to a different future. The people refused and set their will against God's. In the end, they shattered themselves on the rocks of sin and folly – spiritual, moral and political. In prophetic word and historical fulfilment, God won. The verdict of the supreme Judge was carried out.

But in the end Jeremiah is a book of the victory of God's love and grace. The words themselves do not occur often in the book, but when they do they are a powerful combination. They come together beautifully in the Book of Consolation (chs. 30 – 33), in the twin phrases, 'favour in the wilderness', and 'loved with an everlasting love' (31:2–3). God's love for his people, and through them for the world, is eternal and cannot be defeated, even by their sin. The title of Gordon McConville's study of Deuteronomic theology is superbly appropriate to Jeremiah as well: *grace in the end.*

While we have seen that the first half of the book is predominantly filled with judgment, and the major promises of hope and blessing in the future come in the second half, nevertheless there are promises of salvation woven through that first half also.[31] Even God's threats and warnings of judgment must be seen as actions of God's grace, since they are explicitly given in the hope of bringing the people to repentance so that the judgment need not fall. We are alerted through God's commission to Jeremiah in chapter 1 that beyond the tearing down and uprooting, God will build and plant. And it is that redemptive, reconstructive work of God that fills the future horizon of the book.

What we shall see, however, when we come to study those great chapters (30 – 33) is that it is a future wholly created by the grace of God. It is a future, we shall see, that defies human logic and is dependent only on the power of God to create something new, something that has roots in God's past work but is not merely a return to the past nor generated out of the past. For Jeremiah's own generation, the fall of Jerusalem and exile in Babylon were 'the end'. For them there was no future beyond death in exile under the judgment of God. But for Israel as a people, Israel as the people to whom God had made promises as unbreakable as his own oath, Israel to whom God had remained faithful from generation to generation, Israel as the people through whom God's plan was to bring blessing to all nations on earth – for *that* people there was a future. But they needed to understand (as we also need to) that it was a future guaranteed, not by their amazing ability to survive all historical disasters, but by God's amazing grace, God's ability to bring life out of death, God's determination to bring redemption beyond judgment.

It was a future that Jeremiah never saw with the eyes in his head, only portrayed with the eyes of his faith. It was a future that was first realized within the horizon of the Old Testament itself, when later generations of exiles from Judah came back to the land and rebuilt their city in the years after 538 BC, under the auspices of the Persian Empire. But it was also a future that we can see fulfilled at the New Testament horizon through the life, death and resurrection of Jesus, the Messiah, the king who can rightly be called 'The Lord our Righteousness', the one who inaugurated the new covenant through his own blood. And it is a future that we still anticipate when, at the ultimate horizon of the Bible's narrative, God will build and plant his redeemed people in the new creation and dwell with them in perfect goodness and joy forever.[32]

---

[31] E.g. 3:15–18; 12:14–16; 16:14–15; 23:5–8; 24:4–7.
[32] Jer. 32:38–41; Rev. 21 – 22.

Jeremiah 1:1–3
1. The beginning – and the end

It would be very easy to hurry past these opening verses as nothing more than a few details of personal and historical background. But that would be seriously to miss several key ways in which they contribute to our initial orientation to the book and our understanding of it as a whole. At one level, of course, these verses function in exactly the same way as comparable editorial introductions to prophetic books. We have surveyed the historical framework that they summarize so succinctly in the Introduction.[1]

However, four aspects of the content of these three verses will prove essential for us to keep in mind all the way through our reading of the book. The editor has given us this opening paragraph not just to satisfy our biographical or historical curiosity, but to pinpoint for us the things that are fundamental to interpreting the book we are about to read.

1. The family Jeremiah came from

We are introduced to Jeremiah as *one of the priests at Anathoth*. Anathoth was (and still is) a small village in easy walking distance of Jerusalem, about three miles to the north-east, close to the edge of the wilderness that led down to the Dead Sea. We know two other things about Anathoth. First, it was one of the places set aside for the Levites within the territory of the tribe of Benjamin[2] – which is why it would have had priestly families living there. And secondly, it was the ancestral home of Abiathar.

Abiathar was, you might say, the 'loser' in the great conflict between two branches of the priestly descendants of Aaron that took

---

[1] Pp. 21–23.
[2] Josh. 21:18.

place during the closing years of David's reign and the early years of Solomon. The other contender was Zadok. Abiathar, having served David faithfully before and during his reign, had aligned himself with Solomon's older brother and rival, Adonijah, at the time of the succession. So after Zadok had sided with Solomon by anointing him king, one of Solomon's earliest acts (after murdering Adonijah), was to banish Abiathar to his home village of Anathoth.[3] The Zadokite clan remained in control of the Jerusalem priestly guild from then on. Abiathar's family no doubt nursed their resentment through the generations in the obscurity of Anathoth.

Now it is possible (though not certain, of course) that Jeremiah from Anathoth was a member of the priestly family descended from Abiathar. So Jeremiah's life would have been steeped in the traditions of this priestly lineage and well-educated in the historical and theological heritage of his people. And Abiathar's family went even further back to include Eli, priest at Shiloh during the early ministry of Samuel. This would explain Jeremiah's familiarity with the fate of Shiloh, for example (7:12–15; 26:6), and his love for Hosea, the northern Israelite prophet of the previous century whom Jeremiah quotes or alludes to often. The life of Jeremiah would also create an uncanny echo of the words of the anonymous prophet who condemned the house of Eli, saying that any who survived would do so 'only to destroy your sight and sap your strength'.[4] Jeremiah certainly fits that description.

But the most formative influence of such a family background on Jeremiah would be in relation to the ruling priestly establishment in the Jerusalem temple and its corrupt and compromised alliance with the monarchy there. One can imagine that the residents of Anathoth took a jaundiced view of those who wielded power between the temple and the palace, and Jeremiah put his prophetic finger on their unholy behaviour with painful force. If, however, Jeremiah's hostile posture towards the Jerusalem establishment was connected to his family roots, we will be left wondering what it was that later brought him into so much disfavour with his family that they plotted against his life (11:18–23).

2. The governments Jeremiah lived under

Three kings set the boundaries of Jeremiah's ministry – Josiah, Jehoiakim and Zedekiah. Actually there were two other short-lived reigns as well, Shallum and Jehoiachin, but the latter was taken off

[3] 1 Kgs 2:26–27.
[4] 1 Sam. 2:27–36 (33).

into exile almost as soon as he came to the throne in 597. So although his regnal years continued to be counted in exile (see 52:31), he had no reign in Jerusalem.

Once again, it would be easy to view these names as nothing more than date markers, indicating that the ministry of Jeremiah spanned the roughly forty-year period that we would now designate as 627 – 587 BC. But there is more here than mere chronology. The readers of this book would know that these three kings also represented extremes of good and bad government in the final decades of the independent kingdom of Judah. Josiah was the only king of Judah to have a virtually unblemished record of faithfulness to God's law in the exercise of practical and compassionate justice.[5] Jehoiakim and Zedekiah both did 'evil in the eyes of the LORD' according to 2 Kings. The book of Jeremiah shows Jehoiakim to have been arrogant, contemptuous of Jeremiah and the word of God through him, and oppressively lavish in self-aggrandisement. And Zedekiah was weak and vacillating in the face of the terrible international threat that was to engulf him and his kingdom.

Accordingly, the naming of these three kings sets the framework for the intensely political nature of the book that follows. For all of Jeremiah's ministry would take place not just at the time of these governments, but in constant interaction and engagement with them. From an early age, Jeremiah was a controversial figure, and as the years went by and as the international crisis and domestic turmoil grew worse, he found himself relentlessly compelled to be a thorn in the government's side.

3. The word Jeremiah delivered

Both of the preceding points only really matter because of this one. That is to say, the mere fact that there happened to be a man called Jeremiah living in Anathoth during the reigns of the last three kings of Judah would be empty of all significance if were not for the fact that he had *words* (1), which constituted *the word of the LORD* (2). The emphasis on 'words' and 'speaking' (the same verbal root in Hebrew) is unmistakeable in this chapter. The noun opens verses 1, 2, 4, 11 and 13; the verb is central to verses 6 and 7 and repeated in verse 17; in verse 9 God says 'I have put my words in your mouth'; and in verse 12 God reassures Jeremiah, 'I am watching to see that my word is fulfilled'.

So the reader is alerted to the fact that this book is neither a biography of one of the priests of Anathoth, nor a historiography

---

[5] 2 Kgs 23:24–25; Jer. 22:15–16 (which refer to Josiah).

45

of the later kings of Judah, but is fundamentally a book *about* the word of God and its impact on priests and kings alike, and also a book that *constitutes* the word of God in the form of the words of Jeremiah. It is the words of a man (1), and the word of *the LORD* (2). And one of the most fascinating things we will discover is how the identities of the man, the word and the Lord seem to oscillate and flow together in the passion and pathos of the text. Indeed, so pervasive is the presence of the word of God that Andrew Shead goes so far as to argue that it is virtually personified as one of the main living and active *dramatis personae* of the whole book.[6]

Furthermore, the reader of the whole book knows that the priests and kings, who stand under the threatening judgment of God in this opening chapter (18), will be devastatingly destroyed by the time we reach the final chapter – but the word of God will reign supreme, embodied in Jeremiah's person in his lifetime and secured in his book thereafter. The book will show how those pillars of the religious and political establishment of a whole generation were exposed to the word of God through the fearlessly persistent ministry of Jeremiah. It will show how they wriggled, resisted, rejected and even burnt it – but could never destroy it or thwart its sovereign declared intent. In the lives and pretensions of human kings, the word of God rules. History moves according to the word of God, not according to the will of kings alone. 'The working out of Yahweh's word as Jeremiah's word has as its purpose and intent the ending of Jerusalem, the dismantling of that royal world, the termination of the recital of the kings in Jerusalem.'[7]

The simplicity of these opening verses then headline a truth that will resound throughout the book: the Lord himself is 'ruler of the kings of the earth'.[8] How the government of God intersects with the governments of men (and it usually is men) is one of the most challenging theological legacies that Jeremiah bequeathed to believers in both Testaments and ever since.

4. The tragedy Jeremiah witnessed

Five words (in Hebrew) bring verse 3 to an end: *until the captivity of Jerusalem in the fifth month* (ESV). But this 'awesome and dreadful

---

[6] 'The word of God is the subject of the book of Jeremiah, addressing us just as it once addressed him . . . It is like a human character, and indeed it is effectively the main character in the book of Jeremiah . . . [which] more than any other book in the Old Testament, demands to be understood as a systematic exposition of the word of God' (Shead, *A Mouth Full of Fire*, p. 62). See also Introduction, p. 33.

[7] Brueggemann (1988), p. 21.

[8] Rev. 1:5.

formula'[9] anticipates four words at the end of the whole book, 'so Judah went into captivity, away from her land' (52:27b). So right here in the introduction we are being told the end of the story to which the whole book is heading. This has several consequences.

First, it means that the reader knows from the start the terrible tragedy that lies at the end. Robert Harris's novel *Pompeii*[10] exploits a similar tragic irony. Readers know from history that the book must end with the catastrophic eruption of Vesuvius that will destroy everything and everybody (well almost) in the end. So we read the novel in the gathering darkness of volcanic extinction, yet with glimmers of hope. Similarly, it is impossible for us now to read the book of Jeremiah without knowing how it will end – which creates an atmosphere of sharp irony in the struggle of the prophet to alert the people and his pleading that they take steps to avert the tragedy.

Secondly, this note in the introduction signals that the book as a whole comes from the hands of those for whom this last line of verse 3 was a reality. That included Jeremiah himself, of course, who witnessed the final destruction of Jerusalem. This means for us as contemporary readers that (as noted in the Introduction) we have a double listening to do as we hear each part of the text: we need to stand in the shoes of the original listeners to the preaching of Jeremiah before the calamity fell (apart from the final chapters that come after the fall of Jerusalem); but we also need to sit with the exiles for whom the book summed up the previous four decades of refusing to heed the word of God that could have spared them the calamity. We need to hear with the ears of those for whom 587 BC had been a future and unthinkable impossibility, and with the ears of those for whom it was now a real and unfathomable fact of their recent past. Was it indeed the end, or could there still be hope?

Thirdly, then, the book as a whole functions as a vindication of the ministry of Jeremiah. The event which is anticipated in its third verse and described in its final chapter, was the event that demonstrated beyond all doubt his integrity as a true prophet of God (even though there were still those who refused to accept this). However, this is not to suggest that the whole book is in the canon simply to prove Jeremiah was a true prophet. The point of preserving in such detail his forty years of preaching was to provide the exiles with an *understanding* of what had now fallen upon them – and out of that understanding to build hope. In other words, the book of Jeremiah, in its profound anticipation and explanation of the exile, is not Jeremiah's gloating 'I told you so', but rather his tear-filled, 'I told you *why*'.

---

[9] Brueggemann, ibid.
[10] London: Arrow Books, 2004.

Jeremiah 1:4–19
2. Jeremiah's appointment as prophet

The introduction (1:1–3) locates Jeremiah's call chronologically in the reign of Josiah and geographically sets him in Anathoth, Jerusalem and Judah. However, the opening speech of God (5), as we shift to Jeremiah's first-person testimony, takes us much further back in the mind of God (before Jeremiah was born) and sets a much wider stage (the world of *the nations*). God's perspective is always bigger than the immediate moment. The other comparable prophetic call accounts show a similar sudden expansion of horizon. Moses was looking after sheep in the wilderness when God announced his concern for a whole people trapped in an empire.[1] Amos was tending sheep and sycamore-fig trees in Tekoa when God 'took' him and sent him to the neighbouring country.[2] Isaiah was in the modest-sized temple when he had his vision of the Lord on the throne of universal government filling the whole earth with his glory and the temple with but the hem of his robe.[3] God's invasion of the world of this young lad from Anathoth transformed his self-perception, expanded his horizons, and rewrote whatever agenda he might have had for a career. He could not have foreseen the next forty years, but they all flowed from the day in 627 BC when *the word of the LORD came to me* (or, more literally, 'became', or 'happened' to me).

1. God's choice (4–5)

The first thing Jeremiah learns in this encounter was the sovereignty of God. The same theme would shape a life-time of learning to come. God's call on Jeremiah's life begins by locating that calling before

[1] Exod. 3.
[2] Amos 7:14–15.
[3] Isa. 6.

his birth. This was an unusual feature of such call narratives, reminiscent of the anonymous servant of the Lord,[4] John the Baptist and Jesus himself. It shows that the moment of Jeremiah's call was not a sudden divine response to an immediate or unforeseen crisis, but simply the implementation in the present of something long since planned for.

Jeremiah's mission, therefore, was not his own freely chosen path of service, but a participation in a divine purpose that was being shaped in the mind of God before Jeremiah was being shaped in his mother's womb. Even that first verb, *I formed you*, speaks of God's personal involvement, for it is the word regularly used of a potter shaping a vessel according to his own intentions. Jeremiah would later turn this word into a powerful metaphor of God's sovereign governance of international history (18:1–12). For the moment, it spoke of God's intimate oversight of his individual biology.

Three matching and reinforcing phrases further underline the point.

a. I knew you

The word indicates not just cognitive awareness, but an act of personal commitment to a relationship; for that reason it is sometimes translated as 'I chose you'.[5] By making it clear that this foreknowledge and choice had happened before his birth, God removes any grounds for pride. Jeremiah's selection for this task had nothing to do with him being 'a good boy' so far. So, though it may not have felt like it as his life wore on, it was divine grace as well as divine sovereignty that had determined Jeremiah's place in history.

b. I set you apart

The verb is the same as that regularly used about Israel as having been set apart by God for himself as a holy people[6] (as in 2:3). It is often translated 'consecrated'. Whether of people (like the priests), or things (like sacred vessels), the central idea is of separation from the common realm for a purpose determined by God. But this is not just a matter of someone dedicating themselves to God ('Take my life, and let it be / Consecrated, Lord, to thee'[7]). The initiative in all three verbs belongs to God. God had identified Jeremiah and marked him out for this purpose before his birth. And this act of divine setting apart

---

[4] Isa. 49:1.
[5] As in Gen. 18:19; Amos 3:2.
[6] Lev. 20:26.
[7] Frances Ridley Havergal, 1874.

49

would have its consequences in Jeremiah's daily life, as he found himself increasingly 'set apart' from his family, his local community, his fellow priests and prophets, successive kings, and the direction of government policy. Such lonely sanctification was the cost of bearing the word of God that confronted all of these realms.

c. I appointed you

Literally, 'prophet to the nations I have given you [to be]'. In other words, it is not so much that God gives a job to Jeremiah as that God gives Jeremiah to the job. 'The message requires the messenger.'[8] Jeremiah is not a driven man, but a given man. This accounts for the sense of inescapable compulsion that we will find throughout Jeremiah's ministry and book. He was not *forced* into this role, but simply being aware that his very existence was for the sake of carrying out this job produced its own inner pressure – which he felt free to resist but could never evade. This was not a task that he had chosen, but a task for which God had chosen him.

Generations of believers have found in God's word to Jeremiah something paradigmatic for all servants of God. There was, of course, a unique historical context and canonical dimension to the specific call of Jeremiah that applied to none but Jeremiah himself. Nevertheless the Bible makes similar affirmations in a generic sense about the calling of all God's people. Not that we are all called to be prophets, but we are all called – called to be saints, as Paul would say to so many of his scattered congregations in the cosmopolitan centres of his day.

The account of Jeremiah's call, then, should not be used simply as a model for pastors or missionaries. Doubtless there is a calling to the ministry of the word, for which the stories of the call of the prophets have a particular resonance. But if we accept the biblical truth that God has a purpose in calling every one of us to himself, then there is a matching sense in which each of us needs to seek the outworking of God's calling in daily life and work.

2. God's command (6–7)

Verse 6 is a surprise. After such an emphatic declaration of God's sovereignty, Jeremiah feels free to object! Right at the start we are encountering what will be a marked feature of the whole book – constant dialogue. It is one of the rhetorical strategies of the book to portray the unremitting argument that went on at multiple levels

[8] Brueggemann (1988), p. 25.

during those tumultuous years, reflecting, no doubt, the street-level encounters that peppered Jeremiah's daily life. Jeremiah argues with the people; the people argue back. God accuses the people; the people question God. Jeremiah argues with God; God responds to Jeremiah, sometimes with rebuke, more often with encouragement. Jeremiah argues with kings, prophets, priests, governors and diplomats. And when the dialogue can no longer be face to face, it continues through written scrolls (chs. 29, 36, 50 – 51). But what we must keep in mind is that it is the record of *all* these words in many mouths that constitute the scriptural word of God through the words of the book of Jeremiah, not only the words spoken by the prophet Jeremiah.

Jeremiah was not a robot or a mere dictaphone for God. He was an inexperienced youth who naturally shrank back from what he was hearing. In this respect the story of his call matches others. Moses voiced his unwillingness. Isaiah voiced his unworthiness. Jeremiah voices his immaturity: *I am too young [a child]*. The word means a youth of uncertain age; possibly Jeremiah was a late teenager (in our terms). This was not stubborn refusal (or even prolonged resistance like that of Moses), but probably a simple statement of the facts as he saw them – he had no experience of public speaking, so should God not find somebody else with better credentials?

God does not rebuke Jeremiah (7), but simply dismisses his point as true but irrelevant. What mattered was not Jeremiah's confidence (or lack of it), but God's command, and that is now put into unmistakeably clear terms. Literally:

> *To everyone to whom I send you, you shall go,*
> *and everything which I command you, you shall speak.*

So God gives Jeremiah an unlimited mission and an unlimited message. He would have no free choice of audience (those who might like to hear what he had to say), and no free choice of message (what he thought they would want to hear). In that respect he would stick out like a funeral director at a wedding, in stark contrast to the many prophets around him who would happily choose their audience and their message to suit their popularity.

As his long ministry wore on, Jeremiah would struggle with both these dimensions of his mandate – audience and message. There would come days when he would call curses on his audience, and other days when he would try to stifle the message. But in the end, the audience heard the word, and would go on hearing it through the book when the message they had refused to believe finally was vindicated.

Once again, we need to preserve the uniqueness of Jeremiah's prophetic ministry, and yet also hear the universality of its challenge to all those who submit to the lordship of Christ. To go where he sends, and to speak what he commands, are responsibilities not confined to biblical prophets, but an essential part of that witnessing task entrusted to all disciples.

In the months before my wife and I went to India (where I taught for several years in a seminary), we became frustrated with the tendency of churches to put cross-cultural missionaries on a pedestal for their allegedly heroic and self-sacrificial obedience to God's call. I remember saying to churches that we visited, 'All we are doing is this: we are going where we believe God wants us to go, to do what we believe God wants us to do. What makes us so special, then? Is that not what should be true of all disciples of Christ?'

3. God's care (8)

a. The power of fear

Jeremiah had not said he was afraid, but God could see him probably trembling at the prospect of the task ahead of him. As in so many other similar situations, God utters the words that constitute statistically the most frequent divine command in the Bible: *Do not be afraid.* With these words God recognizes the reality and power of fear. God did not deny or dismiss it as unreal or ridiculous. He knew better than Jeremiah the struggles and dangers that lay ahead for him.

Fear is real, and nothing to be ashamed of. Jesus feared the cross and shrank back from it, as any sane human being would. But his greater fear was that he might fail to do the will of God his Father. For fear is undoubtedly one of the most potent obstacles to obedience. In Jeremiah's case, his understandable fear would be directed to *them* (literally, 'their faces'), the people to whom he was being sent with the unpalatable word of God. The only antidote to that kind of fear of other people was obedience to the simple command of God *not* to fear them, and trust in the immediately following promise.

b. The presence of God

To his most frequent command, God adds his most precious promise, *I am with you.* The presence of God in the midst of his people was a key blessing in the historical experience of Israel – so much so that Moses once refused to move unless God continued to guarantee it.[9] If battle-hardened Joshua needed this reassurance,[10] how much more

[9] Exod. 33:14–16.
[10] Josh. 1:5.

did the scared young son of a village priest? And for ourselves, we recall how the one who came to embody this promise as Immanuel, God with us, renewed it for the rest of history for those who carry forward his mission to the nations.[11]

Wonderful though the promised presence of God would be (and sometimes it would be the only presence Jeremiah would have in his loneliness), it was not passive but purposeful: 'in order to *rescue you*'. The verb, which means to deliver someone by snatching them out of danger,[12] is a veteran of the exodus vocabulary. What God had done for Israel in Egypt he now promises to do for Jeremiah, implying ominously that Jeremiah will need it as much as the Hebrew slaves had done.[13]

And indeed he would. Jeremiah was going to need this promise to be kept repeatedly, especially in the later years of his ministry when things turned distinctly nasty. He would be disowned by his family, arrested, beaten and imprisoned, threatened more than once with death, cheated by a relative, and would spend much time in hiding. But God made this promise, reinforced it from time to time, and always kept it. The book as a whole, therefore, by recording this promise in the opening verses, stands as a monument to the faithful care of God over those who are determined to live in costly obedience to his calling.

4. God's commission (9–10)

At this point we realize that Jeremiah's encounter with God is not purely auditory, but has some visual element as well, for he sees God stretch out his hand to touch his mouth. The action, similar to the experience of Isaiah and Ezekiel,[14] confirmed the primary organ of Jeremiah's prophetic ministry – his mouth. And the words that accompanied the action defined the source of his prophetic message, the scope of his prophetic authority, and the balance of his prophetic task.

a. The source of his prophetic message (9)

I have put my words in your mouth. The words immediately recall the promise that God had made to Moses in virtually identical phrasing: 'I will raise up for them a prophet like you from among

---

[11] Matt. 1:23; 28:20.
[12] As David claims God had done for him from the paw of a lion and bear (1 Sam. 17:37).
[13] Exod. 3:8; 5:23; 6:6; etc.
[14] Isa. 6:6–7; Ezek. 2:9; 3:3.

their brothers; I will put my words in his mouth, and he will tell them everything I command him.'[15]

This is one of several indications in the book that Jeremiah came to see himself as one in whom that promise had been fulfilled – not only in having God's words placed in his mouth, but also in being 'a prophet like Moses'. There were similar features in the call and ministry of Moses and Jeremiah:

- both had a dramatic experience of God's call;
- both shrank back and objected;
- both heard words of God's over-ruling and promise of protection;
- both were commissioned to speak truth to power – confronting human authorities at various levels;
- both had a passion for God's honour and a horror at the unfaithfulness of God's people.

But what is highlighted here is the identity between the words of God and the mouth of Jeremiah. He would speak what he was given to speak. Hearing Jeremiah, people were hearing the Lord.

For forty years the original recipients of Jeremiah's preaching challenged precisely this point. On occasions they explicitly denied that what he was saying came from Yahweh, preferring the more soothing words of other prophets. But those who later had to read this book in the context of exile realized the truth of these words. What Jeremiah had said had come from God. So they found themselves facing the rest of what God had said to Moses: 'I myself will call to account anyone who does not listen to my words that the prophet speaks in my name.'[16] That accounting had begun.

For ourselves, reading these words within the canon of Scripture, they express what is meant by divine inspiration, namely the dual authorship of the text. The mouth was Jeremiah's; the words were God's. And yet the prophet spoke words that undoubtedly came from his own intellect, background, reflections and emotions. Jeremiah's words were as human as he was, and yet they conveyed the message (the word) God wished to be communicated.[17] Paul makes a similar claim when he says, 'we speak, not in words taught us by human wisdom but in words taught by the Spirit'.[18] Peter likewise affirms, 'prophecy never had its origin in the human will,

[15] Deut. 18:18.
[16] Deut. 18:19.
[17] Andrew Shead, *A Mouth Full of Fire*, is a sustained reflection on this point.
[18] 1 Cor. 2:13.

but prophets, though human, spoke from God as they were carried along by the Holy Spirit'.[19]

b. The scope of his prophetic authority (10a)

In case Jeremiah had missed the significance of the last phrase of verse 5, *prophet to the nations* [plural], God now spells it out in detail: *today I appoint you over nations and kingdoms.* Not quite what this son of a village priest had in mind as a career plan, and of course never literally true in any political sense. The phrase with its international vista takes its truth, however, not from any political or military power that Jeremiah might dream of (in his worst nightmares), but from the immediately preceding verse. Jeremiah himself might never be 'over nations and kingdoms', but the word of God certainly was, and Jeremiah would be the mouthpiece of that sovereign word as it worked out its governing agency in the affairs of nations. This identification of the prophet himself with the word he spoke, and of both with the sovereign rule of God, is one of the theological affirmations of the book as a whole, laid before us here in God's initial summons and commission.

Other prophets had international ministry. Elisha and Elijah were both involved with kings of other nations. Amos had spoken God's word in relation to a whole noose of nations surrounding Israel, tightening it dramatically when he turned to Israel itself, and declared that they too stood among the enemies of God facing his judgment. Isaiah had caricatured the mighty Assyrian empire as nothing but a stick in the hands of Yahweh, being used to punish Judah and then to be cast aside. But Jeremiah takes the conviction of Yahweh's rule over all history and all nations to new heights of rhetorical and theological assertion, as we shall see most sharply in chapters 18, 27 and 29. The words of this puny young prophet will embody the word of the living God in his government of the world, from the tiniest neighbouring states to the dominant world empire.

c. The balance of his prophetic task (10b)

But they were not 'mere words'. God's government, exercised in the outworking of the words Jeremiah would deliver, would be radically transforming in both negative and positive ways. Six verbs describe what God intends to be the effect of Jeremiah's delivery of God's word. They are drawn from the worlds of agriculture, construction and warfare, and arranged concentrically in such a way that agriculture

[19] 2 Pet. 1:21.

begins and ends the list (*to uproot* and *to plant*), construction immediately inside that (*to tear down* and *to build*), while the two warfare metaphors dominate the centre (*to destroy and overthrow*). The effect thus created is both to give the heaviest weight to the destructive metaphors, while ending with the constructive verbs of hope.

Jeremiah's heaviest task would be delivering words of searing rebuke and judgment, tearing down strongholds of political and religious arrogance and prejudice, dismantling traditional certainties of faith, and announcing the uprooting of a whole nation and the destruction of its most precious assets. But out of the dug soil new planting could begin. After the demolition of an unreliable edifice, new building could happen. So, for those reading these words in the trauma of exile, scarred with memories of the rubble of Jerusalem and the ashes of the temple, the four negative metaphors had become reality. But the two metaphors of new beginnings could bring hope – hope for a future they would not see with their own eyes but to which they could lift up eyes and hearts of faith. God's purpose in history – ancient, modern, or eschatological – is that when God brings catastrophic endings it is to prepare the way for unimaginable new beginnings.

5. God's confirmation (11–19)

Two visions conclude this account of Jeremiah's call. The repetition of the phrase *the word of the LORD came to me* (11, 13) suggests that they may not have happened on the same occasion as the call itself, but shortly afterwards as confirmation. They are then followed by a summarizing reinforcement of the total message (17–19).

a. The almond branch (11–12)

This may not have been a 'vision' in the sense of something 'only in his head'. Very probably he was simply enjoying looking at the beauty of a blossoming almond tree near his home, but then God attached a prophetic meaning to his gaze through a word association generated by a simple question.

The Hebrew word for almond tree is *šāqēd*. The participle of the verb 'to watch' is *šōqēd*. The consonants are identical; only the first vowel point modifies. So in answer to God's question, 'What are you looking at?' Jeremiah replies, '*šāqēd* is what I am seeing'. And in response God says, '*šōqēd* is what I am doing, over my word to do it'. From then on, every time Jeremiah saw the almond blossom in spring, he would be reminded of the divine watcher, keeping watch over his word. And in his long ministry he would need such reassurance in the face of those who taunted him with the apparent non-fulfilment of his prophetic message. There would be many springs before the word would be performed, but God was watching. It would not fail.[20]

b. The boiling pot (13–16)

Another ordinary experience provides an ominous message. Jeremiah sees a pot of stew (perhaps) boiling over an open fire, but tilting badly on its stones, threatening to spill its contents and maybe a danger to any child playing nearby. And it happens to be tilting from the north. The prophetic symbolism clicks into Jeremiah's mind: *from the north disaster will be poured out on all who live in the land* . . . Three points emerge:

First, the threat of 'the foe from the north' rumbles repeatedly through the early preaching of Jeremiah. Initially, it was an unnamed enemy. But as the Assyrian empire collapsed and was replaced by rising Babylon, it became clear who was meant, as the exiles sitting in Babylon knew only too well. Babylon lay to the east of Judah, of course, but any attack on the lands of Israel and Judah necessarily came down the roads from the north.

Second, Judah needed to know who was in charge, even as the enemy approached (which would not be for decades yet): '*I am about to summon all the peoples of the northern kingdoms,*' declares the LORD. The threat would consist of Nebuchadnezzar and his very human armies and imperial ambitions. But the commander-in-chief was YHWH, for whom whole nations were simply platoons that must answer his muster. This message would prove deeply unpopular in the years ahead, when Jeremiah delivered it not only to the government in Jerusalem, but even to the ambassadors of external nations.

Third, the fundamental reason for all the suffering that lay ahead as the pot poured out its scalding contents was God's judgment on the wickedness of his people (16). In other words, whatever might be the political or military dimensions of the convulsions that would shake the whole region and shatter Jerusalem, the core issue in God's governance was moral and spiritual. And the core of that issue was idolatry, and all its dismal consequences in the religious and social life of the nation. We should not imagine, however, that such idolatry was a 'merely religious' matter. The separation of religion and politics is a modern quirk that would make no sense in the biblical world – for Judah or Babylon. Judah's flirting with *other gods* was tied up with international alliances and the obsession with putting

[20] Jer. 31:27–28. Cf. Isa. 55:10–11.

self-constructed national security above covenantal loyalty and trust. All the calculations and manoeuvrings of states and empires in the coming decades could not excuse Judah from this fundamental charge or protect them from the inevitable divine judgment it incurred. This would be the message of Jeremiah, resisted for years but finally demonstrated beyond all doubt.

c. Promises and warnings (17–19)

Get yourself ready! is literally 'gird up your loins' – that is, for hard work, or even for battle. The combination of challenge, command, and promise, is very similar to the commissioning of Joshua,[21] which shows that the prophetic career stretching before him was as daunting as the conquest of Canaan, except that the 'Canaanites' were now his own people.

The basic command is repeated (17a): Jeremiah was to be the mouthpiece of God. And he must either do that without fear, or find himself paralyzed by the fear of God, in public embarrassment. The warning of verse 16b is brutally realistic – there would be terrifying moments ahead. But if Jeremiah allowed himself to retreat from his task through fear of his audience, he would face a sterner source of terror. For 'a man who fears man has also God to fear'.[22]

Theological and expository reflections

Preaching from Jeremiah 1 often concentrates on the personal call of Jeremiah and the commands and promises God made to him as a model for our own lives. Along with that it is important to pay due attention to the affirmation that in the words of Jeremiah the word of God was heard and that in the book that now carries his words, the word of God still comes to us.

Also, it is important to remember that this chapter is the introduction to a public ministry in the political arena and to reflect on the ways in which the words of the prophets engaged their historical contexts and how, by implication, their message can address issues in our world. None of us stands, like Jeremiah, as having been 'appointed' *over nations and kingdoms*, but we are called to bear witness to the word of the God whose sovereignty extends to the ends of the earth.

---

[21] Deut. 31:6–8; Josh. 1:6–9.
[22] Thompson, p. 157.

Jeremiah 2:1 – 3:5
3. From honeymoon to divorce

God tells Jeremiah to take a walk. It was only a few miles to Jerusalem, a journey he must have made many times already, but it would never have felt longer than the day he had to *go and proclaim in the hearing of Jerusalem* the message that is recorded for us in this chapter.

Chapters 2 – 6 seem to form a connected whole section, and probably represent a sampler[1] of the preaching of Jeremiah in the early years of his ministry, probably during the reign of Josiah. It has three main movements:

1. Here in 2:1 – 3:5 we have a sustained lament by God, accusing Israel of betrayal.
2. This is followed in 3:6 – 4:4 by an appeal for repentance and return to the Lord.
3. Then in 4:5 – 6:30, assuming the failure of that appeal (though it continued unabated for years), we hear a declaration of terrible judgment to come that was tearful even to contemplate.

As we study this sample of Jeremiah's early preaching, look out for three features of it that are extensively illustrated in 2:1 – 3:5, and are very characteristic of his rhetorical style all through the book:

- *Questions*. There are at least sixteen questions in this section. Some are rhetorical, immediately followed by strong accusation; others seem to express genuine pain and puzzlement in the heart of God. It is worth marking them and reading them in sequence to feel the rhetorical impact of this feature of Jeremiah's style.
- *Imagery*. At least nineteen times Jeremiah finds some image, metaphor or comparison with which to give dynamic vividness

[1] Dearman, p. 61.

to the point he is making. Some of these are poignant and nostalgic; others are painful and shocking. All of them are creative and effective tools of communication.

- *Dialogue.* Nine times Jeremiah quotes directly from words the people were saying, and twice he refers to things they *should* have said, but didn't. Jeremiah probably preached into a highly charged atmosphere in which a good deal of heckling and dialogue actually happened. This gives to the written record of his words a real-life directness, which would have continued to challenge those who read the book in exile. As they were confronted with the record of what they used to say, the challenge was: had they changed their tune, or were the same attitudes still prevailing?

The reign of King Josiah was a time of great religious ferment and national resurgence.[2] It was all very impressive. But what was God's point of view? According to Jeremiah God sees a people who are a disappointment to God, who are being disloyal to their covenant relationship with God, who are already feeling the shock of disasters that foreshadow worse to come, and who are living in brazen denial and delusion. It is a frightening mirror to hold up to the people of God in any generation, with stark relevance to our own.

1. Disappointment: unfulfilled promise (2:1–3)

Our text begins with a honeymoon (2:1–3) and ends in divorce (3:1–5). This nostalgic beginning and poignant ending highlight the essentially *relational* nature of the issue. There are echoes of a law-court (especially the charge list beginning at v. 9), and this in turn connects Jeremiah's technique to the familiar 'covenant law-suit' that other prophets had perfected before him. But the burning question is not so much broken laws (though it included that), as a broken relationship, broken promises (Israel's), and a broken heart (God's). Jeremiah's message contains sharp accusation, severe warning, and chilling threat, but these are embedded in a passionate lament that pours out the pain of God – the pain and anger of betrayed love. It will be important to bear this in mind as we move through the book. For we will find plenty more searing passages of accusation and judgment. But this opening chapter calls us back again and again (as do the tears of Jeremiah himself) to remember that the God who speaks and acts thus is the divine Lover, the divine Husband, whose anger is drenched in the pain of love.

[2] See Introduction, p. 19.

a. A promising marriage (2)

I remember, says God (2). Happy memories become painful nostalgia when the present fails to fulfil the promise of the past. And that is what God expresses here – divine nostalgia. God remembers the first flush of marital love in the early days of his relationship with Israel as a nation (2–3), but only to contrast it bitterly with the ungrateful and unfaithful betrayal of their present behaviour (4–8).

Jeremiah looks back to the exodus and wilderness period in verse 2, and describes it as a honeymoon. God tells Israel that he remembers *the **devotion** of your youth, your **love** as a bride* (ESV), using two words frequently used of the love of God himself. *Ḥesed* means trustworthy commitment within a covenanted relationship. *'ahăbâ* means emotional love demonstrated in faithful and whole-hearted allegiance. And where does God find the evidence for such first love? In the fact that Israel had been prepared to follow YHWH, her covenant 'husband', out into the danger and uncertainties of the *wilderness,* trusting him to protect and provide.

But the wilderness was a time of repeated grumbling and rebellion! Jeremiah must have known the traditions recorded in the book of Numbers. So this rosy view of that generation of Israel's history is a remarkable perspective. It is very similar to the way Hosea also presents the wilderness period in a positive light.

> When I found Israel,
>   it was like finding grapes in the desert;
> when I saw your ancestors,
>   it was like seeing the early fruit on the fig-tree.
>
> When Israel was a child, I loved him,
>   and out of Egypt I called my son.[3]

Probably Hosea and Jeremiah were both drawing on the Song of Moses in Deuteronomy 32, which contrasts the early promise of Israel before the Promised Land with their abysmal backsliding in it.[4] The point lies not so much in what is being said about the wilderness period in itself, but in the jarring contrast with the state of God's people now. Compared with the vile promiscuity of the present, the wilderness was pure honeymoon.

---

[3] Hos. 9:10a; 11:1.
[4] Deut. 32:10–18.

b. A promising harvest (3)

The metaphor changes at verse 3, from the early promise of newly-weds to the early hopes of a good *harvest*, once the *firstfruits* are in.[5] The point here is more extensive in its reach, for it hints at God's wider plan for the nations, and we recall that Jeremiah had been appointed 'as a prophet to the nations' (1:5, 10). Just as the description of Israel as 'my firstborn son'[6] points to the expectation that there would be other sons drawn from other nations, so the description of Israel as *the firstfruits of his harvest*, points to the expectation of a wider harvest of the nations to fill out the roll-call of the people of God.[7]

This missional hope is never as explicit in Jeremiah as it is in Isaiah, but it rests on the same basic theology: YHWH is sovereign over all nations. In Israelite agriculture, firstfruits were the guarantee of the rest of the harvest. So giving them to God symbolized that the whole future harvest really belonged to him. Thus, *Israel's* unique belonging to God (being *holy*), symbolized God's claim over *the whole world* of nature and nations. Paul applies the metaphor to the resurrection of Christ in relation to the rest of the redeemed while James applies it to all Christian believers in relation to creation as a whole.[8]

Back in the wilderness, Israel had been set apart for the Lord, as a bride for her husband or as firstfruits for the priests, and (thinking again of the nations) God had defended her from the attacks of *all who devoured her*. But now, exposed in her infidelity and with God's marital protection withdrawn, those same enemy nations would be released to do their worst (2:15–19).

So then, Israel's relationship with God had been full of promise, whether viewed as the first love of a new marriage, or the first fruits of a coming harvest. God had hopes and plans for his people that would be for their blessing and the blessing of the whole world of nations. But God's hopes were blighted by Israel's betrayals. Jeremiah knew how those verses of Hosea (quoted above) continued, and he felt the same upsurge of baffled divine grief.

---

[5] The first fruits of various crops were consecrated to God by being given to the priests (Num. 18:12–13). The ceremony of bringing the firstfruits was filled with rich historical, theological and ethical significance (Deut. 26). So, for Israel themselves to be described as *holy to the* LORD, *the firstfruits of his harvest*, signified a very special role indeed, as the ending of Deut. 26 indicates.

[6] Exod. 4:22; Jer. 31:9.

[7] 'The "harvest" metaphor envisages peoples other than Israel who also belong to God. God begins with Israel within a purpose that is global in its ultimate scope. Israel's election is an initially exclusive move for the sake of a maximally inclusive end' (Fretheim, p. 62; and cf. Wright, *Mission of God*, ch. 6).

[8] 1 Cor. 15:20–23; Jas 1:18.

But when they came to Baal Peor,
> they consecrated themselves to that shameful idol
> and became as vile as the thing they loved.

But the more they were called,
> the more they went away from me.
They sacrificed to the Baals
and they burned incense to images.[9]

The early promise was unfulfilled. Israel had become a disappointment to God, despised by others, and a disaster to themselves. It is a pattern that did not end with Old Testament Israel. The Lord Jesus Christ himself detected the same thing in the church at Ephesus to whom he wrote: 'You have forsaken the love you had at first. Consider how far you have fallen! Repent and do the things you did at first'[10] – words that carry a perennial warning and challenge to us in every generation.

What had caused such failure? An astonishing combination of ingratitude, amnesia and folly (2:4–13).

2. Disloyalty: unnatural ingratitude (2:4–13)

a. The complaint (5–8)

Jeremiah turns from God's nostalgia to more direct diagnosis of Israel's sin – a diagnosis that is comprehensive horizontally (*all . . . the clans of Israel*, 4, not just Judah; the political division and separate fates of the two kingdoms is here deemed irrelevant), and vertically (through all generations since their arrival in the land). All have sinned. And 'at once we meet that mixture of the perverse, the frivolous and the ungrateful which is typical of all sin'.[11]

God opens his complaint with the question, *What fault did your ancestors find in me, that they strayed so far from me?* (5a). The question is rhetorical, but there are several possible ways of understanding the point of it. The expected answer could be, 'None at all', in which case the point is simply to exonerate God from any blame for the coming crisis. If Israel were suffering all kinds of disaster, it was not God's fault. Put the blame where it belonged. Or the question could be an invitation for Israel to spell out their grievance in court. For the fact was that some in Israel *did* blame Yahweh for their misfortunes, or at least for not ending them (2:29, 35; 3:5). They were

---

[9] Hos. 9:10b; 11:2; my italics.
[10] Rev. 2:4–5.
[11] Kidner, p. 31.

as quick to blame God as Adam was to blame God for giving him Eve, or as even atheists are today to blame the God they claim does not exist for all the wrong things he ought to prevent if he did. So perhaps God is challenging the Israelites to lay out their case, if they can, in defence of their ancestors. Or it could simply be God's heartfelt amazement at his people's inexplicable fickleness. Since he had done no wrong to them, why, oh why had they wandered away from him?

The following verses give no answer to that question, but simply sharpen the diagnosis. What was Israel's real problem?

(i) The pursuit of what was worthless (5b)

The Hebrew is blunt and brutal: 'They went after[12] the worthless and they worthless-ized.' The word translated *worthless idols* is the single word *hebel*, and it means a puff of wind, a triviality, something of no value, benefit or worth, something completely futile. It is the word regularly translated 'vanity' or 'emptiness' in the book of Ecclesiastes. And here it is Jeremiah's verdict on the worship of Ba'al and all the ritualized sexuality that went with it. The cult of fertility was a cult of futility, in which there was neither substance nor salvation.

But the sting in the tail is the final verb. *They . . . became worthless themselves.* They became like what they worshipped – which is a fact of life as much today as in ancient Israel.[13] Worshippers (which means all human beings, for it is our very nature) become like the object of their worship. Since we were created in the image of the living God, to worship him is to become more like him. But when we make gods in our own image, to worship them is to become like them. And so the cult of worthless gods spawned a people characterized by delusion, vanity and emptiness.

Writing as a resident of the Western world, I find this a devastatingly true observation on the hollowing out of a whole culture that used to be rich in Christian assumptions and symbolism (however much defaced by the dubious syncretisms of Christendom). So much that passes for popular 'culture' in the West seems empty and shallow. We see the narcissism of self-promoting talentless celebrities, and freak shows like *Big Brother* masquerading as 'reality' television. It is not surprising then that in the collective idolatry that worships such triviality, human beings find their own lives unbearably

[12] Notice the intentional contrast with v. 2. There Israel 'walked after' God; in v. 5 they 'walked after' worthlessness.
[13] Once again it is likely Jeremiah is echoing Hosea here, who said of Israel, 'they consecrated themselves to the thing of shame, and became detestable like the thing they loved' (Hos. 9:10, ESV).

worthless and futile. And in such a culture of worthlessness, human life itself becomes cheap and expendable. If consumerism is the culture's supreme god, then humans themselves eventually become consumer goods. We use and exploit one another for our own pleasure or fantasy.

(ii) The waste of what was precious (6–7)
Jeremiah here reminds Israel of their historical faith, with a list of things that should have stirred their gratitude but no longer did. Look at how these verses list the rich inheritance of memory that they were squandering:

- redemption out of Egypt;
- guidance in the wilderness;
- provision for all their needs;
- the gift of the land;
- the blessings of abundance and fruitfulness.

But not only did they no longer ask where it all came from (that is, they forgot the Giver[14]), they had actually *defiled my land and made my inheritance detestable* (7). The contrast with verse 3 is pointed. Israel whom God had made holy had become the polluters of the very thing God had entrusted to them. They had abused it by squandering and belittling the precious blessings of God.

Think of all the blessings of God that we as Christians enjoy. There is our historical faith – beginning with the story we share with Old Testament Israel, but for us of course including the life, death and resurrection of Jesus and the New Testament church. But beyond that there is the rich heritage of Christian faith, worship, tradition and history over twenty centuries. And finally there is the inventory of God's blessings in our personal lives. How much of this do we treasure and reinvest for fruitfulness in God's kingdom? And how much do we abuse and squander in careless amnesia?

Those of us who live in the English-speaking Western world are especially vulnerable to this charge, for the Christian resources available to us are simply incalculable. Take the number of Bibles in the English language alone (in a world where there are at least 2,000 languages without any part of the Bible as yet). Apart from the wide range of different translations, there is the almost obscene proliferation of marketing packages. A random check one day in a Christian bookstore offered me a choice of the following 'Bibles' (in each case

[14] Cf. Deut. 8:12–14.

add the word *Bible* to the word or phrase listed): *Devotional, Daily, Men's, Women's, Women and Faith, Life Application, Everyday Life, New Spirit-Filled Life, Family Foundations, Discovery, Business, Chequebook, Amplified, Chronological, New Believers, Ultimate Teen, Extreme Teen, Student, Youth, Boys, Faith Girlz, Giant, Slim, Ultra Slim* and even the Holy Bible.

But what have we done with this profusion, other than being grossly spoiled for choice? For the level of Bible knowledge and even reading has shrunk among Western Christians in startling inverse proportion to the availability of the Bible itself. By contrast, a brother from D. R. Congo told me that in his congregation, when someone in a family is able to afford to buy a Bible of their own, they cut it up (literally), and share it out among the family so that everybody has some part of this infinitely precious possession.

That is just one example. God has given us so much. What have we done with it in terms of bearing fruit for his kingdom, in being salt and light in the world, in participating in God's mission?

(iii) The failure of those in leadership (8)

If verse 6 accuses the people in general of failing to ask the right questions in their abandonment of God, verse 8 lays the blame for such national decline where it really belonged – on the shoulders of those who should have known better, the national leaders (cf. 2:26 and 5:5). In this tactic, Jeremiah also followed the example of Hosea.[15]

Jeremiah accuses all four categories of leaders in Israel who have failed in their duty: *the priests* (since they spent their days in the temple, their failure to ask 'Where is the LORD' is all the more astonishing)*; those who deal with the law* (i.e. the legal authorities – which would include priests who were supposed to teach the law and elders who administered justice in the local courts); *the leaders* (i.e. the political ruling class linked to the king); *the prophets* (many of whom probably also had a professional role in the temple and palace).

So those who were entrusted with the enormous responsibility of leading the people of God in the ways of God did not even know God for themselves, or have any desire to do so. They were no longer asking the right questions or seeking the presence of God; far from it, they were in rebellion against God. They were just as dumbed-down by the cult of worthlessness as the rest of the populace.

---

[15] Hos. 4:4–9. Malachi shows that the failure persisted through the Old Testament period (Mal. 2:5–8), and Jesus picks it up in his own generation.

Once again it takes little effort to transfer Jeremiah's insight to the contemporary church. For are we not also aware that there are pastors who care little for their flock; preachers who never teach the Bible; theological educators who undermine the faith of those they teach; and ecclesiastical leaders who give their blessing to behaviours that the Bible condemns as not pleasing to God?

So then, Jeremiah voices God's complaint, with its ancient and modern relevance,[16] as he exposes the triple scandal of a cult of worthlessness, a waste of inheritance and a failure of leadership. How can we respond, except in repentance where we recognize such trends in ourselves?

b. The charge (9–13)

Therefore I bring charges against you again; the formal accusation is now recorded for the court, as it were. Fundamentally the charge is disloyalty to the covenant relationship with Yahweh. They have deserted the God to whom they were committed. How can Jeremiah convey something of the sheer enormity of what Israel has been doing – to God and to themselves? Answer: by stressing that it was so *unnatural* that there was no parallel to it (among the nations or in nature), and that it was so *irrational* that there was no profit from it.

(i) Their apostasy was unparalleled (10–12)

Go west, or go east,[17] says Jeremiah, and you will find other nations worshipping other gods. All Israelites knew that. And they also knew, with smug superiority, that those gods were not really gods at all. They had no transcendent divine reality or power (as ch. 10 will emphasize). But look more closely, urges Jeremiah. Do your research. Do they ever change those gods? No! The gods of the nations are not really gods at all, but at least the nations are loyal to the non-gods they have!

But in stark and unbelievable contrast, Israel knows the one and only true and living God, *their Glory* (ESV), the only real God of substance, life and power, and what have they done with that God? Swapped him for utter triviality (worthlessness again)! What kind of deal is that, to trade the living God for something as dead as driftwood?

[16] The text itself declares its transgenerational challenge, as Jeremiah speaks first of all about 'your fathers/ancestors' (5), then 'you' (7, 9a), and then 'your children's children' (9b). Clearly the preaching spans his first original hearers and his later exilic readers – and thus continues to address God's people in any generation wherever the charge sticks.

[17] *Cyprus* (Kittim) is in the sea to the west; *Kedar* was Arabia to the east.

Even the creation itself would be appalled at such inexplicable disloyalty. The *heavens* had been summoned to witness the making of the covenant; now they must be summoned back to witness its breaking with shuddering *horror* (12).[18]

The sin of idolatry is bad enough among nations who do not know God. But the prophets (and Jesus) reserve their fiercest condemnation for those of God's own people who *do* know the living God and yet reject him for flashy flimsy alternatives. Idolatry among the people of God is fundamentally unnatural and astonishing – and sadly still prevalent. It is to be found wherever Christians live by the same idolatries as the world around them. This applies to any culture, but in the West it includes the pervasive idolatries of consumerism, militarism, racism, uncritical patriotism and self-centred narcissism. Even Christians get sucked into going after such things, loving and adoring them, treating things that are ultimately worthless as though they were of ultimate value, trusting things that are as transient as a puff of smoke as though they could provide total security. What appalling folly, if only we had the eyes of the prophet.

(ii) Their idolatry was unprofitable (13)

But the tragedy that really broke Jeremiah's heart was that he saw the *cost* of all this idolatry in the lives of those around him. They were deserting God and going after all kinds of other seductive alternatives, *and yet none of it satisfied*. He saw the huge investment of religious sweat, blood and tears in these cults of Ba'al, the eager longings for success, fertility and prosperity that drove them. And he saw them repeatedly frustrated, for false gods never fail to fail. That is the only thing you can depend on about false gods. Whatever they promise, and whatever you pay, the result is the same: shattering disappointment.

But people who are caught up in the great myths of these idolatries rarely see them for the deception they are (any more today than in Jeremiah's day). How then could Jeremiah convey the *stupidity* and the *futility* of abandoning the living God and trying to fix up their own needs by their own resources? At this point Jeremiah came up with the most memorably haunting picture in this chapter that is full of pictures (13).

My people have committed two sins, he begins. At which point he could have concluded, 'apostasy and idolatry', and hearers or readers would yawn with déjà vu. Instead he portrays the first through a picture of absurd agricultural stupidity, and the second through a picture of wrenching physical futility.

[18] Deut. 30:19; 32:1; Isa. 1:2; cf. Mic. 6:1 which similarly appeals to the mountains.

Imagine a farmer fortunate enough to have a perennial spring of water on his land. Such good fortune was extremely rare in a land almost entirely dependent on rainfall. Never again would he need to worry about irrigation for his crops. The spring provides for all his life's needs – directly or indirectly, harvest after harvest. Can you even imagine someone stupid enough to willingly abandon such a priceless asset?[19] What would be the alternative?

Well, imagine the same farmer, hacking away for years in the back-breaking work of carving out a big underground tank in the solid rock beneath the soil. These cisterns, some the size of large rooms, can still be seen in Palestine, and their purpose was to collect the rainfall and store it in hopefully sufficient quantity to see you through the dry season, for irrigation and personal needs (though the water was often stale and infested). But after all the sweat and effort, the rock is found to be cracked and the water drains away. All the effort was in vain. All you hoped for has dribbled away. The whole thing is a pointless, needless waste.

We may think of comparable images in our own day and culture, but Jeremiah's is hard to beat. He exposes apostasy as the height of stupidity and idolatry as the depths of futility. How can people who have experienced the *spring of living water* in the limitless grace, love and provision of the living God, turn their back on him? How can those who know God as the source of all that makes life worth living try insatiably to find satisfaction, life, security and fulfilment in the flawed work of their own hands, *broken cisterns that cannot hold water*?

No wonder Jesus, who grieved like Jeremiah at the heart-breaking struggle of those around him, urged them to find their satisfaction and sustenance in him. 'Come to me', he invited, 'and I will give you rest.' Picking up and expanding Jeremiah's metaphor he offers himself as the water of life and the bread of life, the sole sufficient source of life and fulfilment.[20]

Disloyalty and desertion in the face of such divine generosity deserve the scathing denunciation that Jeremiah pours upon them. Broken promises, broken cisterns, broken hearts.

3. Disaster: unprofitable alliances (2:14–19)

Jeremiah moves on to point out the consequences of such behaviour – consequences that had already begun to be felt in the nation's life,

---

[19] Loss of (or ignorance of) a spring on one's land is part of the poignant theme of the powerful French movies set in Provence, *Jean de Florette* and *Manon des Sources* (1986).
[20] Matt. 11:28–30; John 4:14; 6:35; 7:37–38.

but would get much worse if there were no change in their attitude and actions.

A barrage of rhetorical questions expose the painful fact that Judah was reeling from some recent devastating punitive attacks by Assyria (15) and Egypt (16, *Memphis and Tahpanhes* were two important cities in Egypt). They had taken a beating such as *a slave* might expect (14) – what a comedown for the bride and firstborn of verses 2 and 3. They had deserted their protector (3b), played with predators, and become an easy prey. And yet they continued to play the same dangerous game, running east and west trying to fix up political alliances with the great river empires of *the Nile* and *the Euphrates* – Egypt and Mesopotamia (18). The water imagery of verse 18 continues the metaphor of verse 13. Having abandoned the living water of their covenant Lord, they would be as disappointed by the tainted river waters of untrustworthy political alliances as they were by the broken cisterns of Canaanite fertility cults. 'When the treaty with God had been broken, no treaty with Egypt or Assyria could mend the damage.'[21] Isaiah had warned Judah of the futility of putting any trust in the protection of Egypt a generation earlier, but they had not learned.[22]

The disastrous results of this fickleness, however, were not caused merely by political folly and miscalculation. The roots were profoundly spiritual and moral. It was their abandonment of God (17) and their deliberate social wickedness (19) that brought such disaster upon them – as a punishment that was built into the very offence itself (19a). As so often, we have to feel the impact of Jeremiah's words not only through the ears of those who first heard them preached (when they were a warning and an appeal before the axe fell), but also through the eyes of those who read them in exile, where they had no option but to *drink water from the Euphrates.* For that generation, all the scheming of successive governments had led to inexorable ruin, and verse 19 was no longer a warning for the future but an explanation of the present.

To the political leaders, of course, the idolatry described here would not have seemed like idolatry at all, but as simple political prudence and calculation. Basically, Judah was trying to fix up their own security by playing on the international stage and strengthening their military capability, with no trust in the covenant promises of God that stretched back to their miraculous experiences of *God's* capability in the exodus and wilderness. It is a temptation

[21] Craigie, Kelley and Drinkard, p. 33.
[22] Isa. 30:1–5.

that has never gone away, and can take personal as well as national shape.[23]

Of course there is a proper place for behaving with due care and prudence, as Proverbs repeatedly impresses upon the young. But we can become so obsessed with buying protection or making our lives totally risk-free, that we not only waste precious time and resources, but also rule out any willingness to live with the risks of obedient faith as disciples of the One who had nowhere to lay his head. If the generations of early pioneer missionaries had applied to some mission agencies today, they would never have got past the first paragraph of the health and safety rules, or the first submission of their plans to risk assessment.

A few years ago I read two bumper stickers side by side on a car in the USA: the familiar 'In God We Trust' alongside 'Support Our Troops'. I'm sure there is an appropriate legitimacy to both admonitions. But the second can generate a powerful and very expensive idolatry of almost limitless military spending. Jeremiah would probably protest, 'Which do you really mean?' For in the end, trying to buy ultimate security (at unimaginable cost of national debt) is an illusion that leaves nothing but evil and bitterness in its wake, especially since the cost of such extravagance is usually borne by those least able to afford it – the poor, whose needs are overlooked in budgets that allocate far more to weapons of death than to the means of preserving or improving life.[24]

> *Consider then and realise*
> *how evil and bitter it is for you*
> *when you forsake the LORD your God*
> *and have no awe of me* (19).

---

[23] This whole section of ch. 2 fills out the programmatic accusation of 1:16, according to Rob Barrett (unpublished paper at the 2012 Society for Biblical Literature). There, the reason given for the coming disaster (both of which govern the whole book of Jeremiah) is that the people have forsaken YHWH and are worshipping other gods. This constitutes 'wickedness' – their fundamental evil. But it is not just a matter of religious or ritual activity. Jeremiah interprets everything from reckless political alliances to social and economic injustices as ultimately the fruit of idolatry. All Israel's offences are one form or another of idolatry, ways of abandoning covenant loyalty to YHWH. To abandon this God was to abandon his ways and his laws. Spiritual idolatry and social evil are integrally connected (then as now).

[24] 'Many people today still invest huge sums of money in seeking protection, security and peace, without ever finding them. Unfortunately, such people are even found in churches. They are always asking whether the protection that the Lord Jesus promises is really effective against all dangers. Then they run hither and thither in a frantic search for stronger protection, and fail to recognize that all that they are doing is enriching charlatans of all kinds' (Coulibaly, p. 857).

4. Delusion: unhidden guilt (2:20–37)

a. Exposing the confusion of the people's self-defence

How the people of Judah deluded themselves! Jeremiah records
seven direct quotations from the words of the people. By this means
he cleverly exposes how they swing back and forth between brazen
denial of their sin and abject acceptance of it. There words are simultaneously self-excusing and self-condemning. Here are the quotes
in sequence.

> 'I will not serve you!' (20)

> 'I am not defiled; I have not run after the Baals.' (23)

> 'It's no use! I love foreign gods, and I must go after them.' (25)

> They say to wood, 'You are my father,' and to stone, 'You gave me
> birth.' (27)

> 'Come and save us!' (27)

> 'We are free to roam; we will come to you no more' (31)

> 'I am innocent; he is not angry with me . . . I have not sinned.' (35)

The confusion is astonishing. But it is simply what happens when
people become so embroiled in sin that they can no longer think
straight. In verse 20, they declare their rejection of covenant obligation to Yahweh, but in verse 23, they claim they are not breaking
the covenant by going after other gods. But then in verse 25 they
admit what they denied in verse 23. In verse 27a they address the
sexual symbols of fertility as their parental providers and protectors,
but in verse 27b they cry out to Yahweh to save them, when those
gods manifestly cannot. In verse 31 they treat God in the way that
the prodigal son treated his father, yet in verse 35 they deny all culp-
ability. 'Religious doublethink' had become a skilled art form.[25]

Read together verses 25 and 35 point to addiction. The former (25)
seems to be an admission of defeat, as if to say that their sin is com-
pulsive, something over which they have no control. The latter (35)
is then a claim of innocence, which is one of the hallmarks of
addiction. 'Most likely [verse 35] is revealing of an addictive

[25] Kidner, p. 34.

personality, claiming innocence for actions that are beyond personal control: I cannot be blamed for what I cannot help but do!'[26] These insights of Jeremiah show that the psychology of addiction is not confined to individuals, but can come to characterize a whole community. God's response in 35b shows that such a specious defence will simply not stand up in his court.

b. Exposing the magnitude of the people's sin

Alongside this barrage of quotations comes a profusion of metaphors, as Jeremiah ruthlessly exposes what their sin actually looked like to God. Almost every verse puts a fresh image before our eyes.

20a: Like an unruly ox, Israel has thrown off the *yoke* of serving Yahweh in the covenant bond.[27]

20b: Israel had behaved like a *prostitute*. Since the fertility cults of Ba'al took place on wooded hills, the picture of wanton sexual promiscuity is both literally descriptive of what went on, and figurative of Israel's unfaithfulness to Yahweh as a form of prostitution to other gods.

21: Israel had reverted from the carefully cultivated *choice vine* that Yahweh had planted into a *wild vine*, bearing nothing but useless fruit. The note of disappointment and frustration is evident again.[28]

22: Their guilt was like a *stain* that could not be washed away by *soap* and water. Perhaps this was Jeremiah's assessment of the reforms of Josiah: externally cosmetic, but without radical cleansing.

23–25: In this most daring of all the images in the chapter, Jeremiah compares Israel's behaviour to female animals in *heat* – restless and flighty, and eager to mate with any males they can find. Israel's unfaithfulness to their covenant God was as blatant and as shameless as that: the most holy relationship reduced to animal instincts.

---

[26] McKane, p. 56.

[27] The MT pointing reads 'Long ago I [= YHWH] broke off your yoke and tore off your bonds', which would of course refer to God saving Israel from slavery in Egypt. This would make Israel's words, 'I will not serve you' all the more reprehensible. However, comparison with 5:5b makes the NIV's acceptance of the LXX's reading, 'you broke off', more probable.

[28] On the vine as an image for Israel – positive and negative – see Ps. 80:8–16; Isa. 5:1–7; Ezek. 15, and of course John 15:1–8.

26:     Any disgrace that Israel might feel was not because of
their behaviour in itself, but only because of being
caught and exposed in the spotlight of the prophet's
perceptiveness, like a *thief* caught in the act.

30:     Jeremiah knows how prophets before him had given
God's warnings, and what had happened to them. They
had been executed by the tyrannical state behaving like
a *ravening lion.* Chapter 26:20–23 makes it clear that
this was no paranoid exaggeration.

31:     Israel had wandered away from God, as though God
had been as trackless as a *desert* or as impenetrable as
darkness. Knowing just how much of himself and his
ways God had in fact revealed to these people, God
simply cannot understand such fickleness.

32:     The joys and treasures of *marriage* are again contrasted
with the treacherous amnesia of God's *bride.*

33:     In fact, though brides should take no lessons from
Israel's behaviour, prostitutes (*the worst of women*)
could learn a lot from their wanton ways.

34–35:   Thieves caught breaking into a house at night risked
being killed, without the householder being guilty of
murder.[29] But the Israelites were shedding *the lifeblood
of the innocent poor,* through ruthless social and
economic oppression, while brazenly claiming to be
innocent themselves. The blood-soaked reign of
Manasseh may have been in the mind of Jeremiah, who
was born towards the end of it.[30] Social injustice always
follows corrupted religion. Since covetousness is
idolatry, the idolatry of greed quickly marginalizes the
poor and tears a society apart.

What a kaleidoscope of imagery, and what a catalogue of sin. And
underlying the whole charge sheet is the fundamental sin of covenant
unfaithfulness, of going after other gods (27–28), whether through
the temptations of political and military power games, or the
seduction of the cults of fertility, health, wealth and sexual promiscuity. Such glamorous alternatives to a life of humble trusting
obedience to the living God ('glamorous' because it is remarkable
how violence and sex go so closely together in popular imagination),
still exercise powerful and fatal attraction – even for Christians who
can get caught up in their promising myths, in public or private life.

[29] Exod. 22:2–3.
[30] 2 Kgs 21:16.

And still the message of Jeremiah rings simple and clear – there is no salvation in such things, no matter what they promise. And when real trouble exposes this truth, and people turn back to the God to whom they had turned their backsides (27), they should not be surprised when he allows them to suffer the devastating impotence of the very things they chose to trust in (28). For the exiles, reading verse 28 must have been unbearably painful. The miracle would be that out of such desperate confrontation with the truth there would eventually be a fresh experience of the saving grace of God. But that message was for another day. The immediate prospect was the appalling suffering and public shame of surrender and deportation (37).

Unless Israel could be brought to repentance . . .

And indeed, the next main movement of this great sample of Jeremiah's early preaching will be a passionate plea for the nation to repent, to turn back to God and avoid the terrible judgment that otherwise lay inexorably ahead. But such repentance was problematic. Could Israel just come back to God as if nothing had happened?

5. Divorce – unlawful hopes (3:1–5)

These verses, 3:1–5, form a kind of hinge passage. On the one hand, they bring closure (*divorce*) to the preaching that began with the honeymoon of 2:1–3. But on the other hand, it also opens up the issue that will occupy the prophet's message until 4:4, namely, the meaning of true repentance.

Josiah's reforms seemed to be a great turning back to YHWH. At least that's what Josiah intended. There was a great deal of religious reform going on. Priests were being summoned to serve in Jerusalem, or not at all. The bric-a-brac of idolatry was piling up in the rubbish pit outside Jerusalem. The temple was being restored. The Book of the Law had been found! The king himself had modelled personal repentance and covenant renewal.[31]

But that same Book of the Law itself suddenly presented an obstacle. If the prospect of Israel returning to her covenant Lord was like a wife returning to her husband (as Jeremiah so strongly emphasized, drawing the metaphor from Hosea's profound exposition and experience), what did the law have to say about that?

Shock and horror! *The law forbade any such thing.* The law that regulated divorce in Deuteronomy 24:1–4 prohibited a man from taking back a wife he had officially divorced if, in the meantime, she had been married to another man who had then also divorced her. In its own context, the purpose of the law was undoubtedly to

---

[31] For all these details on the reforms of Josiah, read 2 Kgs 22 – 23.

protect a woman from being treated like a sexual football, getting kicked back and forth from one fickle man to another.[32] Such behaviour was defiling and detestable to the Lord.

So Jeremiah's question in 3:1a would have to be answered, by those who knew the law, with an emphatic 'No'. If the divorced wife had married another man, the original marriage could not simply be reconstituted just like that. If the people of Judah were so complacent that they thought they could flit back to YHWH when their other gods proved unsatisfactory, they needed the shock of this lesson from their own law. For they had not merely been married to *one* other husband; they had cavorted with *multiple* lovers. Repentance could be nothing so shallow as just walking back through the door of the marital home. 'This kingdom of Judah was no passive shuttle-cock between one husband and another, but brazenly promiscuous, installing her lovers, her gods and goddesses, on every hilltop (2), to charm the rain out of the sky and the corn out of the earth in the time-honoured way of Canaan.'[33]

The irony was that those efforts at fertility had been in vain, frustrated by the judgment of the God they had deserted. The ecological effects of their sin were already apparent (3), but caused not the slightest blush of shame. On the contrary, they still managed to talk to God with the same old language of familiar affection. Such words now seemed as obscenely inappropriate as an adulterous spouse mouthing the old sweetheart words of the marriage bed (4–5). For people in such an advanced stage of evil-doing to talk of 'Yahweh's fatherhood, friendship and forbearance' was 'insufferable'.[34]

What hope could there be then?

The only hint of a possible future lies in comparing the form of the two questions that Jeremiah poses in verse 1. The first, *should he return to her again?* is part of the hypothetical legal case being cited, in which 'he' is the first husband. The second, *would you now return to me?* addresses the actual reality of the people. In the light of the way Jeremiah describes their gross unfaithfulness, the answer to the second question has to be no, or at least – not without a great deal more sincerity and radical change than they had shown so far.

But the answer to the first question is more ambiguous and intriguing. The law is framed in terms of what the first husband may wish to do, and prohibits him returning to his original wife after she

---

[32] 'This law ... was aimed against what would amount to virtually *lending* one's partner to another – for if an authoritarian husband could dismiss his wife and have her back when the next man had finished with her, it would degrade not only her but marriage itself and the society that accepted such a practice' (Kidner, p. 35).

[33] Ibid.

[34] Ibid., p. 36.

has belonged to another. But what if that husband is God? Was God bound by the law? Was God prevented by his own statute from ever taking Israel back? If so, what would be the point of Jeremiah's passionate and prolonged appeals to Israel to turn back to God, starting in the very next verses?

The fact that the question is even raised at all shows that the redemptive potential of God's grace transcends the regulatory power of the law. 'The law provides no way into a future for Israel and Yahweh. The law, strictly interpreted, means permanent divorce from Yahweh. The only way for the relationship between Yahweh and Israel to be continued would be on the basis of promise and grace.'[35]

But then, promise and grace were the basis on which the relationship had been founded in the first place – promise (to Abraham) and grace (in Egypt and the wilderness). The law (and particularly this one, which even Jesus understood to be an exercise in damage limitation, softening the effects of the hardness of hearts), was a response to our fallenness, not a limitation on the grace of God. The love of God could redeem and transform the places where the law could not reach. Hosea had proved this truth, in his costly obedience to the command of God to 'love again' the wife who had left him for a life of adultery and prostitution.[36] Hosea, the husband, took the redemptive initiative out of pure love and grace. So would God.

So if the first question in verse 1 is asked in terms of its legal precedent in human divorce law, and translated, '*should he [the husband] return to her*' [that is, 'is he legally allowed to?'], the answer could only be no. But if it is asked in terms of the One to whom the metaphor refers, YHWH himself, and translated as, '*will he [God] return to her?*' [will God take the initiative], the answer has to be more hopeful. We must wait and see. The decision rests with God and his grace, not with the letter of the law.

And it is to the grace of God that we turn in the next section of this great sample of Jeremiah's preaching, as he appeals for a genuine repentance that will have transforming implications for Israel and the world.

Theological and expository reflections

- The theme of first love (like a honeymoon) abandoned later on is a powerful challenge to complacent Christian living. It is echoed in Christ's words to the church in Ephesus in Revelation 2:4–5, a text that could be preached alongside Jeremiah 2:1–3.

---

[35] Fretheim, p. 75.
[36] Hos. 3:1–3.

- The subtlety of idolatry is exposed in this chapter. We see that it was not only a matter of 'other gods' in physical form – the idols and statues of other religions – but also the matter of allegiances and alliances in which people placed their supposed security, or from which they hoped to get great gain. What are the comparable idols within the world church today, and what are the costs and losses involved in going after them?
- Repentance is essential. But it is not 'cheap'. These chapters force us to confront the cost *to God* of bringing us back to himself. The question is not merely whether we can come back to God; but will God take us back and in that sense 'return' to us? Only the death and resurrection of Jesus would answer that question with an eternal 'Yes'.

Jeremiah 3:6 – 4:4
4. Turn, turn, turn

Out of one very small word, Jeremiah made a very big thing, rhetorically, theologically, ethically, and even geographically. The word
is just three letters in Hebrew – *šûb* (pronounced *shoove*). Its simplest
meaning is 'to turn', but Jeremiah (pardon the pun) turned it in all
kinds of ways. It can mean to turn towards someone, or to turn away
from them, or to turn back (in repentance), or to return (physically
to a place). Jeremiah uses it with all these meanings, in a variety of
verbal forms, some fifteen times in this section – which is a profound
reflection on the meaning of repentance.

We are still in the early years of Jeremiah's ministry (6). However,
the breaks in the material, the oscillation between poetry and prose,
and the shifts of perspective between the past, the present and the
future, suggest that a number of distinct messages have been woven
together on the basis of their common theme. If we remember to
listen to these words initially with the ears of those to whom they
were first delivered and then also with the ears of the exiles hearing
them in the form of the edited book, the message goes through a
subtle transformation. Initially, this was a call to repentance that was
never in fact heeded. The hopes of Jeremiah (and God) that Judah
could be spared the wrath to come were dashed in the conflagration
of 587 BC. However, hearing these words in the aftermath of that
catastrophe, the exiles were being challenged once again to feel the
pain in the heart of God and respond at last in a true repentance that
could lead to the future God promised. And it is in that key that the
words still speak across the centuries to our own hearts.

For as we listen to the words of Jeremiah, first preached in
Jerusalem, then later read in exile, they still speak into our own day.
These words give us a glimpse into the pathos of God's broken-
hearted longing for intimacy with his people. They surprise us with
the initiative of God's forgiving grace. They warn us of the cost and

the shame of idolatry. And they lift up our eyes to the missional potential of true repentance among God's people.

1. Shocking comparison: a lesson that hadn't been learned (3:6–11)

About one hundred years before Jeremiah, the northern kingdom of Israel had sunk into an advanced stage of apostasy and idolatry under a succession of weak kings and the impact of Assyrian domination. The warnings of the great northern prophets of the eighth century, Amos and Hosea, had been ignored. The nation fell under the judgment of God and the hammer of Assyria. Samaria was destroyed and the population decimated and exiled in 721 BC – an event which Jeremiah interprets as a certified divorce in 3:8.

And who was watching? The southern kingdom of Judah (7b), to which, doubtless, some of the inhabitants of the north fled as refugees with horror stories of their suffering. Now at that time, Judah was under the relatively godly and reforming government of King Hezekiah. So you might have thought that Judah would have learned a permanent lesson from the destruction of Israel, never to go down the road of such covenant-breaking disloyalty. But sadly not. The king who followed Hezekiah, Manasseh, utterly reversed his political and religious policies and led Judah into half a century of the worst excesses of idolatry, cruelty and bloodshed that the nation had ever known.[1] That was the background to the early ministry of Jeremiah, even as the new king, Josiah, was giving some hope of change.

Incredibly, Judah had become even worse than her northern sister, and Israel's fate was an object lesson that had gone completely unheeded (10–11).

Two points in this message of Jeremiah would have been particularly shocking. First, if people imagined that the reforms being instituted by Josiah constituted an adequate national repentance, they were deceiving themselves. This seems to be the point of verse 10, which implies that some efforts at *return* had been made in Judah, but they were a deceptive sham with no deep down reality (such as 4:1–2 will explain). Jeremiah would spend a great deal of energy trying (and failing) to get that part of his message to sink in.

Secondly, for the staunch citizens of Judah to find themselves compared unfavourably with the proverbially depraved northern tribes, would have been mortally insulting. 2 Kings 17 shows us exactly what the south thought of the north. Yet Jeremiah compounds it by saying that Judah was so much worse as to make Israel appear

[1] 2 Kgs 21:1–18.

relatively righteous (11)! The words are clearly rhetorical, not theo-logically literal. The adjectives linked to both kingdoms (*faithless*, or apostate; *unfaithful*, or treacherous) make the message clear: 'there is no difference; all have sinned and fallen short'.[2] Ezekiel would push this rhetorical technique to even more unbearable lengths, telling Jerusalem that their sins made not only Samaria but even Sodom seem righteous.[3] Jesus offended his hometowns with the same unflattering method.[4]

But what if the lesson could now at last be learned in exile? Perhaps verse 10 could yet be reversed, if the remnant of Israel, south and north, would return to the Lord with all their heart, and not in pretence. Then the appeal and the promises of the Lord himself could come into operation, as we move to the next section.

2. Unexpected promise: a lifeline that hadn't been grasped (3:12–18)

The surprise here is that God, the offended husband who had sent his unfaithful wife away with a certificate of divorce (8), suddenly makes an appeal for her to return (14). Jeremiah is more moved by the example of Hosea than bound by the logic of 3:1 or the law of Deuteronomy 24.

The original setting of this passionate preaching may have been the attempt by Josiah to extend his reforms north of his border into the lands of former Israel (which by this time, of course, had become a province of the Assyrian empire). Josiah seems to have had a vision of a purified and reunited greater Israel.[5] Perhaps Jeremiah here endorses that hope, making God's appeal to the remnants of the northern tribes (whether living in that territory, or possibly as refugees in Judah), to come back home – spiritually to God, and physically to Zion. We have no evidence that the appeal was heeded, though the mocking rejection that greeted Hezekiah's similar appeal a century earlier,[6] makes it very unlikely. Yet the text of this failed appeal stands here in Scripture – both as proof that God had done all he could to bring his people back, and also as a renewed appeal to those who still had ears to hear, even in exile.

Return, faithless Israel. The appeal that comes three times in this chapter (12, 14 and 22), uses our key word twice in a poignant rhyme that is hard to express in English: *šûbâ, mĕšubâ;* lit. 'Turn, you

[2] Rom. 3:22–23.
[3] Ezek. 16.
[4] Matt. 11:20–24.
[5] 2 Kgs 23:15–23.
[6] 2 Chr. 30:1–11.

turning one', or 'Turn back, turning-away-Israel'. 'Come back,' pleads the Lord. 'Come back to me, come back home.' The appeal rests on a truth about God, sets a single condition for the people, and makes a promise for the future.

a. A simple truth (12)

A question had been asked about God in 3:5, which, even though it was asked out of the hypocrisy of appealing to God's forbearance while continuing in wickedness, demanded an answer. 'Will you always be angry? Will your wrath continue forever?'[7] Verse 12 is God's straightforward, blunt, unambiguous answer: 'No.' God declares that his unchanging character is to be faithful: *for I am faithful (ḥāsîd)*. His anger is not forever. This is a truth affirmed in Israel's history and worship. While we must affirm the Bible's insistence on the reality of both the love and the anger of God, we should not regard them as equivalent. Love is an attribute of God, part of his eternal being and character. Anger is the response of God to evil and to human sin. Repentance and rejection of that evil and sin leads to the ending of the anger. God will be love eternally. God *will not be angry forever*. God himself says so.

God's own initiative of forgiving grace enables this appeal to be made. It is not *motivated* by anything that Israel has done or could do, though it is *conditioned* on the one thing that Israel must do.

b. A single condition (13)

Only acknowledge your guilt. It sounds so simple. But these are the people, we remember from chapter 2, who habitually deny any wrongdoing altogether. Guilt? What guilt? (2:23, 35). The first step on the journey back to God is an act of self-knowledge, as the prodigal son found. *Acknowledge*, is simply 'know'. Before the will can become engaged in the process of true repentance, the mind must face reality, without excuse or pretence. And that reality had been nothing less than rebellion, apostasy, and turning a deaf ear to the voice of the Lord. Accept the facts, and the first homeward step has been taken.

Verses 12 and 13 together show us the tension within the heart of God that human sin produces. There is the powerful yearning of the merciful husband (12), alongside the profound recognition of the sheer evil of evil and the assault that it makes upon his will and

---

[7] The same anguished question brings the book of Lamentations to a close, Lam. 5:20–22.

integrity (13). 'The tension so felt and spoken by the poet tears the heart of God, who yearns, but will not be mocked, trivialized, or used.'[8]

The tension would only finally be resolved when God's heart was torn on the cross itself, when in the person of his Son Jesus Christ God took our guilt, rebellion and disobedience upon himself and bore its just consequences. The forgiving grace that God offered to Israel flowed from the same source, available from eternity and accomplished in a history that was as yet future from Jeremiah's standpoint.

c. A complex promise (14–18)

There is something of a crescendo in these verses. They begin with what sounds like an original word to any stragglers from the former northern kingdom – they could return to Zion and find the Lord's welcome there, along with a government pleasing to him (*shepherds after my own heart*). However, as they gather pace, the promises point to a future that would include the loss of *the ark of the covenant* (16) – and thus to the destruction of the temple – i.e. the exile of Judah itself. However, says God, this will no longer matter. The remarkable dismissal of the ark from memory or manufacture may point to two possible expectations: first that Jerusalem itself would become *the throne* of God, not just the ark (17); and second, that the law which had been housed in the ark[9] would ultimately be housed in the hearts of God's people. But that is a feature of Jeremiah's new covenant prophecy that we must keep for later (31:33). The promises escalate even further to envisage a future for *all nations*, whose worship and ethics will be transformed (17),[10] and a unification of the people of God that will transcend the centuries-old political division (18, cf. Ezek. 37:15–28).

It is rather typical of Jeremiah and other prophets that something that starts out as a simple expectation in relation to their contemporary political situation and finds some measure of fulfilment at that level also should suddenly explode like the release of a champagne

---

[8] Brueggemann (1988), p. 43.

[9] Deut. 10:5.

[10] It is a further irony that Jeremiah here envisages *foreign* nations being purged of *the stubbornness of their evil hearts*, at a time when he was battling to get *Israel* to recognize that this was precisely God's verdict on themselves. In the promised future, the nations will no longer be like Israel is now! On the missiological significance of Jeremiah's various visions regarding the nations, see the Introduction. On Jerusalem/Zion as an eschatological symbol of the unity of the nations in worshipping God, cf. Isa. 2:2–5; 56:6–8; 60:11–14.

cork into a fizzing vision that points to a New Testament fulfilment
in Christ, and to an ultimate future that still lies ahead.

In the short run, a band of exiles from Judah, with a sprinkling
from the other tribes, would return from Babylon to Zion and
struggle to rebuild their temple, their city and their way of life.
But in the long run, all of this would be transcended. What is said
here of the *shepherds* (*i.e.* rulers) and of the ark and the nations
reveals the scale of this transformation, with God's people ideally
governed (15), his earthly throne no longer a mere ark but his
entire city . . . ; his Jerusalem the rallying point of all nations, now
converted; and his divided Israel home and reunited. It brings us
right into the era of the new covenant, and indeed to the new
heavens and earth and the 'New Jerusalem' of Revelation 21 – 22,
whose 'temple is the Lord God' (Rev. 21:22), and whose open gates
admit 'the glory and honour of the nations' (Rev. 21:26).

If so distant a prospect was worth unveiling to the old Israel,
six centuries before Christ, it must be doubly relevant to us who
have reached its foothills.[11]

3. Painful lament: a longing that hadn't been fulfilled (3:19–20)

We return to the yearning heart of God. There is both longing and
lament in these two verses. The longing of verse 19 is similar to the
honeymoon nostalgia that we heard in 2:2–3. Here YHWH is
the generous father who has done everything to give his son the
most lavish inheritance possible.[12] The land of Israel was the most
tangible, monumental proof of the relationship between YHWH
and Israel. Repeatedly described as Israel's inheritance, it portrays
that relationship as one between father and son.[13] In view of such
loving generosity, the divine Father felt sure of his son's enduring
affection and loyalty. *I thought you would call me '[My] Father' and*

[11] Kidner, pp. 36–37. Later, in relation to chapters 30 – 33, I shall refer to these as
three horizons of the prophetic texts: Horizon 1 is the Old Testament era itself;
Horizon 2 is the New Testament gospel of Messiah Jesus; Horizon 3 is the eschatological vision of new creation.
[12] The phrase is literally: 'a land of desire, an inheritance of the beauty of beauties
of nations'. The hint that Israel would be one among YHWH's sons (even if the most
favoured), with an inheritance among the nations (even if the most beautiful), suggests
again the missiological significance of Israel's place and role among the nations – that
is explicit at 4:1–2. The concept has very ancient roots; cf. Deut. 32:8–9.
[13] On this very important part of Israel's conception of their relationship with God
(as son to father), more intimate even than the covenant dimension, see, e.g. Exod.
4:22; Deut. 8:5; 14:1; 32:6, 18; Hos. 11:1, and even Jer. 3:4; 31:9, 20. See also Wright,
Knowing God the Father.

not turn away [šûb] *from following me.* But his hopes were to be dashed. The only time Israel addressed such words to their God was when their desperation drove them to assail God like grumbling children but without any moral change (3:4–5). Most of the time they sank to saying these very words to sticks and stones (2:27)!

The lament of verse 20 switches the metaphor back to marriage. Jeremiah feels the pathos of God as the betrayal of both parental and marital love. The love between parent and child and between husband and wife comprise the most profound depths and sublime heights of which human affections are capable. For that very reason they have limitless capacity for causing pain when they are abused or betrayed. The heart of God is torn by the behaviour of an ungrateful delinquent son and an unfaithful promiscuous wife. Once again we must hear the language of God's judgment through the tears of God's grief.

That is what the exiles would hear through the words of Jeremiah when they sat under that very judgment. What could they say in response to such grieving divine love, since they had so culpably ignored it for generations? Perhaps they could make use of a litany that Jeremiah had written years before.

4. Shamed confession: a litany that hadn't been used (3:21–25)

This passage and the next can be read as a kind of dialogue, or litany, with the following voices:

- Israel (21)
- God (22)
- Israel (23–25)
- God (4:1–2)

It may indeed originally have been a litany of confession that Jeremiah hoped the people might use as they turned back in radical repentance to God. Such words (23–25) would be real, sincere, and powerful, in contrast to the shallow assumptions of an easy return that God had already rejected in 3:1–5. In his early ministry Jeremiah seems to have genuinely hoped that the nation would repent and avoid judgment. After years of appeal and warning, though, he came to see the former as impossible and the latter as inevitable.

The litany begins with *a cry . . . on the barren heights, the weeping and pleading of the people of Israel* (21). They have at last come to recognize the futility of what they were doing on those hillsides in the wretched idolatry of the fertility cults, and how terribly they had abandoned their divine father and husband.

So God issues for the third time his appeal (cf. 12, 14), but this time with a remarkable promise (22). Once again Jeremiah plays on the potential of his keyword – *šûb*. Literally, God calls: 'Turn, you turning-away sons, and I will heal your turnings.' The language is strongly reminiscent of, and probably a deliberate echo of, Hosea 14:1, 4. God's promise to *heal* the multiple apostasy of his people is a promise that goes even beyond simply forgiving them. 'Healing is a more comprehensive and holistic divine action – including forgiveness – that affects the entire person and more fully speaks to issues of shame.'[14]

Jeremiah gives the people words that begin with covenant recognition (*you are the LORD our God*, 22b) but end with covenant contrition (*we have not obeyed the LORD our God*, 25b). In between, he calls them to recognize three things about their idolatry, which remain cuttingly relevant to this day.

a. False gods deceive you (23)

All the worship of Ba'al on the mountains was for the sake of health, wealth and fertility, but in the end, it delivers nothing of the kind, and cannot save you when you need it. Salvation is to be found nowhere else than in the living God of Israel, YHWH himself. The sheer impotence of the false gods that humans honour and fall down before is staggeringly demonstrated again and again in human history – but just as staggeringly ignored in every fresh generation. You might have thought we would have learned by now that those who live by the sword eventually die by the sword, but apparently not. Or that we might have learned that markets that go up on a corrupt bubble of greed and gambling can come crashing down when the debt implodes, but apparently not.

b. False gods cost you (24)

Jeremiah leads the horrified people to see the scale of what their idolatries have consumed. The cost has been incalculable in material and human terms. They have sacrificed their substance and their families, for no benefit. And what are we to make of the jaw-dropping cost of our worship before the idol of militarism today – consuming astronomical amounts of the world's wealth (in rich and poor countries) on swords, when people desperately need ploughs? And when we looked to mammon to save us all, we found that it cost us *trillions* of dollars and pounds simply to keep its temples of casino finance in business, in the banking crisis of 2008.

---

[14] Fretheim, p. 86.

c. False gods shame you (25)

When you are exposed under the spotlight of how much you have been deceived and how much that deception has cost you (and how you ignored all warnings), one response is inevitable – profound shame. Jeremiah actually calls the god Ba'al by the derogatory nickname the prophets reserved for him – Ha Bosheth, The Shame (24). And he has already observed that people become like what they worship (2:5). So the only place to go is to hide under the blankets of disgrace in a bed of shame and confess the enormity of what you have done.

Such was the litany of confession that Jeremiah gave his people, if they were to avail themselves of God's offer of healing and home-coming. But it was never used in his own day, as the following chapters will quickly show. Could it become the liturgy of a people languishing in exile, now fully aware of the truth of all it affirmed? That must have been the hope of those who preserved the book of Jeremiah among the exiles.

But God had one more thing to say, because the God of Israel had the rest of the world in view.

5. Worldwide consequences: a long-term vision that hadn't been realized (4:1–4)

For the last time (in this section), the *šûb*-word comes again, but in a cryptic form that could be taken several ways. Literally, God says simply, 'If you will turn, Israel (oracle of YHWH), to me you will turn.' Three interpretations suggest themselves:

Placing the emphasis on 'to me', would suggest: 'If you do want to return, make sure it is truly *to me* that you return' – that is, in complete rejection of all other gods and total allegiance to me as your sole covenant Lord.

Or, we may recall that the whole section began in 3:1 by putting the very possibility of any return under question. By the law of Deuteronomy 24, a husband cannot divorce a wife and then 'return to her' after another failed marriage. So after Israel's flagrant promiscuity, when God had asked in 3:1, 'Will you return to me?', 'Not according to the law,' had to be the answer. But now a different answer is given: 'If you will *repent*, then you may indeed return to me after all.' You are not under law. Grace wins.

Or (and this is my own preference), we could take the second phrase ('to me you will turn') as a continuation of the first phrase, leading on to two further 'ifs' in verses 1b and 2a, with the final apodosis in verse 2b, in which the result of Israel's return to YHWH is seen to affect the nations. This would produce the following exegesis:

> *IF* you return, Israel – that is, if to me you return –
>   [by which I mean:]
> if you put your abominations out of my sight and
>   do not wander off,
> and if you swear, 'as the LORD lives', in truth,
>   in justice and in righteousness,
> *THEN*, nations will call themselves blessed in him
>   and in him they will render praise.

This remarkable text puts before us both the nature of true repentance and the astonishing breadth of what is at stake in it.

a. Repentance and ethics

Repentance must be both spiritual (1b) and ethical (2a). Israel must first recognize all other gods than YHWH as 'abomination', and ruthlessly reject them, and stop wandering off in dazed devotion to them. But secondly, their return to YHWH-centred worship and life ('as YHWH lives' was a phrase used not only in worship but in social situations where truth and trust were paramount, such as the courts and business deals) must be marked by a return to YHWH-like qualities – truth, justice and righteousness. It was not just a matter of purging the religious landscape of false gods. It was also a matter of purging the social, economic and political landscape of lies, injustice and oppression. The two things, of course, are integrally intertwined. Idolatry and injustice always go together. Repentance is unavoidably ethical in its demands – as John the Baptist saw and taught clearly.[15]

b. Repentance and mission

If Israel would truly repent in the radically ethical way just described, and return to whole-hearted covenant allegiance to the Lord, then what? We might have expected Jeremiah to say something like, 'Then God will have mercy on his people and spare them the threatened judgment.' But it is almost as if Jeremiah skips over that as too obvious to mention ('Yes, yes, of course it is true that if Israel repents, *Israel* will be blessed and forgiven'), and lifts our eyes to a much wider horizon, reminding us of the very reason why Israel existed

---

[15] Luke 3:1–20.

in the world at all, namely, to be the vehicle of God's blessing *other nations*. This was the whole point of their election.

And so, in a clear allusion to the language of the covenant with Abraham,[16] God envisages that the fruit of Israel's repentance would be seen in the extension of YHWH's blessing and the praise of YHWH among the nations. 'It becomes clear that true repentance on Israel's part would have far-reaching consequences not merely for Israel, but also for mankind in general (cf. Isa. 42:6, 49:6).'[17]

This indicates sharply what is at stake when God's people either obey him, or fail to. It shows what is at stake when they repent, or stubbornly refuse to. It is not just a matter of their own relationship with God. It is not just that disobedience will cost them and grieve God. The fact is that, since God's people exist in the world fundamentally for the purpose of God's mission to bring blessing to the nations, then either our obedience will facilitate that divine purpose (and fulfil our own mission), or our disobedience will frustrate and hinder it (and deny our own mission). Effectively God is saying, 'Let my people come back to *their mission*, back to being the people they are meant to be – back to living as the people of God in the midst of the world of nations, and let me then get back to *my* mission of bringing blessing to the nations through them, and praise and glory to myself among all nations.'

There is no biblical mission without biblical ethics.

c. Repentance and new beginnings (3–4)

Jeremiah uses two metaphors to capture the kind of repentance needed.

First, *break up your unploughed ground* (3). That is, don't try to work in the old field that is choked with thorns, but start completely afresh on virgin soil. Jeremiah is probably once more echoing his prophetic hero (cf. Hos. 10:12).

Second, *circumcise yourselves* (4). To which the answer might well have been, 'We are already circumcised'. But Jeremiah insists, like Deuteronomy 10:16 and 30:6, that this must be a circumcision of the heart (an idea that was not invented by Paul, though he gladly used it).[18] Circumcision, like baptism, was the entry point into the

---

[16] Gen. 12:3, and four more times in Genesis. For in-depth discussion of the missional significance of the Abrahamic covenant, see Wright, *The Mission of God*, chs. 6 and 7.

[17] Thompson, p. 213. See also the further discussion of the missiological dimensions of Jeremiah's message in the Introduction, pp. 35–39.

[18] Rom. 2:25–29.

covenant relationship. So telling them to circumcise themselves was in effect saying, 'Start again. Come through the door again' – rather as Hosea had envisaged God bringing Israel back to the wilderness in order to start all over again with them.[19]

The double metaphor, then, makes a single point. Repentance involves a radical new beginning with God, with a fresh surrender of heart, mind and will, of worship and life, to him as covenant Lord. With such a new beginning, all things are possible with God. This was a message the exiles needed to hear, and indeed Jeremiah would repeat it to them decades in the future (see ch. 29). But without it, there could be nothing ahead but judgment for the generation to whom Jeremiah first spoke. The rest of chapter 4 will spell out its horrific reality.

Which means, before we turn on to the darkness of the next section, that the appeals of this passionate poem fell on deaf ears at the time it was preached. And yet, they still hold out their message of the 'wounded hope of God',[20] first to the exiles engulfed in that darkness, and then to all subsequent generations of God's people caught up in the snares of idolatry and sin. The intense poetry oscillates between the impossibility of return (imposed by the divorce law in God's Torah), and the longing for return (expressing the grieving love in God's heart).

> The torah establishes that Judah has no right to return. The torah establishes that YHWH has no obligation to take her back. The themes of guilt and betrayal are stated with overriding power and clarity. None of that quite touches the central affirmation of the poem, however. The truth of the matter is that, after the requirements of torah are acknowledged, there is the unfinished business of the relationship that the torah cannot contain . . . The real issue is that *YHWH is hurt* and filled with humiliated indignation. Nonetheless, *YHWH is open* to restoration.[21]

How can these be reconciled? As we have said, ultimately only the cross of Christ and the New Testament's reflection on it could give the full answer and sustain the righteousness of God in both dimensions. Jeremiah, meanwhile, is caught in the agonizing tension of declaring both truths – law and grace, the threat of judgment and the appeal to come home – with equal power and faithfulness.

---

[19] Hos. 2:14–23.
[20] Brueggemann (1988), p. 48.
[21] Ibid.

Theological and expository reflections

What lessons might we learn from pondering the powerful pathos of Jeremiah's poetry? What kind of responses might an expository application suggest?

- The danger of paying no heed when God puts object lessons in front of our eyes concerning the terrible consequences of ignoring his warnings and persisting in sin.
- The hurt in the heart of God over the sins of his people, and the gospel power of his thrice-repeated, grace-filled, promise-laden appeal, 'Come back, come back to me.'
- The awesome cost and loathsome shame of idolatry. False gods never fail to fail; we just never fail to forget that truth. But in the end we pay the cost and bear the shame – until we return to the One who did both on our behalf.
- The ethical core of repentance, and its missional impact. If God's people seek restoration, or revival, or renewal, or reformation (or whatever word best suits the ecclesiastical context), then that has to penetrate to the core of their behaviour as covenant-keeping disciples of Christ in the midst of the nations. But if they *do* repent in such fashion, then there are no limits to what God may do through them in his mission of blessing the nations.

Jeremiah 4:5 – 6:30
5. Disaster from the north

'Come back, come back to me,' God pleaded with his people throughout chapter 3. To no avail. With increasing sorrow Jeremiah realizes that the call to repentance may never be heeded. And if it is not, then the outpouring of the pot of judgment (1:13–14) became increasingly inevitable. The precise source of that danger is not yet specified – except that it would come from the north, the direction from which most enemies attacked Judah. But the sheer terror of it fills these remaining chapters of Jeremiah's earliest preaching.

There is some flow of thought in this section. The rest of chapter 4 is mostly filled with a graphic portrayal of the horrors and destructiveness of invasion, siege and conquest. Chapter 5 focuses on the moral decay of the people and the scandalous complacency of the religious leaders. Chapter 6 returns to the horrors of the coming siege, but concentrates on God's analysis of the stubbornness of his people and the moral necessity of the judgment. And in the midst of all these recurring themes, we get glimpses of the agony going on in the heart of Jeremiah himself, as he speaks the words of God and feels the pain of God.

However, for the sake of a reasonably ordered exposition of the tumultuous poetry, rather than moving verse by verse we will identify four major themes within it and trace them through all three chapters. First, we hear the ominous background music of the whole section – the *external terror* of coming invasion. Secondly, we feel the *internal turmoil* in the emotions of Jeremiah, with which he also expresses the emotions in the heart of God. In contrast to that, thirdly, we witness the scandalous *religious complacency* of those who should have been leading the people in better ways. And finally, we listen to God's own *analysis and explanation*, as God first exposes the sordid and stubborn behaviour of the people and then pleads that they were leaving him with no other morally possible option than purging judgment.

1. External terror: the coming invasion

a. Warning (4:5–8, 11–18)

Completely out of touch with reality. That's how Jeremiah's early preaching in the reign of Josiah must have seemed. At that time there was no external threat. On the contrary, the great hundred-year enemy – Assyria – was creaking at the seams. Yet Jeremiah cries out about an imminent invasion. It did not actually take place till forty years later, and it came from Babylon not Assyria, but his words here must have haunted those who first heard the warning but took no notice and then lived to have seen them come horrifically true.

An enemy is already on the move against Judah, bent on terrifying destruction (7, 13, 16). But his plans are not just his own; for God affirms, *I am bringing disaster from the north* (6), such that the devastation will be the work of *the fierce anger of the LORD* (8). But what is arousing God's anger? Verses 17b and 18 explain. Fundamentally, the evil Judah will reap is the evil she has sown. *This is your punishment*, is literally, 'this is your own evil' – the same word, *rā'â*, translated *disaster* in verse 6. God's judgment is in fact their own rebellious *conduct and actions* rebounding on their own heads. If it was *bitter* and *piercing* to contemplate in advance (18), how much more so must it have been to reflect on it after the event.

But where does the warning come from? It is a strange paradox that the one who has unleashed the agents of judgment is the same one who gives his people warning of their approach – as if to give them time to flee to safety (5–6). Strange – but not unique. Ezekiel found himself posted as God's sentry to give warning to his people that God was on his way against them.[1] What human enemy appoints a sentry to give warning to the very city they are about to attack? But that is God's way – even when judgment is irreversible, God's prophets are sounding warnings, warnings that flow from the baffled, longing heart of God himself, as verse 14 makes clear. Even at this late stage God and Jeremiah urge Jerusalem to flee, not to the flimsy sanctuary of a fortified city, but to the only thing that could be their salvation – repentance. *Wash the evil* [rā'â] *from your heart. How long* would they persist in wickedness without remorse (14)? Answer: until it was tragically too late.

[1] Ezek. 3:16–21.

b. Catastrophic ruin (4:23–28)

Cormac McCarthy's book *The Road*[2] paints an unremittingly bleak and searing picture of the world after some terminal catastrophe (we are left wondering if it was the result of climate change or some nuclear holocaust). Everything in the landscape is dead and desolate, and only a few scavenging and murderously desperate human beings survive.

Jeremiah manages to convey the same sense of apocalyptic horror in the space of four verses, all beginning with the tolling bell, *I looked . . .* (23–26). In his awful vision, everywhere he looks, he sees the undoing of creation itself. The language clearly recalls Genesis 1 and 2, but in terrible negative reversal. At one level, of course, Jeremiah is putting into graphic poetic form the destructiveness of warfare, in which invading forces consume or destroy everything in their path, leaving a wasteland behind them. But at another level, his use of creation (or 'un-creation') language makes it clear that the work of the human enemy will be the work of the *fierce anger* of the Lord (26), and that, just as the word of God had *spoken* creation into existence, so the same God now says of his devastating work of judgment, *I have spoken and will not relent* (28). And at yet a third level, this text (like others in Jeremiah that we shall notice), points us to the cosmic and creational impact of human sin. The wickedness that brings the judgment of God simultaneously brings grief to creation. The two are linked inextricably, for since we are of the earth and were created to care for the earth, our persistent rebellion inevitably has ecologically destructive effects on our relationship with the earth.

Amidst the horror, one ray of hope shines through: the destruction will not be total (27). God's devastating judgment would seem to roll back the very fabric of creation itself, but its outcome would leave a remnant (as other prophets put it) – a fact which those who would read these words in exile would understand with the rueful agreement of survivors. The land lay in ruins, but not without hope for the future (cf. 5:10, 18). Much later in his ministry, Jeremiah would amplify such words of hope into whole chapters of comforting reassurance, as we shall see – but not for a long time yet!

c. Invasion (4:29–31)

The final three verses of the chapter return to the noise and confusion of actual invasion, and picture three reactions that people will have

---

[2] Picador, 2009.

in those terrifying moments. Some will try to escape through taking flight – running for safety to any scrap of cover they can find (29). Some will try to seduce the invader in a last pathetic attempt to play the harlot. Verse 30 may portray literal attempts by desperate women to placate the enemy by offering whatever charms they had left, or more likely it is another of Jeremiah's parodies on Judah's attempts to buy favour with other nations that would in the end tear them to pieces. But finally, for many, the only futile refuge will be the breathless scream of the dying victims of war's brutality (31). Such a fate would have seemed unthinkable to the beautiful *Daughter of Zion* in the days of the young Jeremiah and his zealous king, Josiah.

d. Destruction (5:10–11, 15–17; 6:1–5, 22–26)

These four passages in chapters 5 and 6 keep coming back relentlessly and brutally to the theme of imminent invasion and siege: the enemy is on his way, and when he arrives, the devastation will be terrible. The resources of the country, material, animal, vegetable and human, will be consumed (5:16–17). But what that enemy will do is portrayed as if it were a direct command from YHWH the God of Israel himself (5:10). The shock is that the people of Judah would have been expecting God to do exactly the opposite. Surely God was there to *protect* their vineyards from the enemy. Not so; their rebellion is so great that God has virtually disowned them. The final phrase of 5:10 is shattering – *these people do not belong to the LORD* (cf. 6:30). It would take a miracle of grace to reverse that verdict.

All of this must have sounded wildly alarmist in the days Jeremiah first preached. He was pointing forward to something that only he could see with the clarity of prophetic vision. When he first spoke such words, it was still a long way off. But imagine reading these graphic predictions in exile, no longer as a distant warning of things to come but as an all too realistic (and probably even inadequate) description of the traumatic reality that the exiles had endured. Would the message at last sink in – the message of *why* it had all happened and what they must now do in repentant response?

2. Internal turmoil: the personal struggles of Jeremiah

So what was it like to be a prophet called to proclaim such a message? Did you just stand up and rattle off the words and go home for dinner, and then wait calmly till the next message dropped into your mind? Very, very far from it. The personal stress and struggle of having to visualize and then articulate such dire messages was enormous. Later in the book we will find whole passages in which

95

Jeremiah pours out his heart, wrestling with God in the most brutally honest words we find on the lips of any biblical character. But here, even in this early preaching, we get some glimpses of the toll it took on his mind and emotions. For Jeremiah, the message itself caused him a mixture of confusion and anguish. And the experience of delivering it was like a bursting flask or a blasting furnace. Come and see these effects. Come and feel the confusion, anguish, bursting and blasting.

a. Confusion (4:10)

'*Ah, Sovereign Lord,*' says Jeremiah, in an echo of his first protest to God (1:6). This time, however, it seems not so much a protest as a genuine puzzle: *how completely you have deceived this people and Jerusalem* . . . What on earth led Jeremiah to think such a thing?

This verse is probably a window on the confused world of multiple prophets in Jerusalem. Now we know (with hindsight) that most of the prophets contemporary with Jeremiah were false, and that he was virtually alone in bearing the true word of God. However, that distinction would not have been so obvious at the time to many of the people, and perhaps not even sometimes to Jeremiah himself. After all, prophets did not wear name-badges: 'Jeremiah: True Prophet'; 'Hananiah: False Prophet'. And all those other prophets confidently prefaced their words with 'This is what YHWH says', just as vigorously as Jeremiah. If they contradicted one another, who were you supposed to believe?

This verse is puzzling but it may suggest that, for a while at least, Jeremiah thought that the other prophets were in fact bringing a word from the Lord, when they told the people of Jerusalem, '*You will have peace*'. But Jeremiah *knew* that God was actually planning an invasion of disastrous destructiveness: *the sword is at our throats.* So his only explanation was that God was somehow deliberately deceiving the people through those *other* prophets.

If this is the right way to understand this verse, then it is a remarkable example of how God has allowed his inspired word to include words spoken by human beings even in confusion and misunderstanding. These words of Jeremiah, though confused, come to us in their own context as part of the word of God. There was no truth in Jeremiah's assumption here, as he would later see very clearly, when he grasped the depth of deception to which the other prophets had sunk (see section 3 below). It was certainly not *God* who was deceiving anybody! But Jeremiah was human, and human beings get confused, and God allowed him to voice that confusion, and corrected it later.

b. Anguish (4:19–21)

Oh my anguish, my anguish! Whose voice is this? God is the speaker
in the verses immediately before and after (18, 22). So at first sight
this cry also seems to come from the grieving heart of God himself.
But the reference to a pounding heart, and the visual anticipation of
battle scenes, makes it clear that Jeremiah is the one venting his pain
here. Nevertheless, there can be no doubt that the emotions of the
prophet reflect those of his God, for if the heart that is pounding in
agony in verse 19 belongs to Jeremiah, the heart that is pierced with
bitterness at the end of verse 18 belongs to God.

My anguish is literally, 'my belly'. The staccato words of verse 19
speak of a churning stomach and a throbbing rib-cage – the effects of
violent emotional stress, as Jeremiah experiences the shocking sights
and sounds of battle. There is no glorying in warfare, no gloating over
a people and land suffering what they are said to deserve as judgment.
Nothing but pain and anguish at the 'evil' these people have brought
upon themselves. We are reminded yet again that the language of
God's judgment must be heard through the agony of God's heart.

c. Bursting (6:9–12)

Burdened with yet another message from God portraying the coming
judgment as a thorough gleaning of every last grape on the vine (9),
Jeremiah wonders if anybody will ever listen to his message (10),
and not for the first or last time decides (probably), that there is
simply no point in dinning into deaf ear-drums (cf. 20:7–9). But
silence is more painful than speaking, for the accumulating message
within him makes him feel like a vessel filling up to bursting point,
till the terrible contents can no longer be held in (11a).

The frightful message of verses 11b–12 does not mean that God
targets especially the children or the old in his anger, but rather that
the coming judgment (the rebound of the people's evil on their own
heads) will leave no section of society unaffected. The grim realities
of invasion, conquest and exile would engulf the nation and be
inescapable for young and old especially. In ancient as in modern
times, war is no respecter of little people. Every scene of war that
we witness on our TV is at its most unbearable when we see what
happens to children and women.

d. Testing (6:27–30)

The closing verses of this whole section that has run through chapters
2 – 6, assigns to Jeremiah a role that was fierce in its operation, but

tragically futile in its failure. He was to be like the fire of a blast-furnace, testing and refining metals, burning up the dross, in the hope of finding some precious metal. *The bellows blow fiercely* (29), may well have been an image that the people of Jerusalem mockingly applied to Jeremiah himself and his preaching. But sadly, in spite of all God's efforts to use Jeremiah in this purging and refining way, *the refining goes on in vain; the wicked are not purged out* (29).

The final verse of the whole section must have been chilling when it was first uttered, and even more frightening when it hung over those who sat in exile – the place of experienced rejection. *They are called rejected silver, because the* LORD *has rejected them* (30).

By God's amazing grace, there would be a reversal of this verdict, and Jeremiah himself would later bring words of hope and a future beyond the fires of judgment. But that day was not yet.

3. Religious complacency: the reaction of leaders and prophets

Jeremiah was far from alone as a prophet in Jerusalem. The religious and political leadership included professional prophets among their number. But their only contribution, in the face of the catastrophe that Jeremiah foresaw, was to stand resolutely between the people and the only action that would have prevented that catastrophe – namely genuine repentance, demonstrated in religious and social change. The complacency of the leaders only served to compound the crisis and make it all the more inevitable.

a. Collapsed lies (4:9; 5:12–13)

When the disaster would eventually fall (*in that day,* 4:9), then the whole political and religious establishment would collapse in appalled disbelief. The whole fabric of lies and self-delusion that they had woven for decades (indeed for centuries, as we shall see in the next chapter), would be shredded before their eyes. If Jeremiah had for a moment thought that the other prophets were right in their optimism (such that *God* was deceiving the people through them (4:10), then he quickly understood the real truth. Their cosy dismissal of any danger amounted to one damning fact: *they have lied about the* LORD (5:12) – not the most sensible strategy for anyone claiming to speak in his name. Their message in verse 12 is of course a direct denial of the word that Jeremiah was bringing. It has the same flavour as the flat denial of God's word with which the serpent tempted Eve,[3] and these people would tragically believe the prophets' lies just as Eve

---

[3] Gen. 3:4.

believed the serpent's lie, and with the same deathly result – shame and expulsion from the place of God's blessing and presence.

b. Collusion in delusion (5:30–31; 6:13–15)

But false prophecy requires willing listeners. There is a double delusion going on – of the deceiver and the (willingly) deceived. This is what 5:30–31 sees as *a horrible and shocking thing*. A religion of lies and a politics of lies require people who prefer to inhabit a universe of lies than face up to the truth – a people who *love it this way*. But when that people claim to be *my people*, it is unbearably tragic.

When such collusion between those who peddle the lies and those who profit from them becomes established, it poisons the whole culture with greed, *from the least to the greatest* (6:13). And when greed becomes 'good', the eyes become blind and the conscience atrophies like an unused muscle. If the conscience is not exercised, it withers away out of all memory or even recognition. There is something astonishingly perceptive, and perennially relevant about Jeremiah's analysis. He sees the combination of religious and social shamelessness, the anaesthesia of the most fundamental human response to wickedness. Forget *shame*; those who collude long enough in greed-fuelled unethical conduct lose the capacity even to be *embarrassed* about it: *they do not even know how to blush* (6:15). The financial crisis of late 2008 gave us ample evidence of such jaw-dropping shamelessness. Far from feeling any shame or making any change, those who precipitated the crisis, as soon as they had been rescued by public money at tax-payers' expense, promptly returned to the same tainted practices as before. Utterly shameless.

4. Divine verdict: God's analysis and explanation

In the middle of chapter 5 we hear the people's key question that the coming conflagration would raise: 'Why?' *Why has the LORD our God done all this to us?* (5:19). Jeremiah provides God's answer in advance. Throughout these chapters there are interspersed passages of direct divine explanation. Essentially, God says, the people of Judah have sunk to such a level of social depravity, and at the same time risen to such a level of stubborn resistance, that they leave God no other course of action than to bring judgment upon them through the fruit of their own unrestrained wickedness. *What else could God do without denying his own character?* God answers their question with that question of his own.

a. Social evils

(i) A search for honesty (5:1–6)

God sends Jeremiah on another visit to the city (cf. 2:2), this time on a research mission. There is probably some rhetorical exaggeration in the quest: *if you can find but one person who deals honestly and seeks the truth*. Baruch, for example, and some of his family, represented at least a rump of godly folk in the city, and Jeremiah was not entirely without friends in later life (including the compassionate black African, Ebed-Melek, 38:7–13). However, the point is clear: the whole culture of the city had become one of cheating (on one another) and contempt (for the truth and holiness of God). *As surely as the LORD lives*, was an expression in common use in places where truthful speech was expected (e.g. in giving evidence in court, or making business deals), but where it was now grotesquely absent (2b).

The form of the challenge in 5:1 recalls Abraham's questions to God in Genesis 18:23–33. Abraham had found to his surprise that God was only too eager to be merciful to Sodom and Gomorrah – far more so than Abraham ever expected. 'Spare the city for the sake of fifty righteous people? Of course! I'd be willing to do it for ten, if you can find them!' The fact that Jeremiah could not even find *one* righteous person (rhetorically speaking) in Jerusalem makes a very ugly comparison indeed. If God would have spared Sodom, how much more did God long to *forgive this city*, if he could find the slenderest justification to do so? But Jeremiah could find none – nor even any hope of any, given the stony-faced refusal that his pleading words encountered (3b).

Jeremiah's change of tactics in verses 4–5 may have been genuine; as a boy from the village he may have been shocked by the scale of cheating on the streets of the city, but hopeful of a higher level of morality among the 'great and the good'. If so, his hopes were dashed as he found among the social elite exactly the same deliberate ignoring of the fundamentals of covenant faith and ethics (*the way of the LORD, the requirements of their God*). The whole society is rotten from top to bottom.

The repetition of that key phrase in verses 4b and 5b shows that this really is the nub of the matter. This is Torah language. This is covenantal and ethical language. This is the repeated phraseology of Deuteronomy. So if Deuteronomy was in fact 'the book of the law' that had been so recently found and promulgated by Josiah, the effect was precisely zero on the streets, no matter how many royal robes were torn in the palace.[4] For such covenant-breaking *rebellion*,

---

[4] 2 Kgs 22:11.

covenant curses would fall, in the form of enemies whose ferocity could be portrayed as devouring wild animals (6; cf. Deut 28:49–52, and Hos. 13:7–8).

(ii) Oppression and covetousness (5:26–28; 6:6–8)
The whole society has been gripped by the tentacles of dishonesty (5:1) and greed (6:13). In such a culture there are those who profit with gross obscenity while others languish voiceless and defenceless at the bottom of the pile. A culture of aggressive, predatory covetousness is accurately described in 5:26–28a, in which some people make themselves exceedingly rich on the basis of ruthlessness and deceit. Yet at the same time, and very close by, are those they *could* have helped, but deliberately choose not to (28b). It is hard to escape the comparison with the economic crisis of late 2008 and after, when trillions of dollars and pounds were found from somewhere to shore up the wealth of those whose reckless greed and financial folly had brought the whole system virtually to the point of implosion, while the poor of the earth (indeed, the poor in the same Western countries) are denied even the scraps that fall from the rich man's table, so that widows and orphans die for lack of the clean water and affordable medicines that a mere fraction of such astronomical quantities of national treasure could provide.

Such a society and social system is like a well that is polluted with some toxic, virulent poison (6:7). As the well pours out its store of wickedness, so those who drink from it fall victim to the *sickness and wounds* that it produces in the form of unending *violence and destruction*. What future can there be for such a self-replenishing wellspring of wickedness? *This city must be punished; it is filled with oppression* (6:6). The city Jeremiah had in mind was Jerusalem, but the same thing was said of Sodom, and has lost none of its moral necessity in the cities of today's world.

b. Stubborn attitudes

(i) Foolish people (4:22; 5:20–25)
'The fear of the Lord is the beginning of knowledge.'[5] So to choose deliberately *not* to know the Lord is the essence of folly. This explains the stark equation that launches 4:22: *My people are fools; they do not know me.* The rest of the verse reads like a photographic negative of Proverbs 1:1–7, where the moral and spiritual values of wisdom are listed. The phrase, *they are skilled*, is literally 'they are wise', but

---

[5] Prov. 1:7; cf. 4:22.

with sharp irony the prophet says that the only way these people are 'wise', is in *doing evil*.[6]

Continuing to draw on the Wisdom tradition, 5:20–25 makes the accusation that the people are *foolish and senseless,* and as blind and deaf as the idols they worshipped.[7] Their lack of fear of the Lord (5:22) is lack of wisdom. The imagery drawn from creation (a typical Wisdom comparison) reinforces their stubborn rebellion. When the ocean (symbol of rebellion and chaos) actually obeys the limits God has set for it, how appalling it is that God's own people transgress the moral boundaries God has set for them. What kind of unnatural, incorrigible rebellion is that? Indeed, is there *any* way in which these people will acknowledge the living God at all? They refuse to acknowledge him as their redeemer (2:5–7). Now they learn no lesson from him as the creator either (5:24).

(ii) Walking the wrong way (6:16–21)
If Deuteronomy was indeed the book found in the temple in the course of Josiah's reforms, then it probably provides the background for this concise oracle of judgment. Deuteronomy constantly urges the people to walk in the *way* of the Lord and not turn aside from it.[8] And Deuteronomy contains severe covenant *warnings* about the consequences if they should do so.[9] But the people of Jeremiah's day refused both the ways of God and the warnings of God.

The exhortation of verse 16 speaks of *ancient paths* and *the good way,* almost certainly meaning the original covenant faith of Sinai, as summarized in Deuteronomy. Such an understanding of the terms is reinforced by the phrases at the end of verse 19, *my words . . . my law.* So yet again, God calls his people back to their written, known, covenant law – a call that was all the more poignant in the wake of the publication of the Book of the Law, and made their refusal to obey it all the more culpable. For if only they had returned to covenant obedience, they would have found *rest* for themselves (16). That is, they would have found peace and harmony with God, with one another, and with the world around them. This is the verse that was probably in Jesus' mind when he urged people to submit to the yoke of obedience to himself (thus controversially placing himself in the role of the law).[10]

---

[6] The word order of the end of v. 22 brings out this irony and bitter contrast: 'Wise they are – towards the evil; but as for doing good, they don't even know how to.'
[7] Cf. Ps. 115:4–8.
[8] E.g. Deut. 5:32–33; 10:12–13; 26:17; 30:16; etc.
[9] Especially, Deut. 27 – 30.
[10] Matt. 11:28–30.

So there is a shocking stubbornness in the repeated blank refusal of the people to heed either the exhortation of the law (*we will not walk in it*, 16), or the warning of the prophets (*we will not listen*, 17). All that the Scripture-based reforms of Josiah had done was to make even clearer the way they would *not* walk in and the warning they would *not* listen to. Such stubbornness troubled Jeremiah greatly. He complains of it again and again, indicating that it was characteristic of the response to his preaching all through his career as a prophet.[11]

The verdict and sentence in verses 18–21 similarly follow the form of a covenant lawsuit, in which *nations* and *earth* are summoned as witnesses to hear the charge.[12] As Deuteronomy had spelled out, the way of persistent disobedience brings its own in-built retribution. God will 'bring' it, of course – for he decreed it in the first place. But the evil that will happen to them under God's judgment (19: *disaster* is simply 'evil'), is nothing less than *the fruit of their schemes*, the guaranteed end result of persistent rebellion (cf. 4:18). And indeed, when Babylon's wrath would fall on them it would indeed be the result of their incorrigible international scheming. God's judgment consisted in the price they paid for their own political machinations.

And God's judgment could not be bought off with religious rituals, either, however costly and exotic (20).[13] Extravagant imports for the temple could not compensate for extortionate dishonesty on the streets (5:1). This verse is not a rejection of the sacrificial system in and of itself, but rather saying that religious activity was *not acceptable* to God when it was offered from the hands of such people. *Your burnt offerings . . . your sacrifices*; if *you* are living blatantly in a way that does *not please* God, then don't expect your religious activity to please him. He neither needs it nor wants it.[14]

c. The logic and limits of judgment

Finally, in God's analysis, we need to take note of the struggle going on within God's own self. On the one hand, there are the rhetorical questions, which ask the people what alternative was open to God, other than purging judgment. If God be God, then there is a moral

[11] See, e.g., Jer. 3:17; 5:23; 7:24; 9:14; 11:8; 13:10; 16:12; 23:17.

[12] Cf. Deut. 32:1; Isa. 1:2; Mic. 6:2.

[13] *Sheba* was in south-west Arabia, the source of very expensive incense. *Calamus* is a form of sweetcane that may possibly have come from south-west India.

[14] In this rejection of the sacrifices of people whose lives offend God, Jeremiah shares the same perspective as Amos (5:21–24), Hosea (6:6), Isaiah (1:10–17) and Micah (6:6–8) before him.

necessity for God to act consistently with God's own character. And yet, on the other hand, there is such *reluctance* to do so, such grief in the doing itself, and such relief that the destructive acids of judgment will not dissolve the people out of all existence. There remains a future beyond a judgment that will have limits. Judgment is logically necessary, but mercifully limited.

(i) The logic (4:18; 5:7, 9, 19, 29)
The emphasis here is that when people persist in rampant evil, judgment becomes unavoidable in every sense. But to show that this is not merely some impersonal and implacable law of cause and effect, God invites the very same people to agree with him, through a series of rhetorical questions that they cannot answer truthfully without implicating themselves. There is a powerful rhetoric and an even more compelling logic at work in this series of questions:

> *Why should I forgive you?* (5:7)

> *Should I not punish them for this?* (5:9, 29)

> *Why has the LORD our God done all this to us?* (5:19)

> *Should I not avenge myself on such a nation as this?* (5:29)

(ii) The limit (4:27; 5:10, 18)
Judgment has become inevitable, not because of some iron law that even God must submit to, but rather because of the refusal of the people to do the one thing that would allow God to respond in forgiveness, namely to repent and change. But at the same time, judgment is also seen as limited. The devastation to come will be horrendous, but it will not be total. In each of the above verses, the common phrase is *not . . . completely.* So even in these early chapters of almost unrelieved gloom, there is an anticipation of the great chapters that will come later in the book. There is a future beyond judgment that filled the prophet with hope and held an open future before those in exile who would later read his words in the midst of that judgment.

Theological and expository reflections

As we draw our survey of these three searing chapters to a close, how might we summarize some of the key challenges that a preacher might wish to reflect on and apply?

- God gives warning of judgment to come in the hope of repentance, and God goes on doing so even when there seems no further hope of that. God's warnings are intrinsic to his mercy in at least two ways. On the one hand, such warnings are (one might say) unnecessary. We *know* the penalty of sin and its dire consequences. God could act in judgment, without warning but with perfect justification. Yet he chooses to warn, again and again, while delaying judgment to the point where it simply cannot be suspended any longer without damage to his name and character. But on the other hand, the whole point of the warning is the hope of bringing about repentance and change, *so that the judgment can be spared*. Declaring judgment was in itself an act of grace. That was the lesson Jonah found difficult to swallow.
- To bring such a message is costly, and is a matter of grief, never of gloating or anticipation. The language of the prophet in these chapters is severe, but again and again one senses the grief and pain that were part of the cost of delivering such words. Sadly, there are those whose preaching of judgment is little more than a kind of gloating *schadenfreude*. Sinners will get their due, and about time too! But the true prophet weeps his message, and would prefer anything than to see it fulfilled.
- It is a terrible thing to mislead God's people into falsehood, complacency and immorality, to be chaplains to the unrepentant, and to collude in the culture of lies. The condemnation of false prophets here will be intensified when we reach chapter 23, but already we are alerted to the grave sin of such apostate ministry among God's people.
- There is real danger for churches and Christians who know the truth, who understand the 'ancient ways' (namely the received truths of the biblical faith and the ethical demands that accompany them), but who refuse to walk in such ways (of true doctrine or godly living), ignore the warnings, carry on with the ecclesiastical rituals, but end up falling over their own feet.
- The kind of social evil that aroused God's anger in Judah in the sixth century BC must still do so today. If God responded in judgment by allowing the built-in moral retribution of such evil to fall upon society, are there marks of God's judgment in evidence in our own day, and how do we discern them in our own culture and context?
- Even in anger, God continues to long for any other alternative than judgment. If we perish it is ultimately the choice we make, as our persistent sin leaves God no choice but to exercise his own character in its settled and inescapable opposition to all that is evil in his world.

105

Jeremiah 7:1 – 8:3
6. The temple sermon

Spiralling through the tumultuous poetry of chapters 4 – 6 could leave our heads reeling. That was the intention, the editors of the book might respond. Only the clamouring collage of clashing images, the searing descriptions of disaster, the penetrating questions and grief-sodden answers that are all piled together in those three chapters could give us any idea of what it was like for Jeremiah to bring such a message to the people. Only thus could we feel the emotional intensity of the passions poured out in his poetry. But our editors have the wisdom to know that readers cannot cope with such intensity without a pause for breath. That is most probably the reason why they inserted 7:1 – 8:3 here to bring a change of pace, a change from wild poetry to more steady prose, from flashing imagery to the more linear argument of a sermon – though the message is no less powerful.

For it is indeed 'inserted', in the sense that this sermon was preached much later in Jeremiah's life than the surrounding text, which, as we have said, is probably an anthology of his earlier preaching. Almost certainly, 7:1–15 is the content of what Jeremiah preached on the occasion described in Jeremiah 26. There it is dated as a message preached in the courtyard of the temple in the early reign of Jehoiakim, i.e. in 609 or 608 BC, about eighteen years after his call during the reign of Josiah. It was a sermon that almost cost him his life, as we shall see when we get to chapter 26. This chapter will help us understand why.

Why then has this prose sermon been inserted here?[1] Not only because it gives a change of pace, but because it functions to

---

[1] By saying that the editors of the book have 'inserted' this prose sermon at this point I do not at all imply that it is not the words of Jeremiah. That is the view of some critical scholars who argue that the prose sections of the book represent later sermons composed by followers of Jeremiah in the exile itself, on the assumption that Jeremiah himself only spoke or wrote in poetry. However, it seems to me an absurd

summarize and consolidate the key messages of the preceding chapters of poetry. Remember that the book in its final edited form addresses the exiles. They had paid no heed to Jeremiah's predictions when they first heard them but now they ached under the fulfilment of them. A key question was asked at 5:19: 'Why?' Why had such terrible destruction fallen on the temple, the land and the people? And a key part of the answer was given in 6:17–19; the people simply did not, would not, listen to all the words and warnings God had given them for centuries. These two points are now picked up again, with detailed explanation and accusation, in chapter 7. The main text of the sermon in 7:1–15 answers the 'why?' question with devastating logic, while 7:21–28 expands the theme of non-listening by repeating the Hebrew word for listen (*šāmaʿ*) five times (sometimes translated 'obey').

After this prose interlude, we will be launched once again on a rollercoaster of poetry in chapters 8 – 10, followed by another prose section that summarizes, consolidates and reinforces the message (11:1–14). This oscillation between turbulent poetry and calm prose makes sure that we miss neither the passion of Jeremiah's preaching, nor the clear point of it.

1. Commanded to preach (7:1–15)

Imagine, then, the scene. Jeremiah, by now well known for his radically unpopular perspectives on contemporary society, is sent to stand just inside *the gate of the LORD's house* – in the courtyard of the temple (26:2) – and *there proclaim this message*. It would be where the crush of people coming through the gate into the courtyard would be greatest – the perfect place to be heard. It would also be the place from which everybody who heard his words would go out and tell friends and family about the appalling, scandalous, treacherous things Jeremiah had said – and how he had only just escaped being lynched by the mob (ch. 26). It was a day to remember.

It helps our understanding if we notice that Jeremiah does what many good preachers do: he states his two main points first (3–4),

---

assumption that powerful poetry and prose cannot be the work of a single mind and voice, or that the same person could not, on different occasions, deliver both passionate short oracles and also more linear sermonic discourses. Are we to assume that the Jesus who could tell parables in the street could not also argue at length with Jewish leaders (as some scholars say, who contrast the 'authentic' Synoptic Jesus with the 'constructed' Johannine one)? Which, then, is the true John Donne – the brilliant poet, or the powerful prose sermon writer? Many great preachers also write poetry (Don Carson for one), and great hymn-writers are not incapable of preaching expository sermons (e.g. Timothy Dudley-Smith). I have no difficulty at all in hearing the voice of Jeremiah speaking both through the poetry and the prose of the book.

and then explains each of them in turn. Thus, the main thrust of his message (which he may have repeated again and again as people flocked into the courtyard) is first a *command* (3) and secondly a *warning* (4). Then, verses 5–7 explain what the command really entails (the verb *reform . . . change* is the same in Hebrew), while verses 8–11 explain what the warning means by *deceptive words* (4; picking up the identical phrase again in v. 8). So the structure is: verse 3 expanded in 5–7; verse 4 expanded in 8–11.

a. Change their ways (3 and 5–7)

It all started like any other day when the worshippers would habitually *come through these gates to worship the LORD*. But the message they heard this time was truly shocking. They must change their behaviour if they want to live with God *in this place* as before. Verse 3 sounds like a promise (*I will let you live*), but of course it is a dire warning: if they would not change, God would *not* let them live there any longer. It is, in short, a threat of expulsion, a threat to the temple, and by implication to the land itself.

The implied threat could be taken in two possible ways, depending on the meaning of *this place*. The Hebrew of the end of verse 3 can be read either as:

(1) *I will let you dwell in this place*, or

(2) *I will dwell with you in this place*.[2]

In reading (1), 'this place' would refer to Jerusalem or to the land – the place where the people lived. In that case, the implied threat is that if they refuse to change, God will no longer let them live there – by driving them out into exile away from the city and land.

In reading (2), 'this place' would refer to the temple – the dwelling-place of God with his people. In that case, the implied threat is that God will either destroy the temple or abandon it – an unthinkable, unspeakable prospect for the worshippers.

Now when we set verse 3 alongside verse 4, it would seem more natural to think that 'this place' means the temple, and read it as (2). But in verse 7, 'this place' is defined as *in the land*, which assumes (1). Most probably the words are intentionally ambiguous since both meanings are integrally connected, equally threatening, and were in fact fulfilled (people exiled from the land, temple destroyed).

---

[2] The difference is a matter of very small changes in the vowel points only. The MT is pointed to read (i), while two ancient versions, Aquila and the Vulgate, read it as (ii).

But the point of the message was utterly unambiguous. It was a massive, blatant threat to everything the people held dear – their land, their city, their temple, and their assumed relationship with their God. 'All doomed,' cries Jeremiah, 'unless you change your ways. And if you do not, the only future ahead is exile, destruction and abandonment: you will not live here and God will not live with you.'

But what did he mean, *change your ways*? Verses 5–7 spell it out. Jeremiah was not talking about greater sincerity in their worship. He was not talking about greater piety or better attitudes; nor about sounder doctrine or deeper prayer. His demand reaches, as it always did with God's prophets, to the practical, social and ethical level of everyday life in the public arena. It was the familiar demand of Old Testament covenant law:

- do justice with one another in the community;
- no oppression of the weak and vulnerable – the homeless and family-less;
- no violence against the innocent;
- no self-destructive hankering after the false gods of surrounding cultures.

These had been the covenant conditions of dwelling in God's land ever since they had been spelt out so comprehensively in Deuteronomy.[3] Verse 7 embodies a sharp tension that runs through the Old Testament, most strongly in Deuteronomy. On the one hand, there is a condition: *If* in verse 5, comes to its *then* in verse 7. *If* the people would change, *then* God would let them live in the land. The stark implication is, 'But if *not*, then *not*'. God would drive them away from the land, or rather take the land away from them, since it was God's land. But on the other hand, verse 7 ends with the official theology of the land, expressed in countless texts since Genesis: it is *the land I gave to your ancestors for ever and ever*. But if it had been given *for ever*, how could it be taken away? Was the land an unconditional gift, or a conditional one? The fact is that the Old Testament affirms both, and both are theologically important.

On the one hand, yes, the land had been promised to Abraham, and then given to his descendants in faithfulness to that promise. The land was a monumental, tangible proof of the faithfulness of YHWH, God of Israel (7b). In that sense it was unconditional – they had done nothing to deserve it. They owed it solely to God's redemptive grace. But on the other hand, it remained YHWH's land. He

[3] E.g. Deut. 4, 11, 28.

was the divine landlord,[4] and he determined the conditions under which the people of Israel could enjoy life in the land (5–7a). Those conditions were obedience to the covenant law, living together as a people of justice and compassion, in every dimension of economic, social, political, judicial and religious life. Those were the conditions of secure enjoyment of the land. They were warned from the start that to stay in God's land depended on walking in God's ways.

The tension, in other words, is the fully biblical relationship between grace and obedience. The land was an unconditional gift of grace. Ongoing life in the land required an obedient response to that grace. Obedience was never the means of earning the land. But it was the condition in which the grace-gift could be possessed and enjoyed. Grace comes first. Obedience must come second. The principle resounds through the Old Testament and on into the teaching of Jesus and the apostles.

This is a crucial balance that corrects two false assumptions. On the one hand, it rules out legalism and merit. We do not, we cannot, earn our way to God's favour and blessing. We receive God's gift of grace as the only basis for our relationship with him. But on the other hand, it rules out the idea that once you have got God's promise tucked away, it doesn't matter how you live. Obedience is the only way to enjoy the blessing of God's promise.[5] So, the paradox of verse 7 is that it links Israel's possession of the land *both* to the promise made to their ancestors *and* to their present obedience. It is a balance in tension between indicative and imperative, between the givenness of grace and the conditionality of obedience.

b. Challenging their assumptions (4 and 8–11)

The first shock of Jeremiah's sermon, then, was an implied threat. The second shock was an explicit accusation of deception.

---

[4] Lev. 25:23.

[5] This principle also stands against the idea that if you happen to be fulfilling some prophecy or promise of God, then you are immune to all moral critique by the standards of God's laws. There are cases in the Old Testament itself where someone fulfilled a prophecy but is later condemned for how they then lived (e.g. Jeroboam the son of Nebat and Jehu). Likewise in the modern era, there are those who interpret the return of Jews to the land of Palestine in the mid twentieth century as a fulfilment of Old Testament prophecies. I have difficulty with that view, and would place the matter of a safe homeland for Jewish people within the sovereign providence of God, not specific prophetic fulfilment. However, even if one does adopt the view that Old Testament prophecy is being fulfilled in the modern Middle East, God clearly and repeatedly told Israel that his condition for their continued enjoyment of the land of promise was that they should do justice, show compassion, avoid bloodshed, and not oppress foreigners in their land. The modern Israeli state can be challenged on such issues, even if (especially if) it is claimed to be fulfilling prophecy.

In times of uncertainty and danger you want to have a safe place to go. And as the Babylonian threat began to loom larger, the people of Judah thought they had one sure shelter from the storm – the temple. So Jeremiah hears them chanting, as if in auto-reassurance, '*This is the temple of the* LORD', over and over again (4). But he calls out to them – 'That's a lie! You're trusting in a deception!'[6]

What could he possibly mean? Was that not the truth?

Indeed it was, of course. The building and its courts were the temple that Solomon had built and dedicated to YHWH.[7] It's origins went right back to God's promise to David, and it now carried the full weight of a centuries-long tradition of the presence of God in Zion, in the city and temple that bore his name. They had stories to tell about it and hymns to sing about it.[8] More than that, they thought they had God's guarantee to protect it. Isaiah, over a hundred years earlier, had seen off the terrifying threat of the Assyrian king Sennacherib with words of superb dismissal from God: 'I will defend this city and save it, for my sake and for the sake of David my servant!'[9]

And indeed God had defended Jerusalem and its temple at that time. Spectacularly so. The problem was that the people had turned that historic deliverance into a complacent belief that Jerusalem was inviolable. God would *never* let it be destroyed. God would always defend his temple. So, while the words of the worshippers in Jeremiah's day were true in themselves, they had become a deception. God was not bound to these buildings or this city. YHWH's name-tag on the temple was not a divine insurance policy against the consequences of disobedience and rebellion. The truth (it was the temple of the Lord) had become a lie (if they imagined God could never let it be destroyed and them with it).

For all their chanting, they were deceived in regarding the temple as their ultimate security. Get in there and you'll be safe from any enemy, they thought (10). Right, said Jeremiah – unless you make God himself your enemy, then it becomes a rather dangerous place to be. And that is exactly what they were doing with their persistent covenant-breaking.

Having made the stark point in verse 4, Jeremiah returns to it in verses 8–11, to explain why the words are *deceptive* and *worthless*. The lives of the people have become a daily round of breaking the

---

[6] He uses a graphic word: *šeqer.* It is the climactic word of condemnation of the false idols of the pagan worshipper in Isa. 44:20. For thorough exploration of the concept of falsehood and deception, see Overholt, *The Threat of Falsehood.*

[7] 1 Kgs 6 – 8.

[8] 2 Sam. 7:1–17; Pss 46, 48, 72, 76, 78, 89, and especially 132.

[9] Isa. 37:33–35. See the whole of Isa. 36 – 37 for the full story.

Ten Commandments. He lists the sixth, seventh, eighth and ninth
– which between them include violence and bloodshed, sexual
promiscuity, economic oppression and judicial corruption. But every
weekend (so to speak) they would flock to the temple to claim the
protection of YHWH on a society that ignored him all week.
Jeremiah mercilessly exposes 'the nonsense – and the effrontery – of
tearing up the ten commandments and turning up in church (10), as
though saved to sin'.[10] Their worship was deluded and divorced
from morality. Their lives made a mockery of the words they spoke
in God's presence. Sadly, it was a practice that did not end with Old
Testament Israel but remains a temptation among God's people to
this day.

They had turned the temple into *a den of robbers*. This scandalous
comparison likens the temple to the hideout where robbers flee after
committing their crime, a place where they could stay safe and
unseen by the authorities. But not safe from God, for *I have been
watching!* – watching not only what was going on in the temple,
but also all that was going on in the public arena, where the crimes,
oppression and corruption were rife. Jesus quoted this verse in his
prophetic enactment of the destruction of the temple. But his point
was not merely that he didn't like buying and selling in the
temple courts. Jesus was not objecting to commerce in a holy place.
Rather, it was the fact that the temple commerce was linked to a
whole system of oppression and exploitation of the poor. 'God
will not inhabit space Jerusalem has violated by mistreating its
poor.'[11]

If we are to preach what Jeremiah preached, what might his words
attack today? His point was that there was something that the people
were convinced was a truth they could rely on, but which had
become, in fact, a deception – a complacent and dangerously false
sense of security. It is a temptation that is still with us and may apply
to a range of things: words and traditions we like to repeat for the
feeling they give us of secure orthodoxy, but without lives to match;
places, organizations and institutions we have come to think of as
having a charmed permanence, even if they have long passed their
usefulness to God's kingdom; causes, convictions, positions that
God once blessed in the past, but that have turned into shibboleths
or gained a kind of sanctity that none dare challenge. Once-great
truths can turn into deceptions when they generate a security that
is not grounded in a living and obedient response to God in the
present.

[10] Kidner, p. 49.
[11] Stulman, p. 90.

c. Check their history (12–15)

Remember *Shiloh?* Jeremiah asks his stunned listeners. They knew
it well. It was a few miles north in what had been the northern
kingdom of Israel, but was now a province of Assyria. By Jeremiah's
day it would have been an overgrown ruin, an embryonic archaeo-
logical site, a future tourist attraction. But it had once been 'my place'
(lit.), says God, *where I first made a dwelling for my Name.* Indeed,
it had once been the place where the ark of the covenant had been
stationed, where there had been a central sanctuary for the tribes of
Israel while Jerusalem was still a Jebusite city. Samuel had grown up
there.[12] It had been YHWH's home, as much as anywhere could be,
centuries before the temple was built in Jerusalem.

But now? Abandoned. Derelict. Most likely destroyed by the
Philistines in the mid eleventh century BC. Go to Shiloh and have a
good look, says Jeremiah, and see the future of *this* place you are so
proud of and in which you feel so safe (14).

What made this comparison even worse was that the people of
Jerusalem actually liked to contrast Jerusalem in all its glory with
the rejected Shiloh. For Shiloh was in the hated northern kingdom
of Israel, which God had destroyed and sent into exile over a century
earlier.[13] *They* were so wicked and look what happened to *them,*
they thought. *We,* on the other hand, stand under God's favour and
blessing, because of God's choice of David. The great historical Psalm
78 describes the sins of Israel from the exodus to the emergence of
the kingdom of David. But it is easy to see how sentiments like Psalm
78:58–72 could feed popular belief that what happened to Shiloh
could *never* happen to Jerusalem.

On the contrary, says Jeremiah, what happened to Shiloh is
precisely what God *will now do to* the temple in Jerusalem. Judah
is doomed to exile, just as *the people of Ephraim* (Israel) had been.
That was the unthinkable conclusion to an intolerable sermon. That
was the point at which the crowd seized Jeremiah, intent on killing
him for such dangerous blasphemy (26:6–9), anticipating the similar
reaction to Stephen when he also dared to challenge the assumptions
of another generation of temple-trusters.[14]

Jeremiah survived. So did some of those who first heard his sermon
preached, and now read the record of it again in exile, when its dire
prediction had become reality. It would have had two effects. First,
it provided the explanation for the catastrophic destruction that had
fallen on their city and temple. But secondly, it also provided a

[12] Josh. 21:1–2; 1 Sam. 1 – 3.
[13] See 2 Kgs 17 for an obituary.
[14] Acts 7:48–60.

glimmer of hope. If YHWH was not bound to any place (Shiloh or Jerusalem), then the message was not only, negatively, that *no* place could claim him forever, but also, positively, that *any* place could be where he might show up for his people in their worship and prayer. Could that include Babylon, the graveyard of exile? Jeremiah would later write and tell them exactly that (29:7). But it would be Ezekiel who would minister the very presence of YHWH in the midst of the exiles themselves.

2. Forbidden to pray (7:16–20)

Prophets not only preached, they also prayed. It was part of the prophetic calling. Moses, the model prophet, was the model inter-cessor. Samuel, Isaiah and Amos did the same.[15] Jeremiah, then, would have been praying for his people – until God told him to stop. This people were so far gone in rebellion that they were past praying for. It was such a habit for Jeremiah, however, that God had to repeat the instruction several times[16] – making it even more stark in its implications. The triple prohibition of 7:16 is emphatic, and shows the kind of urgent, pleading prayer that must have exercised Jeremiah's voice when it wasn't being used for preaching to the people; prayers, pleas and petitions, all now must fall silent.

For I will not listen to you – or to them (11:14; 14:11–12). The words seem harsh and unfeeling, until we set them in the context. Who was not listening to whom? The fact that God now refuses to listen to his people's prayers is set in the context of repeated emphasis on how they have persistently refused to listen to God's commands and appeals.[17] Those who will not listen will in the end not be heard either.

The analysis of idolatry in 7:18–20 is perceptive and relevant – once we make some cultural transposition to our own day.[18]

First, Jeremiah observes that the worship of false gods is not confined to the religious leaders in the temple. Whole families are involved in it in everyday domestic life (18). *The Queen of Heaven* was probably the Mesopotamian goddess Ishtar (who bore that title), though she may have been identified with the Canaanite goddess Astarte or Asherah. She was the goddess of war and – more relevantly to families – of fertility (of crops, animals and women). So the women of Israel enlisted children and fathers in the preparation of sacred

[15] Exod. 32 – 34; Num. 14; 1 Sam. 7:5–9; 2 Kgs 19:1–4; Amos 7:1–6.
[16] Here, and see also 11:14; 14:11; 15:1.
[17] 6:17, 19; 7:13, 24, 26, 27, 28.
[18] For a comprehensive analysis of the biblical category of idolatry, its sources, its forms, and the various missional responses that the Bible portrays, see Wright, *The Mission of God*, ch. 5, 'The living God confronts idolatry'.

JEREMIAH 7:1 – 8:3

cakes (cut to the shape of the goddess, or stamped with her image), and pouring out drink-offerings. The worship of other gods has become normalized at family level. Children grow up thinking this is simply the way it is, by parental instruction and example. 'Worship of "the Queen of Heaven" has become a cottage industry that engages the entire domestic economy.'[19] The Western quasi-religion of consumerism has similar characteristics. Children become targets of marketing and allies in the drive to possess, to pour out libations at the altars of profit in the side-chapels of the vast cathedrals of mammon we know as shopping malls. Are Christian families any different from the ambient culture and its idolatry? And even in the fast-growing churches of the majority world, it is a common phenomenon that families who have nominally converted to Christianity will continue with traditional practices 'out of church', for their daily needs and problem-solving.

Second, idolatry is self-harm (19). Such behaviour by God's people will inevitably *arouse my anger,* says God. But it is not simply that God is angered by our sin, but that we damage ourselves. The verb 'arouse/provoke' in verse 19, speaks of an action that brings hurt, pain and shame. When it is done to someone else (God), it is spiteful and ungrateful. When it is done to oneself it is so irrational. We are perverse creatures. Why do we go on doing something even when we know that it 'can seriously damage your health'? Yet we do – and our whole culture reinforces the refusal to change, even when the signs of damage and suffering pile up, and all the statistics and research point in the same direction. 'Not proven', we reply, in deaf denial. God warns us repeatedly that going after false gods leads to loss, disappointment and futility. God himself is angered by what we do to him, the only living, loving God. But God is grieved by what we do to ourselves (cf. 25:7).

Third, the destructive effects of idolatry are felt at every level (20). The activities of families who worship false gods are 'bounced back' as the comprehensive judgment of the living God. They poured out drink offerings; God will pour out his anger. They lit fires to bake cakes; the fire of God's judgment will consume them. Ominously, the very things they hoped for from their goddess of wealth and fertility will be consumed – humans, animals, crops and trees. In other words, an economy riddled with idolatry will eventually collapse with devastating effects – in their case through war and invasion. And as we have seen in our own generation, when the economic idols fall, the whole society suffers. And always it is the poor who suffer most.

[19] Brueggemann (1988), p. 78.

3. Generations of the deaf (7:21–28)

The camera angle shifts back from cottage kitchens to the temple courts. The great sacrificial system was still in place, still apparently keeping YHWH satisfied, still being conducted according to the distinctions and rules that prescribed which sacrifices must be offered whole (*burnt offerings*) and which ones could be used for a feast ('fellowship offerings').[20] It really doesn't matter any more, Jeremiah says. God couldn't care less if you mix the whole lot up and use the meat for a barbecue (21). The shock of Jeremiah's attack on the temple is made even worse with this sarcastic attack on the most important activity that went on there – the sacrifices.

But had God not commanded these sacrifices? How could Jeremiah say God no longer wanted them? Jeremiah's answer is stunningly simple, 'Read your Bible – in the right order'. What was the first thing God required of Israel when he redeemed them out of Egypt? That they should set up a sacrificial system? No, that they should listen to him, obey him (same word in Hebrew), and walk in his ways as set out in the covenant law (23; cf. Exod. 19:4–6).[21] Only after that had been established at Sinai, agreed by the people and sealed in blood (Exod. 19 – 24), did God speak about a tent, an altar, and sacrifices.

Jeremiah's point is based on the chronological order of events. Not only does the book of Exodus show us that God's initiative of redeeming grace comes before the requirement of responsive obedience (there are eighteen chapters of salvation in the book before a single chapter of law). It also shows us that the ethical dimension of covenant obedience in personal and social life came before the ritual dimension of sacrifices. Without the first, the second was a charade. 'Jeremiah was really indicating that the order of revelation was indicative of the relative value of obedience and cultic observances . . . Where the basic requisite of obedience was lacking, God refused to regard what went on in the temple as a true sacrifice.'[22] There was no point in the people boasting about how well they were keeping the secondary rules on sacrifices if they were ignoring the

[20] See Lev. 1 – 7.
[21] The word 'just' (NIV, *I did not just give them commands about burnt offerings and sacrifices*), is not in the Hebrew text. It has been inserted to soften the contrast, and allow for the fact that, of course, God did give commands about sacrifices to the Israelites. NIV is assuming that this is a case of 'relative negation', that is, sometimes Hebrew says 'A not B', when what is meant is 'A rather than, or more than, B.' The clearest example, which makes the point clear, is Hos. 6:6. However, the text can be true at face value: God did not prescribe the sacrificial system when he brought the Israelites out of Egypt, but months later after the giving of the law and covenant at Sinai.
[22] Thompson, p. 288.

primary thing that God had called for. And they had been doing exactly that right from the start (24–26).

The verb *šāmaʿ* is the five-times repeated heartbeat of this passage. It occurs in every verse but one (25) from 23 to 28. Israel had been deaf to the voice of God ever since the exodus. No generation had listened to the warnings of the past or the messengers of the present – *my servants the prophets*. And now the generation of Jeremiah's contemporaries displayed the same affliction, only worse. Not only would they not listen, neither would they answer when spoken to (27), something that even Cain reluctantly managed to do. Such inveterate, incurable, spiritual deafness and dumbness now defines this people as a whole (28).

They will not take any discipline or correction, so there is no hope for the change called for in verse 3. Since *truth* itself *has perished* (lit. 'cut from their lips'), there is no hope of them giving up the lies and deception of verse 4.

When any culture, or any generation of God's people, turns brazenly deaf ears and dumb mouths to all God's appeals and warnings, there comes a point when all reasoned discipline and truth are lost and nothing remains but the deathly implosion of judgment. No wonder the next verse (29) breaks down in agonized lament.

However, before moving to the searing climax, we should pause to reflect on the apparent contradiction of what God tells Jeremiah in this chapter. Jeremiah is commanded to preach such messages to the people. Yet he is told they will not listen, so there is no point even praying for them. What good is there in preaching then? Why preach to those you can't pray for? Why speak to those who won't listen? Three possible reasons suggest themselves.

First, the preaching serves to expose the hardness of the people's hearts, the persistent, wilful, state of rebellion they were in, and their refusal to pay heed to any of God's pleas. In that sense, through listening but not responding to Jeremiah's words, the people condemn themselves. They show their condemnation to be all the more deserved. This is probably close to what Jesus meant by his puzzling comments on the effect of his preaching on those of his generation who heard his words but refused to change.[23]

Second, the preaching makes it clear that God did not act without warning. Indeed, all through Israel's history God gave warning of his acts of judgment – hoping people would repent so that he could suspend judgment. Paradoxically, Jonah shows a pagan nation responding to such 'space for grace', while Israel refused all the warnings she ever received.

[23] Matt. 13:10–17.

Third, for those in exile who would read the record of Jeremiah's pre-587 BC preaching, the words bore the poignant sub-text, 'You refused to listen before; will you listen now?' The message could bring hope if the written book could achieve what the living voice had not. The written book still speaks with the same implicit appeal to all who read it, including ourselves. Do we listen to God's warnings?

4. Generations of the dead (7:29 – 8:3)

This terrible text begins with a cry of lament and ends in the silence of a living death. The lament, we note, is for *this generation.* God will not abandon his ultimate purpose in the election of Israel, his long-term mission of redemptive blessing, his eternal covenant faithfulness. However, for *these* people – people who had put themselves beyond preaching to and past praying for – there is no hope: *the LORD has rejected and abandoned this generation that is under his wrath* (7:29).

The climax of all the people's wrongdoing lies in the 'crowning horror of child sacrifice' (7:30–31).[24] *Topheth* is an Aramaic word meaning a fire-pit, but has the vowels of 'bosheth' which means 'shame'. It was apparently a site of sacrifice in the *Valley of Ben Hinnom,* which later became the smouldering rubbish pit outside Jerusalem known as Gehenna, used by Jesus as a picture of the destructive fires of hell. In the late monarchy it had become the site of the sacrifice by fire of little boys and girls – an abomination to God. Israel had descended to crimes against humanity such as had led the land to vomit out the original Canaanite inhabitants in disgust.[25] History was about to repeat itself. And when it did, the valley would be renamed *Slaughter* on account of the heaps of unburied dead – a grisly picture that would have been matched by reality at the end of the siege of Jerusalem. No living human being left among the dead, none of the noise and joys of normal life. The book of Lamentations will capture the scene unforgettably.

If the living have gone to join the dead, the generations of those already dead will not escape the judgment of the living (8:1–2). These verses probably describe the actions of the conquering armies of Nebuchadnezzar by which the shame of defeat was visited even on the dead. Their theological point is stronger still. People might be tempted to think that those who had already died were fortunate to escape God's judgment. Not so. Accountability before God does

[24] Kidner, p. 51.
[25] Deut. 12:31; Lev. 18:21, 24–28.

not end with death. Death is no escape. The picture of exposure of the bones of the dead is the nearest the Old Testament can come to portraying that God's judgment reaches beyond the grave. The New Testament will make it much clearer, affirming that we must all appear before the judgment seat of God, that 'books will be opened', and nothing will be swept under the carpet.

This climactic section of the temple sermon is filled with several terrifying ironies. Domestic idolatry that had involved parents and children lighting fires to bake cakes (7:18) ended up in the flaming horror of parents putting their own children on the fires of demonic idolatry (7:31). People who should have *loved and served and . . . followed and consulted and worshipped* their own covenant Lord and God, Yahweh, had piled up exactly those devotions instead to *the sun and the moon and all the stars of heaven*. But those who had worshipped the sun, moon and stars in life would end up exposed to them in death – exhumed and unburied (8:2).

And most devastating of all: the dead will end up sharing the judgment of the living (8:1–2), while the living will wish they were dead (8:3; cf. Rev. 9:6).

At the start of their journey into the land, Moses had appealed to the people of Israel with evangelistic fervour, to 'choose life':

> This day I call the heavens and the earth as witnesses against you that I have set before you life and death, blessings and curses. Now choose life, so that you and your children may live and that you may love the LORD your God, listen to his voice, and hold fast to him. For the LORD is your life, and he will give you many years in the land he swore to give to your fathers, Abraham, Isaac and Jacob.[26]

But they had chosen death.

And now they had taken that choice to the ultimate level of sacrificing children, symbols of all life's new potential. In their perversion they had chosen death over life. Under judgment, they would prefer death to life, but even that would bring no relief.

Theological and expository reflections

What possible expository themes might inform a sermon built on this chapter, that is itself the record of a sermon (if that is not far too weak a term for what transpired in the temple courts that day in 609 BC)?

---

[26] Deut. 30:19–20.

- The priority of ethical obedience over religious practice. God will not be worshipped acceptably by those who refuse to walk in his ways. And his ways are ways of justice and compassion, exercised in the public arenas as well as in personal life. Without such commitment, all forms of religious ritual – however orthodox in themselves – are an insult to the God they are offered to.
- There is a dangerous false security in 'truths' that have been turned into falsehoods by those who like to repeat them, as slogans, shibboleths, or security blankets. History moves on, and what may have been a word from God in the past may turn into a dangerous self-deception in the present, when divorced from living obedience. God is not bound to any institution, place, organization, tradition, or methodology.
- Idolatry is subtle, deceptive and ultimately destructive. It can infect the apparently innocuous normality of family life, as well as the religious trappings of state pomp and power. But it is self-harming in the end, and can lead to horrors beyond imagining.
- When people abandon the most fundamental moral standards, as embodied in the second table of the Decalogue, the whole of society becomes sick and dysfunctional – but it is the poorest and weakest who suffer most in the inevitable outcomes of judgment.
- There are modern forms of child-sacrifice that may not reek of the fires of Gehenna, but are as destructive on a massive scale. These range from the statistics of social abortion, the suffering of children in broken marriages and confused promiscuity, the abuse of children in pornography, child slavery and sex-trafficking, and the haemorrhage of young life in the military adventures of so many nations.

Jeremiah 8:4 – 10:25
7. Tears in heaven

Jesus wept. He wept when death 'climbed in through the window' (9:21), invading the home of a much-loved family.[1] He wept over Jerusalem, as he anticipated it suffering yet again the same fate that had brought tears to the eyes of Jeremiah. His prediction, like Jeremiah's, was fulfilled in the horrors of siege, blood and death.

> As he approached Jerusalem and saw the city, he wept over it and said, 'If you, even you, had only known on this day what would bring you peace – but now it is hidden from your eyes. The days will come upon you when your enemies will build an embankment against you and encircle you and hem you in on every side. They will dash you to the ground, you and the children within your walls. They will not leave one stone on another, because you did not recognise the time of God's coming to you.'[2]

The passage before us is filled with the same sense of foreboding, the same looming danger, the same wilful blindness and missed opportunities, the same fearful violence – and above all, the same tears. For the tears of the weeping Messiah mirrored the tears of the weeping prophet, and the tears in the heart of God himself.

After the sermonic prose of chapter 7, we return to Jeremiah's passion and poetry in chapters 8 – 10, which immediately take us back to the world of chapters 4 – 6. Once again we reel in a torrent of rhetorical questions, graphic imagery, fierce accusation, dire predictions of invasion, and anticipated lament for a doomed society. It would be a mistake, however, to rush through these chapters

[1] John 11:35.
[2] Luke 19:41–44.

imagining we've heard it all before. At one level, we have. The basic core message has already been stated and is easily summarized:

- Israel has rejected their covenant Lord God, broken his covenant laws and refused all pleas to repent and return to him.
- As a result they face the full weight of covenant judgment, which will fall upon them in the form of enemy invasion from the north.
- This can no longer be averted, and no religious rituals or sacred places will provide protection from the wrath to come.

The whole sequence is summarized for us in the text itself in 9:12–16.

However, that core message is nuanced in two major ways through the poetry of these chapters. On the one hand, there is penetrating insight into the sheer *perversity of sin*, along with the *destructiveness of idolatry*. False gods always fail, but they drag their worshippers down in baffled rage and suffering as they do so. Social and economic breakdown is not something separate from corrupt religion; they are integrally linked to each other.

On the other hand, there is the pathos of divine grief.[3] So intense is the poetry, and so seamless in the way it switches from one speaker to another, that it is hard to decide at many points whether we are hearing the voice of Jeremiah or of God. Probably we should not try to decide, for the voice of one expresses the heart of the other, and the tears of one flowed for the grief of the other. There are few places in the whole Bible where we have a more telling glimpse into the inner emotional life of our God than here – only at Calvary do we see and hear more.

1. Perversity, panic and pain (8:4 – 9:1)

a. Irrational behaviour (8:4–7)

The thrust of the questions in verse 4 and the comparisons in verse 7 is that Israel's behaviour is both inexplicable and unnatural. There is a self-correcting rhythm about ordinary life: you fall down, you get up again; you go off on a journey, you come back home (4). But *these people* of *Jerusalem* have perfected the art of perpetual motion in a single direction – *away . . . away* (5a). It is like a parent struggling to speak to a child face to face, but wherever the parent moves, the child swings around to face the other way.

[3] For a profound reflection on divine pathos in the prophets in general and Jeremiah in particular, see Heschel, *The Prophets*.

Israel would admit to no wrongdoing. Indeed, they lack any faculty of self-criticism or self-questioning (6a). It is a very advanced state of hardness when people are so convinced of their own integrity, even while *they cling to deceit*, that they ask no questions and want no questions to be asked. 'There is no alternative!' they cry. It is frightening to wonder at what point any society has become so committed to its own immoral paths that it has passed the point of no return. Western culture may already have done so.

Other prophets noticed that when it comes to behaving sensibly, animals regularly outperform humans. Isaiah reckoned that the farmer's ox and donkey knew where to find a meal better than Israel knew how to find their God.[4] Jesus commended the birds as an object lesson in freedom from worry.[5] More ominously, Jesus saw more intelligence in chicks snuggling for protection under their mother hen than in the people of Jerusalem who refused the safety of trust in God.[6] Jeremiah watches the great stork migrations through Palestine – south to Africa in the autumn and back north to Europe and Asia in the spring – and sees a lesson in the require-ments of nature.[7] In stark contrast, God's own people[8] *do not know the requirements of the LORD* (7).

It is a tough thing to speak to those who claim to be God's people – Christians by name – and who *ought* to know the requirements of the Lord, but live as though they had never heard of them. One of the most disfiguring features of the world church is the widespread ignorance of the basic demands of discipleship, of obeying the requirements of the Lord Jesus Christ himself. Shallow and hasty evangelism, with more zeal to count decisions than to make disciples, can lead to such nominalism. And when those who have been evan-gelized but not discipled are then exploited by unaccountable leaders who care more for their own status and wealth than for the teaching and example of Christ, then the church itself becomes a scandal, a denial of the gospel. So Jeremiah turns next, and rightly, to the leaders.

[4] Isa. 1:3.
[5] Matt. 6:25–27.
[6] Luke 13:34–35.
[7] Jeremiah's words 'may well be the first definite reference to bird migration in the literature of the world' (John Stott, *The Birds Our Teachers* [Abingdon: Candle Books, 1999], p. 18). Stott goes on, 'What birds do by instinct (by inbuilt, inherited navi-gational skills which scientists have not yet fully fathomed), we human beings should do by deliberate choice, returning from our self-centred ways to the living God our Creator' (p. 20).
[8] *My people* (7), the personal relationship that is so poignantly repeated throughout.

b. Delusional leadership (8:8–13)

Sometimes we can sense the flow of thought in a prophetic text by imagining the other side of the living dialogue with those who first heard him. Jeremiah's accusation that the people did not know the requirements of their God is met with protest from the leaders, who pick up on the legal meaning of the word 'requirements'. In Hebrew it is *mišpāṭîm* – which can have a general sense of what is right and just, the requirements of a situation (just as the birds know the requirements of their migration patterns). But it also means 'laws' – particularly the case-laws of the Book of the Covenant in Exodus 21 – 23.

'*You do not know the requirements / laws* [*mišpāṭîm*] *of the* LORD,' accuses Jeremiah.

'Of course we do!' the leaders protest. 'Wise leaders that we are, we have them right here with us in *the law* [tôrâ] *of the* LORD' (8a).

But Jeremiah counters that smug claim with two more of his devastating ripostes:

- 'Your scribes have turned it (the Torah!) into a lie' (8b);
- 'You may possess the written *law of the* LORD, but you are rejecting *the word of the* LORD' (9).

Jeremiah's first point (8) is as brazen as calling the temple a lie (7:4), and uses the same word – *šeqer,* lie or deception. Literally he says, 'the pen-of-lies of the scribes has made [it] a lie'. What did he mean? Clearly he is referring to written law. Possibly the verse may refer to the discovery of the Book of the Law in the temple during the reign of Josiah. However, the scribes (who were professional teachers and administrators) had *handled it falsely.* Almost certainly, this does not mean that they had somehow changed the written text. Rather, like the same class of people accused by Jesus, they had found ways of avoiding the harder challenges of the 'weightier matters' of God's law by interpretations that were more accommodating to popular demand.[9] So they avoided the warnings in the law about the consequences of disobedience (11). They left the people as falsely complacent in merely possessing the Torah as they were in merely being present in the temple. But to trust in Torah or temple without obeying the God who gave the one and dwelt in the other, was to turn both into 'a lie'. The real test was whether they were *living* in accordance with the law they possessed, whether their lives in the world tallied with the words they used in the temple. On both counts, says Jeremiah, they were living a lie and trusting a lie.

[9] Cf. Matt. 23:16–24.

The *lie* . . . is their interpretation of the law. Theirs is an interpretation that reinforces the message of *peace* and complacency given by the prophets and hence cannot be the word of the Lord (11). Their 'soft' use of the law never convicts anyone, never moves people to ask, 'What have I done?' (6). They find ways of using the law to conceal the problem rather than to reveal it.[10]

Jeremiah's second point (9b) is intriguing. It sets up a contrast between possessing the written *law of the LORD*, and rejecting *the word of the LORD*. He was not, of course, suggesting that the written law was not part of the word of God. He was, however, putting his finger on a very relevant temptation that has never gone away – the perverse ability of God's people to pay lip-service to the text of the Bible while living in disobedience to it, and to find clever ways of interpreting it in such a way as to justify their disobedience. Jeremiah would surely challenge us: when people make great claims about honouring the text of Scripture, while rejecting the word of the Lord, what kind of wisdom do they have?

Verses 10–12 repeat 6:13–15, with their picture of complacent, self-serving leadership that has corrupted society from top to bottom to the point where it has forgotten what shame even feels like. When the judgment falls, these leaders will not be immune. The brutal effects of war will engulf them too, and the things they have coveted will be stripped away (10a, 12b–13).

c. Crushing grief (8:14 – 9:1)

The natural response to the stubbornness of the people and the complacency of their leaders would be *anger*. And there is plenty of that (19b). But the dominant emotion of this section is a mixture of panic and fear (among the people) and overwhelming pain and grief (for God and his prophet).

Enemy invasion is terrifying. Cavalry squadrons were the tank regiments of ancient conquerors. Their noise, their wanton pillage and destruction of all in their path, were as fearful as an earthquake (16). Shifting from the noisy to the sinister, the terror is compared to a silent invasion of poisonous and inescapable *snakes* (17). The response of the people is at first a dark bravado: 'Let's take to the forts. We're doomed to die anyway, so let's at least die fighting' (14). If there is some acknowledgement of the underlying cause of their predicament (14b), it hardly amounts to a repentant confession, more a statement of bald fact.

[10] Fretheim, p. 150.

They lurch from fear to bitterly accusing God for failing them in their hour of need. Blame God. It's the oldest and easiest way out of facing up to our own responsibility. But it's so irrational:

- *We hoped for peace* (15). The acute irony here is that the people actually believed the false prophets of peace who had not spoken God's word (11), and then blamed God for not delivering what he had not promised. 'There is no peace for the wicked' – words of Isaiah, not Jeremiah, but totally applicable here.[11]
- *Is the LORD not in Zion?* (19a). The plaintive questions shatter the confidence they had once had in God's permanent presence in the temple and their assumption that he would always be there to protect them. So if Zion was now being attacked, where is YHWH? Why does he not show up at the right place? Shouldn't the Commander-in-Chief (*her King*) stay with his troops and not go AWOL?
- *We are not saved* (20). This haunting cry moves from the round of liturgy in the temple to the round of the seasons in the calendar. If the harvest time had passed but you had not brought in the crops, if the summer had ended and you had not collected the summer fruits, then you had lost all hope of having a safe winter. You have to act at the right time. God needs to show up before it's too late. Now, if ever, was surely the right time for God to act if the people were to be saved from the enemy battalions. But God was not just late. In fact, he was not coming at all. The people's confidence in holy places and set times was a delusion. Walter Brueggemann links the cries of verses 19 and 20:

> The fakery of such an appeal to the holy place of Zion as a place of God's presence is matched in 8:20 by an appeal to time. Now the quoted liturgy reminds God that the saving season is almost over. The community expects to be healed by a certain point on the calendar. God may be a bit behind schedule, so the community attempts to remind God about the proper order of events.[12]

To the people's accusing question, God responds with his own (19b), stating the reason that he will no longer respond to them. God is provoked, hurt, stung, vexed, offended and angered (it is a strong word with that range of meaning), by their continuous idolatry. If they choose to run after other gods, why should the one God they

[11] Isa. 57:21.
[12] Brueggemann (1988), p. 89.

have persistently turned away from come to their aid? It's 2:27–28 revisited.

But this divine anger is drenched in sorrow. It was Ezekiel who heard God say, 'I take no pleasure in the death of the wicked',[13] but it is Jeremiah who witnesses the agony and grief in the heart of God over the suffering of his people in the midst of the violence that God's own judgment has unleashed. Indeed it is Jeremiah who feels it as his own.

The identity of the speaker in verses 8:18 and 8:21 – 9:1 is ambiguous. Who is the 'I', and 'me' of these verses – Jeremiah or God? The sheer physicality of 9:1 (*head, eyes, tears*) seems most naturally to imply the prophet. But the whole oracle runs without a break to the end of 9:3, where 'me' is unquestionably God himself, and the concluding ascription, *declares the* LORD, seems to apply to all that is above it since 8:18.

The brutal fact is, *God* himself is breaking down in agonizing sorrow (8:18).[14] *God* is *crushed* and wounded by the violence inflicted on his people (8:21). *God* wishes he could call for ointment and doctors to heal the wounds (8:22).[15] *God* is dissolving in tears over the mountains of those slain in siege and battle (9:1). *God* is inflicting all this as the unavoidable consequence of their evil ways (see 9:7–9), but those on whom it falls are still *my people*. This phrase, which has the piteous overtone of 'my poor, poor people', is a refrain throughout these terrible lines (8:7, 11, 19, 21, 22; 9:1, 2, 7). God is holding his head in his hands, sobbing through the tears, 'My people, my people, my poor people', just as David sobbed for his rebel son Absalom.[16]

The suffering of God is something that Western theology has not felt comfortable with, but it is an unquestionably biblical dimension of God's interaction with the world. God reacts to sin and evil with both anger (in relation to what it does to God's love and goodness), and with pain (in relation to what it does to humans and to the rest of his creation). We should not set either of these against the other.

---

[13] Ezek. 18:23; 33:11.

[14] *O my Comforter* is an attempt at an otherwise unknown word in the Hebrew, and makes the verse definitely spoken by Jeremiah. A more likely translation is 'my grimace of pain in my sorrow', which could equally be spoken by God.

[15] *Gilead* was known for its balsam trees. An ointment was made from their resin which was used in healing wounds (giving us the word *balm*; cf. Gen. 37:25). But for this generation, there would be no ointment, no doctors, *no healing*. No human medical expertise could avert the disaster of invasion and exile. God himself, however, would step in as the divine healer for a future generation, when healing would include rebuilding, cleansing, forgiveness, obedience and peace (33:6–9). God, not Gilead, would be the source of their healing.

[16] 2 Sam. 18:33.

We must not think, for example, that if God is grieved by our sin he cannot also be angry about it or punish us for it. On the contrary, the very nature of the relationship is such that terrible anger and desperate grief are both simultaneously appropriate reactions, as those who have experienced or witnessed a marriage breakdown will immediately agree. Jeremiah has already portrayed the relationship between YHWH and Israel as a marriage that began with a honeymoon and ended in divorce. Anger and tears? Absolutely.[17]

2. Death of a culture (9:2–26)

a. Breakdown at the heart of society (2–8)

The first two verses of chapter 9 both begin with the same expression – a wish or longing. However the emotions in each are entirely different: verse 1 longs for a head full of enough water for the tears that need to be shed for the suffering of the people; verse 2 is the longing to get away from the people altogether in exasperation at their corrupt ways.

Once again we face the question: who is speaking? It could well have been Jeremiah, wanting to get away from the people who hated him. But could it be God? It is certainly God speaking in verse 3, so could verse 2 be God also, shockingly wishing that he could just get away somewhere by himself – anywhere else but in the company of such people? If so (and I think the text warrants that reading), then three thoughts follow.

First, God echoes the lyrics of a psalm composed by someone suffering the hatred of the wicked, and applies them to himself in an astonishing emotional outburst (see Ps. 55:6–8). Perhaps it is not so astonishing. Already we have heard nostalgia on the lips of God (2:1–3), sarcasm (2:27–28), shock (2:11–13), and wistfulness (3:19). If we are troubled that such portrayals of the emotions of God seem too human, we should ask ourselves, 'In whose image are we humans created? From where do we get the emotions we are reluctant to attribute to the God who made us?'

Second, God is thinking the unthinkable – just as his people were. 'Could God ever really leave them?' they wondered (8:19a). 'If only . . .' says God. They were afraid God might leave. God wishes he could. 'Because of the people's sin, their worst fear has become the fantasy of God.'[18] This is a fearful thought to even imagine.

---

[17] See Fretheim, p. 153, and also his superb study on the suffering of God: Fretheim, *The Suffering of God*.

[18] Craigie, Kelley and Drinkard, p. 144. In another sense, the people's fears were fulfilled, as Ezekiel described the glory of the Lord lifting up, leaving the temple, and

But thirdly, though the longing expresses God's revulsion at the people's sin, it was not an intention he would (or could) ever carry out. For although God would certainly judge this generation and, in a sense, abandon them to their fate at the hands of the Babylonians, he would never abandon his ultimate commitment to the people of Abraham to whom he had sworn on his own life and being that they would be his people and he their God.[19] That was a truth of God's own character that Moses fully understood. He even boldly reminded God of it on earlier occasions when God's exasperation with his people reached the level of ultimate threats.[20] And it was a truth that Jeremiah would hold out as a lifeline for the exiles later, but not until the axe of judgment had fallen on this generation.

What precipitated this unthinkable longing, if indeed it comes from God's lips? Basically, Judah's society had become rotten to the core, filled with lies, deceit and untrustworthiness – that is, the diametric opposite of the character of God himself (3–6, 8). No wonder God couldn't stand their company any longer.

Social breakdown has rarely been more accurately and poignantly described than in these verses. After generations of trusting false gods that have let them down, the whole culture has become a stinking swamp of slander, spin and smears. Even the natural human bonds of friendship and kinship can no longer restrain the evils of cheating (4). Lying has become an art-form, a well-honed skill (5). Words have become weapons to pierce, wound and entrap (3, 8). The rot corrodes individual relationships (*friends, anyone*), and society as a whole (*a crowd of unfaithful people*, 2).

Verse 6 summarizes the truth and the truth behind the truth – as much for our contemporary culture as for ancient Israel. We live in the midst of deception, and the biggest deception has been Western culture's three centuries of pragmatic public atheism – assuming that God and God's standards need not be 'known' for society to carry on its business as usual.

b. Brokenness in the heart of God (7–11)

Once again Jeremiah gives us a window into the heart of God and the clash of emotions going on there. God bounces the question back

moving out of the city (Ezek. 10). The purpose of Ezekiel's vision, however, was to prepare for the radical freedom of God to appear to Ezekiel in Babylon, and later to return to his temple. Jeremiah's metaphor rather expresses the exasperation of God with his people and his longing to get far away from their corrupting company.

[19] Gen. 15; 17:3–8; 22:16–18; Heb. 6:13–20.
[20] Exod. 32:11–14; Deut. 9:25–29.

THE MESSAGE OF JEREMIAH

at those who want to question his final, but reluctant, decision to act in punishment upon *such a nation as this. What else can I do?* God pleads. *Should I not punish them for this?* (7, 9) In other words, God says, 'You be the judge. What would you do in my place? What would your own courts do to people found guilty of gross fraud? What, then, is the simple moral logic of the position you put *me* in? If I do *not* act to punish wrongdoing on such a scale, then I lose all claim to be the moral judge of the universe. Shall not the Judge of all the earth do right?'

But the questions also voice the struggle within God. This is the God whose first definition of his own identity begins, 'The LORD, the LORD, the compassionate and gracious God, *slow to anger, abounding in love . . .*' but continues, 'yet he does not leave the guilty unpunished'.[21] God can no longer let the guilty go unpunished, but the act of punishment will be carried out with the grief of suffering love and the pain of tormented compassion. This tension is simply set side by side in verses 10–11.

Verse 11 describes what will happen *and* affirms that it will happen by God's decree (*I will . . .*). The deed would be done by Nebuchadnezzar, but the decision was made by God.

But verse 10 describes the emotional cost – to God. For whatever ambiguity there may be over the speakers in 8:18 – 9:1, there is no ambiguity here. The 'I' is continuous from verse 7 to verse 11. This is *God* who *will weep and wail.* This is God in tears. This is God crying out loud. This is God hugging the very creation that is now desolate. This is God bereaved not only of his human loved ones, but of his beasts and birds in the mountains, fields and forests. War then, as now, was environmentally devastating and God grieves at the destruction, the eerie death-filled silence of abandoned farms with no bellowing or birdsong. This is a picture of un-creation, like 4:23–28. Human sin takes a terrible toxic toll on our whole created world, for we are part of it. Judgment on us tears at the fabric of the environment God made for us. Creation suffers in silence and the only sound is the sobbing of the Creator.

c. The rationale of judgment (12–16)

The overwhelming emotion of such poetry needs another pause. Our skilled editor knows when we must stand back for a moment and dry our own tears. And while we do so, he provides another short prose passage that makes the point crystal clear. If the reader – in exile or later – is moved by the ghastly scene of verses 10–11 to

---

[21] Exod. 34:6

ask, '*Why?*' (12), then the answer is simply distilled from all the surrounding preaching of Jeremiah. It is a straightforward equation: apostasy (13) plus idolatry (14) leads to judgment – exile and death (15–16). Deuteronomy anticipated the same question and gave the same answer.[22]

d. Lament! The grim reaper is coming (17–22)

The prose pause is over. The poetry resumes and reaches its grisly climax in verse 22. The chapter began with the tears of Jeremiah and God (9:1). It has peaked with the weeping and wailing of God himself (9:10). But God will not weep alone. The scale of the tragedy calls for an army of wailers. Israel, like many traditional societies still today, had grief-professionals – women who were *skilful* in providing appropriate songs of lament and all the culturally expected accompaniments of mourning that would honour the dead and support the bereaved. Their finest hour has come, says God. Send for them and let the wailing and weeping fill the air for the ruin of *Zion* – city and people (17–19).

Then God addresses these same dismal women. If you have *daughters*, teach them to wail too – the grief will last into the next generation. Childhood songs of fun and joy will be silenced by the mounting death toll in a city besieged and then captured with appalling violence and slaughter by Nebuchadnezzar's armies. Death is personified as an omnipresent intruder – climbing through windows, smashing down hiding places, slaying the children and youth, at home, in the streets, in the fields – mercilessly slaughtering, splattering the dead everywhere, reaping like a harvester who cuts down the grain but never picks it up. Death, the grim reaper, reaping the awful harvest of all that this people have sown (21–22).

And so the last word goes to the women, and it is lament. For if there is another 'why?', it has to be, 'Why is it the women who suffer most for the sins of humanity?'

War is cruel not only to those who become battlefield casualties but also to those who are left behind to grieve their loss. More often than not these are women – wives, as well as mothers. The scene is re-enacted over and over again on our television screens. Black-robed women stand beside open graves in the not-so-holy land, lifting clenched hands towards heaven or beating upon their breasts. What else can they do when the men they love lie dead

[22] Deut. 29:22–28.

before them? Why must women always bear an unequal share of the world's sorrow? Why must they teach their own daughters to lament? Why must Rachel grieve over her departed children? Why must Mary weep alone at the cross?[23]

e. The crucial choice (23–24)

In such circumstances, any kind of *boasting* would seem utterly out of place. It may be that these two carefully crafted verses come from a different occasion and certainly they can stand on their own and deliver a powerfully coherent message about relative priorities in life. They list three things that human beings value, and which are good gifts of God in themselves. But when they are the subject of boasting, *wisdom* becomes intellectual pride and folly; *strength* becomes naked power and violence; *riches* become idolatrous greed. On the other side, they list three things that God most values – *kindness, justice and righteousness.* That is what brings pleasure to God when they are done *on earth.* And they can be practised only by those who, at the pivotal point of choice that stands between the two groups of three, have chosen to *understand and know* God as he is revealed in the person and character of YHWH.

However, our editors have placed these two verses here and we owe it to them to discern their reasoning.

The disaster that was coming would not be averted by any human capacity. Three human capacities in particular have had some mention already in the preceding poetry. Those who claimed to be *wise* in Israel's governing and religious elite have already been exposed as frauds (8:8–9). The *strong* of Jerusalem's military[24] will be unable to defend Judah's forts (8:14), and will eventually be food for scavengers in the streets and fields (21–22). The *rich* had gained their wealth through covetous greed and manipulative, exploiting religion (8:10). No such flawed *wisdom, strength* or *riches* would withstand the power of God's judgment. They had trusted, they had boasted in such things. They had made a profoundly wrong choice. Fatally wrong.

So, for the benefit of those who would read the book in the aftermath of the events, what choice *should* they have made? What choice was still open to those who survived? They could, at last, choose to do what the generations before them had refused to do (8:7; 9:6) – to understand and know YHWH their God, and in knowing him, to live according to *his* character, not according to their own foolish boasting.

[23] Craigie, Kelley and Drinkard, p. 151. See 31:15; Matt. 2:16–18.
[24] The word for 'strong man' commonly referred to mighty young men of military prowess.

The lesson is clear: those who know what God delights in should go and do likewise. But there is a further, and more challenging, theological dimension to verse 24 that cannot be avoided because of the context in which it is placed. Following a chapter filled with tragedy and tears, with death and mourning, how can we possibly speak of God's *kindness? Justice and righteousness* we can understand, for the moral necessity of punishment on persistent, unrepentant wickedness has been explained again and again. But kindness?

The word is *hesed*, the faithful, loving commitment of God to his covenant promise. The paradox is that God calls on the reader in verse 24 to understand something profound about God himself, which is that even in the terrible execution of his anger against sin God is being true to his own essential character of love *and* justice. And to understand that we need to step back to a wider perspective.

God's purpose in and through the very existence of Israel was the ultimate blessing of the nations (cf. 4:1–2). All his dealings with Israel – in redemption, and in judgment, and beyond judgment in restoration – were geared towards that universal saving mission. All that God does *on earth* serves that purpose and is consistent with his essential character. The paradoxical message of Jeremiah 9:24 in the context of a chapter describing God's outpoured judgment on Israel in 587 BC is the same as Psalm 47. There, the nations are summoned to give YHWH a round of applause. Why? Because YHWH had subdued the nations under Israel – referring of course to the conquest of Canaan. How can such an event be a reason for thanksgiving *among the nations*? Because in the long story of God's mission that will span the rest of the Bible, the nations will have reason to praise God for the history of Israel, even including the conquest, for it will become an integral part of the whole story of salvation that ultimately led to Calvary and opened the gate of eternal life to all nations.[25]

Similarly, the remnant of Israel will come to see the name and character of YHWH vindicated *both* in the exile as an act of his righteous judgment *and* in the restoration as an act of his loving grace. God is sovereign in punishing sin and in bringing salvation. And in both dimensions God acts in holy love and justice. Ultimately, only the cross of Christ could adequately contain both truths simultaneously.

[25] Paul perceives this paradox, citing Deut. 32:15, as he anticipates the Gentile nations coming to rejoice in God, even though the immediate means by which they have come to hear the gospel and turn to God for salvation was God's judgment on those Jews who had rejected their Messiah (Rom. 15:10; following Rom. 9 – 11).

f. Israel among the nations (9:25–26)

The final insult. Was it not enough to say that Israel's trust in the temple was a lie (7:4)? Was it not enough to say that their pride in the law was a lie (8:8)? Must their distinctive mark of covenant identity also be nullified? For that is what circumcision had meant ever since God first required it of Abraham as a sign of God's covenant promise to him and his descendants.[26] It had been the first act of Joshua when the people moved into the land of promise.[27] Now that God was about to expel them from that land, he makes the point that even circumcision in itself as an outward physical mark was no proof of covenant loyalty, no cause for boasting superiority above other nations, and no guarantee of continued survival in the land.

Circumcision was in fact practised by several other nations, including those listed here. What is shocking here is that Jeremiah simply inserts Judah into a list of other circumcising nations – and not even the first on the list – as if to say, 'There really is no difference between you and all these other nations you so despise. They all practise physical circumcision as you do. But you are just as uncircumcised in reality as they are. You have become no different from the other nations in heart or flesh.'

Circumcision of the flesh was supposed to be a sign of covenant obedience of the heart. The Apostle Paul made this clear when he distinguishes sharply between Israel 'after the flesh' – i.e. those physically circumcised – and the true Israel who were circumcised in heart, through faith and obedience. In comparison with that true circumcision of heart (which he linked to faith in Christ and baptism), physical circumcision was of no value in itself, one way or another.[28] However, Paul did not invent this language of 'circumcision of the heart'. He was simply connecting the clear teaching of the Old Testament itself to Christ. Deuteronomy and Jeremiah both call for such spiritual circumcision, lived out through hearing and heeding the word of God in covenant obedience.[29]

3. The final cost of idolatry (10:1–25)

The nations form the link between the end of chapter 9 and the beginning of chapter 10. Likewise, Jeremiah 10 begins and ends with *the nations* (1 and 25). This not only gives us a clue as to why the

[26] Gen. 17:1–14.
[27] Josh. 5:1–8.
[28] Rom. 2:25–29; 9:6–7; Col. 2:11–13; Gal. 5:1–6.
[29] Deut. 10:16; 30:6; Jer. 4:4; 6:10. Cf. Lev. 26:41.

editors have put together the two otherwise unconnected parts of chapter 10 itself, it also points us to another important Old Testament text that certainly influenced Jeremiah and may well provide the framework of ideas that lie behind this whole edited digest of Jeremiah's preaching in 8:4 – 10:25. That is, the Song of Moses in Deuteronomy 32:1–43.[30]

a. The living God or dead idols? (1–16)

The nations in general run after their false gods, but Israel knows better – or should do – and is warned not to *learn the ways of the nations*. For they, Israel, have the privilege of knowing the living God as their own (16), and need to see again the sheer folly of exchanging him for anything else.

Jeremiah 10 is very similar to the great preaching of Isaiah 40 – 48. It has its own distinctiveness, however. Whereas Isaiah focuses repeatedly on YHWH's power to predict and interpret history, Jeremiah does not mention that here, but concentrates on his power in creation. In its context, this highlights even more strongly the wrong choice that Israel had made in abandoning YHWH for other gods (cf. 9:14), and prepares the way for the anticipation that God will eventually judge the nations that walk the ways of such folly (25).

The poem falls into four sections, in each of which some feature of the idols is mocked and then contrasted with YHWH, the living God. This creates an antiphonal effect of alternating negative and positive voices.

---

[30] Deut. 32:1–43 is an anticipation of the Old Testament history of Israel in a vigorous and graphic poem (which Paul also turned into an anticipated history of the way God would bring about the salvation of the nations, in Romans 9 – 11). It has the following main features, all of which (except the last) are explicitly reflected in Jer. 8:4 – 10:25:
- It characterizes Israel as warped, corrupt, crooked, ungrateful, perverse and unfaithful.
- It portrays the prime sin of Israel as rejection of YHWH and going after other gods.
- It contrasts the worthlessness of those gods with the greatness and power of the living God.
- It portrays God's punishment in terms of violent attack (including the imagery of venomous snakes) that will devour people, land and harvests, spreading death in the homes and streets, and ending in exile.
- It sees the nations as the agent of God's judgment. But in a sudden switch, anticipates that God will turn to judge those enemy nations too, and ultimately save his people from total destruction.
- It ends with a mysterious invitation to the nations to join in rejoicing at the work of God (something which Paul linked to the spread of the gospel among the Gentiles, Rom. 15:10).

THE MESSAGE OF JEREMIAH

(i) Impotence vs. power (2–7)
Are idols something or nothing? That is, are the false gods that human beings worship 'real' in any way, or simply imaginary? The question needs careful definition. If we ask it in relation to human culture and behaviour, then, yes, idolatry is a powerful force, whether one thinks of the named gods of major human religions, or the unnamed but equally idolatrous gods of so-called secular cultures, such as consumerism, militarism, narcissism, etc. There is 'something' there in the spiritual power of religions and ideologies. But if we ask the question in relation to the only true and living God, then the answer is 'no'; in comparison to *God*, all false gods are nothing at all. Or to be more precise, and more biblical, they are no-gods, not-God things. They are, in fact, 'the work of men's hands'. That is the phrase most commonly used for them. The idols we worship are human constructs.

Now, at the physical level, the point is obvious. Statues of the gods may be terribly fancy and expensive, but they are no more in essence than *a scarecrow in a cucumber field* (possibly the most richly comic metaphor for idolatry ever invented), and no more able-bodied either. The Old Testament generally has a lot of fun with the absurdity of idols that have all the human body parts but can't do a thing with them (5).[31] But the point is actually very serious. For it is not just the statues that are the product of human hands, but the gods themselves – they too are figments, constructs, fabrications.[32] Once exposed as impotent frauds, they are not to be feared or trusted, for *they can do no harm, nor can they do any good.*

By contrast, YHWH is incomparable in his greatness and power, and his sovereignty over all nations (6–7), a truth that Israel had known since Moses turned it into triumphant song in Exodus 15.

(ii) Manufactured objects vs. eternal King (8–10)
The point of this shorter stanza is much the same as the last one. 'The glamour of gods that are made to measure disappears',[33] and the glory of the *true, living* and *eternal King* shines forth.

(iii) Doomed to perish vs. creator of the universe (11–13)
Since these false gods did not make the heavens and the earth (as God did – the echo of Gen. 1:1 is clear), they can only be objects *within* the created order, and therefore they must be perishable by nature like all other created things. And that indeed will be their fate.

---

[31] Pss 115:5–7; 135:15–18; Isa. 44:9–20.
[32] This is an important point that I have explored more fully in Wright, *Mission of God*, ch. 5.
[33] Kidner, p. 56.

And has been. Where, after all, are the gods we know by name as the gods of Egypt, Babylon, Assyria, Greece, Rome, ancient Britain . . . ? Some of them seemed to rule the world of their day. Now we know them only through archaeology and ancient texts and legends. History is the graveyard of the gods. They do indeed *perish from the earth and from under the heavens.* Sadly our human capacity to resurrect and refurbish them by different names seems limitless.

Verses 12 and 13 echo many psalms, perhaps particularly recalling Psalm 33:6–9, and the great creation traditions of the Wisdom literature such as Job 38 – 41.

(iv) Worthless fraud vs. the God of Israel (14–16)

The fact that Israel has not been mentioned hitherto highlights the universal claim that the poem is making. YHWH *is* the God of Israel, yes, but before and beyond that he is the sovereign Lord, Creator of the universe and governor of all nations. In comparison, the idols are objects of shame, precisely because their claims are fraudulent. They suck the life and treasure out of a nation (the cost of all our idolatry is stupendous), but they always fail when you need them most. Idolatry is fundamentally a fool's game, but we never learn until it is too late.

By contrast, Israel, the people of God to whom we belong through faith in Jesus Christ, have the inestimable privilege and responsibility of knowing this God as our own. The sheer grace in that relationship is pin-pointed by describing God as *the Portion of Jacob* – Jacob the cheat, the deceiver! Jacob who gave his name to the whole nation of cheats that has sprung from him.[34] But this perverse people have been entrusted with the knowledge of the living God. *The Maker of all things* has chosen to make Israel, and all of us who are in Christ, *his inheritance* – his family treasure. The language of verse 16 is reciprocal. We belong to him, as he belongs to us.

b. Thrown out at last (17–22)

Our editors could not have achieved a greater shock than putting this final description of the exile and its shattering grief immediately after the hymn of praise to the greatness and glory of God. People who had the Creator of the universe as their *portion*, and the privilege of being his *inheritance* – terms of identity, security and anticipation (16), are pictured packing up their last wretched *belongings* and

---

[34] In 9:4, the line *every one of them is a deceiver*, is literally in Hebrew, 'every brother is a "Jacob"', a supplanter.

taking to the road as nameless, hopeless, future-less refugees, as they are slung out of the land they thought was theirs forever. But since they had insisted on exchanging the glory of their God for the worthlessness of idols, they would pay the cost in exchanging the blessing of their land for the curse of exile.

And so to a final outpouring of grief from the prophet, as Jeremiah accepts the fact that he will have to endure what the people themselves would suffer (as indeed he did, though he was not taken by the Babylonians but by his own people to Egypt). Once again we hear the dual voice of Jeremiah (19), and of God (20). God now feels himself as homeless as his people, the people so senselessly betrayed by their own leaders (21). Nothing is left now but to wait for the invasion from the north (22) that Jeremiah had been foreseeing since his vision of the boiling pot in chapter 1.

c. A prayer and a hope (23–25)

And finally, a closing prayer. This whole sprawling collection since 8:4 has strained our imagination and emotions to the depths. Now, having given us a window into God's heart, it concludes with a word in God's ear. These words, especially verse 25, entered into the prayer life of the exiles as well, as is clear from the way they are built into a psalm of lament that clearly comes from the stinging trauma of those who survived the destruction Jeremiah foretold – Psalm 79 (see especially vv. 6–7).

The prayer begins with humble acceptance of human limits and God's sovereignty (23), moves on to plead for God's mercy (24), and concludes by appealing for God's justice (25).

While verse 24 is cast as a personal request, it is most likely that in speaking of *me* Jeremiah identifies himself with the people as a whole (as he so often did). If there must be punishment – and it is accepted now that there must be (9:9) – let it be disciplinary and not totally destructive. A glimmer of hope appears: the destruction and suffering of the fall of Jerusalem would be intense. But in God's ultimate purpose it would not be The End. There will be a future. Grace will triumph (31:11; 46:28).

Deuteronomy 32:27–42 describes how God, having used the nations as agents of his judgment on Israel, would in turn act in judgment on the nations themselves. Jeremiah turns that expectation into a prayer, a plea that God would vindicate his own justice (25).

But we cannot miss the glaring irony of this prayer, placed climactically at the end of this whole section. For if God is to judge nations that *do not acknowledge* him (the Hebrew is simply 'do not know you'), *peoples who do not call on your name*, who can possibly fit that description better than Israel itself? It was Israel who had refused to acknowledge God (9:3, 6). It was Israel who kept calling on every other god but the Lord. So who most deserves the judgment here prayed for? Once again, the text of Jeremiah is radically levelling. If the nations are to be judged and punished, then so must Israel be.

But what about the converse? If there can be hope for Israel's future, can there be hope for the nations? That question is not answered here. But it will be. And the answer will be yet another surprise (12:14–17).

Theological and expository reflections

- Perhaps the most challenging dimension of these chapters is the combination of anger and pain in the heart of God. How can we hold these together and preach them appropriately? The comments above on 8:16 – 9:1 may help us at least avoid falsely setting one against the other. The spectrum of emotions in marriage breakdown also call us to remember the deeply personal nature of God's relationship with his people.

- Consider how easy it is for people to affirm the written scriptures while 'rejecting the word of the Lord' in practice (8:9). We may think, at first, of theologians and church leaders who provide clever arguments for limiting the ethical standards of biblical faith to the ancient cultures in which the texts emerged, leaving themselves and their followers free to approve what the Bible condemns and condemn those who seek to live by what the Bible approves. But then there are those who affirm the truth and authority of the Bible in their confessions of faith, while their obedience to the Bible is a highly selective mixture of hotspots and blind spots. Some people, for example, are very vocal and active on defending biblical sexual standards, but silent about the even stronger biblical teaching on issues of injustice, poverty, race, corruption, and the care of God's creation. Some who claim the highest ground in their doctrine of biblical authority seem happy to behave in very unbiblical ways in conducting their disagreements with other Christian sisters and brothers.

- It would be hard to find a more succinctly accurate description than 9:2–6 of the culture of 'disinformation' (the contemporary euphemism for public lying) to which much Western society has sunk. What do we see?

  – the pollution of the media by propaganda pretending to be news;

139

- the control of so many media by so few powerful global empires;
- the strangulation of truly investigative journalism that at least makes some attempt to expose and tell the truth;
- the 'public relations' industry that will create any story you like for a price, and the laziness of media, politicians and public who will swallow it, bait and hook;
- the perversion of science by the vested commercial interests of those who stand to lose if the truth be known (whether about tobacco, pharmaceutical research, the weapons trade, 'collateral damage' in war, environmental destruction, or climate change);
- the obsession of politicians with information control and 'spin', and their rigorous training in question avoidance;
- and among the general population frightening statistics of the number of those who see no harm in lying to employers.

The breakdown of trust pervades the whole culture, from the boardroom to the bedroom, and the price is astronomical.

Jeremiah 11:1 – 12:17
8. Broken covenant and broken hearts

Pause for prose. Once again our editors slow down the pace and passion of Jeremiah's poetry with a pillar of more sermonic prose. Once again the main reason is to summarize the message with clear rationale. And once again, we find that the pain of Jeremiah is a window into the grieving heart of God. This time, however, Jeremiah faces a very specific threat – a conspiracy against him from those of his own home and family. When Jeremiah challenges God as to why God allows such wickedness to continue, God answers with a direct parallel to himself. He too is the victim of a conspiracy from his own home and family. Whatever pain and anger Jeremiah feels is vastly amplified in the heart of God, and Jeremiah's cry for justice will be answered – but with a surprising twist of compassion in the end.

The opening sermon (11:1–17) introduces the third major section of the whole book, running from here to the end of chapter 17. This section is suspended between two prose sermons that emphasize the demands of the Sinai covenant. The overall message is the dismantling of Israel's trust in their covenant relationship with YHWH. They needed to be reminded that the Sinai covenant itself included threat and curse, along with promise and demand. The covenant had now become so broken and disregarded that nothing remained but the outworking of its curse in the horrors of invasion, defeat and exile.

This third section of the book (chs. 11 – 17), then, builds on the second section (chs. 7 – 10), where the major thrust was to dismantle Israel's trust in the *temple* and declare it 'a lie'. Now Jeremiah turns his full attention to the *covenant* in all its scriptural weight, and declares it *broken* (11:10).

1. The curse of a broken covenant (11:1–17)

It is possible that the preaching contained in this chapter comes initially from the period of the great reformation under Josiah.[1] That reformation was accelerated by the discovery of the Book of the Law in the temple, which is usually assumed to be some form of what we now call Deuteronomy. And the echoes of Deuteronomy are particularly frequent and pointed in this passage of Jeremiah. However, even if Jeremiah preached in support of Josiah's reformation it is clear that he became disappointed with its long-term effectiveness. There seemed to be little change in the hearts, minds and behaviour of the people.

There are strong similarities between the temple sermon in chapter 7 and this one in chapter 11,[2] which suggests that these themes probably occupied the constant preaching of Jeremiah over a sustained period from the heady days of Josiah's reformation to the dark days of its reversal under Jehoiakim. And for the exiles, reading these words written, the message would remind them of the words, the prophet and the God they had rejected. But for them, it was a message not without hope.

The sermon has three sections, introduced by the formula of a word from God (1, 6 and 9), though the third section is somewhat disjointed.

a. Listen to your scriptures (1–5)

Good preaching starts with the biblical text and moves on to contemporary application. Jeremiah knew the technique. If the public reading of the Book of the Law during Josiah's reformation was a repeated ceremony, then Jeremiah had his scriptural text ready to hand. This first part of his message is almost entirely made up of quotes from Deuteronomy.[3] Verses 3 and 5 reflect the curse texts of Deuteronomy 27. Jeremiah even chimes in with the *amen* that the people were supposed to say to the list of curses that sanctioned the covenant (5b).

The message is clear. God had given his people the great promise that he would give them the *land flowing with milk and honey* (5). But enjoyment of that gift was conditional on their willingness to *obey me and do everything I command you* (4b). This command was

[1] For a full account, see 2 Chr. 34.
[2] The comparisons can be clearly seen: compare 11:1–5 with 7:22–23; 11:7–8 with 7:24–26; and 11:14 with 7:16.
[3] Notice how common phrases occur in 11:4 and Deut. 4:20; 11:5 and Deut. 7:8; 11:8 and Deut. 4:13.

itself sanctioned in two ways. First, it was based on the past grace of historical salvation, for it was given *when I brought them out of Egypt* (4a). The exodus preceded Sinai. And secondly, it was backed by a curse on those who would not *obey the terms of this covenant* (3).

This is the paradox of the book of Deuteronomy itself – between God's unconditional promise and saving action on the one hand, and the conditional nature of continued enjoyment of the fruit of God's promise and action on the other. Israel had received the land because God had delivered them from Egypt and kept his promise to Abraham. That was a narrative of unconditional sovereign saving grace alone. Yet God calls for obedient listening to the terms (lit. 'words') of the covenant. Obedience would be, *not* the means of *earning or deserving* God's salvation, but the means of *continued living* within the sphere of God's covenant blessing that had already been granted by saving grace. Outside that sphere of responsive obedience and blessing lay only one thing – the curse.

So Jeremiah begins his sermon with the curse in Deuteronomy 27 (3), but immediately jumps back to the positive foundation for Israel's obedience – God's saving grace in the exodus (4). The order of verse 4 clearly reflects Exodus 19:4–6: salvation first, obedience second. In building his message on the foundation of such authoritative scriptures, Jeremiah was leaving his listeners no option but to repeat after him the *amen* his text called for.

b. Look at your history (6–8)

The sermon moves from text to application, from hermeneutics to history. Ever since that first act of salvation (the exodus), and that first giving of the command (Sinai), the history of the people has been an uninterrupted refusal to listen and obey (7–8). Stubborn evil reigned in place of covenant obedience. So what could possibly be left of covenant reality? Certainly no longer the promised blessings they vainly wanted to hang onto. God is as serious about the covenant threats as he is faithful in his covenant promises. The people's own actions have determined which they will experience. God remains sovereign, but the people bear their own responsibility.

The sermon is thus a combination of scriptural foundations, historical perspectives, and inevitable conclusions. There is a simple homiletical logic:

- This is what the scriptures say.
- This is what you have done.
- This is what is now going to happen, in fulfilment of the scriptures.

143

So the sermon brings into sharp focus the essential principles that underlie the poetry of the previous chapters, where these same points had been painted on a broader canvas in slashing brush strokes laden with lurid colours and wet with tears.

c. Face the inescapable (9–17)

The Sinai covenant reflects the form of international treaties imposed by victorious empires on their vassal subject kingdoms. Such treaties were laced with severe threats against anybody foolhardy enough to conspire or rebel against the ruling empire. Jeremiah draws on that political metaphor when God declares that *there is a conspiracy among the people of Judah and those who live in Jerusalem* (9). Since they knew the dire consequences of conspiracy and rebellion in the political arena, they should know what would be in store for them if they persisted in conspiracy against their covenant Lord.

Repeatedly Jeremiah had urged the people to 'turn back' (*šûb*) to God in repentance. Far from turning back to God, however, they had turned back (same verb) *to the sins of their ancestors*, with the same deliberate deafness (10).

The same international treaties prohibited vassals from making any kind of alliance with other states, in rivalry to the one imposing the treaty. The consequences for such disloyalty were very severe. Likewise, in the covenant between YHWH and Israel, there was the demand for total allegiance to YHWH as their covenant Lord, to the exclusion of all rival gods. Making alliances with others (other nations or other gods) constituted treaty-breaking. Accordingly, now for the first time Jeremiah states clearly and unequivocally that both kingdoms, Israel and Judah, *have broken the covenant I made with their ancestors* (10).

This stark reality – a broken covenant – produces stark results that are now unavoidable. *Therefore* (11), pronounces the verdict that removes all possibility of escape. *Therefore this is what the* LORD *says: 'I will bring on them a disaster they cannot escape.'* And in support of this terrible pronouncement, four reasons are given as to why the coming disaster is inevitable. There is no escape because:

(i) God won't listen to them (11b, 14b)

This may seem harsh, but it is nothing more than God returning upon their own heads the Israelites' own persistent refusal to listen to God. The Hebrew for 'listen' and 'obey' is the same word (with a different preposition) – *šāma'*. It has occurred seven times already in the first part of the sermon, climaxing in Israel's habitual refusal to listen in verse 10. This is a very similar sequence to what we saw in chapter 7, where the same word occurs repeatedly, both as a characteristic of Israel through history (7:24–26), and as their continuing stubborn stance in the present (7:27). There too, God says he will no longer listen to them or to prayers on their behalf (7:16). They can't plead their way out of their fate. People who resolutely refuse to listen to God cannot complain when God says he will not listen to them.

(ii) Their other gods won't help them (12–13)
Once again, the sermonic prose emphasizes things that have been said already in the poetic oracles. False gods promise life, prosperity and success. But they deliver death, poverty and disaster. And when God's judgment falls in the form of the disasters that we bring on ourselves by the folly of idolatry, then the gods we put so much faith in simply disappear in embarrassed impotence. These verses are a summary of all that had been said in chapter 2, especially 2:26–28.

(iii) Jeremiah won't pray for them (14)
Once more (cf. 7:16), Jeremiah is told not to pray for his own people – a command that implies that this was something that he *was* doing, as part of his prophetic calling and task. But with agonizing finality, God tells Jeremiah that these people are past praying for. This generation will suffer the weight of God's judgment. Having refused to listen to God they will find out what it means to have God not listen to them. And not even a prophet's prayers will help.

(iv) Their sacrifices won't work (15)
But the pain in the heart of God even as he speaks such words is felt in the next line. For who are these people? *My beloved!* The word is a term of special affection – built into the name Jedidiah – 'beloved by the LORD'.[4] Israel had proved an unfaithful lover in the covenant bond, but God still thinks of himself as lover and them as his beloved – a sad irony. To be angry with someone you love is extraordinarily painful, especially if the anger is caused by perceived betrayal. But the two emotions are so closely intertwined because each is a legitimate dimension of the other. That is why, when we read so much in Jeremiah of the boiling anger of God, we must see it coming out of a heart filled with love, longing, grief and pain. In his anger, God does not cease to be the God who is love.[5]

Where were those whom God still regarded as *my beloved* – false though they were? In his temple, carrying on their sacrifices as if all

---

[4] Solomon's other name, 2 Sam. 12:24–25.
[5] See the discussion on the passion of God in the Introduction, pp. 28–31.

was well in heaven and earth. Jeremiah sees the thronging courts and multiplying sacrifices – and is totally unimpressed. As he had said in chapter 7, sacred rites in the temple could not compensate for social wrongs in the city. No amount of sacrificial exuberance could cancel out their planned evil and its inevitable punishment.

And so the sermon ends (16–17) with another change of image. Israel the beloved, becomes Israel *a thriving olive tree* – beautiful in its fruit and its shape (16). Elsewhere Israel is portrayed as a vine.[6] The agricultural metaphors speak of deliberate planting and loving care – Israel's history in the land where God had planted and protected them for so long. But the prospect now was the raging fire of judgment that would destroy both people and land together. The pain of such action – for God the planter and farmer – would be acute (45:4).

2. The complaint of a rejected prophet (11:18 – 12:6)

Jeremiah's preaching was not calculated to make him popular – to say the least. In fact it put him in danger of his life. But the biggest surprise to Jeremiah was where that threat first came from – his own village and family. The shock of it leads to the first of what have come to be called 'The Confessions of Jeremiah' – though that is not a very good term. From here until the climax in which he curses the day he was born (20:14–18), we have interwoven a series of deeply personal encounters between Jeremiah and God. They are a mixture of complaint, protest, grief, self-pity, loneliness and pain – closely similar to the psalms of lament, and doubtless owing some of their language and imagery to that source.[7]

a. 'A lamb led to the slaughter' (11:18–23)

The death-threat was so unexpected that Jeremiah says he would not even have guessed it if God had not warned him. It seems he had become vaguely aware of a plot being hatched in the village (19). But in his innocence he had no idea that 'it was *against me* they were scheming their schemes' (lit. word order). In comparison to their vicious intention to obliterate him, he had been like a vulnerable *lamb led to the slaughter* – an image that connects the suffering of Jeremiah with the suffering servant of Isaiah 53:7 and is another item in the list of ways in which Jeremiah prefigures Jesus.

With dramatic effect, the text reveals the identity of the conspirators piece by piece. At first, we hear only that threats have been

[6] Jer. 2:21; Ps. 80:8–16; Isa. 5:1–7.
[7] See the Introduction, p. 28, for further discussion of their significance.

made against Jeremiah's life, by persons unknown (19). Then we discover, from God's response, that the conspirators were in Jeremiah's home village – *people of Anathoth* (21). Finally, and worst of all, we learn that they come from Jeremiah's own closest family – *your relatives, members of your own family* (12:6).

What could have caused such violent reaction to one of their own kith and kin (a question that could have been asked in Nazareth regarding its most famous son)? There are two possible answers.

If the reforms of Josiah provided the background to Jeremiah's preaching and if Jeremiah had expressed his support for those reforms (even if he saw how ineffective they ended up), then Jeremiah may have found himself on the wrong side of the religious and political arguments in his own village. Anathoth was a village of priestly families (1:1). Josiah's reforms involved the destruction of local sanctuaries and the demand that local village priests come to the temple in Jerusalem to do their work – or face redundancy.[8] One can easily understand that this would have been keenly resented in places like Anathoth, if members of Jeremiah's own family lost their livelihoods. Jeremiah's support for the royal policy would have been perceived as a treacherous betrayal of family honour and loyalties.

That is a possible, though speculative, reason. But there is another one much more clearly rooted in the text. Jeremiah was engaged in a systematic attack upon the key pillars of Israel's self-identity and worldview. We have seen how he dismantled the people's confidence in the *temple*, in the *land*, in the written *law*, in *circumcision*, and now in the very *covenant* with YHWH itself. None of these things, Jeremiah argued, could provide security from the wrath of God now being unleashed. But all of these things had ancient tradition and profound theological weight behind them. To attack such precious foundational beliefs must have seemed radically undermining of all that the people's life and faith were built upon. In fact, his relentless attacks probably appeared blasphemous. And that would explain the *fatwa* – the declaration that Jeremiah must be put to death. Their words, *Do not prophesy in the name of the LORD or you will die by our hands* (21), suggest that they may have come to regard Jeremiah as a false prophet in the terms of Deuteronomy 13. He was claiming to speak in the name of YHWH, but (in their opinion) he was in fact leading the people away from their ancient faith. Even though he was from their own family, he must be expelled and expunged like poison. That's what the law of Deuteronomy 13 demanded.

The truth of the matter, of course, was the precise opposite – as Jeremiah knew, and knew that God knew (20a). Jeremiah was truly

---

[8] 2 Kgs 23:8–9.

speaking the words of the Lord (cf. 1:9) and those who sought to silence him were therefore setting themselves up against God, again by a principle clearly expressed in Deuteronomy (18:18–19). For that offence, God promises, they will suffer the same judgment that was about to fall upon the nation as a whole (22–23).

In making that prediction (of the forthcoming punishment of Jeremiah's attackers), God was answering Jeremiah's petition in verse 20b. Now that petition may seem harsh. Certainly, it is one place where Jeremiah differed from Jesus. They may both have been like *a gentle lamb led to the slaughter*, but whereas Jeremiah cried out, Jesus was silent. Whereas Jeremiah asked God for retribution on his unjust attackers, Jesus asked for their forgiveness. Nevertheless, we should understand Jeremiah's cry in its own Old Testament context. And when we do that, several points can be made.

First, he did not launch into retaliation or take personal vengeance. He knew that was forbidden and so he, rightly, entrusted his case to God alone (as did Jesus).[9] Secondly, however, he knew that YHWH is the one truly just judge who will always judge righteously. In this conviction, expressed twice (11:20 and 12:1), he stands alongside Abraham.[10] 'Thus the petition is based on a fundamental conviction Israel has about God.'[11] Thirdly we must remember that, as in many of the lament psalms, Jeremiah is in a deeply dangerous and unfair situation, the victim of false accusation and death threats. His only appeal is to God for protection and vindication. He simply asks for God to do what God repeatedly declares he will do – deal with the wicked. Fourthly, we should take note of the legal nature of Jeremiah's language. He sees this as a case at court and appeals to the divine judge for a verdict, sentence and penalty – so that justice can be seen to be done.

> When the juridical language is recognized, the plea for 'vengeance' is not a request for blind capricious retaliation, but for the implementation of a just legal claim and the implementation of YHWH's justice on which the speaker has every right to count. This is the court petition of one unjustly treated, addressed to a reliable judge against the unjust perpetrators.[12]

Fifthly, God's response (21–23) shows that God does in fact accept the justice of Jeremiah's plea and promises to act accordingly. The divine court hands down the judgment that Jeremiah had requested.

[9] 1 Pet. 2:21–23.
[10] Gen. 18:25.
[11] Brueggemann (1988), p. 110.
[12] Ibid., p. 111.

And that, we might have thought, should be that. Case heard. Sentence pronounced. Case closed. Court adjourned. But not so fast. Jeremiah wants a word with the Judge.

b. 'Why? . . . How long?' (12:1–6)

Jeremiah trusts in God's ultimate justice, of course, and so he begins his second 'complaint' most politely by affirming it (1a). But Jeremiah's problem is: why does justice have to be delayed for so long, allowing the wicked not only to get away with their evil ways but also to prosper in doing so? The question (1b–2) echoes some of the most powerful lament psalms which agonize over the same problem – a problem which is no less acute for believers today than it ever was.[13] And what makes the complaint even sharper is the element of frustrated innocence on the part of the complainer. God has already accepted the truth of what Jeremiah claimed in 11:20a – namely that he, Jeremiah, was innocent. But that only made his 'righteous anger' all the worse in the long delay between the sentence and its execution (12:3a). Jeremiah might have joined those protest marches with their antiphonal demands: 'What do we want?' '*Justice*!' 'When do we want it?' '*Now*!'

> The assurance of divine judgment only further torments Jeremiah (12:1–6), for his own local context, his own specific situation in life, contradicts such claims. Jeremiah's world is still terribly fractured and in utter disarray. There is no evidence of justice, no visible sign of equilibrium, and no moral logic. The 'guilty prosper,' the 'treacherous thrive,' and YHWH appears blind or even in collusion . . . (12:2). In contrast, the righteous prophet suffers for no apparent reason ('my heart is with you,' 12:3). His charge against God is therefore no theoretical whim about rewards and punishment but a deeply personal cry. His queries are not philosophic but existential; they grow out of raw disappointment and pain.[14]

Such disappointment and frustration are common feelings, and those who seek to spend their lives serving God can feel them too. Indeed, those who try to serve God the most can feel the most hurt when others thrive and they are left to suffer and struggle. It all seems so unfair. Gerard Manley Hopkins drew on the opening lines of Jeremiah's complaint to voice his own disappointed endeavours.

[13] Job 21:1–21 expresses very similar sentiments.
[14] Stulman, p. 126.

149

> Thou art indeed just, Lord, if I contend
> With thee; but sir, so[15] what I plead is just.
> Why do sinners' ways prosper? and why must
> Disappointment all I endeavour end?
>
> Wert thou my enemy, O thou my friend,
> How wouldst thou worse[16], I wonder, than thou dost
> Defeat, thwart me? Oh, the sots and thralls of lust[17]
> Do in spare hours more thrive than I that spend,
> Sir, life upon thy cause. See, banks and breaks[18]
> Now leavèd how thick! Lacèd they are again
> With fretty chervil, look, and fresh wind shakes
> Them; birds build[19] – but not I build; no, but strain,
> Time's eunuch, and breed not one work that wakes.
> Mine, O thou lord of life, send my roots rain.[20]

We easily feel angry when law-abiding citizens are clobbered with one blow after another – unfair discrimination at work, higher taxes, loss of employment, unrelieved poverty and debt, austerity measures and welfare cuts, or any of life's other adversities – while greedy and influential people in high places or high office can twist the system to their own advantage and enrich themselves with immunity. Especially if the law-abiding citizen is oneself. And how much worse when the extreme wickedness of tyrants and dictators goes unpunished while their riches pile up in foreign bank accounts? Somehow, the calm logic of Deuteronomy's simple moral equations, as summarized in the sermonic discourse of 11:1–17, cannot contain the emotions generated by this inconsistency. We can believe that *ultimately* the wicked will suffer God's judgment and that the moral equilibrium of the universe will be eschatologically restored as God intended it. We can believe all that will happen in the end. But in the meantime. . . ? What about now? The delay is hard to bear.

Peter tells us that God delays his judgment in order to allow time for repentance, to give space for grace.[21] But for Jeremiah, it was not theological explanation that he wanted, but decisive and deserved

---

[15] In the sense of 'also'.

[16] In the sense: 'How could you do any worse than you already do to me?'

[17] I.e. the wicked.

[18] I.e. river banks and hillsides.

[19] Even nature achieves beauty and building without 'effort', in contrast to the author's inability to accomplish what he hopes.

[20] From *Poems* (London, 1918).

[21] 2 Pet. 3:8–9.

action right now. Verse 3 is the cry of someone not only deeply hurt by unjust attack, but whose life was now in danger. He had said that he felt 'like a gentle lamb let to the slaughter' (11:19). Now he tells God to make his enemies face the same fate (12:3b). Once again, we witness his deeply human feelings and we can understand them, for who of us would not be tempted to react the same way sometimes? And again we have to contrast them with those of Jesus, and remind ourselves that it is the example of Jesus, not of Jeremiah, that we are commanded to imitate.

Verse 4 moves beyond Jeremiah's concern for himself and issues a cry on behalf of *the land*. Whatever the precise circumstances that verse 4a refers to (it appears to be prolonged drought – cf. ch. 14), Jeremiah's heart goes out to the suffering of the non-human creation (*land, grass, field, animals and birds*), and connects it with the wickedness of the human inhabitants of the land (4b). This connection between human behaviour and ecological suffering is often articulated by Jeremiah.[22] It may be another theological and ethical perspective that he learned from Hosea.[23]

In our day, we can and should share Jeremiah's anger and his desperate sense of impatience when we see the scale of global devastation of creation caused by human greed, toxic consumerism and political impotence. If climate change is the result of human behaviour (which may once have been unwitting but is now done in full knowledge of, but appalling indifference to, its likely results), then Jeremiah's anger and longing for divine intervention is appropriate, not only for the poor of the earth who will suffer most and soonest, but for God's suffering creation itself.

God's answer to Jeremiah's complaint begins with no comfort for Jeremiah's pain (5–6), but then goes on with no comfort for the even greater pain felt by God (7–13). In response to the plea that Jeremiah has put before the heavenly court in verse 1, 'the divine judge refuses to take the case but issues an advisory brief'.[24] God simply says, 'If you think this is tough,[25] worse is yet to come' (5–6). As indeed it would come, in the later years of Jeremiah's persecuted life. The warning may have given Jeremiah some self-protective wisdom (*do not trust them*), but nothing else – other than God's continuing promise since 1:19.

[22] Jer. 2:7; 3:2–3; 4:2–28; 9:10.
[23] Hos. 4:1–3.
[24] Allen, p. 150.
[25] A small indication of how God's speech is marked out by word connections can be seen in comparing v. 5, where *safe country* translates, lit., 'a land of peace', with v. 12, where the land is described as a place where *no one will be safe*, lit. 'no flesh has peace'.

3. The lament of the rejected God (12:7–13)

If Jeremiah has a *family* who are treating him like an enemy, so has YHWH. There is a word-link between verse 6 (*your own family*, which is lit. 'your father's house'), and verse 7 (*my house*). Verse 7 expresses the agony of God with the double possessive, *my house, my inheritance,* and the repetition from 11:15 of the language of a dearly loved one (lit. 'the beloved of my soul').

What must it cost God to *give the one I love into the hands of her enemies?* Imagine that in purely human terms to feel its horror and pain. The poetry of the verse, with its repeated, rhyming first person possessive suffixes and verbal endings, intensifies the feeling of deep personal pain in the actions that follow. The personal emotion is sustained by continuous emphasis on *my: my house, my inheritance* (three times), *my vineyard, my field, my pleasant field.* All of these, and especially 'inheritance', can refer to the people, the land and the temple. All three were bound together as belonging to God, and all three would suffer in the judgment to come.

So although the last line of verse 11 expresses the appalling indifference of the people to their sins and their consequences, it was not wholly true that *there is no one who cares* (lit. 'there is no man who takes it to heart'). Maybe no *man* cared, but *God* cared with all his infinite heart. It was because God cared so much that he could not simply let things go on as they were.

The imagery of verses 8–9 is exceptionally striking. First of all God portrays *himself* as a lion's prey (8)! The lion, in this case, is his own people, who have become so viciously hostile to their loving God that, for God, it feels like being mauled by a lion. God himself is the victim being torn to pieces by the ones he loves! The metaphors of Psalm 22:12–16 are here transferred to God, and were actually experienced by him in the person of his Son on the cross, dying at the hands of the ones he loved. The shocking words, *therefore I hate her* (8b), do not mean that God had ceased to love. At a simple human psychological level they express the familiar 'love-hate' relationship that can occur when people are bound together in an intimacy that is both immensely strong and immensely vulnerable in the face of betrayal. But in the biblical context, it implies that God will necessarily have to treat Israel as his enemy, in response to the fact that they are treating him as theirs. The echo of Deuteronomy 7:9–10, in both its dimensions, is very clear.[26] If a lion attacks you, you cannot but treat it as an enemy. That is what God feels in response to his people's behaviour towards him.

[26] Cf. also Pss 5:4–6; 11:5; Hos. 9:15.

But secondly, in verse 9, the imagery reverses, as God portrays Israel itself as the ones who will become a prey to their enemies. As observant of raptors as of storks, Jeremiah had witnessed a lone *bird of prey* being attacked by others, and foresees Israel being similarly attacked by the surrounding predatory nations. The remainder of the passage (10–13) then describes the suffering and desolation that will be caused by the invasions of foreign enemy kings (*many shepherds*, 10). There will be destruction and death throughout the whole land (and yet again, the suffering of the land itself is kept in focus). But though the hand that wields it will be the foreign enemy, the sword itself will be *the sword of the LORD* (12). God's judgment will be mediated through enemy invasion, but the people need to know whose anger they were truly facing (13). For the exiles, who had suffered the anger of Nebuchadnezzar, it was crucial that they absorb this truth (that it was the result of God's anger), since it was only in doing so that they could experience the mercy and compassion of the same God – to which Jeremiah will surprisingly turn next.

4. The surprise of God's compassion (12:14–17)

Put yourself for a moment into the mind of those exiles in Babylon, reading the words of the book of Jeremiah. The reality of what is described in 12:10–13 was a raw and recent memory. Their land had been invaded and their city destroyed by the wicked Babylonians. What would be your emotion and your strong desire? Would it not be the same longing expressed by Jeremiah against his personal enemies, for God to deal with these national enemies with justified vengeance (11:20b; 12:3)? We know that this indeed was the mood on the streets of Babylon among the first wave of exiles. Psalm 137 says it all. They longed for the judgment of God to fall not only on Babylon but also on all the little nations around Judah that had taken quick advantage of Jerusalem's fate, and had attacked and pillaged the land.

So God's response in 12:14–17 is surprising indeed. Jeremiah had plenty of oracles of doom against surrounding nations (chs. 46 – 51). But on this occasion, he holds out an amazing offer of *compassion* and restoration – to foreign *nations* – on exactly the same terms as he had been extending to the people of Judah. If these *wicked neighbours* would, in the wake of God's judgement, turn to YHWH as the true and living God, then they could be as much established and incorporated within the people of God (*among my people*) as any native-born citizen of *my people Israel.* But if not, not.

And that, I think, is precisely the point, and explains why this strange short passage is included here. It expresses the consistency

153

of God's character and ways – on the universal stage – a message that will be graphically reinforced in chapter 18, as we shall see. Israel in exile had to learn first that their identity as God's covenant people provided them with no immunity from the righteous judgment of God. If they behaved like other nations (and especially like the Canaanites of old), then they would find that God would treat them just as much as enemies as they had been required to treat the Canaanites who stood under God's judgment for their wicked ways.[27] God has his covenant people, but God has no favourites. Whether Canaanite, or Babylonian – or Israelite – the wicked stand under the judgment of God.

However, the converse lesson also needed to be learned by the exiles. If they longed for God to act once again in salvation towards them, to extend to them the hand of compassion and restorative grace beyond the fires of judgment, then they must realize that such saving grace would never be confined to them alone. That offer of grace was characteristic of God's dealings with all people and all nations all the time. God is consistent. The principles of judgment *and* of salvation apply to all. Isaiah had a similar insight when his vision of the reigning, returning, redeeming God bringing his people back from exile is expanded to anticipate that 'all the ends of the earth will see the salvation of our God', and can thus call on people of all nations to 'turn to me and be saved, all you ends of the earth'.[28] Ezekiel also, with pointed absence of flattery, says that God's restoration of his people Israel will be not so much for their sake as to make him known among the nations (Ezek. 36:22–32).

This sudden broadening out of the horizon of the text is consistent with Jeremiah's calling to be God's 'prophet to the nations'. His was not just a message for Israel only, but was a part of that wider narrative of God's mission, ever since his promise to Abraham, to bring blessing to all nations on earth – of whom the little countries around Israel were a tiny but significant representative group at this moment.

> God will have compassion on them, and return them again to their heritage/land. Hence the focus on land is finally not simply on the land of promise, but on the heritage/land of all peoples. God's concern about land has universal dimensions (see the positive words in the oracles against the nations, 46:26; 48:47; 49:6, 39). Jeremiah is truly a prophet to the nations (1:5,10).[29]

[27] Lev. 18 and 20.
[28] Isa. 52:7–10; 45:22.
[29] Fretheim, p. 198.

This astonishing message blurs the distinction between insiders and outsiders. It declares that God's mercy extends beyond national borders to all people on the earth.[30]

This is a passage that militates against the narrow exclusivist tendency that seems endemic among God's people, when we so emphasize the amazing privilege of having been called, saved and sanctified by God's grace and included among his covenant people, that we lose sight of the universal missional love of God for people of all nations. It is a note that we already heard sounding at 4:1–2, and will hear again later in the book.

Theological and expository reflections

- Missiologically, we might ponder the implications of a section that begins with condemnation of God's own people and ends with the offer of compassion to foreign nations. What is the greater obstacle to the mission of God to bring blessing to all nations and the whole earth – the ignorance and idolatry of people who do not yet know God, or the syncretism and idolatry of those who claim they already do?
- Pastorally, as we face the suffering and complaints of people around us – within and outside the church – what can we helpfully learn from Jeremiah's questioning of God, and God's response?
- Homiletically, what kind of model for biblical preaching might we discern in Jeremiah's use of Scripture?

[30] Stulman, p. 129.

Jeremiah 13:1–27
9. An unwearable people and an unbearable future

This chapter begins with a piece of clothing so ruined that its owner would be ashamed to wear it, and ends with clothing being torn off as a symbol of the ruin and shame the people would suffer. In between come warnings of the coming darkness and doom, along with more of the bitter tears that flow from the eyes of the prophet and the heart of God.

1. Unwearable in disgrace (13:1–11)

a. Surprising behaviour (1–7)

God sends Jeremiah shopping. He was to buy a new piece of clothing for wearing around his waist. What exactly the garment was and how it was worn is not entirely clear. The word (*'ēzôr*) is rather rare, but it seems to have been a short skirt bound tightly around the waist and reaching some way down the thighs. Some commentators assume it was an undergarment, and translate 'loincloth'. Others, however, envisage it being worn outside a man's main long outer garment, as a waistband (NIV *belt* is too small and thin for what would have been a sizeable piece of cloth). It might have been decorative, but would have served also to carry small tools, weapons or a pouch of coins. Like a waistband, sash or girdle.

Two features help us visualize the garment better. First, it was designed to fit snugly around the waist, and cling tightly to the wearer (11a). The verb *dābaq* means to cling or hold fast to something or someone – as indeed Israel was supposed to do to their God. This feature would apply both to an inner loincloth and also to an outer waistband. In either case, it needed to be tight enough not to drop down or fall off! But secondly, the final comparison that God makes between Jeremiah's garment and the people of Israel was that it, and they, were meant to be *for renown and praise and honour* (11b).This strongly suggests an outer garment that would be visible (intentionally so), and would draw admiration from all who met the wearer. Somehow, comparing Israel to YHWH's inner loincloth, though it would certainly speak of close-fitting intimacy, would hardly suggest admiration and praise for something that nobody could see.

So my own view is that God sent Jeremiah to buy a fresh and attractive linen external waistband, which he was then to wear in public. Linen, of course, was the fabric of the clothing of priests,[1] and Jeremiah came from a priestly family. So he may have attracted comment as to whether he was, after all, reclaiming his priestly credentials. Of course, our text does not specify that he was to wear it in order to be seen, but it seems most likely. The point was probably to arouse surprise. 'If Jeremiah [normally] wore the traditional prophetic garb he would have been clothed in a fairly tight tunic of coarse material with a hair cloak over it. A linen girdle around his waist, such as was worn by priests and the rich nobility, would have made him something of a spectacle.'[2] Rather like meeting an old friend you've only ever seen in jeans and a T-shirt suddenly going around in a suit and tie.

Then comes the surprise (3–5). God tells Jeremiah to go and hide his attractive accessory in the ground. Even more surprising is the burial place. Literally the Hebrew says 'the Euphrates'. Now that great river lay some 500 miles to the north-east, so if Jeremiah actually did that, it would have meant a thousand-mile round trip taking several months. And then he would have had to do it all over again (6). Rather than assume that this whole story is simply a parable of the imagination (which would hardly support the public meaning God gives it), many scholars think that he was to go to a nearby wadi by the name of Perath (as in NIV). The consonants of that name are identical to the Euphrates in Hebrew; there is just one vowel-point difference. This would have meant a shorter journey and the effect on the cloth would have been the same. But possibly the play on words would have been noticed by the people, later at least – given that Euphrates was the great river of Babylon to which themselves would later be exiled.

Wherever he buried it, God sent him back a long time later to find the thing again (6), and to nobody's surprise *it was ruined and*

[1] Lev. 16:4.
[2] Thompson, p. 363. 'Usually *'ezor* is rendered "loincloth", an undergarment, but the reference in v. 11 to "renown, praise and glory" reflects the ornamental quality that a girdle or "waist-sash" can have' (Allen, p. 156).

completely useless (7). After lying in the damp soil so long, the piece of fresh linen, once so decorative and admirable, had become a stained and rotting rag. Jeremiah certainly wasn't going to be seen around Jerusalem wearing that! Probably, though, he carried it around to show the tattered shreds to the people who had once so admired it when it was new and pristine. A thing of beauty, a thing you could wrap around yourself with pride – now ruined and useless for the purpose it had been bought for.

b. Startling message (8–11)

The message in verses 9–11 picks up the actions of the story in reverse order, making it clear from the start (by using the verb 'ruin' for both the cloth and the people, 7 and 9) that the waistband was a metaphor for Israel.

First (9), God was about to *ruin the pride of Judah and the great pride of Jerusalem,* just as the linen cloth, for all its 'pride' of appearance, had been ruined. Judah had a monarchy and a city stretching back unbroken to David and a temple built by Solomon. These were things they felt pride in. But all of them would suffer the fate of Jeremiah's linen sash: monarchy, city and temple would all be reduced to ruins. 'Look at this cloth,' said Jeremiah, 'and see your own future.'

Secondly (10), the fact that the cloth had 'gone off' to a foreign land (at least metaphorically, if the village of Perath symbolized the Euphrates), spoke of the way Israel had strayed from their 'wearer' and gone after other gods. We have heard Jeremiah say it so often: Israel simply *refuse to listen . . . they have not listened* (10a, 11b). Their stubborn rejection of their God was the reason for their rotting and ruin.

Thirdly, however (11), comes the most startling part of the message. Going back to the beginning, Jeremiah turns the human action of choosing, buying and wearing a piece of clothing into a metaphor for God's relationship with Israel through election and covenant. And the snug fit of a waistband was a picture of how God wanted his people to cling close to him. *'The close cling of a sash to a man's waist is like the way I made Israel's entire community and Judah's entire community cling to me,'* declared Yahweh, *'so that they would become my people, a source of my renown, praise and glory'* (11).[3]

The imagery is striking. *God wanted to 'put his people on'* like *clothing!* And not just as a man might wear a cloak loosely thrown

---

[3] As translated by Allen, p. 155.

over the shoulders, but as a close fitting, clinging, waistband. And not just for warmth, but for show! Both these points seem to be included in Jeremiah's message.

On the one hand, God had bound Israel to himself in a covenant relationship in which they were to cling to, or hold fast, to him in covenant loyalty, trust and obedience. This is a strong emphasis in Deuteronomy.[4] But that is exactly what they had failed to do, to their own ruin.

On the other hand, God wanted 'to look good' wearing Israel. That is to say, as a whole community they would be a credit to the God they worshipped, living in such a visibly different way among the nations that the name of YHWH would be held in praise and honour. Other nations should look at Israel and be attracted to the God Israel worshipped and belonged to (cf. Deut. 4:5–8). When we praise a beautiful piece of clothing, the praise is actually for the person wearing it. A husband who comments on his wife's beautiful new dress is paying *her* the compliment of how beautiful she looks wearing it.

This is how we should understand the other passage where this same triplet of words (*renown and fame and honour*) occurs – in Deuteronomy: 'He [God] has declared that he will set you [Israel] in *praise, fame and honour* high above all the nations he has made and that you will be a people holy to the LORD your God, as he promised.'[5] There, the praise is for Israel, but it is clear that the real destination of such praise is YHWH himself. Whatever praise comes the way of God's people is actually for the God who chose them as his covenant people and shows himself through them.

Jeremiah's graphic point, therefore, is that not only had the people unbound themselves from their covenant Lord, they had become completely unwearable by him. Israel, far from displaying the splendour of YHWH, were rotting in their own disgrace. They were failing to be and do what they had been bought for. They were denying their mission, their reason for existence.

Jeremiah's dramatic metaphor has a powerful implication for our biblical theology of mission. It sets the election of Israel in the context of God's mission to bless the nations.

> . . . in choosing to wear Israel, God had a wider agenda, namely the exaltation of his own name among the nations through what he would ultimately accomplish 'dressed with' Israel.
>
> And it was that wider purpose of God that Israel were so frustrating by their disobedience. They had become as corrupt as a

---

[4] Deut. 4:4; 10:20; 11:22; 13:4; 30:20. Cf. 1 Kgs 11:2; 2 Kgs 3:3; 18:6.
[5] Deut. 26:19, my italics.

new waistband that has lain in wet soil for many months – to return to Jeremiah's graphic acted parable. God simply couldn't wear them anymore. Far from bringing him praise and honour, they brought him shame and disgrace.[6] How could God attract admirers dressed in the filthy rags of such people? Their rottenness would bring him into contempt.

For that reason, if God's purpose for the nations were to proceed, God would have to deal with Israel first. And so it is very significant that the next time we come across that little triplet of words, it is in a promise – the promise that God would once again make his people fit to bring him admiration and praise.

> I will cleanse them from all their iniquity by which they have sinned against Me, and I will pardon all their iniquities by which they have sinned against Me, and by which they have transgressed against Me. And it [the city of Jerusalem, standing for the people of God] shall be to Me a *name of joy, praise, and glory* before all the nations of the earth, which shall hear of all the good that I do for them, and they shall fear and tremble because of all the good and all the peace that I make for it. (Jer. 33:8–9; my italics; 'joy' is added to the original three, 'name, praise and glory/honour').

And so we have to ask, how does our mission as God's people fit this metaphor? Are we living in such a way that the God we claim to worship attracts admiration from those around? Or does God look at us and think, 'I can't be seen wearing people like that!'[7]

2. Smashed in drunkenness (13:12–14)

Every wineskin should be filled with wine. The saying seems very obvious (as the people retort), and may perhaps have been a line of a drinking song or a common proverb. Most likely it had a cheerful, positive ring. Wine in the Bible is normally accompanied by joy, or a symbol of God's blessing and human gladness. So the people's echoing response probably expressed the expectation that the wineskins of their lives and their futures would be filled with joy and blessing. But that easy optimism is very quickly subverted by the other way that wine is used in the Old Testament – namely as the fastest route to self-destructive drunkenness. That sort of wine

---

[6] This is what Ezekiel means in ch. 36 when he speaks of Israel 'profaning the name of YHWH' – i.e. 'bringing YHWH into disrepute'.
[7] Wright, *The Mission of God's People*, p. 138.

filled the cup of God's wrath.[8] To drink such wine was to be, literally, dead drunk.

That would be the fate of the people as a whole. Jeremiah specifies every level of leadership, *the kings . . . the priests, the prophets,* but goes on to include all the citizenry, parents and children. Like staggering drunks they will *smash . . . one against the other* (which may be just adding vividness to the metaphor, or may hint at the internal division and civil violence that would mark the closing years of the monarchy and especially the final siege and fall of Jerusalem).

And when the end comes, it will come pitilessly. For this people in this generation, there could be no last-minute reprieve, since they had refused for so long to listen, repent or change. Even having said that, these words of verse 14b coming in the mouth of the Lord God himself may seem unbearably harsh – *I will allow no pity or mercy or compassion.* We must remember, however, that such mercilessly total destruction was the tool of war wielded by Nebuchadnezzar. Exactly the same three words are used to characterize his attack on Jerusalem (21:7). Since, therefore, Nebuchadnezzar was the agent of God's judgment, the same language is used of both.

> God does not micromanage the actions of the Babylonians; they will act just as kings and armies in that world have historically been known to act. That is predictable . . . and so, God in judgment will not spare, pity, or have compassion, because that is what the Babylonians, the instruments of divine judgment, will not do. And so this is a kind of extreme realism regarding what is about to happen to the people.[9]

3. Weeping in the darkness (13:15–17)

At first sight it might seem that verses 15–16 hold out a hope that repentance might still be possible so that the people could avoid the enveloping darkness – that is, that God's judgment would be suspended. However, it would be hard to see a hope of reprieve in these verses in the light of the utter finality of verse 14 (and see also 19b). The question is not, 'Can the darkness be avoided?' It cannot. It is coming inexorably. The question is, 'With what attitude, with what response to God, will you face it?'

The appeal of verse 15 and 16a, then, is to people who are now being told that their judgment is sealed. Their *hope for light* is forlorn, for God has decreed the *utter darkness* and *deep gloom* of exile. But

<hr />

[8] E.g. Ps. 75:8; Isa. 51:17; Lam. 4:21; Hab. 2:15–16.
[9] Fretheim, p. 213.

161

before that judgment falls on them (as it surely will), they can and should, even now, do what they had failed to do all along, *hear and pay attention* to the voice of God that *has spoken* through his prophet.

The command that opens verse 16, *give glory to the* LORD *your God*, is the primary clue to this reading. These were the precise words of Joshua to Achan at the moment when his guilt had been identified and his punishment determined.[10] It was not a command that would enable Achan to repent and avert execution for his covenant-breaking crime. Rather, it was an invitation to accept his guilt (which he then did), and to acknowledge the rightness of God's justice. In that sense at least, it could be seen as an act of contrition, of accepting the truth, of acknowledging his wrong-doing, and of going to his death agreeing with his God.

That seems to be what Jeremiah holds out to the people here. If they were now irretrievably doomed to go into exile under God's judgment, then it would make all the difference whether they would go in contrite acceptance of God's vindicated justice, thus giving him glory by agreeing with their God and acknowledging the truth of his verdict on them;[11] or whether they would go in undiminished self-righteous anger at the unfairness of it all, bitterly blaming God himself and their ancestors for all that would befall them. For those who would go in a spirit of acceptance, Jeremiah could later bring words of comfort and hope: they would still die in exile, but with sure and certain hope of a glorious future for their posterity. But for those who went in a spirit of defiance, the exile would be bitter beyond belief, and it would take the life and ministry of Ezekiel (and the death of his wife) to pierce that armoured shell of resentment.

Jeremiah, sadly, knew which of the two possible responses would win, because of their incorrigible *pride* (17). For if, true to form, they still would not listen, then it would all end in tears.

And what tears! The sound of weeping overflows verse 17 with its triple repetition, *weep in secret . . . weep bitterly, overflowing with tears . . .* As before, it is hard to tell if this is Jeremiah or if we are again listening to the weeping of God himself. Probably both. For if Jeremiah's pain was all a human heart could contain, how much more filled the infinite heart of God?

Notice again how the language of implacable anger (14) has dissolved into the language of inconsolable grief (17). Verse 17 is surprising. *If you do not listen,* it begins. We might have expected, 'then you will suffer the consequences'. That, of course, would be true and tragic. But Jeremiah looks beyond the obvious and focuses

---

[10] Josh. 7:19–20.
[11] As we see, for example, in the prayers of Dan. 9, Neh. 1 and 9.

on the emotional effect on God and himself. When *the LORD's flock will be taken captive*, there will be no grim pleasure in heaven or earth. Nothing but the secret sobbing of the divine shepherd and his servant. Jeremiah knew as well as Ezekiel that the Lord takes 'no pleasure in the death of the wicked'.[12]

4. Humiliating climbdown (13:18–19)

The catalogue of catastrophe continues. If the people placed any hope in their government to get them out of the approaching devastation, they were doomed to disappointment there too. For no king can survive when the cities of his tiny kingdom have all been *shut up* (presumably by invasion and siege). So the royal family, their *thrones* and their *crowns* will all come crashing down together. Royal altitude will be reduced to street level.

It is not clear which of Judah's kings and queen mothers is the target of this saying, but it doesn't really matter. It could have been Jehoiakim (who first brought Nebuchadnezzar's wrath on the city), and his mother Zebidah.[13] Or it could have been Jehoiachin (who rebelled to such an extent that Nebuchadnezzar attacked the city in 597 BC, deposed Jehoiachin and took him captive to Babylon along with the first group of exiles), and his mother Nehushta.[14] Or it could have been the very last king of Judah, Zedekiah (who led his people into the final siege and destruction of Jerusalem in 587 BC) and his mother Hamutal.[15] Jeremiah had unpleasant dealings with all of them, and all of them in one way or another were brought low in the long-drawn-out death throes of Judah.

Verse 19, for the first time in the book, since the editorial introduction in 1:3, speaks the dreaded word, *exile*, then doubles it, and adds, *completely*. Nothing can now turn back the inevitable. And since it will be the fate of *all Judah*, there will be no advantage in being a king rather than a slave.

5. Inescapable doom (13:20–27)

This final section of the chapter is addressed to Jerusalem, pictured in the feminine singular as a woman – a woman facing a terrible fate. When Babylon's armies invade from the north (20, cf. 1:13–14), what will become of the people – *the flock that was entrusted to you, the sheep of which you boasted?* Jerusalem, the capital city, and its king,

[12] Ezek. 18:32; 33:11.
[13] 2 Kgs. 23:36 – 24:6.
[14] 2 Kgs. 24:8–17.
[15] 2 Kgs. 24:18 – 25:7.

should have been able to defend and care for the country people who trusted in them – as people are entitled to expect of their government. But these kings of Judah were failed shepherds, and had been for generations. In fact it was the spectacular folly of one of them, Ahaz, over a century earlier, that had put Judah into a vassal status with the Assyrian empire. That empire was now collapsing before the Babylonians and all its vassals would share its fate. The consequences of Ahaz's fateful failure to trust in YHWH were now rebounding with a vengeance, as the great Mesopotamian monster Judah had sought to have as a friend turned to devour them (21).

Verse 22 takes the message of all the preceding chapters, condenses it into the single question *Why?* and answers with a summary of all Jeremiah's preaching so far, *it is because of your many sins.* And because of those many sins, judgment would include the most horrific reality that invasion and war can bring – the brutal abuse of women, often in systematic rape. Of course, the image here is that Jerusalem, like a woman at the mercy of a rapist, would be stripped, exposed, shamed and brutalized as a city. But for many of the women living there the image would become terrifying reality. Ancient and modern warfare have changed little when the depravity of men's hearts govern their hands and loins.[16]

And was there any hope of a last-minute change of course – morally, spiritually or even politically – that could avert such a fate? No more than the hope that an African might change his skin colour or a *leopard its spots* (23). What was impossible in the natural world was just as impossible in the entrenched world of Judean rebellion against God and Babylon combined.

And so those who had for centuries enjoyed their *lot* in the land of promise, would find themselves experiencing a very different *lot* – of being scattered like chaff to the winds in exile (24–25). The irony is that the *lot* and *portion* were originally and literally the division of the land to Israel's families, clans and tribes – a symbol of God's faithfulness and blessing. But the divine apportionment now was landlessness. Such would be the fate of those who trusted lies (*false gods* is lit. 'the lie'), and forgot their God.

And so the chapter ends with a repetition of the repulsive nature of Israel's unfaithfulness and spiritual adultery (which took literal,

[16] Amy Kalmanofsky (in an unpublished paper presented at the Society for Biblical Literature, November 2012), points out how the metaphor of clothing opens and closes the chapter. Jeremiah, the man, is shamed by the stripping off of his sash because it is rotten and unwearable. Jerusalem, 'the woman', is shamed by being stripped of her skirts, so that her nakedness is exposed and violated (22, 26). The association of nakedness, shame, and sin, goes back to the Garden of Eden. The tragedy is that Israel re-enacts it all.

physical reality in the promiscuous sexual fertility cults, 27a). From the same symbolic world comes the punishment – shaming of the shameless city before the eyes of the world.[17]

But the final word is a longing – could it even be a hope? The present state of Jerusalem is filthy and unclean (echoing the state of Jeremiah's waistband). But must that go on forever? When might it end? Literally the chapter ends with a woe and a question:

> *'Woe to you Jerusalem, you are not clean!*
> *Until when?* [i.e., how long must this be so?]' (27)

No answer can be given yet. But for the exiles, languishing in an unclean land, the hope must be, 'Not for ever.'

Theological and expository reflections

Jeremiah's acted prophecy – buying a smart brand-new waistband, and then letting it become so rotten it could not be worn – calls for theological reflection on the purpose of our election and the demands of our mission. Paul combines both when he says (twice) that we have been chosen, predestined, to live for the praise of God's glory.[18] He encourages Christian slaves with the perspective that by being hard-working, honest and trustworthy they can 'adorn' the gospel – 'they will make the teaching about God our Saviour attractive'.[19] Both thoughts remind us of Jesus' words about the attractive power of the 'light' of 'good works' that bring praise and glory to our Father.[20]

Part of our mission as God's people, then, is to attract admiration. But, as I discuss elsewhere:

---

[17] The use of such imagery of the abuse of women is disturbing, and some accuse the Bible (and God) of licensing, through such language, the scandal of gender violence. The same accusation is levelled at Ezekiel even more. However, it must be remembered that the language is drawn from the horrific realities of war, which throughout the Bible can be the agency through which God exercises his judgment. What is suffered in war, however, is charged to the account of the human beings who inflict it, and they bear their own moral responsibility when they commit atrocities (as Amos 1 – 2 indicates). The message here is that the nation would suffer appallingly the consequences of their own history of rebellion, and the shame of the coming military defeat and destruction would be comparable to the shame of a violated woman. It does not thereby condone or diminish the utter moral repugnance of such gender violence when literally committed.

[18] Eph. 1:5–6, 11–12.

[19] Tit. 2:10; the verb is *kosmeō*, from which we get 'cosmetic'.

[20] Matt. 5:14–16: 'good works'; the word is *kala*, which has the sense of beautiful and attractive.

I hope it is clear that the admiration is *for God, not for us*. But it still has to be said that if there is fundamentally nothing in the least admirable about the lives of Christians individually, or the collective witness of the church, then there is small hope of the world finding anything to admire in the God we represent.

[Jeremiah's waistband] is an unusual metaphor, but a powerfully suggestive one. It raises challenging questions about our mission in the world. Are we the kind of 'clothing' that God is pleased to wear in order to attract the nations to himself? Or are we so soiled that people wrinkle their noses at us – and at the God we represent?[21]

---

[21] Wright, *The Mission of God's People*, p. 138.

Jeremiah 14:1 – 15:9
10. Too late! Too late!

'It's never too late,' we say. But sometimes it is – for us, if not for God. Sometimes sin and folly set in motion a train of consequences that become irreversible. Remorse and repentance can have eternal results, but they cannot turn the clock of history back, or prevent inevitable consequences. A murderer may repent, but it cannot bring his victim back to life. A business women might regret a foolish or fraudulent deal, but that in itself will not prevent her business collapsing when it all comes to light. An unfaithful spouse may be filled with remorse, but it may be impossible to undo the damage to their marriage and family, or to reverse any infection their action may have brought on themselves or others. Actions have consequences. And no amount of repentance can ward off what has become unavoidable. In Tom Wolfe's searing novel *The Bonfire of the Vanities*, a single act of marital unfaithfulness, combined with a careless phone call and an accidental wrong turn on an urban freeway, lead to a train of disasters that wreck homes and careers with an escalation of social and professional disgrace.

So is there any point in repenting at all, when it seems too late for that? This section explores that tough question, twice over. Twice we hear of terrible situations of suffering; twice we hear words of lamentation, confession and repentance; and twice we hear the terrible word from God, 'I am not listening; the consequences (political and military) of your own wickedness cannot now be averted.'

So what good, then, was their repentance? Once again we need to recall the double audience of our text – those whom Jeremiah first addressed, and the exiles who later read the words in the midst of the judgment that had indeed fallen upon them. In the case of those who first heard these words, we can only assume (the text gives us no hint) that God in his mercy could distinguish between the *collective national* folly that was leading to the inevitable disaster through which his judgment would be outpoured, and the personal *hearts of individuals* in the nation. And if any of them spoke the words of 14:7, 20–22 in genuine contrition and repentance, then we may assume that God met them with grace and forgiveness, and that their eternal destiny was not sealed by the immediate destiny of their nation and city.

But what about the exiles? On them the judgment had already fallen. They had reaped the consequences of generations of unfaithfulness combined with the colossal miscalculation of their political leaders. For them, the words of repentance recorded here were still available for them to use in turning back to God even from the depths of defeat and exile. And on the basis of such repentance a hope for the future could be built, as Jeremiah will later promise. It *was* too late for Jeremiah's own generation to avert the fall of Jerusalem. It was *not* too late for the exiles to seek the face of God again and pray for grace beyond judgment for their children and children's children.

1. Lament in the face of devastating drought (14:1–16)

a. The situation (1–6)

I write in 2011 as reports hit the news of the worst drought in the Horn of Africa for sixty years, causing widespread famine, desperation, the death of livestock and devastation of crops. The pictures of cracked earth, dead animals and dying people are hard to bear. Some such tragedy had afflicted the land of Judah. These verses describe an unspecified but terrible drought and its effects. It becomes the harbinger of an even worse catastrophe to follow – the destruction of land, city and people (17–18).

Four times in four verses (3–6) the terrifying absence is mentioned, like a tolling bell: *no water . . . no rain . . . no grass . . .* [no] *food.* The grim portrayal of a stricken land starts in the city, where *nobles* wealthy enough to have *servants* to fetch water for them cannot by wealth fill empty *cisterns* with something more necessary than wealth. It moves to the country, where farmers can grow nothing since *the ground is cracked* for lack of *rain.* And then, with noticeable sensitivity, we see the suffering of the non-human inhabitants of the land, *the doe* and *her newborn fawn . . . wild donkeys . . . jackals* (cf. Hos. 4:3; Joel 1:18, 20). Once again we notice Jeremiah's inclusion of creation in the consequences of human sin. The suffering of creation mirrors and amplifies the suffering caused and endured by people who reject God. And when God withholds water, the noble in his city is no better off than the farmer in his field. And neither of them is better off than cows, donkeys and jackals. Such is the levelling power of God's hand of judgment, the counterpart to the breadth of his life-giving provision for man and beast in Psalm 104:23–30.

b. The plea (7–9)

The people respond to the crisis as Israel regularly did, and indeed as they were inspired to do by the psalms of communal lament.[1]

The plea begins appropriately (though surprisingly) with words of confession of sin (7). The people accept what Jeremiah has repeatedly affirmed: (lit.) 'many are our turnings away'. YHWH is addressed directly, and asked to act, first because of his own name (*for the sake of your name*, i.e. your reputation), and then because of titles that YHWH had earned through centuries of such saving acts (*the hope of Israel, its Saviour in times of distress*).

But then, from such a promising beginning, the lament brazenly accuses God of being absent when they need him – a mere passing visitor to their homes (8). Yet they were the ones who had spent their lives getting as far from God as they could (10)! They go on to wonder if YHWH had been caught unawares by events (9a), or if he was perhaps no longer the mighty warrior God they once knew (9b). And with unwitting irony they beg God, *do not forsake us!* How many times has Jeremiah warned the people that *they* have been forsaking God for years, with the kind of inconceivable madness that would induce a farmer to abandon a permanent spring of water and chisel out a cistern for himself (2:13)? But now they come running to God when the cisterns were, quite literally, empty. God waits until 15:6 to respond to that absurd insult.

c. The refusal (14:10–16)

So the people cry out to God. And God says 'no'.

That is not what was supposed to happen. In some psalms of communal lament, God responds with assurance of grace, peace and salvation. The clearest example is Psalm 85:8–13. But this time, when the people tell God that *he* is a passing stranger, God quickly reminds them of *their* wandering ways (10a; cf. 2:17–19, 23–25, 31). So instead of an expected word of forgiveness comes the devastating verdict that *the* LORD *does not accept them* (10). That is God's word for the present. For this generation, right *now*, their wickedness *would* be remembered (for judgment); their sins *would* be punished (in exile).

[1] Compare Pss 74; 79; 80; 85; 89:38–52.

A time would come when this verdict would be reversed within the promise of a new covenant. There will be a time when God says, 'I will forgive their wickedness and will remember their sins no more' (31:34). But that time was not yet.

Jeremiah seems to have reacted to the devastating word of verse 10 by interceding for the people (11). And yet again God stops him (cf. 7:16; 11:14). God simply repeats: the coming judgment (*sword, famine and plague,* 12; i.e. the realities of the siege and fall of Jerusalem at the hand of Nebuchadnezzar), had now become irreversible. Neither the prayers of the prophet nor the penitential rituals of the people could ward it off (12).

That leads Jeremiah to try an approach that he had tried before (in 4:10). If he cannot pray for the people, perhaps he can make a plea on their behalf. Perhaps it is not their fault. They are being deceived by prophets who keep promising them a secure future – 'peace in our time' (13). But that excuse carries no weight with God. First he dismisses these other prophets and their message as utterly false – *prophesying lies ... false visions ... delusions of their own minds* (14; cf. ch. 23). Then, God goes on to say that these false prophets will face the same fate as the people, the suffering of the coming siege and its appalling results: death on such a scale that there will be no-one left to bury the dead – a terrible but accurate description of the reality of ancient sieges and their aftermath (15–16). Far from the people having any valid excuse, the coming catastrophe will be nothing other than God (lit.) 'pouring out upon them their own wickedness' (16). The judgment of God would take the form of the outworking of their own wicked folly. 'That is how I will overwhelm them with the consequences of their own bad behaviour.'[2]

2. Lament in the face of the final destruction (14:17 – 15:4)

a. The situation (14:17–18)

The language of devastating destruction returns: enemy invasion ravaging people in the countryside, while famine strangles the city, culminating in the wrenching departure into foreign exile (18). Verse 17, however, following upon verse 16, makes a move that has by now become familiar: from overwhelming wrath to overflowing tears (cf. 4:19; 8:18 – 9:1; 9:9–10; 10:18–19; 13:15–17). And as before, it is hard to say whether the eyes and the tears belong to Jeremiah or God, or both. Certainly the language of *my virgin daughter, my people,*

---

[2] Allen's translation, p. 166.

sounds like God (cf. 31:20 where God speaks of Ephraim as 'my dear son'). The wrath of Nebuchadnezzar against a rebel vassal will mediate the wrath of God against a broken covenant. But as God views the length and breadth of his land (*the country . . . the city*), the suffering he sees everywhere breaks God's own heart.

> The reason for this revelation of the divine emotions is to give readers a glimpse of the inner-divine side of wrath. The God who judges is also the God who weeps. This God is not punitive or uncaring with respect to what the people have had to endure. Such a portrayal of God is important in any interpretation of these events. Exilic readers of this material are reminded that this is the kind of God with whom they are related. This God is genuinely caught up in what has happened and mourns over the disasters experienced by this 'virgin daughter,' responding as any good parent would.[3]

b. The plea (14:19–22)

The language of the psalms returns with even greater passion as the people resume their plea to God. They are so desperate that they hardly know whom to blame. First they attribute their dashed hopes to God's affliction (19; cf. 8:14). Then they acknowledge their own *wickedness and . . . guilt* (20).Then, with brazen lack of awareness, they demand, *remember your covenant with us and do not break it* (21b). Had they not listened to the preaching of Jeremiah (11:1–4)? Who exactly had forgotten the covenant with stunning amnesia? Who had already broken the covenant so persistently that nothing but a miracle of grace would be able to renew it? Will these people ever own their own responsibility?

And so, although the prayer ends with ringing words of confidence and hope (22b), we can't help expecting that, as the Babylonian invasion loomed, such confidence was just as tragically doomed as they were. This generation was beyond hope. For them it was too late.

However, those who would read these words later in exile could pick them up again. Then, as they sat under the judgment of God, these words could once again become words of hope. For indeed, where else could they turn? *It is you, O Lord our God. Therefore our hope is in you, for you are the one who does all this.* And so indeed we find very similar language to 14:19–21 in the appeal of the exiles in Lamentations 5.

---

[3] Fretheim, p. 224.

c. The refusal (15:1–4)

As we expect, from 14:10, the door of heaven is shut to the prayers of *this people*. Not only would Jeremiah's prayer not avail, even the prayers of Moses or Samuel, the most noted (and successful) of Israel's historic intercessors,[4] would not prevail either. Their judgment is sealed and all that is left is the expectation of every form of death and destruction that invasion and siege inevitably inflict upon their victims. The reference to Manasseh points to the accumulated evil of generations, to the point where God's patience has finally come to an end (see also 15:6b).

3. Lament for the victims of a nation's folly (15:5–9)

After the double sequence above (first describing the situation, then entering the people's plea, and finally hearing God's refusal), there comes this final section spoken with emotional intensity by God himself. The people must hear their God. They may blame the false prophets – and that would be partially right. They may blame Nebuchadnezzar – and that would be partially right also. But ultimately there were two parties only in this whole matter: a sinning, backsliding people who had not radically changed at all; and the sovereign Lord God whom they had rejected, but who determines their destiny. That destiny contains long-term hope, but in the immediate future, nothing but disaster.

The rhetorical questions of verse 5 ('*Who will . . . ?*') expect the answer, 'Nobody'. The final destruction of Jerusalem will be without pity or mourning or concern. Nobody cares. Such is the reality of war. And yet, when set alongside verse 6, there is a nuance to the questions as we imagine God himself answering them:

Who will have pity on you, O Jerusalem?
'I would have, if only you had turned to me long before now.'
Who will mourn for you?
'I already do and will continue to weep for your suffering.'
Who will stop to ask how you are?
'I would gladly show my concern for you, but though I am the only one who would do so, I am not welcome among you. I am the very one you have deliberately excluded.'

So verse 6 gives the devastatingly emphatic answer to the people's accusation that God had rejected and forsaken them (14:9, 19). 'On

[4] Exod. 32:7–14; Num. 14:13–19; Deut. 9:6–29; 1 Sam. 7:5–11; 12:17–18; Ps. 99:6–8. And compare a similar comparison with Noah, Daniel and Job in Ezek. 14:14.

the contrary,' exclaims God, '**You** are the ones who *have rejected me*!' *You* is emphatically stressed as the subject of the verb, as is *me* as the object. 'Let us be very clear here,' God is saying, 'about who has rejected whom.'

For all the people's liturgies of repentance, God sees the reality underneath. *You keep on backsliding* (6; lit. 'backwards you keep walking') . . . *they have not changed their ways* (7b; which was the explicit condition on which their survival in the land depended; see 7:3–8). And in the face of such prolonged and incorrigible disobedience – in spite of centuries of warnings by successive prophets – God's patience has finally come to an end.

I am tired of holding back (6) captures the sense of divine weariness. The Hebrew says: 'I have grown weary of relenting.' We might be inclined to interpret this as parental exasperation: 'You've had one "last chance" too many. I'm tired of letting you off.' We know, in human life, that there comes a time when punishment that has been threatened again and again can no longer be postponed. This would be an appropriate reading of the text, for we are told that YHWH is 'slow to anger and abounding in love'.[5] Ezekiel 20 builds a whole history of Israel upon the theme of God repeatedly withholding his judgment until the point where he cannot go on doing so and remain true to his own moral character. 2 Peter speaks of the patience of God in delaying judgment, 'not wanting anyone to perish, but everyone to come to repentance'. But that delay is not forever. 'The day of the Lord will come . . .'.[6] Similarly, Jeremiah is saying that God has grown weary of holding back his threatened judgment time after time. He cannot put it off any longer.

However, we know that God does not just get tired in the way humans do.[7] So there is something more theologically profound here than mere compassion-fatigue.

When Jeremiah speaks about being weary himself, he means the suffering he endures in the task of delivering God's word of judgment. When he tries to hold it in, he grows weary and cannot do so (6:11; 20:9). There is a cost, an expenditure of emotional and spiritual energy, in coping with God's words and actions. If that is so for Jeremiah, then since we have seen how closely Jeremiah's feelings match God's, there must be a corresponding cost and expenditure on the part of God. To put it bluntly, God finds his own people exhausting!

This fits with other texts that speak of God's weariness, always in the context of coping with the sins of his people.[8] Our human

5 Exod. 34:6 and many related texts, such as Ps. 103:8–10.
6 2 Pet. 3:9–10.
7 Isa. 40:28.
8 Isa. 1:14; 7:13; 43:24; Mal. 2:17.

experience of the effort that can be involved in bearing with another person's shortcomings, speaks powerfully of the seriousness of sin and that it is no light matter for God himself to deal with it – to bear it. As often, Terence Fretheim has an instructive word that points us beyond Jeremiah to the One who carried our sins at ultimate cost to himself.

> . . . such texts refer to the expending of the divine life; God's life is in some sense being spent because of the people's unfaithfulness. By bearing the sins of the people over a long period of time, God suffers; such divine forbearance is costly to God. By holding back the judgment they deserve (see Isa. 42:14; 48:9; 57:11; Ezek. 20:21–22; Ps. 78:38; see Rom. 2:4; 3:25), by carrying their sins on the divine shoulders, God chooses to suffer their infidelity in patience. Such continued divine restraint in the face of continual rejection must have meant for an intensification of suffering for God. Weariness entails a self-giving for the sake of the continuing relationship.[9]

For the present generation, that weariness would give way in definitive judgment, though the relationship would indeed continue, as later chapters of the book will show clearly. Fretheim goes on:

> In speaking of a divine weariness, there may be an intimation that God is the kind of God whose suffering on behalf of the people's continuing life will someday take a further step. God will take their sins into the divine life and bear them there (Isa. 43:23–25; Hos. 11:8–9) and, even more, bodily assume the form of a servant to suffering death on a cross (Phil. 2:6–8; see John 4:6). Jeremiah conforms to the weariness of God; Jesus does as well, in an unsurpassable way.[10]

Theological and expository reflections

- These raw chapters force us to raise the difficult question: When (if ever) is it too late for repentance? The question needs to be answered with very careful theological and pastoral sensitivity. On the one hand, God's word does warn us that sin has serious consequences and when people deliberately persist in sinful ways and ignore all warnings of God or his servants, there can come a time when certain results become inevitable and

[9] Fretheim, pp. 232–233.
[10] Fretheim. p. 233.

unavoidable in this life. In that sense, Jeremiah agrees with the 'consequentialist' ethic of Proverbs. Don't play with fire if you don't want to get burned.

- On the other hand, we must avoid driving people into despair and loss of trust in, and assurance of, God's grace and forgiveness. The gospel truth is that God's forgiveness is offered to every truly repentant sinner without limit. In that sense, in relation to the gifts of salvation and eternal life, it is never too late for repentance. Equally, however, that glorious truth is not a reason to continue in sin while counting on some deathbed moment of repentance. God is not mocked.
- And in the closing section, we are reminded of the cost *to God* of bearing with our sin, of the divine patience that serves divine grace, and of the ultimate cost borne by Christ so that when that day of grace ends in the day of judgment we will not be condemned but stand in his righteousness.

175

Jeremiah 15:10–21
11. The pit of self-pity

The strain begins to tell. These wretched words reflect long years of prophetic ministry with no apparent success. Instead Jeremiah met with rejection, ridicule and isolation. This seems to have led to periods of intense depression and almost suicidal despair – all of which he pours out to God and presumably to his friend and secretary, Baruch. The honesty of his words is astonishing, particularly as we recall that in listening to these words of Jeremiah we are still hearing, through them, the word of God.

In the following exposition we will explore the personal dimensions and relevance of Jeremiah's words. But, as Andrew Shead reminds us, even in his individual suffering Jeremiah remains a representative person, embodying paradoxically both the pain of God and the suffering of God's people – a truly awful position to endure. Shead points out that Jeremiah's words echo things already spoken by the people:

> It was the people who said 'we are called by your name' (14:9); it was the people who were shattered by a wound (14:17) and who said 'there is no healing for us' (14:19); and it was the people, throughout chapter 14, to whom God was a spring that failed [15:8, cf. 14:3]. Jeremiah has become the representative Israelite who suffers in his body the judgment God has announced for the nation.[1]

Taking the section as a whole,[2] there seem to be three main ingredients of Jeremiah's distress – all of them very human, and all of them still possible hazards for those in leadership and public ministry.

[1] Shead, *A Mouth Full of Fire*, p. 134.
[2] Omitting vv. 11–14. It is difficult to see the connection between vv. 11–14 and the surrounding text. Vv. 11 and 12 are difficult to translate, as a glimpse at several translations will show. Vv. 13 and 14 seem to be an anticipatory variant of 17:3–4.

1. Disillusionment with his ministry

a. Regret (10)

The struggle here is with frustration and disappointment. Jeremiah wishes he had never been born (10). Later and even more emphatically, he curses the day he was born (20:14–18). But God had appointed him to be a prophet *before* he was born, and he knew it (1:5). So in making such a wish, Jeremiah was effectively regretting and rejecting his very calling to be a prophet. He was so disillusioned with his ministry because all he got was strife, contention, hatred and cursing. So if that was what he had been born for, he wished he'd never been born at all.

But his disillusionment is made even worse by bitter-sweet memories (16). He remembers back to the early joy, delight and pride that he had once had in the word of God – the great privilege it had seemed to be God's spokesman. Perhaps, as a young man, he had had high hopes and expectations of being God's 'prophet to the nations'. *I bear your name*, he says. That was his divine commission and authority. Once it had seemed like a priceless joy. But now it had become a burden, an unbearable torture (18a). And so he falls into disillusionment. He knows God had called him to this job. He knows he has really no other choice and nowhere else to go. But still he hates it and wishes he'd never been called at all. All his dreams and hopes in his ministry are shattered. Life is a mess of disappointment and frustration. It's a tragic picture.

The disillusioned believer (especially in any form of church leadership) sees no good anywhere. He or she is always critical and pessimistic about everything. They sometimes become very sarcastic and cynical. They pour cold water on other people's enthusiasm or good ideas or achievements, finding ways to be maliciously negative about them. Worst of all, in any group or team (especially a leadership team), the disillusioned Christian tends to spread their own disillusionment and thus poison the minds and snuff out the hopes of others. Negativity is horribly infectious.

What then is God's therapeutic word to Jeremiah in response to his disillusionment?

b. Rebuke (19)

First of all comes a gentle rebuke. God tells Jeremiah to repent. *If you repent, I will restore you* (19a). The rebuke is specifically directed at what Jeremiah had been *saying: If you utter worthy, not worthless, words*. All Jeremiah's talk had become negative, destructive and *worthless* – so characteristic of a disillusioned person. God checks and rebukes this.[3]

In place of those negative words, God gives his positive requirement: *worthy . . . words.* That is, God tells Jeremiah to quit all his talk about 'I wish I'd never been born', and get back to what is healthy, positive, constructive – as God's spokesman.

There is a time to talk to ourselves and a time to listen to ourselves. It is important to check our habits of speech. It is not that God does not allow us to question or complain or protest (the psalms are full of such emotions). But we cannot languish in that mood with nothing else to say. God calls us up and out and back from such 'worthless words'.

c. Recommissioning (19–21)

After the rebuke comes the second part of God's 'therapy' for disillusioned Jeremiah, a recommissioning. God did not dismiss Jeremiah – 'If that's how you feel, you can quit. I've no more time for you as my prophet. Go back home.' Rather, God repeated the same call and commission that Jeremiah had heard at the very start, the words that had launched his ministry: *you may serve me . . . you will be my spokesman . . . I am with you* (see 1:7–9). The mission goes on. The job isn't finished.

This is very similar to how God dealt with Elijah when he also fell into acute depression and despair, and literally tried to run away. God took him back to the roots of his faith and his calling, through an encounter with God at Mount Sinai, and then recommissioned him for further ministry.[4] God is gracious. God understands disillusionment. But God does not let his servants wallow in it, but calls us back in repentance and recommissions us to his service once again.

2. Bitterness and resentment

The struggle here is with relentless opposition. Of course, Jeremiah had been warned to expect opposition. Right at his call God had

[3] God's rebuke of Jeremiah's words here has implications for the way we understand the divine inspiration of Scripture. Not everything that the text records of what Jeremiah said was 'the inspired word of God' in the simple or direct sense that 'this is exactly what God *wanted* Jeremiah to say'. Rather, the word of God in a passage like this (that is, the word that God wants the reader to hear and understand) comes through the *combination* of what Jeremiah said that was negative and complaining (and unacceptable), *along with* the words of rebuke that God then spoke to correct him. We must read and hear the text as a whole.

[4] 1 Kgs 19.

warned him that he would need to be like an iron pillar to stand against the prolonged attacks and rejection he would encounter (1:8, 17–19). But surely thirty years of it was more than anybody could endure. And this was not polite theological disagreement in a seminary. Jeremiah was laughed at, taunted, disbelieved, ostracized and isolated, physically threatened, actually beaten and later imprisoned, falsely accused, threatened with death . . . And it went on for year after year – even from his own family and kinship network. Until eventually it ate into his very soul and he became bitter and resentful, longing for vengeance: *avenge me on my persecutors* (15).[5]

There is a frightening frankness in Jeremiah's emotional outbursts that we also find in some psalms. But before we criticize him or them, we may find similar thoughts in our own minds, even if we would never speak them out loud (still less dictate them to a secretary with a pen and scroll in hand).

Bitterness and resentment are among the most poisonous and lethal of all emotions. They are also among the longest lasting. Anger is different. It can flare up and die down very quickly. But bitterness stays; it smoulders on, gnawing away at our minds and hearts. No wonder the New Testament speaks of it as a 'bitter root' (cf. Heb. 12:15–16). It is indeed a root that goes down deep, grows very long, and bears nasty fruit, sometimes for a lifetime. Most seriously of all, bitterness and resentment together raise one of the hardest and most resistant barriers to personal healing and peace. That is because they usually involve a refusal to forgive some other person (or even God) for a wrong that has been done – either real or imaginary. We refuse to forgive. But that in turn prevents us from being forgiven ourselves. And that in turn blocks the flow of cleansing and healing. Jesus was quite specific and emphatic on this point. Those who refuse to forgive others will not experience God's forgiveness themselves (Matt. 6:14–15). And without forgiveness there can be no healing and peace. It is a terrible cost to pay for the 'luxury' of nursing bitterness and resentment.

What is the antidote to such emotions? Ironically, the first element is to be found in Jeremiah's prayer itself. He takes the matter to *God* and asks *God* to deal with his tormentors.

> *LORD, you understand;*
>   *remember me and care for me.*
>   *Avenge me on my persecutors* (15).

[5] See also 12:3; 17:18; 18:19–23; 20:12.

Old Testament law told people not to take vengeance into their own hands, for all vengeance and justice belongs to God.[6] So if there was a real wrong being done, if there was a genuine grievance that needed to be put right (and God agreed with Jeremiah that there was; in v. 21 God recognizes that wicked people were indeed threatening Jeremiah), then the thing to do was to pass it over to God and ask God to deal with it. That is exactly what Jeremiah prays for here and in 11:21–23 and 20:11–12. And God promises to deal with the matter (21).

Jeremiah did not vent his bitterness by jumping to defend himself, to fight back. He entrusted his case to God. That is what the righteous person in the Old Testament was supposed to do. It's what the Servant of the Lord did when he felt under violent attack.[7] It's what Jesus did, according to Peter, in order to set us an example of non-retaliation.[8] And it's what Paul instructs us to do with the same scriptural support.[9] Vengeance and retaliation are simply non-options for obedient believers.

Even if we were to go no further, this Old Testament principle in itself stands out against the chronic tendency among Christians to take immediate angry action in self-defence, or to take combined action in defence of some group or party or interest in the church – usually claiming that some rights have been violated, some wrongs done. Well, that may indeed be true. But the act of angry, bitter, resentful self-defence nearly always ends up making the situation worse. The prayer of Jeremiah, even if we don't like it, points to a different way – leave it to God, entrust your cause to him and wait.

But of course, the New Testament does go much further even than this. The gospel calls us not only not to retaliate, but also to replace the very spirit of vengeance against our enemies and persecutors with love for them. Love for enemies and persecutors is, of course, impossible – apart from the example and the empowering Spirit of the Lord Jesus Christ. For it was Jesus who, even when he was suffering the worst injustice that any human being ever faced, prayed: 'Father forgive them.'[10] At that moment Jesus transcended the Old Testament. Jesus would have known Jeremiah's prayer, 'Do not forgive their crimes',[11] but he prayed exactly the opposite. And so it is in Jesus' name alone that Paul could command us 'forgive each other, just as in Christ God forgave you'.[12] And that is a command.

---

[6] Lev. 19:18; Deut. 32:35.
[7] Isa. 50:7–9.
[8] 1 Pet. 2:21–22.
[9] Rom. 12:19–21.
[10] Luke 23:34.
[11] Jer. 18:23.
[12] Eph. 4:32.

For Christ-imitating forgiveness is the Bible's final and only liberating answer to the bondage of resentment and bitterness.

3. Self-pity

The struggle here is with his own deep emotions. Jeremiah groans in lonely pain about his broken heart and wounded soul (17–18). His loneliness was very real, of course. This is not exaggeration. As we shall see in chapter 16, Jeremiah was instructed by God not to marry and not to go to any of the normal social functions in his community – wedding celebrations or funeral mournings. He was socially isolated in a very painful and embarrassing way. So it is understandable that he felt so sorry for himself eventually.

Now Jeremiah had done plenty of weeping and groaning before. But in earlier passages of the book his grief was poured out *on behalf of his people.* Look again at 8:18 – 9:1. He had felt deep sorrow over the people's persistent sin. He was wracked with terrible anguish at the judgment that was coming upon them. But now, all his emotions seem to be introverted and turned in upon himself. He is wallowing in self-pity.

Self-pity is another crippling and very unhealthy emotion. It usually has an element of wounded pride: 'I deserve better than this.' Like the so-called 'martyr complex', self-pity is by definition self-centred, expecting others to feel sorry for me and my suffering. In fact, it is a very subtle form of sin precisely because it is not recognized as sin at all. 'Don't ask *me* to repent, it's those other sinners who are making my life a misery – they are the ones who need to repent!' And as pointed out above, any barrier to repentance (which self-pity definitely is), is a barrier to forgiveness, healing and wholeness.

Jeremiah's self-pity hurls him into such a pit of bleak despair that he even accuses God of being a failure (18b). He twists one of the most striking images he ever used for accusing the people (the spring of living water and broken cisterns, 2:13), into a rasping accusation of God. 'You God,' he explodes, 'you're a disappointment too. Just when I needed you most you turn out to be like a dry river-bed. Full of promises, but delivering nothing. Where are you? Why do you deceive me?' Now we might react that Jeremiah should not have even thought such things, let alone say them. But the point is – he did. That was exactly how he felt, and so he exposed his inner emotions to God. How well he must have known God to feel free to speak to God with such desperate honesty.

God himself says, 'I the LORD search the heart and examine the mind' (17:10). So God knows our innermost thoughts anyway. What

181

then is the point of hiding them? Unfortunately, in my view, a lot of Christian worship and public speech is full of pretended emotion (saying or singing things we don't feel), or repressed emotion (hiding the things we actually do feel). Jeremiah at least has the honesty to say what he feels – and the courage to say it directly to God (not complain about it to others).

And in immediate response to Jeremiah's agonizing honesty God speaks his word of healing rebuke and gentle restoration (19–21). Honesty is the very first step on the road to healing. For there is no healing without repentance, and there is no repentance without honesty – even if it includes anger with God, questioning, and self-pity. God's response to Jeremiah's self-pity brings us back to verse 19. God tells him to repent. God does not *blame* him for feeling lonely and sorrowful, but he does call him to turn around in his thinking and speaking.

There was a time when my wife and I went through a particularly bad patch of depression and self-pity (during the year before we went, with our young family, to India as mission partners in theological education). A Christian doctor to whom we went for a routine medical check-up discerned this and its damaging effects on our lives. And he said to my wife, 'The only thing to do with self-pity is to repent of it.' That was very hard to hear, because the trouble with self-pity is that it is a 'comfortable' kind of emotion, which you can almost enjoy for a while as you wallow in it. Everybody else needs to repent, not me! But it is only through specific repentance before God of the self-centredness and pride that lie at the core of self-pity, that we can be released from its cloying grip and be raised up to a more healthy way of thinking and feeling.

Theological and expository reflections

Disillusionment, bitterness and resentment, self-pity. What a miserable list of symptoms! Yet how amazing that God has allowed these words of Jeremiah, filled with pain and anger, to be in the inspired scriptures, as part of the word of God. As Paul said, these things are written for our instruction and encouragement, so that we might take heed.[13]

So in preaching such a passage we should aim, with the help of the Holy Spirit, to help people to discern and diagnose such things and to recognize how damaging they are to the spiritual, physical and social life of individuals and the Christian community. What are the things that make people disillusioned today? How do our bright

[13] 1 Cor. 10:11.

expectations and hopes get dashed and betrayed? What corrodes our joy and confidence in the gospel? What causes resentments and bitterness among fellow-believers? How can we distinguish pastorally between genuine suffering and malingering self-pity?

And more importantly, we should then help people to take the road of repentance which will lead, in God's grace, to restoration and recommissioning, along with the fresh promise of God's presence and salvation – the road that Jeremiah trod.

Jeremiah 16:1–21
12. Silver-lined loneliness

Jeremiah wept the tears of God. He entered so much into the mind and heart of God that he became the embodiment of the divine feelings.[1] 'Not only are God's words being spoken by Jeremiah, but God's emotions are being felt by Jeremiah. This is prophetic mediation in reverse: Jeremiah is forbidden from presenting the people's pain to God, but he is commanded to present God's pain to the people.'[2]

But God demanded more of his servant than emotional empathy. His whole life, physical and social, became a living enactment of his message. Like Hosea before him and Ezekiel after him, Jeremiah was a prophet from whom God demanded the most appalling personal cost. Hosea endured his wife's unfaithfulness. Ezekiel saw his wife, 'the delight of his eyes', ripped from him in premature death.[3] Jeremiah was denied a wife altogether. And that was just the beginning of woes.

Any account of the book of Jeremiah, and any preaching from it, needs to be constantly aware of the enormous cost that this man bore in being the mouthpiece of God. Jeremiah bluntly contradicts the 'prosperity gospel' teaching that faith and obedience automatically bring health, wealth and happiness. It was precisely his faithful obedience that thrust Jeremiah into lifelong suffering and sorrow. 'He had to representatively and predictively take up the cross on which the community soon would die.'[4] But beyond the cross lies the resurrection.

[1] See Heschel, *The Prophets,* Part II.
[2] Shead, *A Mouth Full of Fire*, p. 132.
[3] Hos. 1 – 3; Ezek. 24:15–27.
[4] Allen, p. 190.

1. Unseen prophet (1–9)

a. No family (1–4)

The devastating demand of verse 2 must have come early in Jeremiah's life, since most men married relatively young in Israel. It bound him to a life that was so abnormal that there is no known Hebrew word for 'bachelor' – an unmarried man. His continued single state would have been a topic of increasing curiosity, criticism (and doubtless much well-intentioned match-making) among his family – as if his family relationships were not strained enough already.

But not only was singleness socially abnormal in Israel's culture, it would also have seemed counter-creational. Verse 2 naturally links getting married with having sons and daughters, which for Israel was a celebrated part of living in God's creation and fulfilling God's creational mandates. Jeremiah's refusal (on divine orders) to participate in that duty and joy was a disruption in the human realm comparable to the undoing of creation he saw in nature when God's judgment falls (4:23–26).

And why? He was being called to embody in his own bereft existence the reality that would engulf all families in the coming catastrophe (3–4). Jeremiah would never know the joys of parenthood. But those who were enjoying them now would soon lose them forever. Ancient siege warfare was not waged by the rules of the Geneva Convention (not that much modern warfare is either), and 'civilian casualties' would be devastating (4). Only after the fall of Jerusalem and the loss of children *born in this land* (3), would there be opportunity for the exiles to resume the task of building families.[5]

b. No funerals (5–7)

A single man can still find relational richness in the company of family and friends and in the cycle of social events in the community. But not Jeremiah. He was banned from 'the house of mourning'. He was not to participate in *a funeral meal* with the family; not even to *show sympathy*. But to be absent and silent at such times would be hugely offensive to the close-knit community. Jeremiah was being asked to embody, in his withdrawal from human society, the withdrawal of God himself from all loving engagement with his own people.

The triple negative of verse 5b is shocking: *I have withdrawn my blessing, my love and my pity from this people.* The words are: šālôm

[5] Jer. 29:4–6.

(peace); *ḥesed* (faithful love); and *raḥămîm* (compassion, mercy). These are among the 'biggest' of all the words in the Old Testament that express the covenantal commitment of YHWH to his people. For God to say that he is taking these things away does not mean that God himself has ceased to be the God of peace, love and compassion. Jeremiah knew that the steadfast love of YHWH never ends (31:3; 33:11; cf. Ps. 136). The key phrase is *from this people*. These were people who loved to hear the false prophets preaching peace when there was no peace. These were people who liked to appeal to God's love and compassion, but who had shown not an ounce of repentance or practical change. So for them, in such circumstances, God's peace, love and pity would be withdrawn in order to leave room for the exercise of judgment.

Jeremiah's refusal to sympathize with the bereaved, then, embodied God's refusal of mercy to the impenitent. But a further reason is given in verse 6: in the coming cataclysm the scale of death and destruction will be so great that all the normal cultural comforts of mourning will be abandoned. Jeremiah declines to participate now in ceremonies that will be impossible then.

c. No parties (8–9)

Similarly, when the wedding parties came round (lasting sometimes for days), Jeremiah was once again nowhere to be seen, insulting every bride and groom and their respective families for miles around. He was as invisible in the house of feasting (8) as in the house of mourning (5). And the message? The time was coming soon when all such joy and feasting would be at an end for the people of Judah (9).

Jeremiah lived, from this point on, in a state of embarrassing aloneness and exclusion. With no family for daily refuge, and being unable to participate in rituals that brought comfort and joy to the community, he lived out the pain of his terrible message. 'The ban on all forms of public celebration and consolation symbolizes the end of community life as it was known. Jeremiah is to reveal in his body the woeful destruction of structured life, Judah's hour of darkness.'[6] But we remind ourselves again – Jeremiah's pain embodied in a single finite human life the infinite pain in the heart of God. And Jeremiah's forced exclusion from his own flesh and blood embodied what it meant for God to be driven out by the people he loved.

[6] Stulman, p. 162.

2. Unseeing people (10–13)

Jeremiah must have been called to account for his behaviour, since it was socially inexcusable. And he would have answered in line with the verses above. But when he would *tell these people all this*, their response is jaw-dropping. '*Why?*', they ask! One imagines the only response to that must have been, 'Have you not been listening?' But then, of course, that is the one thing they seemed utterly incapable of doing.

The spiritual blindness of the questions is astonishing, '*What wrong have we done? What sin have we committed against the* LORD *our God?*' '. . . this question is almost comical; this issue has been addressed in a regular drumbeat in the preceding chapters. Given this context, this exchange may be considered testimony to the incredible stubbornness of the people, perhaps in the tradition of their denial at 2:35.'[7] With incredible patience, Jeremiah explains again the reason they had heard countless times already – the combined and accumulated forces of apostasy, idolatry and breaking of God's covenant law. And this had been going on for generations – *because your ancestors forsook me* (11).

'But that's not fair!' we can imagine Jeremiah's audience protesting, in between verse 11 and 12. 'Why should we be made to suffer for the sins of our ancestors?' If that's what they thought, Jeremiah responds that in fact they were even *worse* than their ancestors. Jeremiah and Ezekiel both faced the blame-shifting tactics of the people.[8] There was some truth, of course, in their complaint that they were having to bear the brunt of the wrath of God for the accumulated sins of many generations. One might call it the downside of God's patience. By holding back his judgment time after time, waiting to see if his people would repent, God may seem to be unfair when his patience eventually expires. But when the axe finally falls, it must fall somewhere. And Jeremiah and Ezekiel make it very clear that those on whom the axe did fall, in siege, destruction and exile, were by no means innocent victims. They were just as much a wicked generation, and just as deserving of their own fate, as any of the previous generations that had been spared it in the days of God's patience.

So they will be 'hurled out' of the land, as the covenant curses had threatened (13a). And there, with great irony, they will be compelled to do in captivity what they had freely chosen to do in disobedience (13b). They had chosen to serve other gods in defiance of God's

[7] Fretheim, p. 250.
[8] Jer. 31:27–30; Ezek. 18 and 33.

covenant law. Now they will have no choice but to serve the gods of those whom God would use as agents of his covenant anger (cf. 5:18–19).

3. All-seeing God (14–18)

The remainder of the chapter is usually said to be made up from fragments of prophecy from different moments in Jeremiah's ministry, since it jumps so quickly from judgment (13) to restoration (14–15), back to judgment (16–18), and then to even wider hope (19–21). Well, that may be true of course. However, we should perhaps not dismiss too quickly the possibility that Jeremiah himself could mentally move along such a trajectory. Critical scholars commonly regard verses 14–15 as a dislocated fragment that has found its interrupting way here from 23:7–8 (where, admittedly, it fits more naturally), on the grounds that a single author cannot entertain more than a single thought in his head at one time (a curious idea but surprisingly common among critical scholars). If the main theme is judgment, we are told, then any word of hope must be a later editorial insertion. Accordingly, verse 13 must originally have continued at verse 16, and verses 14–15 must have been inserted by someone in the exile.[9]

However, from the very beginning of his ministry Jeremiah had a twofold mandate, 'to uproot and tear down, to destroy and overthrow, *to build and to plant*'.[10] His overwhelmingly dominant message fell into the former category, of course. But Jeremiah had a hope that penetrated beyond the imminent judgment that was falling on his people. It was hope firmly grounded in the scriptures. Deuteronomy 29 – 30 contains exactly this combination of judgment and hope. So do the visions of Hosea. And Jeremiah himself, ten years before the final destruction of the city, had his vision of the two baskets of figs – good and bad (Jer. 24). In his interpretation the bad figs were those in Jerusalem still bent on rebellion against Nebuchadnezzar and facing inevitable destruction, but the good figs were those in exile, for whom there was a future of restoration and

---

[9] Brueggemann, for example, says, 'Critical opinion is unanimous that these verses [14–15] are a late voice in the tradition. They reflect a later generation of exilic hope, for such hope was not available until after 587 B.C.E.' (Brueggemann [1988], p. 147). But that last statement is simply untrue, as the examples in the following paragraph show – unless they are all also deemed to be exilic fabrications. Fortunately, in his interpretation of the text, Brueggemann himself says that 'we should approach the text as it stands and not dissolve the deliberate juxtaposition of Jer. 16:10–13 and vv. 14–15. Both the statement of harsh judgment and of grand homecoming are part of the canonical text.' Exactly.

[10] Jer. 1:10, my italics.

'planting'. Around the same time he wrote a letter to the exiles in Babylon that made the same explicit promises (Jer. 29). And even as Jerusalem was in the death throes of the final siege, the imprisoned Jeremiah bought a field as a courageous prophetic sign of a future when the people and the land would be restored by God's power and grace (Jer. 32). Indeed, as early as 3:16–17, Jeremiah had voiced surprising visions of future hope that are remarkably similar in form and content to what we read here in 16:14–15 and 19. So the idea that Jeremiah could not have followed words of imminent judgment with words of ultimate restoration in the passage before us seems hypercritical and insensitive to the wider balance of Jeremiah's vision.

If we try to interpret this short sequence of sayings as a whole, then, we will find the prophet moving from his own historical horizon to a broader missional horizon that lies even beyond those of us who read his words many centuries later. It is a series of imaginative moves very similar to the leap of logic we found in 4:1–2.

a. A future for Israel (14–15)

Verse 14 actually begins with 'therefore' (*lākēn*), not '*however*'. If we take the word in its usual sense, we have to ask what is the logical connection ('therefore') between the immediate judgment in verse 13 and the prospect of restoration in verses 14–15.[11] The only answer is that the one is the necessary precursor of the other. The second is the outcome of the first. Even when God acts in judgment it is but a stepping-stone to his larger purpose of redemption. Even when a whole generation must fall under the weight of God's anger at a persistently broken covenant (13), God's promised future for the nation as a whole will continue (14–15). Wrath will end. Restoration will follow. There is hope. It was a hope that the present generation would never see with the eyes in their heads, but to which they could lift the eyes of their faith.

As in ch. 3, the deliberate intent of the unit inserted here is reassuringly to jump ahead to a hopeful, post-catastrophe future. In this new context, 'Therefore,' introducing a proclamation of salvation

---

[11] 'Therefore' in the Bible can sometimes produce quite unexpected, paradoxical, following statements, which demand that we probe more deeply into the theological connection between what goes before and what follows. 'You only have I chosen of all the families of the earth; *therefore* . . . I will punish you' (Amos 3:2). 'With you there is forgiveness; *therefore* . . . you are feared' (Ps. 130:4). Similarly here: 'I am about to judge you by hurling you out of this land, as I threatened. *Therefore* . . . a fresh understanding of God's saving power will be the result when I bring you back.'

as in 16:19, blatantly expresses divine logic that defies human pos-sibility, like the new life rising from the grave of exile in Ezek 37:1–14. The oracle announces a radical innovation that launches a fresh era of revelation, as in Jer 3:16–17.[12]

That 'fresh era', that future restoration, would be such a historic, surprising and mighty act of God that it would constitute a relaunch-ing of the very faith of Israel itself. Hitherto, the people of Israel had grounded their sense of identity, as the redeemed people of YHWH, on the exodus. That historical foundation would not be lost or denied. But when they would return from exile Israel would discern another and even greater defining moment in their understanding of the saving power of their God.[13] That moment would generate a fresh form of their confession of faith, as expressed in the form of the oaths they customarily took to substantiate the truth of any statement, claim or case in court (14). God's great acts in history generate the confessions of faith of God's people (as we see in the psalms). So, as one great act of God surpasses another, the confession expands accordingly.

> This text of new historical possibility dares to say that the Exodus memory will now be superseded because Yahweh is about to outdo that miraculous act by an even greater miracle. This new act bursts out beyond Israel's best memory of liberation . . . There is judgment and there is new possibility. There is exile and there is homecoming. There is death and there is resurrection. Both moves are characteristic of this God. Both moves are definitional for this faith, this people, this God.[14]

In Christ, we share this faith, we belong to this people, we are redeemed by this God. We stand now on this side of the greatest of all God's mighty acts of salvation and so our confession of faith embraces and celebrates the whole of the Bible's story and every moment of God's redeeming power. Just as the focus of the returning exiles was no longer only on the God who brought Israel up out of Egypt, so our focus is no longer only on the God who brought the exiles back from Babylon. We worship the God who brought Jesus out from the tomb. We join the writer to the Hebrews – those who

[12] Allen, p. 192.
[13] Jeremiah already uses the idea of 'a new exodus' here, in a way that is expressed with a joyful profusion of poetic metaphor in Isa. 40 – 55. See especially Isa. 40:3–4; 41:17–20; 43:14–21; 51:9–11; 55:12. The theme of exodus and wilderness is used as a vision of future redemption with purging by Ezekiel also (Ezek. 20:34–38).
[14] Brueggemann (1988), p. 148.

were the physical descendants of Abraham and also, in Christ, his spiritual heirs – in the concluding prayer:

> May the God of peace, who through the blood of the eternal covenant brought back from the dead our Lord Jesus, that great Shepherd of the sheep, equip you with everything good for doing his will, and may he work in us what is pleasing to him, through Jesus Christ, to whom be glory for ever and ever.[15]

And Jeremiah would have said, 'Amen'. The promised return from exile is ultimately fulfilled in the death and resurrection of the Messiah. As Paul put it, 'What God promised our ancestors, he has fulfilled for us, their children, by raising up Jesus'.[16]

b. But first: inescapable judgment (16–18)

But now, those who cannot see the blindingly obvious answers to their own questions (10–11) will face the God who can see all, and who is fully aware of all they would rather keep hidden (17). They will find no hiding place from his pursuit, which will be as patient as any fisherman and as thorough as any hunter (16). Wherever they may flee or hide, they will inexorably be caught.[17]

Verse 18 begins with a word that the NIV inexplicably omits – 'first of all'. This indicates that the section is aware of the words of future restoration that precede it. *First* there has to be judgment before there can be a future for Israel (14–15), or a future for the nations for whose ultimate blessing Israel existed (19).

4. Foreseen world (19–21)

And so to the final leap of missional logic. If beyond the coming judgment lay a future restoration of *Israel* to God, then what lay beyond that? Surely the fulfilment of the purpose of Israel's very existence – that *the nations* of the world should also come into the blessing of knowing the living God. Jeremiah here makes exactly the same startling (but theologically justified) connection that he had

[15] Heb. 13:20–21.

[16] Acts 13:32–33.

[17] Cf. also Hab. 1:15. It is typical of Jesus that when he invited disciples (who were fishermen) to respond to, and become agents of, the good news of the kingdom of God, he transformed this negative scriptural metaphor of God's judgment (fishing) into a positive metaphor of evangelism – 'fishing for people' (Mark 1:17). Elsewhere, of course, he could return to the original metaphor and use it as a picture of the discriminating, separating, operation of the kingdom of God within the world (Matt. 13:47–50).

made in 4:1–2.[18] There he had called for Israel's repentance, and had jumped ahead from the prospect that such repentance would suspend God's judgment on *Israel*, to the more ultimate conclusion that it would lead to blessing for the *nations*. Whatever was good for Israel was good for the nations – according to a biblical missional logic that stretched back to the original covenant promise to Abraham which Jeremiah so clearly echoed in 4:2. So here, if it was now too late for Israel to repent, then judgment on Israel must fall (13, 16–18). But if beyond judgment lay restoration and future hope for Israel (14–15), then the ultimate ingathering of the nations would begin (19).

It is a prophetic word, but it is also a very personal word. The passage begins and ends with the personal name of the Lord, YHWH, as its first and last word. It starts with Jeremiah addressing God and concludes with God addressing Jeremiah – and in both cases with words of assurance to each other about the future. Recalling the bleak loneliness of Jeremiah in verses 1–9, it is heart-warming to hear Jeremiah speak again of God as *my strength and my fortress, my refuge in times of distress*, of which there must have been many. The reproachful accusations of 15:18 have been left behind. Jeremiah speaks to God as friend to friend.

Is there even a hint that just as God had comforted Jeremiah in his tribulations (15:20–21), so now Jeremiah comforts God with the reminder that his ultimate goal *will* be achieved?[19] God's heart is filled with pain over the judgment he must inflict on his own people. But let God look forward to the day when his promise to Abraham will be accomplished. *To you*, says Jeremiah to the God who weeps with him, *to you the nations will come from the ends of the earth.* The day will come when the God who has been so spurned by his own people will be the God to whom the nations will flock. The rejected God will be sought, found, and known by the whole earth. Let God take comfort in that.

There is a double irony, however, in Jeremiah's prediction.

First, the foreign nations will acknowledge what Israel had refused to accept – namely that man-made gods are *false* and *worthless* (19b). While Israel had spent their energies running after the gods of the nations (ch. 2), the nations would themselves acknowledge that they had been deceived.

This is a paradox that runs through the Bible. Often God's own people are the last to perceive the futility of their own idolatries. Often 'outsider' people come to see what 'insiders' have refused to

---

[18] And the fact that the connection of thought happens within a single sentence in 4:2 makes it all the more unnecessary to take a critical knife to this passage and sunder these verses from their context.

[19] This tantalizing thought is suggested by Berrigan, *Jeremiah*, p. 78.

accept, or offer correction to those who should have known better. The pagan Abimelech teaches Abraham about truth-telling.[20] Rahab the Canaanite turns to Israel's God and is saved while Achan the Israelite rejects God's commands and is destroyed.[21] The Queen of Sheba told Solomon why the God of Israel had made him king – whereas Solomon himself quickly forgot the point.[22] The Phoenician widow of Zarephath and the Syrian commander Naaman experience life and healing while the kings of Israel reject every word of Elijah and Elisha – a point that Jesus made to outraged listeners one sabbath day in Nazareth.[23] And climactically, it was a Gentile Roman soldier at the cross who recognized the truth about Jesus that Mark announces in the opening verse of his Gospel but the Jewish leaders had utterly rejected.[24] Sadly, Paul confronted the same astonishing paradox in another synagogue.[25] It is an enduring paradox, still with us today, whenever the world exposes the failings of the church, or when outright pagans seem more ready to embrace the gospel than the church is to renounce the idolatries of the world around us.

The second irony in these verses is more cheerful. What we have here is a glorious reversal of the behaviour of the nations that was held up in chapter 2 as a foil for Israel's fickleness.

Everybody knew that the foreign nations worshipped other gods – gods that were really 'no gods' at all. That is the point also of the scathing rhetorical question in verse 20:

Question:	*'Do people make their own gods?'*
Expected answer:	'Yes, it's what people do everywhere.'
Emphatic dismissal:	*'They are not gods!'* (or more likely, 'they are not God').[26]

Now in 2:10–11 Jeremiah had invited Israel to study those other nations and their habits of worship. Did they swap and change their gods? No! The gods of the nations were no-gods, but at least the nations were loyal to their non-existent gods. Whereas in stark contrast Israel, who knew the one true living God – their Glory – had exchanged that living God for the worthless idols of the nations.

[20] Gen. 20.
[21] Josh. 6:22–23; 7:1–26.
[22] 1 Kgs 10:9; 11:9–10.
[23] Luke 4:16–30 (1 Kgs 17:7–24; 2 Kgs 5).
[24] Mark 15:39.
[25] Acts 13:44–48.
[26] There is undoubtedly a play on the fact that in Hebrew 'ĕlōhîm can be either plural ('gods'), or singular (when it refers to YHWH the one true living God). My feeling is that in v. 20, the first is plural while the second is singular: 'There are lots of gods; but they are not God!'

So in chapter 2 the contrast is between Israel's disloyalty to the one true God, and the nation's loyalty to their many non-gods.

But here in 16:19b, in ironic contrast, the nations come to recognize about their own gods what even Israel had refused to acknowledge. And so they will reject those false deceptions and embrace the living God of Israel. *The nations will do what Jeremiah had pleaded all his life for Israel to do.*

And so, in response God will *teach them*. In the context, *them* must refer to the nations who are turning to God. The nations will come to know God. That is the great goal of all God's saving work, that the living God should be known for who he truly is, as creator and redeemer, among all nations and in all creation. God wants to reverse the present fact mentioned in 10:25 ('nations who do not acknowledge you').[27]

And so the logic of the whole section (14–21) has been played out. Israel must be judged, but beyond judgment there lies the restoration of Israel, and beyond that the ingathering of the nations. It is the same missional logic that inspired the New Testament mission to the Gentiles, on the grounds that in the death and resurrection of the Messiah the exile had truly ended and the restoration could begin on the global scale that God's promise to Abraham had always anticipated. 'God's purpose in judgment reaches beyond the judgment to the knowledge of the Lord that will be taught to all the nations of the world.'[28] And then, 'the earth will be filled with the knowledge of the glory of the LORD as the waters cover the sea'.[29]

And so this chapter, which began with the grim social exclusion of one man as a symbol of God's judgment, ends with the glorious saving inclusion of the nations as the summit of God's redemption.

Theological and expository reflections

- Beginning at the end, it is worth reminding ourselves and any congregation of Gentile believers that we are included in verses 19–21. Jeremiah 'foresees the day when far-flung peoples will realize the hollowness of their religions and turn to the Lord. If this seems almost too remote a hope, it can reawaken our

---

[27] The translation, *teach them* unfortunately obscures the emphatic triple use of the verb *yāda'* – to know. Literally God says, 'I will cause them to *know*; this time I will really make them *know* . . . Then they will *know* my name, YHWH'. Jeremiah paves the way for Ezekiel's 'signature'. More than eighty times Ezekiel uses this expression: 'then you will know', 'then they will know'.

[28] Fretheim, p. 253.

[29] Hab. 2:14.

wonder at the fact that most of us who read these words are drawn *from the ends of the earth* (19), as part of their fulfilment'.[30] That ought to remind us of Paul's warnings in Romans 11 that Gentile Christians should remember the grace that has grafted them into God's people, refuse any feelings of superiority over the Jews, but rather long for them to turn to their Messiah Jesus and be saved.

- Reflecting on the irony of verse 19b (above), it is sobering to ask whether much has changed. Should we not recognize that abuses within the church, which are often nothing short of idolatry – running after the gods of the people around us in cultural captivity and blatant syncretism – are a far bigger obstacle to God's mission of bringing his saving gospel to the nations, than the idols of those nations themselves? Sometimes we see 'pagans' fully ready to accept the truth of the gospel when they genuinely hear it and to come running into the arms of the God who longs to save them, while so many Christians stubbornly refuse to heed the clear commands of Christ; for example, to love one another, to walk in integrity, to avoid covetous greed, to forgive one another, etc. The return of the prodigal son is sadly counterbalanced by the refusal of the elder brother.

- How can we express and apply the message of 16:18 that idolatry defiles both people and land?

  > This verse teaches that the practice of idolatry profanes a country and defiles the land. This warning must be taken seriously, for many people do not seem to have understood that the many misfortunes that have saddened our countries are the result of our rejection of God and our widespread occult practices. No occult practice is without consequences. All affect those who practise them, and also their families and environment.[31]

- The cost for Jeremiah of being the embodiment of God's word was enormous. The cost for Jesus of being the incarnate word and the bearer of God's salvation was infinite. Reflecting on the comparison is challenging.

---

[30] Kidner, p. 71.
[31] Coulibaly, p. 868.

195

Jeremiah 17:1–27
13. Heart searching

Editors have an unenviable job. If Baruch was the final compiler of the Jeremiah archive, he must sometimes have wondered how to combine various sayings, especially the shorter ones. However, although Jeremiah 17 is sometimes treated as just a miscellany of unconnected pieces, closer study shows up some fascinating connections through repeated words (which we will point out as we go through the chapter). Then, with a little creative reading between the lines, we can discern theological insights that may well have led these texts to be held together in this way. Whether or not one agrees with the connected interpretation offered below, it still seems important to pay attention to the canonical form of the text and seek its significance.

1. Dialogues of the heart (1–13)

The first connecting thread we observe is *the heart*, which we find in various states in verses 1, 5, 9 and 10.

a. The hard heart (1–4)

Remember there were no chapter and verse divisions in the original text. That makes the contrast between the end of our chapter 16 and the beginning of chapter 17 striking and tragic. While the nations are portrayed as turning away from past generations of idolatry (16:19–21), Judah remains stubbornly determined to inflict their inveterate sin on future generations (2). While the nations will come from the ends of the earth to know God, Judah will be driven away from God to *a land you do not know* (4).

And why? Because their hearts are like stone *tablets* on which their *sin is engraved with an iron tool* (1). The heart, in Hebrew, is not just the seat of the emotions, but much more of the will. It is where decisions are made. The heart speaks of the whole direction of one's life, commitments and priorities. So this metaphor speaks of blatant, incorrigible, unbending refusal to *choose* to change their sinful ways. Israel's wilful rebellion is, as we might say, 'set in concrete'.[1]

Jeremiah focuses again on the sexualized fertility cult (cf. ch. 2). The *Asherah poles* (female fertility symbols) and the lascivious rituals under *spreading trees* were still there in *the high hills*, the mountains and the open fields (2b–3a).[2] The practices have become so ingrained and 'normal' that children take them for granted and the people simply will not live without them.

When sin becomes habitual and we refuse to repent, even after all the appeals of God's word, the warnings of friends, or the protests of our own conscience, it leads to a very dangerous spiritual state, in which it becomes ever harder and harder to repent.[3] Something permanently written in stone is like other pictures of unchangeable conditions: the indelible stain that cannot be removed by mere washing with soap (2:22); the colour of your skin or the spots on a leopard that cannot be changed at will (13:23). Only a miracle of God's grace can intervene to bring about a change of heart when such a state has been reached. And that is precisely what other texts both require and promise. For Jeremiah it was the promise of the new covenant in which God would write his own law on hearts that had once been engraved with sin but would now be cleansed with for-giveness.[4] For Deuteronomy it was the promise of heart circumcision in which God's grace would give what God's law demanded – the love and obedience of the heart.[5] For Ezekiel it was the promise of even more radical heart surgery – a complete heart transplant that would replace hard hearts of stone with hearts of flesh that would be moved to obedience by the regenerating power of God's Spirit.[6]

When Jeremiah says that *Judah's sin is engraved . . . on the horns of their altars* (1), he means that it has penetrated to the heart of their worship, to the very place where they thought forgiveness and pro-tection were guaranteed. 'Moreover, "the horns of the altar," which once provided atonement for sin and protection from pursuing

---

[1] For a wide-ranging biblical survey of the twin themes of idolatry and hardness of heart, see Meadors, *Idolatry and the Hardening of the Heart*.

[2] It seems more likely that 'my mountain, in the field' at the beginning of v. 3 should be taken along with v. 2, rather than as the start of the list of things God plans to 'give away as plunder'.

[3] Cf. Meadors, *Idolatry*.

[4] Jer. 31:33–34.

[5] Deut. 30:1–10; note especially how the circumcised heart of v. 6 answers the requirements 'with all your heart' in vv. 1 and 10.

[6] Ezek. 36:26–27.

197

adversaries (Exod. 29:12; 30:10), now serve as a constant reminder of Judah's guilt before Yahweh. The text transforms symbols of salvation and security into emblems of guilt and danger.[7] To persist in deliberate known sin is dangerous enough. Combining it with regular attendance at church and participating in Holy Communion is a mockery of the grace of God. If there are things that need to be put right, that needs to be done first.[8]

Because they refuse to abandon their sin they will be forced to abandon their most precious things, things that were in fact the greatest symbol of God's blessing upon their nation: the land that was *the inheritance I gave you* (4a); and the accumulated *wealth and all your treasures* (3).[9] The land was the monumental tangible proof of God's covenant faithfulness. So to be ejected from it was bitterest proof of God's covenant *anger* (4b). The threat of expulsion from the land had been clear and repeated.[10] The moral equation was simple: it was *because of sin* and *through your own fault* that the judgment would fall (4a). 'God cannot be mocked. A man reaps what he sows.'[11]

b. The trusting heart (5–8)

'Faith-based' is a term that has entered into contemporary public language, to describe initiatives or projects undertaken by religious believers (whether Christian or of other religions). The expression makes the assumption that some people are 'persons of faith' while others are not. But that is entirely the wrong way to frame the contrast. We are all 'persons of faith' – the only difference lies in the object of our trust. As we come to our decisions, make our plans, and follow up with our actions, we are all exercising faith in some form or another in relation to a future that we cannot ultimately predict or control. The question is: where have you put your faith? In what are you trusting?

---

[7] Stulman, pp. 166–167.

[8] Pss 15; 51:16–19; Matt. 5:23–24; 18:15–17; 1 Cor. 11:27–34.

[9] This is probably the correct location for these lines, which seem to have got mistakenly inserted into v. 3. Cf. 15:13–14.

[10] Lev. 18:24–28; 20:22–24; 26:27–35; Deut. 28:64–68. Note: *It [God's anger] will burn forever* (4); this is an example of how the Heb. *'ōlām* does not always mean 'everlasting' in the temporal sense of something going on forever without end, but rather something that will last a very long time. Lev. 26, Deut. 30, and later promises from Jeremiah himself, make it clear that God's anger, poured out in the events of 587 BC, would not last forever in the absolute sense, but would ultimately come to an end in restoration and return. For those of Jeremiah's own generation, however, who suffered and die in the conflagration, it was most certainly final and forever. There was no future for them, even though there was a hope and a future for their descendants. The word expresses irrevocable finality for those to whom it applies.

[11] Gal. 6:7.

So the contrast in this insightful short poem is not between those who 'have faith' and those who do not (as contemporary secular commentators like to put it), but between those who trust in themselves and those who trust in God. *Both* parties are exercising faith, but their faith is placed in very different locations.

On the one hand (5) is the person *who trusts in man, who draws strength from mere flesh*.[12] The point is not merely that such a person is using human resources (which are in any case God-given), but that they are trusting in them while their *heart turns away from the LORD* (5b). This is not just your average self-sufficient pagan. This is someone who has known the living God but who is now governing the essential core of their life (*heart*) without reference to God. On the other hand (7) is the person *who trusts in the LORD, whose confidence is in him.* The contrast is then presented in matching pictures of a stunted *bush in the wastelands* (6) and *a tree planted by the water* (8). The comparison may have been suggested by meditation on the two ways portrayed in Psalm 1.

The vivid images may seem rather obvious in their meaning – droughted barrenness contrasted with irrigated fruitfulness. But the application in the text (6b and 8b) is more subtle and true to life's ambiguities. The poem does not blithely assert that only bad things happen to those who trust in themselves, or that only good things happen to those who trust in God. Life does not conform to that kind of fairy-tale theology.

On the contrary, 'good' may indeed attend the self-sufficient, self-trusting person, but *he will not see* it – in the sense that ultimately it will bring them no lasting benefit. In fact, even in the midst of *prosperity*, such a person may find that life itself becomes a desert, and their own inner person, cut off from any life-giving nourishment from the God they have rejected, has become spiritually shrivelled and stunted. 'Elsewhere there may be "showers of blessing", but in his spiritual desert he remains untouched (6a). The truth about that desert, the godless world, is summed up with masterly brevity in the three features of 6b: thirst, loneliness and sterility.'[13] And conversely, the person who is trusting in the Lord may well face *heat* and a *year of drought* – i.e. times of stress, pressure, suffering and need (as Jeremiah will testify again a few verses later). But even in and through such tough times, God's faithful ones need not *fear* and can continue to *bear fruit.*

So in stark contrast to the seductive lies of the 'prosperity gospel', these verses open our eyes to the paradox that one can shrivel to death

[12] Lit. 'makes flesh his arm', which may be the inspiration for the lines of the hymn, 'The arm of flesh will fail you, Ye dare not trust your own' (from 'Stand up, stand up for Jesus, ye soldiers of the cross', George Duffield Jr, 1818–88).

[13] Kidner, p. 72.

in the midst of prosperity, or one can be spiritually alive and fruitful in the midst of adversity. What makes the difference is where you put your ultimate trust. Not surprisingly, therefore, when we next hear Jeremiah crying out in his personal adversity, it will be very clear that he knew there was only one place to put his trust in (14).

c. The tested heart (9–13)

The poem of verses 5–8 echoes the familiar advice and promise of Proverbs 3:5–10:

> Trust in the LORD with all your heart
>   and lean not on your own understanding;
> in all your ways submit to him,
>   and he will make your paths straight.
> Do not be wise in your own eyes;
>   fear the Lord and shun evil.
> This will bring health to your body
>   and nourishment to your bones.
> Honour the Lord with your wealth,
>   with the firstfruits of all your crops;
> then your barns will be filled to overflowing,
>   and your vats will brim over with new wine.

That is the kind of general rule Proverbs likes to affirm: a life of obedient trust in God should result in blessing and fulfilment. But life does not always follow the rules. Life is complicated. There is the reality of innocent suffering. There is the apparent futility of death. And there is also the mystery of baffling human behaviour. Why do we behave as we do, in spite of all we have learned from the mistakes of countless generations? So, just as Proverbs is balanced by Job and Ecclesiastes, in the same way, after the proverbial affirmations of verses 5–8, we have balancing questions and reflections of verses 9–13. The connections of thought are not obvious, but let us take it a verse at a time.

(i) Beyond cure (9)

> *The heart is deceitful above all things*
>   *and beyond cure.*
> *Who can understand it?*

This classic summary of our fallen inexplicability echoes the bleak diagnosis of Genesis 6:5: 'The LORD saw how great the wickedness of the human race had become on the earth, and that every inclination of the thoughts of the human heart was only evil all the time.'

The old cliché sums it up well: the heart of the human problem is the problem of the human heart. And that problem is summed up in three words in verse 9 – *deceitful . . . beyond cure,* beyond understanding. We are sly, we are sick and we are inscrutable. The sin that is engraved on our hearts with iron and flint (1) makes us deceitful in our thinking, diseased in our attitudes and darkened in our understanding even of ourselves. The stark truth 'is presented in a triple crescendo: a heart morally insidious beyond compare, sick beyond hope of recovery, and therefore located far beyond the limits of human comprehension.'[14] Indeed, the human heart is almost beyond *divine* comprehension, since God has already voiced his own bafflement at Israel's inexplicable behaviour in some stinging rhetorical questions. Even God asks 'why?' (2:5, 31; 8:5). Almost, but not quite. For the question at the end of verse 9 gets its answer in the opening words of verse 10.

(ii) Searched by God (10)
I the LORD *search the heart. . .* The opening word, *I,* is emphatic. It seems to be a deliberate riposte to the despairing question, *Who can understand it?* 'I can,' says God, '*I the* LORD, the searcher of the heart, the examiner of the inner being.'[15] We may be a mystery to ourselves, but we are no mystery to the One who sees into the deepest recesses of human motives and thoughts.

YHWH is the God who sees and audits the inner realities of all human life. That truth was part of Israel's faith from earliest times. Samuel's mother sang it, and taught the same truth to her son.[16] Psalmists took it to heart as personal comfort, and universalized it to every human being on the planet.[17] David saw it as the dominant motivation for personal integrity.[18] Jeremiah makes it one of his regular themes.[19] Jesus exercised surprising insight into the human heart as one aspect of his divine identity.[20] Thomas Cranmer turned it into the beautifully searching prayer that begins the Anglican service of Holy Communion.

---

[14] Allen, p. 200.
[15] The second word is literally 'the kidneys', which were considered metaphorically the seat of our emotional life and feelings, alongside 'the heart', seat of the intellect and will.
[16] 1 Sam. 2:3; 16:7.
[17] Pss 17:3; 139:1–6, 23; 33:13–15.
[18] 1 Chr. 29:17.
[19] Jer. 7:11; 9:7; 11:20; 12:3; 20:12; 32:19.
[20] John 2:23–25.

Almighty God, unto whom all hearts be open, all desires known, and from whom no secrets are hid: Cleanse the thoughts of our hearts by the inspiration of thy Holy Spirit, that we may perfectly love thee, and worthily magnify thy holy Name; through Christ our Lord. Amen.

And since God possesses such total knowledge of all human motivation, intention and action, he alone is positioned to exercise perfect justice. The second half of verse 10 expresses that link. Because God knows everything about everybody, he is able [lit.] 'to give to each person according to his ways, according to the fruit of his doings'.[21]

(iii) In the end (11)

But if God judges all people according to their deeds, how does it happen that the wicked prosper? This age-old question rebounds in verse 11 against the affirmation of verse 10, in this oscillating dialogue. It is a question that assailed many a psalmist, assaulted Jeremiah repeatedly, and goes on troubling God's suffering faithful ones to this day. The answer given by verse 11 takes the form of proverb that condenses the theology of Psalm 73:16–18, i.e., 'just wait; don't judge too soon, but look what happens *in the end*'.

Somebody *who gains riches by unjust means* is like a bird that *hatches eggs it did not lay* – i.e. a bird that seems to have offspring without the 'effort' of laying the eggs, by hatching the eggs of other birds. It seems unnatural and unfair that a bird should 'get away with it'. How much more so in humans who should know better. But just as the bird's false chicks will fly off or be eaten by predators, so unjust wealth will eventually be lost and the wicked will be shown to be fools. The timescale (*when their lives are half gone*) may frequently prove optimistic, even naïve. But the point is that *in the end* those who accumulate wealth at the expense or neglect of others face the same utter loss and shame of the one Jesus portrayed as 'the rich fool'.[22] So, even if real life seems to contradict the promise of verses 5–8, *in the end*, God will see that justice is done. Jeremiah would agree, but longs for it to be done sooner rather than later (18).

---

[21] The phrase 'fruit of their doings' is another verbal link within the chapter, since it echoes v. 8 where the person who trusts in God *never fails to bear fruit.* There (8), it implies the positive fruit of life-fulfilment. Here (10b), it is neutral, meaning the consequences of our actions, whether good or bad. The NIV's renderings of *reward* (for 'give'), and *deserve* (for 'fruit') add some interpretation to the verse that is not strictly in the original. What we 'get' is what our actions themselves produce as 'fruit': the outcomes, the consequences. God's moral governance ensures that in the end such consequences are indeed 'according to' what we have done.

[22] Luke 12:13–21; Jas 5:1–6.

(iv) The safe hope (12–13)
These verses (which are echoed elsewhere: 3:17; 14:8; Lam. 5:19), affirm two things: first that YHWH is the only safe hope for Israel, and second that the choice presented in principle in verses 5–8 now faces the people as a direct practical challenge. The verbal echoes build the links clearly. *Those who turn away from you* (13) will become like the one *whose heart turns away from the LORD* (5), and will face the same dry and dusty fate. By implication, those who do not *forsake the LORD* will have the abundant water supply not only of *a tree planted by the water* (8), but of *the spring of living water* that is the Lord himself (13; cf. 2:13). With that last line of verse 13 Jeremiah clearly recants the despairing cry of 15:18, in which he had accused God of being 'a deceptive brook . . . a spring that fails'. He has not only repented of that outburst, as God gently urged him to do (15:19), but has returned to that secure and life-giving source of hope – for himself and his people.

Remember who would read these words: the exiles in Bablyon. For them, this personal journey of the prophet needed to become their journey of repentance and trust. They would be painfully aware that some of those who had rejected Jeremiah's message when first delivered were now indeed *written in the dust,* in the death and destruction of Jerusalem. For those who were spared, however, there remained a *throne,* a *sanctuary,* a *hope* – so long as it was placed in YHWH alone.

It is possible to read verse 12 not simply as a statement, but in the vocative. That is, with the same '*O*' of address as at the start of verse 13. It would then read, '[You, Lord], the glorious throne . . . the place of our sanctuary'. In this sense, the verse is more than a standard affirmation about the temple in Jerusalem. It expresses the profound insight that even if that building and city lay in ruins and ashes, the Lord himself was still on the eternal throne of the universe. God himself was *the place of our sanctuary.* Even if none of their own generation would return to their destroyed temple, they could return to their indestructible God. For he was *the hope of Israel,* as he always had been and always would be.

2. Desires of the prophet (14–18)

Jeremiah's struggles were far from over. This cry follows the familiar format of the psalms of lament, with address to God ('you'), complaints about external enemies ('they'), and forlorn self-pity ('I').[23]

---

[23] Cf. Pss 28, 31, 35, etc.

Jeremiah appeals to God to keep his promise 'I am with you to rescue and save you . . . I will save you' (15:20–21): *heal me, Lord, and I will be healed; save me and I will be saved*. The human heart may be humanly incurable, but Jeremiah knew where healing was to be found. The generation he lived among may be beyond saving, but Jeremiah could trust God for his own salvation. And trust God with his laments, his protests, his self-defence and his confused longings.

Jeremiah's complaint on this occasion is the scathing mockery he faced from those who challenged his claim to be a true prophet bringing authentic messages from YHWH. One of the key tests for discerning true from false prophets was the test of fulfilment. According to Deuteronomy 18:21–22, if a prophet's predictions failed to come true, then 'that is a message the LORD has not spoken. That prophet has spoken presumptuously, so do not be alarmed'. 'Quite so,' scoffed Jeremiah's tormentors. 'How many years have you been predicting doom and destruction and not a shot has been fired? Why should we believe you any more?' Or, in words that also find echoes in the Psalms:[24] *'Where is the word of the LORD? Let it now be fulfilled!'*

But this rejection of his word and denial of his credentials as a true prophet of the Lord tore at Jeremiah's heart and stirred up hugely contradictory desires. For the one thing that would prove the truth of his message and vindicate him as a prophet was the very thing he least wanted to happen. The mere thought of it had broken his heart and drowned him in tears since the start of his ministry[25] – the invasion of the land, the destruction of Jerusalem with massive loss of life, and the exile of a miserable remnant of survivors. So in verse 16 he reminds God that he had behaved like a *shepherd* of God's flock and could never wish for the destruction of his own people (another Moses-like moment). God knew that no such wish had ever passed his lips. So how could he cope with the acute tension that was making him sick with stress? Jeremiah longed for people to believe that he was God's true spokesman. But he could not long for the one thing that would prove that he was – namely, the fulfilment of his prophecies. For he loved his people as a shepherd cares for his sheep (16).

Yet such is the churning turmoil of these conflicting emotions that Jeremiah swings in a diametrically opposite direction as far as his tormentors were concerned (17–18). The man who has just said he had *not desired the day of despair* (16), now cries out that God would

---

[24] Cf. Pss 42:3, 10; 79:10; 115:2.
[25] Remember the agonies of passages like 4:19–21; 8:18 – 9:1; 10:17–22; 14:17–18.

*bring on **them** the day of disaster* (18). Jeremiah's heart is trusting (14, 7–8), but his head is still swimming with the unfinished logic of verses 10 and 11. For if verse 10 is true and God deals with people according to their deeds, then why is verse 15 still the case? Why are wicked people scoffing at God's word in stubborn refusal to repent? And since verse 15 *is* true, then why, in the spirit of verse 10, should God not do exactly what verse 18 demands – destroy them? The emotions are strong, the desires are confused.

Stepping back from the stress and emotions of Jeremiah's outburst,[26] we have to ask if such a desire (18) is appropriate? If we can lift it from being a simple cry for revenge, then we can locate it theologically within a proper desire that God should vindicate his own name and character by acting justly, by defending those who are falsely accused and putting down the wicked. This after all is what countless biblical texts affirm that God does do and will do. Why then does he not do it sooner? The question is increasingly urgent as the persecution and suffering of believers all over the world grows in intensity and barbarity.

Peter would answer that God gives time to repent – space for grace, scope for hope.[27] Faced with the mocking persistence of the wicked, including those who do us wrong, we should pray for them to repent and, with Jesus, pray for their forgiveness. Yes, but although the New Testament (as the Old) emphatically prohibits believers from taking revenge and acting in retaliation, it equally emphatically affirms that in the end God will do justice. In some situations it may be not inappropriate to affirm the retributive principle of Jeremiah 17:10, as even the Apostle Paul did in the case of one person who did him great harm.[28] It is hard, but not impossible, to ask God to do justice while also asking him to be merciful and forgive. Both longings reflect essential truths of God's character.

The petition for retribution is more than a self-centred cry for revenge. Jeremiah also speaks for those who suffer derision on account of their faithfulness to God. Jeremiah's cry for vengeance is thus a cry that justice should prevail, that the righteous be vindicated, and that the wicked be thwarted. In other words, the prophet pleads that God would act in character and not be

---

[26] 'It may surprise us that the prayer is so hostile. Such hostility bespeaks the courage and candor of prayer that is characteristic of Israel . . . The one who prays is filled with hurt and rage, and entrusts vengeance to God' (Brueggemann [1988], pp. 156–157).

[27] 2 Pet. 3:9.

[28] 2 Tim. 4:14–15; but note Paul's immediate echo of the words of Jesus and Stephen in v. 16.

indifferent to the plight of the needy . . . The prophet longs for the establishment of God's just rule.[29]

3. Decisions on the sabbath (19–27)

We may well wonder why this lengthy piece of prose preaching about the sabbath, with its similarities to other great sermons in chapters 7 and 11, has been placed at the end of this rather jerky chapter. Clearly it comes from a distinct occasion, as the instructions show (19).[30]

Our surprise as modern readers that such a diatribe on sabbath observance should feature in a prophet we would least suspect of anything we might call legalism only goes to show how far we have strayed from a true appreciation of the significance of the sabbath in its original Old Testament context. The first thing we must do to 'inhabit' a text like this is to free our minds on the one hand from the atmosphere of burdensome legalism and condemnation that hangs over the sabbath in the Gospels (remembering that there are six centuries between Jeremiah's day and Jesus' encounter with the Pharisees), and on the other hand from whatever forms (or memories) of Christian sabbatarianism that we ourselves may practise or condemn on Sundays. Rather, we must ask what the sabbath meant for Old Testament Israel and why Jeremiah could use it as a test of covenant obedience, and as a criterion for the health of the nation's political and religious life.

When we remember that Jeremiah's sermon in the temple listed several others of the Ten Commandments (7:9), it should not be surprising that he has a word here also about the fourth. The sabbath commandment functions as a hinge between the God-oriented first three commandments, and the socially-oriented following six. For the sabbath was to be observed both vertically 'unto the Lord', but decidedly also horizontally for human benefit (as Jesus famously pointed out). It was, in a sense, a test case for the two great commandments – to love God and love the neighbour.

The sabbath was God's unique gift to Israel. It called them to enjoy God's earth with a rhythm of work and rest that would prevent work becoming the dominating idol of all human existence. And it called them to enjoy their release from the Egyptian oppression that had imposed forced labour upon them and to avoid subjecting others in their own community to the same inhuman drudgery.[31] Or to look at it another way, the sabbath is not so much a burdensome

---

[29] Stulman, p. 174.

[30] One clue may be the verbal repetition of the *unquenchable fire* of judgment (4, 27).

[31] The sabbath commandment in Exodus is based on creation, and in Deuteronomy on redemption (Exod. 20:11; Deut. 5:15).

prohibition on work for a day, as a liberating permission to rest for a day. Which is the reason why Jesus was so angry that the Pharisees had turned it into a burden.

The sabbath was a weekly reminder of the God who was creator of the whole earth and the redeemer of Israel. On that foundation it was a weekly reminder also of their covenantal responsibility to God and to one another in society. And it was that second horizontal, socio-economic dimension that was endangered when the sabbath was ignored.

> The liberation from slavery in Egypt and the gift of a land of their own set Israel's world of economic work in a totally new context. They would now work as free people, no longer in the indignity and insecurity of economic bondage. On that basis, they were to avoid oppressing and exploiting the weak and vulnerable in their own society. Hence the sabbath commandment is specifically for the benefit of the whole working population, animal as well as human (Deut. 5:14). That indeed is its express purpose: 'so that your manservant and maidservant may rest, as you do' (cf. Exod. 23:12).
>
> The moral seriousness of the sabbath commandment now comes more clearly into focus, especially for modern people who find it peculiar and inexplicable that the mere observance of such a day should even figure in the Ten Commandments, let alone be sanctioned by the death penalty. As a brake on the accelerating processes of idolatry it *protected the uniqueness of Yahweh* as creator and redeemer, and as a brake on the parallel tendency of human economic exploitation and oppression it preserved the social liberation that *reflected the character of Yahweh* . . . Not surprisingly, prophetic passages that attack sabbath breaking also condemn the guilty ones for their greed, exploitation, and maximizing of gain at the expense of others (Amos 8:4–6; Isa. 58:13f., in the context of the whole ch.; cf. Neh. 13:15–22).[32]

Coming back to Jeremiah 17, we can now see more clearly the connection between this section and the earlier message of the chapter – especially the starkly polarized choice portrayed in verses 5–8. Those who were habitually breaking sabbath by carrying on their work and trade (21–24), or who chafed under its weekly demand for cessation of work, were those who 'trusted in human resources' – to maximize their profits (Amos 8:4–6; Neh. 13:15–22), or to prove their independence and boast of their self-credited wealth creation

---

[32] Wright, *Deuteronomy*, pp. 75–76.

(Deut. 8:17). Sabbath-breakers were behaving as verses 5–6 describe. Covenant curse was their destiny.

Conversely, those who chose to observe the sabbath and cease from their work and trade needed to trust God's ability to provide.[33] And as they did so, the whole of society would benefit from the regular rhythm of rest. They are those who trust in God and prove it in obedience. They fit the description of verses 7–8. Covenant blessing is their joy.

Jeremiah was passionate about the covenant, and he saw the sabbath as a key indicator. Like Isaiah, he recognized that submission to the sabbath was a mark of covenant acceptance,[34] and that it went along with the ending of oppression and active relief of poverty and hunger.[35] These sabbath passages are light years away from legalistic sabbatarianism. They speak of joyful submission to the liberating will and gift of the God who is creator and redeemer, worked out in actions that benefit the community (especially the needy), and challenge the destructive idolatry of mammon.

> The Sabbath, moreover, is a living reminder that life is more than economics, that the sum total of existence is greater than the accumulation of things, unbridled consumption, and feverish accomplishment. Work can cease and life will go on . . . The Sabbath says 'yes' to the sacred, to compassion, to human dignity, and to economic propriety. At the same time it says 'no' to self or national aggrandizement, the insidious need for more, exploitation, and frenzy for upward mobility. As such, it cultivates a just and fair society.[36]

Theological and expository reflections

- The chapter lends itself to exploring the biblical teaching on 'the heart'. The variety of heart-conditions needs careful pastoral discernment and application. When are we called to warn the hard-hearted, to encourage the faint-hearted, to comfort the broken-hearted?
- As often, the comparison between Jeremiah and Jesus stretches our thinking and challenges our faith and actions. How can we help people cope with the violence of Jeremiah's language in verse 18, understand it in the light of Old Testament teaching

---

[33] Cf. the combination of required trust and promised provision in relation to the sabbatical year in Lev. 25:20–22.

[34] Isa. 56:6–7.

[35] Isa. 58:6–14, note v. 13.

[36] Stulman, p. 180.

about the character of God, and yet move beyond it to the love and forgiveness that Jesus commanded and modelled?

- Reflection on the sabbath sermon reminds us that the test of our love for God is our love for our neighbour. The sabbath, like the law itself, was a gift of God's grace for human benefit. Let us avoid the rebuke of Jesus for turning it into a burden of human regulations for nobody's benefit.

Jeremiah 18:1 – 20:6
14. Pots and plots

Come and walk with Jeremiah in these chapters. Come and see how his obedience to God's word takes him from a potter's shop to a public beating, with a spot of pot smashing on the way, at the smouldering rubbish dump outside the city. And come with him also as the core of his message shifts from a final appeal for repentance (18:11) to the announcement of a shattering doom that cannot now be averted (19:11). And come with him to the peaks of rage and the depths of despair, as his prophetic journey moves towards its half-way point and from then on becomes one of increasing hostility, public humiliation and physical suffering.

1. The Potter who can change his plans (18:1–11)

God sends Jeremiah shopping again. Not this time to the tailor as in 13:1, but to the potter. His mission, however, was not to buy anything (yet), but simply to watch and wait for God's *message.*

a. What Jeremiah saw (3–4)

So we see Jeremiah as he greets the potter, sits down to watch and most probably asks the potter what he is making at that moment as he is *working at the wheel* (3).[1] The potter tells Jeremiah his plan for this lump of clay beneath his hands. Jeremiah goes on watching and waiting. Something happens. The clay is *marred* (4).[2] We are not told how or why. Perhaps there was a stone or a lump in the clay. Perhaps

---

[1] It was in fact 'two wheels', still used in traditional non-electrified potteries. The lower large circular stone was turned by the potter's foot, thus turning via a spindle the upper stone on which the potter worked the clay with his hands.
[2] Interestingly, the verb is the same as when Jeremiah's waistcloth was 'spoiled', after his last shopping trip (13:7).

it was too dry. Perhaps there was not enough for the original intent. Perhaps it just got badly misshapen. Whatever it was, clearly something is not right in the clay for the plan the potter had first declared. What will the potter do? Jeremiah watches and sees how the potter [lit.] 'changed/turned and made it into *another pot* according as seemed good in the eyes of the potter to do'. It may well be that Jeremiah saw this happening several times with different lumps of clay and different pots, as the potter laboured on through his daily order book.³ Perhaps Jeremiah asked questions each time as to why the potter had changed his mind about some lumps of clay and why the end product turned out differently from what the potter had first said he planned to make. A patient and obliging potter, we assume. I like to hope he was the one from whom Jeremiah actually bought and paid for a pot another day (19:1).⁴

What had Jeremiah seen? We need to be very careful at this point to avoid a simplistic or one-sided interpretation. On the one hand, he had seen a craftsman in complete control of his medium. The potter decides what he plans to do without seeking the clay's permission or opinion. And the end product is likewise whatever the potter finally decides. The image is a familiar one in other places in the Bible for the sovereignty of God. God plans and God accomplishes what God chooses to do.⁵ And this, indeed, is the initial message that God tells Jeremiah to tell the Israelites in verses 5–6.

However, on the other hand, Jeremiah had witnessed something very interesting in the relationship between potter and clay. While the potter remained in control, it was not entirely a one-sided affair. Sometimes there was something in the clay that caused the potter to change his original intention. True, the potter had the power to do what he chose with the clay. But the clay had the 'power' to cause the potter to change his plans. The final result was a mysterious combination of the sovereign will of the potter on the one hand and the condition of the clay on the other. Whether the first-announced plan was fulfilled seemed to depend not only on the words and hands of the potter, but to some extent also on the 'response' of the clay.

³ The opening verb of v. 4 is imperfect but without the 'waw consecutive', and so could be read as an 'iterative imperfect' – something that happens several times. E.g. 'Now and then a vessel he was making from the clay would be spoilt . . .' (REB); 'Whenever the object of clay which he was making turned out badly . . .' (NAB).

⁴ One imagines the gossip in the potters' quarter: 'First he comes in here and just sits all day, watching me and asking dumb questions and scaring away the customers. Then he goes away without buying so much as an egg-cup. Then he comes back later and buys a huge wine jar, the biggest I've made – and takes it to the rubbish dump and smashes it to bits! Weird or what?'

⁵ Isa. 45:9; Rom. 9:21.

211

And it is this second element of what Jeremiah saw happening in the potter's shop that provides the dominant message that will follow. For us as Bible readers there is an important lesson here in careful interpretation. The same basic source metaphor may be used with a range of different applications in different contexts.[6] So here, when we read that Jeremiah has a message about a potter, we should not jump to equate it with what Isaiah has to say using the same imagery in Isaiah 45:9. Isaiah's point is that it is ludicrous to imagine clay questioning or criticizing a potter's work, so Israel has no right to disagree with God's plan to use Cyrus as his agent of redemption; God is sovereign. Jeremiah's point is different. He is not so much focusing on the sovereign will of the *potter* (though that is assumed in v. 6), as on the 'responsibility' of the *clay*, and on *God's freedom to change his plans* according to what the 'clay' does.[7]

b. What God explained (11)

The message derived from the pottery class begins and ends with a direct address to Israel in general (6) and to Judah and Jerusalem specifically (11). In between come verses which outline a most remarkable theology of God's overarching rule in human history (7–10). They pick up language that Jeremiah had first heard at his call ('uproot', 'tear down', 'build', 'plant'; 1:10) and deploy it in a way that holds in balance (or in creative tension), the truth of verse 6 (that God is sovereign and people have as little ultimate control as clay in the hands of a potter) with the challenge of verse 11 (that when God declares a plan, he expects a response, which in turn has the potential to cause God to change plans and do something different).

Verses 7–10 present two simple and opposite scenarios that are put in the most general possible terms – *at any* unspecified *time*, and about any unspecified *nation or kingdom*. In other words, God is affirming a universal truth about the principles of his divine governance. And

[6] Another example is that of rock or stone. The dominant use of the imagery is that a rock is a secure, safe and dependable place (when used for God). But stone is also hard, and it can be used for the stubbornness of the human heart. Same source metaphor; different applications.

[7] If we need to be careful not to interpret a Bible text too quickly on the basis of a superficial similarity to another one, even more we should avoid interpreting it in the light of hymns or songs it may have generated. Many a sermon on this text has read into it the sentiments of an old hymn: 'Have thine own way, Lord! Have thine own way! / Thou art the Potter, I am the clay / Mold me and make me after thy will / While I am waiting, yielded and still' (Adelaide A. Pollard, 1862–1934). Such aspirations for submission to God's will in one's personal discipleship are very worthy and preachable. But they are not remotely what Jeremiah was talking about. Jeremiah was not talking about personal piety, but about God's international sovereignty in history.

it is this: God will respond to human response to God's declared plans, and God can change those plans for good or ill accordingly. Nothing is 'written in the stars' immutably. We have the capacity to avert God's threatened judgment through repentance; we have the capacity to forfeit God's promised blessing through evil and disobedience. It is not that God is changeable, but that God will consistently respond to *our* changeability. 'The divine potter can accept the once-rejected and reject the once-accepted.'[8] 'That readiness to change – not capricious but self-consistent – corresponds to God's own freedom to revise either his threats (7–8) or his promises (9–10). So every situation becomes an open one: every threat a challenge to repent and see it cancelled; every promise a call to persevere to its fulfilment.'[9]

The overall message is that while God remains sovereign over end results, he takes into full account the way people respond to what he says. The relationship is not one of absolute divine sovereignty of a deterministic nature, nor is it one in which there is no plan or control at all. God's sovereignty responds to human choices; human actions affect the way God implements God's plans. Or as Brueggemann puts it, returning to the target of our text, 'God is free and can respond and . . . Judah's obedience is of decisive importance. In light of both these affirmations, Judah is exhorted to choose carefully how it will act, for its future depends on its action. Yahweh's responsive sovereignty and Judah's determinative obedience are both constitutive of Judah's life.'[10] '*Responsive sovereignty*' is an excellent phrase to capture what is portrayed here.

So what does all this mean for Judah right now? asks Jeremiah. And God gives him the answer, straight from the potter's wheel, in verse 11.

The encounter with the potter, as Jeremiah had observed it, went like this (with a little imagination):

Plan A: 'I intend to make this clay into a wine jar.'
Response: Something in the clay runs counter to that plan.
Plan B: 'I've changed my mind; I will make it into a soup bowl.'

So now, says God to Judah: 'Look! I am preparing[11] a disaster for you and devising a plan against you. So turn from your evil ways,

---

[8] Stulman, p. 186.
[9] Kidner, p. 76.
[10] Brueggemann (1988), p. 161. Cf. also Moberly, *Prophecy and Discernment*, p. 51.
[11] The continuing connection with the potter analogy is sustained here, since the Hebrew verb translated *preparing*, is the same ($y\hat{o}\d{s}\bar{e}r$) as for the work of a potter. God explicitly casts himself as the divine Potter (as in Gen. 2:7 for the forming of the human being).

each one of you, and reform your ways and your actions.' In terms of the logic above this can be rendered:

Plan A:	'I intend to act in judgment against you.'
Response:	'Repent and change – you can counteract Plan A if you choose to.'
Implied Plan B:	'I can change the plan and suspend the judgment. You don't *have to* suffer Plan A, if only you will respond in repentance.'

That last line is not spoken here, but it is clearly implied by the logic of verses 7–10, and it had already been expressly urged upon Israel from the beginning of Jeremiah's ministry, most powerfully in 3:12 – 4:4, and in the temple sermon of 7:3–7 (where the language is very similar to 18:11). In other words, the prime message from the divine Potter is: 'Work with me here; respond to what I say. Change your ways, and I will change my plans.'

2. The people who would not change their plans (18:12–17)

Final offer meets final refusal. Such brazen defiance (12), coming after such an urgent appeal (11), is breathtaking. *They will reply* could be another iterative imperfect: 'They keep on saying . . .' This is the response Jeremiah has heard from the people ever since his earliest appeal (cf. 2:25), repeated yet again but ominously for the last time. *Nô'āš!* – which is the addict's cry, 'No way! It's no use. It's pointless talking to me. I can't change, won't change.'

This stubborn refusal to change (12), set in the context of the logic of verses 7–11, means that Israel has forfeited any chance of moving to the implied Plan B. By their own deliberate choice (or rather, by choosing *not* to make the choice that God urges upon them for their own good), they have left God with no choice but to carry out Plan A (judgment). The divine Potter has met no response in the clay that would cause him to change that plan, which the whole book so far has shown to be utterly justified and deserved.

For those who heard Jeremiah's living voice, God's message from the potter's shop comes to this:

'I offered you every chance to bring about a different future from the one that is staring you in the face. I have been patient and open, willing to adjust my plans to your choices, like a potter working with changeable clay. Even now for the last time I warn you of what lies ahead, and urge you to take the necessary steps to avert it. If you will not, then the full force of my judgment will fall upon you, as Jeremiah has predicted for years. But you will never be able to say I didn't warn you, or that there was no alternative. There was, and you refused it.'

For those who would read these words in exile, the message would be not only a painful reminder of how they had ended up in *that* 'future', when a different one had been possible; it was also a challenge to seek the Lord again, to return to him from the ashes of judgment and hope for a different future yet again, as Deuteronomy 30 had promised, and as Jeremiah will later write to those exiles (29:10–14).[12]

We will continue with our own plans. This defiant stance picks up the other main word that runs like a theme through this section – plans and plots (*maḥšĕbôt*). This word occurs in 18:11 (God's plan against Judah), 18:12 (Judah continuing with their own plans – which are here implied to be against God), 18:18 (the leaders' plots against Jeremiah), 18:23 (plots that included assassination), and 19:7 (the plans of Judah and Jerusalem, that God would ruin).

The two chapters thus reverberate with clashing plans. There is God's imminent plan, which was open to change. And there is Israel's stubborn plan, which they were utterly unwilling to change. Their plan was to silence Jeremiah, permanently if possible (18). But plotting against the prophet was effectively plotting against God. Israel's whole stance was a conspiracy of rejection of the word of God, whether in their scriptures or through his prophet. But in the end, only one plan would win, and it would not be Israel's (19:7). God's would be the only plan in town. A later day would bring a different plan (29:11, where the same word is used), but it could only come through and after the fires of judgment.

The shock of verse 12 throws Jeremiah back into the metaphoric world of nature to express the unnatural horror of Israel's betrayal of their relationship with God (13–17).[13] *The snow of Lebanon* never *vanishes from* [lit. 'never forsakes'] the upper mountain slopes,[14] with the result that streams fed from that source never *stop flowing*. That is something natural and reliable. How unnatural, then, how

---

[12] 'Exilic readers would learn about a God who had been remarkably open to futures other than the one that eventuated and would also hear a call to repentance in their own time and place' (Fretheim, pp. 273–274).

[13] Cf. 2:10–13; 2:21; 5:22–23; 8:7.

[14] Brueggeman comments that snow cannot, of course, 'forsake' the high mountain slopes without ceasing to exist as snow. It can only be snow in that place. Any other place is doom. Likewise for Israel, the only place it can truly be Israel is with YHWH. To forsake YHWH is thus as self-destructive for Israel as forsaking a mountaintop would be for snow (1988, p. 163). That is true, but probably strains the metaphor beyond the meaning that Jeremiah himself draws from it.

inexplicable, that *my people have forgotten me*. Forsaking and forgetting go together (cf. 19:4). They include abandoning *ancient paths* of scriptural teaching (15; 6:16; 8:8–9), but mainly they describe a betrayed and broken relationship. That is where the real pain lies. When a grieving lover says 'You've forgotten me', she is not talking about a lapse of memory. She means, 'All our shared lives and stories, our promises and joys, the whole journey we've made so far – all these things mean nothing to you any more. *I* mean nothing to you any more. You've dropped me and I'm broken.' There can be few things more desolate than being abandoned like that. That is the pain God feels. Those are the tears Jeremiah weeps for God.

The only future left will be the one Jeremiah has been predicting for years (16–17).

3. The prophet who changed his prayers (18:18–23)

The plots thicken. The people who reject God (12), now focus on attacking God's prophet (18). The specific mention of three official authorities (*the priest . . . the wise . . . the prophets*) indicates the powerful coalition that launched the lethal plots that were now being made to silence Jeremiah.

a. Let's attack him! (18)

It is important to feel the weight and seriousness of what is described here – particularly when we come to Jeremiah's blazing response (21–23). This was no polite theological disagreement or scholarly debate. This was a conspiracy at the highest level of the ruling religious establishment of the nation, plotting how to deal with 'the Jeremiah Problem'. Their plans included a campaign of inciting public rejection to all that he said (counter-propaganda), indicting him on legal charges of blasphemy and treason,[15] and finally assassination plots (23). Jeremiah will now endure for the rest of his ministry the kind of vicious opposition that confronted Jesus from the beginning of his. And it will come from the same combination of religious and political leaders.[16] It is a costly thing to speak the truth to those who do not wish to hear it, and whose authority and vested interests are threatened by it.

The trio of offices mentioned here[17] is interesting in several ways.

---

[15] *Attack him with our tongues* probably implies more than gossip and slander, since in v. 19 Jeremiah speaks of them as *accusers*, a legal term for adversaries in court.

[16] Mark 3:6.

[17] They are mentioned again as a trio in Ezek. 7:26. It was clearly a familiar triangular social hierarchy.

It shows where Old Testament Israelite society expected to hear the voice of authority within the theocratic framework of the state. Priests were those trained to know, handle and teach the law.[18] They also of course ran the massively important religio-political institution of the temple itself. *The wise* constituted a class of intellectuals and advisors, offering reflection and guidance on the problems of life and particularly employed as government advisors and consultants. *The prophets* seem also to have become a professional class of people whose job was to deliver words of divine assurance in response to questions and dilemmas (more about them in ch. 23). 'The triad . . . represents the power structure, the knowledge industry, and the religious authority of the establishment.'[19] Or as we might put it, the combined forces of the government, the academy and the media. What a frighteningly powerful coalition all ranged against a single man of God!

What *they said* in verse 18 could be taken in two possible ways. It may be fear. Those in power saw Jeremiah as a real threat (again, like Jesus). 'He is attacking the sacred traditions of our society and threatening our position of authority. He must be stopped.' Or it may be contemptuous. Compare the enormous weight of all those religious experts over against the loss of a single prophet who was probably an imposter anyway. 'If we silence him, one less prophet won't make any difference. Things will go on as before.' How wrong they were.

b. Don't forgive them! (19–23)

Against this background, then, of a state-sponsored campaign of life-threatening opposition, we come to yet another outpouring of Jeremiah's emotion to God.

It would be easy to gasp in disbelief at the raw fierceness of Jeremiah's prayer with its terrible climax in 23b, but we need to begin where Jeremiah does. For this was not at all how he had been praying up to this point (20). Already several times we have read that God had to tell Jeremiah to stop praying for the people, since they had sinned themselves beyond all appeal.[20] This assumes that Jeremiah had indeed been a faithful intercessor on their behalf (like Moses). In 17:16 he claims he had been like a shepherd, not in the least desiring the destruction of the flock. So now here he explicitly reminds God of his efforts to avert God's wrath: *I stood before you and spoke in their behalf to turn your wrath away from them.* It had

[18] Lev. 10:11; Deut. 33:10; 2 Chr. 19:8–11; Neh. 8:7–8; Hos. 4:1–9; Mal. 2:6–7.
[19] Brueggemann (1988), p. 164.
[20] 7:16; 11:14; 14:11.

217

been Jeremiah's lonely struggle in both directions – to speak to the people on behalf of God and to speak to God on behalf of the people. Neither task brought him joy or thanks. Fair enough, that's what a prophet expects.

But what seemed so utterly unfair was that *good should be repaid with evil* (20). And such evil! Had he not suffered enough already – rejection by his family, public mockery and social ostracism? On top of all that, now he hears that he is the target of a malignant campaign by the most powerful forces in the country. He was supposed to believe in the just God of 17:10. How could God allow the brutal injustice of 18:18? Was it not about time for God to arise and start 'rewarding people according to what their deeds deserve'?

And so Jeremiah swings around in his embattled anger. His desires are as confused as before. Earlier he swung from claiming that he had 'not desired the day of despair' (17:16), to demanding exactly that for his persecutors (17:18). Similarly now, this man who had prayed for his people to be spared the wrath of God now prays that his enemies should not be spared at all. One who *had* prayed that they *should* be forgiven (20b), *now* prays that they should *never be* (23). Perhaps nowhere do we see the humanity, vulnerability and honesty of Jeremiah than just here.[21] Perhaps if our reaction is to rebuke him for such wishes, we have never known or imagined what it would be like to endure the fear that the threats of verse 18 would hurl at him for the next twenty years.

The fate that Jeremiah wishes upon those who sought to destroy him (21–22) is partly drawn from the stereotypical language of cursing one's enemies. There were 'ready-made' stock curses, and they were often filled with hyperbole.[22] But Jeremiah's words also reflect the horrific truth of what actually happened in the bloody agonies of siege warfare – which Jeremiah foresaw already as coming upon Jerusalem. His words anticipate a gruesome historical reality.

It helps us theologically to come to terms with Jeremiah's prayer here if we take note that Jeremiah uses almost no words of his own in these verses. All that he asks to come upon his enemies is drawn from what God had already described in even more graphic detail.[23] What Jeremiah asks is that God's threatened judgment would fall

---

[21] 'His wound would have hurt less had he cared less and, paradoxically, prayed less for his people; but the violent swing from love to hate shows us how near the surface are the unruly instincts of the best of us' (Kidner, p. 78).

[22] The same kind of language is found in some of the psalms. Interestingly some of the psalmists similarly complain of how unfair it is that they were being attacked by people whom they had befriended, and indeed for whom they had prayed. E.g. Pss 35:4–6; 58:6–11; 109:9–11.

[23] E.g. 6:11–12; 9:20–21; 14:12; 15:2; 15:7–9.

upon those who were compounding their general sin of rejecting God with the specific *evil* of hounding God's prophet to death. Jeremiah so inhabits the mind of God that his human words and emotions echo those of God – *both* when he is crying out words of broken-hearted love and seeking to avert God's anger, *and* when he is praying for the fulfilment of what he had already prophesied about the outpouring of God's anger. Jeremiah is praying what he prophesied – and finding unrelieved pain in both. The tensions and contradictions in the heart of the prophet mirror those in the heart of God.

And yet, and yet ... When we have done all we can to read Jeremiah's prayer as *humanly* understandable, *historically* true to reality, and *theologically* integrated with the judgment of God, we are still left uncomfortably wondering if such language can be justified, embraced and even used by ourselves? Even if we allow that Jeremiah was not 'wrong' or 'sinful' to voice such a prayer (and there is no following rebuke by God, as in 15:19), could we ever imitate it and make such words our own? Can we pray what Jeremiah prayed?

I believe the answer has to be 'no'. But it is not a superficial negative, for, as I hinted above, those of us who have never suffered what verse 18 describes are in no position to criticize Christians in our world today who do endure such things (and worse) at the hands of the enemies of God, and who legitimately cry out to God to rescue them and exercise justice on their behalf against their oppressors. The Bible assures us that God hears the cries of those who suffer the hatred and violence of enemies.

But to pray that God should *not forgive their crimes*? That God should *not blot out their sins*? Can we ever pray that? Again, I say 'no'. Our exemplar, standing on this side of the cross and resurrection, has to be Jesus, not Jeremiah. For even when we make all the allowances above in understanding the context of Jeremiah's prayer, we will still find that 'the gulf between praying down famine on even the adversaries' children ... and praying forgiveness on one's tormentors, is the gulf between the resentful "lamb led to the slaughter" (as Jeremiah described himself, 11:19) and the uncomplaining Lamb of God (Isa. 53:7; 1 Pet. 2:22–24)'.[24]

We are bound by the explicit prohibition of both Jesus and Paul on hating and cursing our enemies.

> You have heard that it was said, 'Love your neighbour and hate your enemy.' But I tell you, love your enemies and pray for those who persecute you.[25]

[24] Kidner, p. 78.
[25] Matt. 5:43–44.

Bless those who persecute you; bless and do not curse . . . Do not take revenge, my dear friends, but leave room for God's wrath, for it is written: 'It is mine to avenge; I will repay,' says the Lord.

'If your enemy is hungry, feed him;
    if he is thirsty, give him something to drink.
In doing this, you will heap burning coals on his head.'

Do not be overcome by evil, but overcome evil with good.[26]

And above all we have the example of Jesus himself, who when his sufferings infinitely exceeded those of Jeremiah, yet prayed, 'Father forgive them'.[27] Given that Jesus knew Jeremiah's prophecies so well and was compared to him, it is possible that Jesus uttered these words in conscious replacement of Jeremiah's.[28] And if so, then Stephen learned the lesson well, for he uttered at the point of his martyrdom words that very similarly countermand those of Jeremiah in 18:23.[29] Luke has given us the double example of Jesus and Stephen to show us that in such circumstances they, not Jeremiah, should be our model.

4. The pot broken beyond repair (19:1–15)

The theme of pots and plots continues through this chapter. Jeremiah returns to the potters' quarter to buy a large *clay jar* that would have been used to carry water or wine. Perhaps he actually filled it before taking it as instructed to the site of his prophetic audio-visual display, since he may have poured out the contents while delivering verse 7 before smashing it to pieces in verse 10.

a. Rubbish heap (1–6)

The location was superbly appropriate; *the Valley of Ben Hinnom* was the city rubbish dump, and the road to it was littered with broken pottery – hence the name of the gate – *Potsherd Gate* ('potsherds' were fragments of broken clay pots and plates). Jeremiah pointedly took *some of the elders of the people and of the priests* to the place that would symbolize their own destiny (11–12) – the place

[26] Rom. 12:14, 19–21.
[27] Luke 23:34.
[28] And indeed, in sharp contrast to what is known of the way Jewish Maccabean martyrs had gone to their deaths calling down the judgment of God on their persecutors.
[29] Acts 7:60.

of brokenness, abandonment, and rotting death. How he persuaded such VIPs to accompany him there we can only speculate, since they represented the very people whom 18:18 has now shown to be his sworn enemies. It would not have been a convivial little procession outside the city walls.

Once the party has uncomfortably assembled amidst the rubbish, Jeremiah delivers the accusation, summarizing the message of the previous chapters. One additional detail, though, is the mention of child sacrifice (5), which was such an enormity that even God says he never imagined it. It was, of course, something known within the pagan religion of the Canaanites,[30] and for that reason Jeremiah uses a very strong word for what the Israelites have done. Verse 4 literally begins, 'for the reason that you have forsaken me and "made foreign" this place'. 'This place' was a hallowed way of speaking of Jerusalem and particularly the temple (7:3–7). But God says, 'You have Canaanized it. You have turned it into a foreign country. I am no longer at home here, not even welcome here.'

b. Wine jar (7–9)

The word for the large wine jar Jeremiah was holding was *baqbuq.* It was probably onomatopoeic – the sound of the word matching the sound of water or wine gurgling out of the narrow neck. And the word translated *'ruin'* in verse 7 is *bāqaq* – meaning 'to empty out, make void, nullify'. The wordplay (noted in the NIV footnote), suggests that as Jeremiah declared that God was about to 'empty' *the plans of Judah and Jerusalem,* he dramatically poured the whole contents of the jar out on the rubbish dump. And as he did so, he went on to describe what was going to happen to the city, in language which everybody would recognize as the terrible fate of cities under prolonged siege. With gruesome irony, people who could stoop to the extremity of sacrificing their own children (5), would be reduced to the extremity of eating them in the starvation of siege (9; something which the writer of Lam. 4:10 had seen with his own eyes).

c. Shattering (10–15)

If such appalling words made the people flinch with disgust, the grand finale of the drama must have startled them. With a sudden grand gesture Jeremiah raises the heavy jar and smashes it loudly into a thousand pieces on the ground (10), interpreting the meaning unmistakeably in the words that follow (11–13).

[30] Deut. 12:30–31.

The meaning of this single action was clear enough – *this nation and this city* would be *smashed* like the shattered wine jar that now lay among all the other piles of broken pottery outside the city in the valley beyond the 'Broken Pots Gate'. But when set along-side the pottery image of the previous chapter, there is an added dimension. As long as the people could be compared to clay in the Potter's hand, there was some hope of change. If they would repent, God would change Plan A to Plan B, taking away the threat of judgment. But they had refused all appeals to do so. They had become as hard in their stubbornness as a baked pot (18:12). 'If there is nothing so workable as a clay pot in the making, there is nothing so unalterable as the finished article. If it is wrong by then, that is that.'[31] And if a finished pot is smashed to the ground, it *cannot be repaired* (11).

The tragic message, then, that spans the trajectory running from 18:4 through 18:12 to 19:11, is this. 'You have made your last refusal. All hope of reshaping the clay has now been forfeited by this gener-ation. The shattering finale is upon you, and it is beyond repair (lit. "it cannot be healed").' And indeed, from this point on, Jeremiah offers no further appeal for repentance. The doom of the city is sealed, by their own intractable determination to reject every appeal they have ever heard from him or other prophets. 'This is the point of no return. This destruction is not for chastening or for discipline. There is no invitation to repent. It is not intended to "teach a lesson." There is no escape clause. The judgment is final, massive, decisive, unarguable.'[32]

Nothing now awaits Jeremiah's hearers but the stinking, corpse-filled rubbish heap of Topheth (11–12). But what about Jeremiah's *readers* – the exiles? What might await them? For them there could be hope beyond judgment, but it would depend on their response to the message of the book of the prophet they had rejected at such dreadful cost (29:10–14).

We should not overlook the sheer courage of Jeremiah's final action in this chapter (14–15). It was one thing to take his enemies to a public place outside the city for a message that would have enraged them. It was another thing to take the same message right into the den of lions that the temple had become as far as Jeremiah was concerned. That was the very HQ of all the forces ranged against him. To stand *in the court of the temple* and preach that it would be destroyed was asking for trouble (as Jesus found in the same place). And trouble, to put it mildly, is what he got.

[31] Kidner, p. 78.
[32] Brueggemann (1988), pp. 169–170.

5. The prophet beaten but not silenced (20:1–6)

The story that started in a potter's shop ends in a prison's stocks. Pashhur's action in having Jeremiah *beaten* (probably a fairly severe flogging) and *put in the stocks* for twenty-four hours (2), was not a matter of personal spite. Pashhur was *the official in charge of the temple of the LORD*.[33] As such, he was merely carrying out the official policy that had been declared at 18:18. If Jeremiah would not desist, he must be taught a lesson. Perhaps a flogging and a night in the stocks[34] might change his attitude. If that was the plan, it misfired badly.

You could shut Jeremiah in, but never shut him up. This brief indignity under Pashhur becomes the first of many physical assaults, in which Jeremiah proved that however much they might imprison him, they could not imprison the word of God from his mouth.

For Pashhur, however, it was a humiliating verbal turning of the tables. He himself would suffer the *terror* that the official whispering campaign was whipping up against Jeremiah (10). And worst of all, from his prestigious position in the most holy place in the land of Israel he would be cast out to die and be buried in the unclean land of Babylon (6).

For Babylon indeed it will be. Here, for the first time in the book, the 'foe from the north' is identified. The repetition of *Babylon*, and *all* in verse 4 and 5 makes the fate of Judah unmistakeably clear, both in its destiny and in its comprehensiveness.

Lies! The very last word of the whole section (6) brings it to a depressing close that sums up all that has gone before. It was in the very same place, the temple, that Jeremiah had dared to call the whole charade of Israel's worship, along with their official state ideology, identity and security, *lies* (7:3–8). It's the same word here: *šeqer* – deception, falsehood, illusion, lies. For generations Israel had lived under the delusion that covenant blessings could be enjoyed without covenant faithfulness, that YHWH was bound to prosper and protect those who claimed his name, no matter how they chose to behave in their social, economic, political, judicial and religious life. When you go on believing such lies, even after their falsehood is ruthlessly

---

[33] It is ironic (as Jeremiah notes) that the one who was in charge of the Lord's house should do violence against the Lord's prophet. Pashhur was attacking the envoy of the God he was supposed to be serving.

[34] It is not entirely clear what this punishment involved. It may have been a kind of pillory – intended for public humiliation, or (according to Kidner), some kind of twisting cage that would have caused increasing pain and cramps. Similar punishment was threatened against the prophet Micaiah by Ahab (1 Kgs 22:27), used against the prophet Hanani by Asa (2 Chr. 16:10), and recommended for all pestilential prophets by Shemaiah (Jer. 29:26).

223

pointed out, nothing is left but the crash when the lies implode and the truth rushes in to expose the vacuum of their hollowness.

Theological and expository reflections

It is hard, but sometimes necessary, to warn people that the time may come in the life of a person or a whole community that they have 'had their last chance'. Israel was sick beyond healing because they repeatedly rejected all God's calls to change. This speaks ominously to all cultures. Of course, no nation today stands in the same covenant relationship with God as Old Testament Israel, and no Christian preacher has the infallible authority of the words of the prophets that have been recorded in the inspired Scriptures. Nevertheless these things were 'written for our learning', and as warnings that apply more widely in principle.

Israel absorbed several toxic assumptions that dominated their cultural mindset and collective worldview. Some of their illusions are with us still and need to be exposed:

- that neglect of the poor, heartless oppression, and growing social and economic inequality, do not really matter, and life can go on as normal for the wealthy;
- that false gods that were thought to be the providers of all good things – fertility, health, wealth, business success – can be worshipped at any sacrifice (including the sacrifice of family and children);
- that national security depends on stacking up your military power and juggling your pack of cards in international diplomacy and alliances.

We live in a world where the Western cultures that still dominate the world's economics, politics and cultures are saturated with comparable toxic idolatrous assumptions. The decline and fall of Western empires and cultures, slow at first during the twentieth century, is accelerating, and the warning signs of imminent implosion are there for those who have eyes to see and ears to hear. The tragedy is that the grip of globalization is so strong and all-encompassing that the effects of cultural and economic collapse in one region affects the whole world. Indeed the result of our folly could eventually make some parts of the planet uninhabitable for millions of the world's poorest nations. At what point, one wonders, after God sends so many warnings, does the drama move from clay that can be moulded to produce a different future, to the hopelessness of a pot smashed beyond all repair?

Jeremiah 20:7–18
15. 'Perplexed but not in despair; persecuted but not abandoned'

The Apostle Paul uttered the words of our title in circumstances of crushing stress.[1] The same kind of stress led to Jeremiah's outburst in this, the last of his personal laments recorded in the book. For both Jeremiah and Paul there was the pain of rejection and desertion even by former close friends.[2] For both men the experience was like a sentence of death – feared or wished for.[3] Yet both of them managed to turn their struggles around towards renewed faith in God's power and protection.[4] For Jeremiah, however, such dogged faith did not eliminate the dark agony of the lonely burden he carried. What for Paul seems to have been a devastating crisis, was for Jeremiah a prolonged nightmare that blighted at least twenty years of his life with physical suffering, emotional trauma and social shame.

So who was to blame? Jeremiah was only too aware of the human targets of his complaint – he points them out with frightening detail in verse 10. But behind all human activity lies the mysteriously sovereign hand and watching eye of God (as he would have affirmed in line with Ps. 33:10–15). But knowing that God was somehow involved raised a far more disturbing train of thought.

1. 'It's all God's fault' (7–13)

Jeremiah had accused God of letting him down before, comparing God to the stream in a wadi that runs dry just when you most need it (15:18). Here he uses a breathtakingly blunt word for what he feels

[1] 2 Cor. 4:8–9.
[2] Jer. 20:10; 2 Tim. 1:15.
[3] Jer. 20:17; 2 Cor. 1:8–9.
[4] Jer. 20:11–13; 2 Cor. 1:9–10.

God has done to him and what he himself had let happen. *You tricked me, LORD, and I let myself be tricked.* The word (*pātâ*) is translated in a variety of ways – 'deceived, seduced, duped, made a fool of me' – are some options. It occurs elsewhere in contexts that imply enticing in a wrong or dangerous direction, often involving some kind of deception.[5] It can even denote sexual seduction amounting to rape.[6] We must be careful not to import all its possible meanings into this text, but clearly Jeremiah feels that all his suffering (human rejection and ostracism, ridicule and mockery [7], *insult and reproach* [8], along with actual physical violence [20:1–2]), amounts to having been in some way cheated or manipulated *by God himself*. A fearsome accusation.

It is hard to say exactly what Jeremiah means by this. Is it that he feels God had somehow lured him into being a prophet, only to discover that it meant a life of hostility and rejection? If so, he must be forgetting the fate of most of the prophets who went before him. Or is it that, although God had indeed warned him at his call that things would get tough and terrifying (1:17–19), he had no idea at the time just how tough and terrifying (20:1–3)? Or is it that he remembers that God had promised to protect and deliver him, but it seems such a long time coming that he angrily accuses God of failing to keep his promise? Or is it that he suddenly thinks that maybe God had indeed deceived him into being a *false* prophet, that his words would *never* come true and his enemies were right. Such a possibility would shred to pieces his whole identity and vocation. If that thought did cross his mind, it seems to have been quickly dispelled by his renewed affirmation of the truth of the word of God within him – a word he was powerless to silence (9). He feels trapped as well as tricked.

a. With God, you can't win (7–10)

For it was not merely that he felt he had been tricked; he also felt powerless to resist. It was an unequal contest: *you overpowered me and prevailed.* If you get into an arm-wrestling contest with God, who is going to win? Not me, moans Jeremiah.

There is a clever play on the word *prevail* in these verses. It occurs not only in verses 7, 10 and 11, but also comes as the very last word of verse 9, *I cannot.* The force of the repetition can be seen like this:[7]

---

[5] Judg. 14:15; 16:5; 1 Kgs 22:20; Prov. 1:10.
[6] Exod. 22:16.
[7] Following Allen, p. 222, who translates the verb *ykl* in this passage as 'to win' – i.e. to gain dominance or achieve some objective.

- *'You won'* (7): God's overpowering of Jeremiah.
- *I can't win'* (9): Jeremiah's inability to hold back the word of God, no matter what he suffers for speaking it.
- *'We will win'* (10): the nasty plans of Jeremiah's former friends, plotting to turn him over to the authorities.
- *'They won't win'* (11): Jeremiah's stubborn confidence that God will defend him and frustrate the plans of his enemies.

'I can't win', is exactly the ending of verse 9. For it expresses that sense of quandary, of hopelessness between two impossible alternatives. On the one hand, when he speaks the words God gives him, he is faced with violent rejection and opposition from human beings *all day long* (8).[8] But on the other hand, when he tries to get some relief from such daily trauma by deciding, *I will not mention his word or speak any more in his name,* he feels an accumulating agony of compulsion from God, like *a fire shut up in my bones.*

'I can't win!' Jeremiah cries. 'If I speak up, they burn me outside. If I keep quiet, God burns me inside.'

But in the end, it is God who wins, for Jeremiah has to speak. The divine compulsion is too strong. A prophet's gotta do what a prophet's gotta do.

If we still feel shocked and disapproving over Jeremiah's outburst against God in verse 7a, perhaps we need to tremble awhile with him in the fear and pain of verse 10. Perhaps we should read it in the light of the similar emotions of Psalm 31:9–13, and through the eyes of faithful believers in today's world who face similar terrors on every side. Jeremiah's life from this point on seems to be one of constant danger. He could expect any minute to be falsely accused, betrayed even by his friends, denounced to hostile political authorities, subjected to the revenge of his enemies. Is it at all surprising if his relationship with God oscillated between desperation and hope, between angry accusation and patient trust? His honesty in expressing both emotional and spiritual extremes with equal vigour is part of the measure and message of the man.

b. With God, you can't lose (11–13)

With astonishing resilience, Jeremiah's faith bounces back into action. Such sudden turns from complaining despair back to

---

[8] In v. 8, it is probable that *violence and destruction* are not, here, the content of the message that Jeremiah was *proclaiming* (though his messages were of course full of that kind of language), but rather describe the reaction he was getting from his audience. What the verse probably means is, 'Whenever I open my mouth, I have to cry for help: "Violence! Assault!".' The second half of the verse supports this reading.

reaffirmed confidence in God (11), trusting petition (12), and even call to *praise* (13), are characteristic of some psalms of lament. Such swings of mood are not (for the psalmists or for Jeremiah) a sign of emotional instability or some kind of bipolar disorder. Still less should they be considered evidence for a disordered text. Rather it is strong evidence for the robust nature of the faith and worship of Old Testament Israel and how mature they could be in relationship with God. Jeremiah knew that the highest form of praise was not just to say nice things to God or about God. Rather real praise meant to acknowledge the reality and presence of God in all situations and circumstances, no matter how fraught with contradiction. To go to God with your pain and protest, your anger and anxiety – and to give full vent to them before God's face – is also a form of praise. It might get you some gentle rebuke (15:19), but it could also get you renewed promise (15:20–21) and fresh faith for the hard road.

So in verse 11 Jeremiah reclaims the promise he first heard as a boy (1:8), and had recently heard again (15:20). If his enemies are bent on victory and revenge, they will find themselves up against a stronger foe than powerless Jeremiah. It is the Lord himself who will confront them as *a mighty warrior*. God will make them trip over themselves in their pursuit of Jeremiah (*stumble*) and fall into the shame that they had planned for him.

In verse 12 Jeremiah repeats almost verbatim the request that he had put before the divine Judge in 11:20 and expanded in Technicolor in 18:19–23.[9] We should recall not only the viciousness of the attacks he was suffering, which drew forth this plea for God to act in judgment, but also the correctness of his response in Old Testament terms. Even if Jeremiah could have wielded any kind of force to take revenge on his persecutors, such retaliation was forbidden.[10] He takes his case to the highest court and files it there. Let God vindicate his cause. Let the Judge of all the earth do right.

And having done so, he calls for a round of anticipatory applause for the protection he now expects (13; cf. Ps. 22:22–23). Jeremiah makes it personal: the call to sing and praise is in the plural, but *the needy* (i.e. the needy person) is singular and clearly means himself.

So who wins? Verse 10 is the pivot of the seesaw. The relentless attacks of his enemies make Jeremiah complain that God has won in the power struggle with his own prophet. Jeremiah can't win. He must speak (7–9). But if his enemies thought that they would win against this pestilential prophet of doom (10), then they were so wrong. For with God on Jeremiah's side (11–13), his enemies could

[9] See commentary there, ch. 14.
[10] Lev. 19:18; Deut. 32:35.

not win. And with God on his side, Jeremiah can't lose. Against God, he can't win. With God, he can't lose. Hallelujah! (as verse 13 actually says).

2. 'It's all the parents' fault' (14–18)

But Jeremiah's 'hallelujah' in verse 13 seems to die on his lips, or barely to squeeze itself out through gritted teeth. Verse 14 is such a shock immediately after verse 13 that some commentators think either that verses 14–18 come from a different time, or that verse 13 has got hopelessly misplaced by being inserted here from some more appropriate location. Even taking 20:7–18 as a whole (as I believe we should), we might like a more emotionally satisfying and 'theologically correct' order by keeping verse 13 to the end – light at the end of the tunnel, so to speak. But the text is as we have it. And its violent mood swing (from the depth of v. 7 to the height of v. 13 and then back to the depths in v. 14) is probably an accurate reflection of Jeremiah's thoughts and feelings.

According to Israelite law, cursing your father or mother was an offence that carried the death penalty.[11] Jeremiah just narrowly avoided doing both, in this climactic howl of protest at the misery his life had become. Instead, he pronounces a curse on the day his mother bore him (14) and a curse on the man who cheerfully told his father he'd arrived (15). How can we handle such stridently bitter language? Three perspectives will help:

First we can notice the similarity with Job's cry from the heart (Job 3). This kind of language is what emerges when you are thrown out on the rubbish dump of life, when all that makes life worth living has been wrenched away from you, and when even your friends treat you like an enemy. If we compare Jeremiah to Job, his language becomes more understandable. This is the voice of intense pain, not theological affirmation.[12] We should be careful, therefore, not to read too much theology out of it. 'Interpreters should be careful to assess what difference it makes that this is a lament and not a carefully crafted theological statement. What pray-ers say about God in their screams in the night they may not want integrated into a credal statement.'[13] The theology in Jeremiah's head is given voice in verses 11–13. The pain in Jeremiah's heart is given voice in verses 14–18. The marvel is that the scriptures let us hear both voices. For

[11] Exod. 21:17.
[12] 'What these curses convey, therefore, is a state of mind, not a prosaic plea. The heightened language is not there to be analysed: it is there to bowl us over' (Kidner, p. 81).
[13] Fretheim, p. 299.

in our own lives we often need both, when the truth we know in our heads faces the brutal assault of the emotions we feel in our hearts.

Secondly, Jeremiah is not so much making wishes as stating facts. That is, the verbs in his sentences are not strictly speaking wishes or commands, 'Cursed be . . .' or 'May he be cursed . . .', but simple indicatives, 'Cursed is . . .', 'He will be like . . . he will hear.' This makes a subtle difference to the meaning. Since the events he refers to now lie in the past, he could not, in a sense, directly curse the day or the persons involved. They are beyond the power of any effective cursing that he could do. Rather what he is saying is that, whereas most people regard their birthday as a day to celebrate, Jeremiah regards his as a day of mourning and regret. Since he wishes he had never been born (15:10), his birthday might as well be a cursed day in the calendar, not a blessed one.

As for the man who brought the news of Jeremiah's birth, there is dark irony in Jeremiah's words about him. The man thought he was a messenger of good news,[14] but if he had known what this newborn child would grow up to be, he would not have been so cheerful. As God's prophet, chosen before he was even formed in the womb, baby Jeremiah would become the man who would prophetically initiate the death throes of Judah. So, if that man is still alive, he will indeed experience all that verse 16 describes when Jerusalem is besieged and destroyed. Jeremiah is not so much wishing these things upon him as simply describing the things that will happen in the lifetime of the baby whose birth he announced. And perhaps, Jeremiah ponders in his morbid imagination, if the man had instead killed both mother and foetus, he might have been spared all that was going to happen. That, of course, is purely hypothetical and imaginary, for Jeremiah 'certainly could not have seriously consigned his father's friend to misery and death for not perpetrating a double murder!'[15]

Thirdly, we should be careful not to psychologize about Jeremiah's state of mind here. It is not that Jeremiah has sunk into a suicidal depression, or that he is wallowing in self-hatred, or in some kind of existential angst about the meaninglessness of his own existence. This is not a rejection of his own *life* itself, but an agonized struggle with his *vocation* as a prophet (since that was what he had been born to be, 1:5). He knew that the word of God within him was the truth that had to be spoken. But he railed against the fact that *it had to be him* stuck with the inescapable burden of delivering it. And so the

[14] The verb *bāśar* ('*brought . . . the news*') is always used of bringing *good* news, not just any message. It is the root of the 'evangel' words, through the LXX translation of its use in Ps. 96:1–3, and in Isa. 52:7.
[15] Kidner, p. 81.

climactic, screaming *why?* of verse 18 is not simply demanding, 'Why did I have to be born at all?', but rather, 'Why did I have to be the one born for *this* terrible task, born into the life of misery and shame it has condemned me to?' Once again we can see some similarity between Jeremiah and Moses. For when Moses faced life-threatening hostility in the midst of years of unrelenting stress from the mob that he dragged out of Egypt, he too complained to God about how unfairly he felt God was treating him, and he too concludes with the bitter, dark humour of a death wish, saying in effect, 'If you really love me, shoot me now'.[16]

More profoundly however than Job and Moses, we can compare and contrast the struggles of Jeremiah here with the experience of Jesus. The Servant of the Lord, in Isaiah 49:4, testifies that he went through rejection and apparent failure. But, like Jeremiah, the Servant entrusts his case to God and battles on. Of course, just as Jesus never called on God *not* to forgive his enemies as Jeremiah did, so we can be sure that Jesus never accused God of deceiving him and never cursed the day he was born. Nevertheless, we do know that Jesus' ministry brought him acute pain, suffering and rejection, exactly as Jeremiah 20:10 describes, and the Gospels record that it started long before the cross itself. We also know that Jesus wrestled personally and profoundly with the terrifying implications of his mission – in the wilderness after his baptism, and in the mysterious agony of Gethsemane. But whereas such wrestling led Jeremiah to words of accusation and rejection, it led Jesus to words of trust and submission to his Father and to forgiveness of his enemies. And whereas Jeremiah wished he'd never been born to live the life he did, Jesus knew that he had been born to give the life he had, as a sacrifice for us. For, in the greatest contrast of all, Jesus did not dream of losing his life in order to avoid his mission (like Jeremiah), but chose rather to lay down his life in order to fulfil God's mission.

Theological and expository reflections

We must think hard about how to handle Jeremiah's sense of being cheated or manipulated by God. Even if it is not the objective truth (God does not cheat or deceive), it is certainly a subjective feeling that many people have experienced. Jeremiah's words speak for many, including some, almost certainly, in any average congregation of Christians gathered for worship. If God was willing to allow Jeremiah's words to be in the Bible (though they are untrue about God, but true about how Jeremiah felt) – what does that say to our

[16] Num. 11:4–15; cf. ch. 14.

pastoral and preaching responsibility towards people who suffer so much that they have the same kind of thoughts – even if they would not express them in such outspoken words?

And we must also think about how to handle the extreme swings of this text, from accusation to trust, from agony to praise, from assurance of deliverance to rejection of life itself. Once again, we should be grateful that Scripture provides us with such extremes, for sometimes they do truly reflect the emotional and spiritual reality that many people experience in the pressures of life.

> The lament and the spirituality that produced it throb with pain and ambivalence. The prophet accuses and acclaims, celebrates and despairs, denounces and extols, doubts and hopes . . . Like his ancestor Jacob, Jeremiah strives with Yahweh and entrusts his problems to God all while God *is* his problem. Such understandings are complex, and reflect a piety that is comfortable with ambiguity and protest, as well as with public displays of grief. This piety, moreover, bears witness to a fresh understanding of misfortune: suffering and persecution are no longer associated with wrongdoing but with doing God's will. Jeremiah suffers *because* he has faithfully fulfilled his service to Yahweh.[17]

For that reason (the last line of that quotation), the whole book of Jeremiah is a robust exposure of the blatant falsehood of so much Prosperity Gospel teaching. According to such teaching, the rewards of faith and obedience are health, wealth and success. Sickness, poverty and failure are the result of lack of faith. On the contrary, Jeremiah suffers in ways beyond our imagining *precisely because* he persisted in trusting and obeying God.

[17] Stulman, p. 200.

Jeremiah 21:1 – 23:8
16. Kings: alive and dead and yet to be born

Jeremiah stood almost alone. The hierarchy of priests rejected him (20:1–3). The governments of successive kings resented him, eventually condemning him to rot in prison. And the professional class of special advisors to the kings (the prophets) taunted him as being completely out of step with their comfortable consensus. Prophets, priests and kings – a powerful coalition of state and religious authority. Here, in the central section of the book, we have an edited collection of sayings related to several kings of Judah (21:1 – 23:8), followed by a further collection attacking the false prophets that surrounded Jeremiah throughout his ministry (23:9–40).

This section includes reference to all the kings of Jeremiah's own lifetime. It has been carefully structured, not chronologically (it begins with the last king in Jerusalem), but theologically. For it opens with words of judgment and the threat of exile, but it closes with words of hope and the ending of exile (23:5–8). In between it lays bare the rottenness that permeated Judah's governments and made the exile inevitable.

1. If God be *against* us ... (21:1–10)

a. A refusal of hope to the government (1–7)

We jump into the story at the end, during the final invasion by *Nebuchadnezzar king of Babylon* that led to the siege and destruction of Jerusalem (21:2). The date of this encounter must therefore be around 588 BC in the final year of the ten-year reign of King Zedekiah. In the face of the menacing approach of this enemy (now named for the first time in the book), the government of King Zedekiah turns to the prophet who had been predicting his arrival for decades.

The bare-faced cynicism of their enquiry is evident in two ways. First, this *Pashhur*[1] hated Jeremiah so much that when he heard Jeremiah's response in 21:8–11 he successfully proposed that he be dumped in the stinking pit that was the royal prison at the time (38:1–6), expecting him to die there. So to ask the man whose words from God they so persistently ignored now to entreat that same God on their behalf was as crass as it was callous.

And secondly, consider how presumptuous is their appeal: *Perhaps the LORD will perform wonders for us as in times past* (2b). They want God to do just another miracle please. Something like the exodus or conquest would be nice. Or perhaps God could send that impressive angel again – the one that shredded Sennacherib's army in Isaiah's day.[2] It was precisely this kind of arrogant complacency (thinking God was at their beck and call, that God would always keep Jerusalem safe), that Jeremiah had attacked in his temple sermon in chapter 7. And those great traditions of Israel's history – the *wonders . . . as in times past* – were the very things that Israel had forgotten as they abandoned their covenant loyalty to the God who had done them (ch. 2). Having ignored them for centuries, it was a bit late to expect God to repeat them in the face of the judgment that they had brought upon themselves.

So Jeremiah responds with biting negatives (3–7). But he goes much further than simply saying, 'Sorry, chaps, no deal. Request denied'. He actually makes Nebuchadnezzar the least of their problems. Their real enemy is infinitely greater and more to be feared. Judah's enemy is the Lord God himself. And all the *weapons of war* that Zedekiah had accumulated to defend himself will be turned *against* himself, for they will be useless against God (4). The language of verse 5 is the way prophets customarily spoke about God fighting against his enemies. That's how Exodus spoke about the fate of Egypt. That's how Deuteronomy spoke about the destruction of Canaan. Tragically, now it was Israel in the same position. God's own people were now facing God as their enemy. *I myself will fight against you with an outstretched hand and mighty arm in furious anger and in great wrath.*

Nebuchadnezzar's armies, of course, would be the human agent of the destruction to follow (7). But the repeated '*I*' in verses 5, 6 and 7 (emphatic at the start of v. 5), leaves no doubt that it was the hand of God wielding the hammer of Nebuchadnezzar. This combination of human agency and divine will is fundamental to Jeremiah's theology of judgment – and also of hope (see commentary on 29:1–14).

---

[1] A different man from the priest who had Jeremiah flogged (20:1).
[2] 2 Kgs 19:35–36.

b. An offer of hope to the people (8–10)

So much for the cynical hopes of the government. They were uncere-
moniously dashed. But Jeremiah was a man of the ordinary people.
He had prayed for them, until told to stop. He had wept oceans of
tears for the fate that he saw coming upon them. Ever since the
implacable response to his message after his visit to the potter
(18:11–12), he no longer had any hope of a government-led national
repentance that might lead to the suspension of God's inevitable
judgment on the whole city and nation. The city would fall and
burn. The potter's plan is now irrevocable (notice how 21:10 echoes
18:11). But Jeremiah could at least help some of the people save their
own lives.

And so he delivers a piece of advice to *the people*. Ironically, he
clothes it in the same language as the great evangelistic appeal of
Deuteronomy 30 – the choice between *the way of life and the way
of death*. Most of his fellow-Israelites would have assumed that the
way they should hold fast to the Lord (Deut. 30:20) was by staying
in his city and trusting in his temple. Not at all, Jeremiah says. That
way now lies certain death *by the sword, famine or plague*. The safest
option is to leave the city and surrender *to the Babylonians!*

Earlier in the reign of Zedekiah, Jeremiah had urged this strategy
upon all the governments of the region (including Judah). He told
them that for the time being Nebuchadnezzar was actually acting for
God as 'my servant' (27:1–15). The government in Jerusalem had
refused that as a viable option. But the people in Jerusalem still had a
choice (this must have been before Nebuchadnezzar's siege locked
the city into a deadly embrace and sealed its doom). One wonders
how many individuals or families may have heeded Jeremiah's advice.

In a time of approaching war the last thing a government needs is
a voice urging people to surrender and make their peace with the
enemy. When war arrives, such voices can be ruthlessly silenced by
accusations of treason. Thus it was for Jeremiah who, from this point
on, suffered all the expected harassment meted out to perceived
traitors. Later passages in the book will describe his sufferings,[3] but
for the moment, we return to his struggle with the government.

2. The responsibilities of governments (21:11 – 22:9)

The sayings in this section may come from different times in
Jeremiah's long ministry, but by being combined and placed here
they gain significant power and relevance. There is some tension in

[3] See chs. 37 – 38 especially.

that some of the words imply an element of conditionality and hope (22:3–4), whereas others speak of a punishment that has now become irreversible because the conditions have been flagrantly flouted (21:13–14). Basically, what the text is saying (in its present location and as it would have been heard by the exiles), is that successive governments of Judah knew perfectly well the demands and standards to which God held them accountable. And if they had sought to honour those, they could have continued to prosper. But since generation after generation in the royal line of David had failed to do so, they must now meet their judgment.

The passage highlights the priorities that God holds before any government.

a. The ideals and their source (21:11–12a; 22:1–4)

What are the primary duties of governments? Some people today would agree with those who asked Samuel for a king and put military defence of the state at the top of the list.[4] But Jeremiah puts justice top of the list, and argues that if the state would concentrate on defending the rights of the needy, God would look after the defence of the nation.

It is remarkable how this emphasis on 'doing justice and defending the needy' (21:12a) as the chief role of government is found through-out the strata of the Old Testament. It features in the book of Psalms (far more than in any book of Christian hymns).[5] It is a repeated theme in Israel's Wisdom literature, which has at least some of its origins in advice for those in government.[6] It colours several narratives: David began this way, but departed from it in later life.[7] Tragically, Solomon followed suit. [8] Only a few notable kings are recorded as striving after this ideal – such as Jehoshaphat and Josiah.[9]

All of these expressions of the ideals of government have their roots in the soil of the Sinai covenant. For there, unmistakeably, the responsibilities of civil leadership are laid down – whether for judges[10] or for kings.[11] Those who are entrusted with social power are supposed to act and to speak on behalf of those who lack social power – especially those who lack natural protections, the landless,

---

[4] 1 Sam. 8:19–20.
[5] Pss 12; 58; 72; 82; 101.
[6] Prov. 14:31; 16:12–13; 17:5; 19:17; 21:1–3; 22:22–23; 25:4–5; 29:7; 31:1–9; Job 29.
[7] 2 Sam. 8:15; 15:3–4.
[8] 1 Kgs 3:7–11, 28; 10:9; 12:1–15.
[9] 2 Chr. 19; Jer. 22:15–16.
[10] Exod. 23:1–9; Deut. 16:18–20.
[11] Deut. 17:14–20.

the homeless, the family-less. The primary test of the moral legitimacy and credentials of any government is how it acts on behalf of the poorest and neediest in society.

Jeremiah's threat to the Davidic government in 21:12 and 22:5, and his conditional promise to them in 22:4, clearly prioritizes the ethical demands of the Sinai Covenant over any biological claims on the basis of descent from David. God's promise to the house of David had been explicit on this point. If he and his successors remained obedient to God, they would prosper. If they did not, then God would punish them.[12] That time had come. The ideals had hit the buffers of reality.

b. The realities and their cost (21:12b–14; 22:5–9)

The language of these verses is familiar by now. Jerusalem would be attacked and destroyed, in spite of its strong defensive position (21:13–14). It would be consumed by the fiery judgment of God. And all the flaunted wealth of the king in Jerusalem, which seemed as spectacular as the flourishing mountain forests of *Gilead* and *Lebanon* (from which the expensive woodwork of the palace and temple had come), would be reduced to smouldering rubble. All this would indeed come true.

However, Jeremiah concludes (22:8–9) with a glance at the wider international arena and quotes from Deuteronomy 29:24–28. Israel had never lived in vacuum-sealed isolation from the rest of the nations. What God had done for Israel in redemption had been visible and known.[13] What God would now do in judgment would likewise be a matter of international knowledge and wonder.[14] But if questions were asked, the answer was ready, and it comes directly out of the logic of the covenant itself. Indeed, the question and answer of 22:8–9 is a condensed summary of all the preaching of Jeremiah so far. The question is put in the mouths of foreign nations but if any of the exiles were still inclined to ask the same question, then the list of kings that immediately follows would remind them. It was the sin of successive evil governments that had caused the final downfall of the nation.

3. A catalogue of kings (22:10–30)

Having begun the section with an event from the reign of Zedekiah, the last king of Judah, our editors step back some twenty years to

[12] 2 Sam. 7:5–16.
[13] Exod. 15:13–16.
[14] See also Ezek. 36.

THE MESSAGE OF JEREMIAH

record oracles that Jeremiah spoke in relation to three kings who had reigned between the death of Josiah in 609 BC and the beginning of Zedekiah's reign in 597: Shallum (or Jehoahaz, his throne name), Jehoiakim and Jehoiachin. But since the first and last managed to reign only three months each, the spotlight of condemnation falls mainly on Jehoiakim, whose extravagant evils broke every line of 22:3.[15]

a. Jehoahaz [Shallum] (10–12)

In 609 BC Josiah was killed in battle at Megiddo, in a futile attempt to stop the Egyptian army from marching north to assist the Assyrians against the rising power of Babylon. Josiah was relatively young, and his death very unexpected. Jeremiah, who seems to have been so supportive of his reforms in his earlier years, joined in the outpouring of national mourning.[16]

This short oracle, however, says that the weeping is misdirected. People should *not weep for the dead king* [Josiah], but *rather, weep bitterly for him who is exiled* [Jehoahaz]. After Josiah's defeat, his son Jehoahaz took the throne. But Judah fell under the power of victorious Egypt for a while and Pharaoh Necho removed Jehoahaz and took him to Egypt after reigning a mere dozen weeks. He never returned to his native land and died in exile, as Jeremiah predicted.[17]

b. Jehoiakim (13–15a, 17–19)

And so we come to the king whose eleven-year reign[18] so defined the central portion of Jeremiah's ministry and threw him into almost constant conflict with government policies and actions. There was no love lost between the king and the prophet. The climactic moment of the king's violent contempt for Jeremiah is recorded in chapter 36, when he personally sliced and burned the scroll that contained two decades worth of the word of God through Jeremiah, even while it was being read to him. If that expressed what Jehoiakim thought of Jeremiah, these verses tell us what Jeremiah thought of his king.

What a catalogue of abuses Jeremiah hurls at Jehoiakim in accusation, headed by the dread word, *Woe!*, which combines a curse with a funeral dirge. The man is addressed as though already dead, which he virtually was in unrepented sin. The list includes:

[15] For more historical background, see the Introduction, pp. 20–21.
[16] 2 Chr. 35:23–25.
[17] 2 Kgs 23:29–35.
[18] From 609 to 598 BC; see 2 Kgs 23:26 – 24:6.

- Exploitation of workers by failing to pay fair wages (13). This basic injustice was prohibited in Deuteronomy 24:14–15 as something that rendered the offending employer 'guilty of sin'.
- Conspicuous affluence and consumption (14). Penthouse chambers (*spacious upper rooms*) on the roof with *large windows* were for luxury and display; *cedar* was the most expensive kind of wood; vermilion *red* dye was the most expensive and showy form of paint. It is not clear whether this was a new palace to replace the one that Solomon had spent thirteen years building,[19] or costly enhancements to that building. Either way, it was a vanity project, extremely insensitive when the early years of his reign were dominated by a heavy burden of tribute that had to be paid to Egypt.
- Fraud and greed (17a). *Your eyes and heart are set only on dishonest gain*, speaks both of the inner lusts fuelled by greed and the illegal means of satisfying them. Clearly Jehoiakim was not troubled by thoughts of social inequality as he gave more to himself and his wealthy class while adding to the burdens of the working poor.
- Bloodshed, violence and murder (17b). *Shedding innocent blood* is an evil that God warned judges and kings to avoid, yet it had become endemic in the history of Israel's ruling political class. The treatment of Naboth by Ahab and Jezebel is the most notorious example,[20] but the habit went back even to David and Solomon and reached systemic proportions under Manasseh.
- Oppression and extortion (17c). Probably the best description of how a whole corrupt system of oppressive government had been operating under the late monarchy is found in Ezekiel 22:6–12; words written from exile but describing the reality back in Jerusalem.

This is a picture of the abuse of governmental power and privilege that is all too familiar in the modern world too. And not just among notoriously corrupt regimes in the majority world. Western governments too have colluded in allowing (indeed rewarding) excessive greed and accumulation of phenomenal wealth by a tiny few, while the social and economic cost of their casino-banking disasters is disproportionately loaded onto the shoulders of the increasingly impoverished tax-paying population. Jeremiah's charges would stick in some very glossy high places today.

[19] 1 Kgs 7:1, taking nearly twice as long to build a palace for himself as it took to build a temple for the Lord.
[20] 1 Kgs 21.

Jeremiah's rejection of Jehoiakim is extended to universal rejection of him even in death (18–19; repeated at 36:30). The tragic portrayal of a death unmourned by anybody, a death no different from a dead donkey dumped on the city rubbish tip, is the ultimate insult to one who lived in ill-gotten luxury. The picture is more atmospheric than predictive, since in fact Jehoiakim was dragged off in chains to Babylon,[21] where presumably his death was as ignominiously unmourned as Jeremiah portrays.

c. Josiah (15b–16)

In the middle of his accusation against Jehoiakim, Jeremiah diverts to a scathing comparison with his godly and much-lamented father, Josiah. What Jeremiah says about Josiah is brief but profoundly challenging. I have commented on this elsewhere, in words that may appropriately be quoted here:

- He did righteousness and justice (which God delights in).
- He defended the poor and needy (whom God cares for).

And so, comments Jeremiah, 'It was good for him'. He was good. His reign was good. Things were good, under a king who put God's priorities above his own selfishness.

And then come the startling words at the end of verse 16: *'Is not this to know me?' saying of Yahweh* (my translation).

I find this a remarkable statement, and an infinitely challenging one. For in the midst of all our spiritualizing, pious, devotional, even mystical, verbosity over what 'knowing God' is all about, here is a stark four-word question (in Hebrew) that stands like a lighthouse on a rock in the middle of a tossing sea of words. We come wondering how to steer a course towards truly knowing God, and here we find a biblical, prophetic, inspired, luminous, *definition* of what knowing God is. Its simplicity and clarity defies all obfuscation. Doing righteousness and justice; defending the poor and needy – *that* is to know God. Where does this leave our limp evangelical pietism, or our suspicion of all forms of social engagement, or the rationalizations by which we excuse ourselves from the ideological and practical battlefields of economics and politics? We do not all have Josiah's calling into political authority. But if we wish to be among those who know God and are worthy of his verdict – 'good', then we had better share Josiah's commitment to social justice and action for the poor and needy.

[21] 2 Chr. 36:6.

. . .

We are told very little about Josiah's inner spiritual life, other than that he had come to seek the God of his father David early in life (2 Chron. 34:3) – possibly referring to a kind of personal conversion experience, in the wake of the whole generation of evil led by his grandfather Manasseh and his father Amon. But we *are* told about his intentional obedience to the law with its deep saturation with concern for the poor and needy, the marginalized and vulnerable – the widow, orphan and alien. As a result, Josiah goes down in the record as the only king of Israel in the whole Old Testament who gets an unsullied A+ on his ethical report card. This is the verdict of the historian (who was also imbued with the spirit of Deuteronomy).

> Neither before nor after Josiah was there a king like him who turned to the LORD as he did – with all his heart and with all his soul and with all his strength, in accordance with all the Law of Moses (2 Kgs. 23:25).

Josiah, in short, knew the Lord. And the proof was practical and ethical. And the affirmation that he did know the Lord, came not from his own boasting, but posthumously from God himself through his prophet Jeremiah.[22]

d. Interlude on Jerusalem (20–23)

You in this short oracle addresses the people of Jerusalem or Judah. It has probably been placed here because the phrase *all your shepherds* actually refers to the kings of Judah (cf. 23:1–7). *All your allies* (20, 22) is literally 'all your lovers'. Judah's constant changing of political allegiance during these tumultuous years is again portrayed as adulterous unfaithfulness to their true husband (as in ch. 2), which has persisted *from your youth* (3:24–25; 31:19; 32:30). Israel's history had been one long tale of refusal to listen or obey. But when the storm of God's anger breaks (22), it will blast away not only the kings of Israel but also all those unreliable allies they had placed their hopes in. Then kings like Jehoiakim who had lived in the luxury of *cedar buildings* (wood imported from *Lebanon*) will be exposed to shame and disgrace.

---

[22] Wright, *Knowing God the Father*, pp. 147–148. The New Testament similarly insists that knowing God involves obeying him in practical ways that include care for the needy. E.g. 1 John 2:3 (an astonishingly epistemological affirmation on the link between knowledge and obedience); 1 John 3:16–18.

e. Jehoiachin [Coniah] (24–30)

Jehoiakim died (or perhaps was murdered) as Nebuchadnezzar bore down upon Jerusalem in his punitive raid in 598. His son Coniah became king with the throne name Jehoiachin. Promptly (and wisely) he surrendered the city to Nebuchadnezzar. It bought time for the city but brought no joy to its king. Along with a contingent of 10,000 prominent people, Jehoiachin was taken into exile in the First Deportation of 597 BC (a deportation that included twenty-five-year-old Ezekiel).[23]

Jeremiah's words about Coniah split in two. Verses 24–27 clearly came in those short weeks after his accession to the throne but before he was taken off into captivity. It was hardly the kind of congratulatory speech he (and his mother) wanted to hear at his coronation. But it was abruptly fulfilled, as was the chilling prediction of verse 27.

Verses 28–30, however, probably come from the time when Jehoiachin was already in exile. It seems to pick up the bewilderment of the people, including the exiles. Was Jehoiachin *a despised, broken pot, an object no one wants?* No indeed. He was the rightful king of Judah in the line of David. *Why,* then, had he and his family been *hurled out, cast into a land they do not know?*[24] It was a question that the exiles could scarcely bear to answer. For if this 'why?' got the same answer as the earlier one (22:8–9), then could there be any hope for David's line, or for Israel itself? Verse 30 gives the implacable answer as far as the man himself was concerned. It does not mean that he would be literally *childless.* He did in fact have seven sons.[25] But he was without a royal heir. He was replaced in Jerusalem not by one of his sons but by his uncle Mattaniah, installed by Nebuchadnezzar and renamed Zedekiah. Zedekiah was the last king ever to sit on the throne in Jerusalem. As far as Jehoiachin was concerned, *none of his offspring* would ever *sit on the throne of David* ... until ... until one of his descendants, 'great David's greater Son' would come to reign in a way no son of David ever had before.[26] And that indeed is a prospect to which our text now directs our vision.

[23] 2 Kgs 24:1–17.
[24] The verbs are perfect, and probably the past tense is correct, rather than the future (NIV). The event had already happened, but the shock of it still raises the question 'why?'
[25] 1 Chr. 3:17–18.
[26] In Matthew's genealogy of Jesus, 'Jeconiah' (Matt. 1:12), is this Jehoiachin, otherwise known in our text as Coniah.

4. From bad shepherds to the Saviour King (23:1–8)

a. The failure of Israel's kings (1–4)

The clouds begin to lift. The dark era of evil kings will come to an end. And since they had been the ones primarily to blame for the catastrophe engulfing the people, that is good news. Of course, Jeremiah's words have been directed for years at the people as a whole. But he saw very clearly that in many ways the ordinary people of the land were the victims of corrupt, greedy and oppressive governments, led by 'shepherds' (kings) who cared little for those they ruled. In a subtle play on the word *pāqad* (to visit upon, attend to), God accuses the kings that they had not attended to the needs of the people, so he would attend to their punishment.

This dichotomy between the kings and the people is seen in the way the people are repeatedly described as 'mine' – *the sheep of my pasture* (cf. Ps. 100); *my people; my flock*. In spite of all the condemnation and the appalling judgment of exile, this people still belongs to God. The term *my people* occurs more than forty times in the book of Jeremiah (see especially 30 – 33).

There is hope also to be found in the sovereignty of God, which is at work behind the action of human beings – even wicked ones. Who was responsible for the Israelites being *scattered* and *driven* into exile? Verse 2 gives the human answer: the kings whose persistent rebellion (against God and against Nebuchadnezzar) had brought upon the nation the inevitable political and military consequences – invasion, siege, capture and exile. Verse 3, however, speaks boldly of the divine control of events, by referring to *all the countries where I have driven them.*[27] Here is a sudden shaft of light and hope: if God's hand was sovereign in judgment it could be sovereign also in restoration. And that is precisely the prospect that Jeremiah now holds out.

Sit with the exiles in Babylon and read these verses with them. Scattered and shattered because of the wicked follies of their kings, they are promised a future based on good governance and security. There would be a return to the land, and there would be more conscientious rulers. On the horizon of the Old Testament itself, the post-exilic era certainly included the first and some measure of the second (one thinks of Nehemiah and Ezra).

The language of verse 3, however, ripples out to a wider horizon that will be glimpsed only in the following verses. To *be fruitful* is the blessing of creation. And to *increase in number* is the blessing of Abraham. These creational and Abrahamic resonances are developed

---

[27] This is exactly the same double agency as we find in Jer. 29:1 and 4.

quite explicitly in 31:35–37 and 33:20–26. The exiles were being given hints of a vision beyond their imagining: the ending of exile, when it comes, would be a whole fresh start for God's plan and purpose for the world and for his people. So indeed it would be, but in ways they could not yet dream of.

b. The LORD our Righteousness (5–6)

God is full of surprises. Having declared that the present royal son of David (Jehoiachin) will never have an heir to the throne (22:30), God now declares the paradox that the ending of the line of human kings descended from David will not mean that God's promise to David himself would fail. At some unspecified future date God himself will *raise up to David a righteous Branch*. And *this* son of David will be the one who will combine a reign of righteousness and justice with the blessing of salvation. Jeremiah here follows Isaiah[28] and prepares the ground for Ezekiel[29] in prophesying a coming Davidic king who will exercise the kingship of God himself and will be the Saviour of his whole people.

The name given to this coming One is *YHWH ṣidkēnû*, 'The LORD our righteousness'.[30] This includes both dimensions of God's righteousness in Old Testament terms – doing justice and bringing salvation (5b–6a). YHWH is, as Isaiah definitively put it, 'a righteous God *and* a Saviour'.[31] It has this sense because when God acts in justice (as at the exodus), it has the effect of judging the oppressor and delivering the oppressed. Similarly, in a human court, when the judge exercises justice against the wrongdoer it has the effect of saving the one who is being wronged. It is this saving sense of the righteousness of God that prepares the way for its full exposition in relation to Jesus Christ in the New Testament, and explains the NIV's translation: *the LORD our Righteous Saviour*.

c. The significance of the end of exile (7–8)

These verses may seem to be unconnected to what has just gone before, but there is good reason why they have been repeated here

[28] Isa. 9:1–7; 11:1–9.

[29] Ezek. 34:22–31. Ezekiel 34 is a colourfully expanded meditation on Jer. 23:1–6.

[30] Ironically, the name that Nebuchadnezzar had given to the man he put on the throne in Jerusalem (whose given name was Mattaniah, Jehoiachin's uncle), was almost the same: Zedekiah means 'YHWH is righteousness'. Jeremiah prophesies that God will raise up a king in the line of David who will justifiably bear such a name.

[31] Isa. 45:21. It is important to read that verse *not* as meaning: 'A righteous God, *but nevertheless*, a Saviour' (as if God's salvation stood in contrast to his righteousness), but rather, 'A righteous God *and therefore* a Saviour'.

from their original location in 16:14–15. They put the promise of verses 1–6 into a wider and richer biblical horizon and draw out the full significance of what they prophesy.

What was the greatest act of God's redemption in Old Testament history? Answer: the exodus. It was the monumental proof of the saving power of the living God, and was appealed to by Israelites at any time they needed to invoke the name and power of God (7). But when God brings his people back from exile, it will be the beginning of something even greater, something that will ultimately redefine the very meaning and foundation of redemption. The end of exile will be a moment of redemption to celebrate, in a way that will transcend even the celebration of the exodus (not that the exodus would ever be displaced or forgotten).

But although the ending of exile would happen, on the Old Testament horizon, when the exiles of Judah would be released to return to their own land (as many of them did when Cyrus passed his decree in 538 BC), the *true* ending of exile would come only through the reign of the *righteous Branch* whom God would raise up to David. Only in him would there be lasting righteousness and salvation (6). And that extends the vista of our text to its New Testament horizon and sets it alongside the gospel announcement of the kingdom of God in the person of the One 'who as to his earthly life was a descendant of David, and who through the Spirit of holiness was appointed the Son of God in power by his resurrection from the dead: Jesus Christ our Lord'.[32]

Reading the whole of 23:5–8 together is important. It means that the arrival of this King, *the LORD our righteous Saviour* (5–6) would herald the true ending of exile (7–8). And *that* ending would then become the definitive act of redemption that will be celebrated afterwards forever just as they now celebrate the exodus. And this is indeed the way the New Testament interprets the coming of Christ, and 'the "exodus" he accomplished in Jerusalem' – as Elijah and Moses discussed with him on the Mount of Transfiguration.[33] It was exile ended.

What amazing biblical themes, then, Jeremiah 23:1–8 weaves into its tapestry of hope. What lies ahead, according to God's promise, is a renewal of the blessing of creation, a fulfilment of the promise to Abraham, a new exodus, and a truly righteous Son of David.

Let the exiles breathe again.

---

[32] Rom. 1:3–4. We shall reflect further on the different 'horizons' of prophetic texts when we come to the promises of hope in chs. 30 – 33.

[33] Luke 9:31, my translation. 'Exodus' is the Greek word Luke uses, translated in the NIV as 'his departure, which he was about to bring to fulfilment at Jerusalem'.

Theological and expository reflections

- There is a popular song that I have heard at full volume in Christian worship lately which takes its repeated refrain from Romans 8:31, 'If God is for us, who can be against us?'[34] It is a tremendously reassuring text and a great song! What would it mean, however, for us to recognize – as individuals or as churches – that there are ways of life, actions and behaviour, in which God is *not* for us, but '*against*' us (21:4–5)? 'And if our God's against us, then who can stand at all?' – those would be words we wouldn't want to sing quite so loud.

- Jeremiah highlights biblical standards for human governments. We might reflect on why it is that Christians tend to get far more vocal over the sexual agenda of secular culture than over the effects of government policy and legislation on the poor, marginalized and vulnerable. The Bible, of course, is clear in what it says on both, but more extensive on the latter.

- What does it mean to 'know God', if God says that Josiah provides the definition God approves (22:15–16)?

[34] Chris Tomlin, 'Our God is greater, our God is stronger', 2010.

Jeremiah 23:9–40
17. Prophets not on a mission from God

'Without justice a nation suffers, but without truth it sickens.'[1] Derek Kidner's pithy comment connects the theme of this section to the preceding one. Chapter 22 condemns the *political* leaders of Judah for their destructive greed and arrogance which had caused so much suffering among the poor and needy. Chapter 23:9–40 turns from the political class to the *religious* leaders who provided a convenient veneer of patriotic ideology that endorsed the status quo and raised no challenge to wickedness in high places. These were the prophets and priests who claimed to speak in the name of YHWH, but had no mission, message or mandate from God at all.

When religion is harnessed to provide justification for social evil and political folly, when the truth is suppressed or mocked, then indeed a kind of national and cultural sickness takes over. The great danger is that a sick culture feels perfectly normal to those living in it, oblivious to the signs of approaching culture death. That was the situation Jeremiah faced as he confronted the religious leaders of his own day.

This chapter is a sustained critique of what we now call 'false prophets' – though we need to remember that they did not wear lapel badges stating that identity! For the ordinary people it must have been very confusing (then as now) to have contradictory voices all claiming to be preaching 'what God says'. The criteria that Jeremiah sets out as his reasons for rejecting them should have rung alarm bells for those who knew the roots of their historical faith, the demands of the covenant, and the consistent message of earlier prophets. But, as today, the temptation to go along with the culture in believing what seems plausible (and convenient) will always

---

[1] Kidner, p. 91.

outweigh any willingness to listen and face up to the truth spoken by the courageous few.

In the text of Jeremiah 23:9–40 our editors have combined what may have been separate denunciations of these false religious leaders on different occasions into a composite diatribe – the most sustained of its kind in the Old Testament.[2] As before, we need to read these words not just as if listening to them for the first time when Jeremiah spoke them, but also through the ears of the exiles who were paying the cost of having listened to the false prophets rather than paying attention to the word of God through Jeremiah. In spite of that, it seems that even in exile they were still plagued by peddlers of false hopes (ch. 29).

1. Corrupt religious leaders exposed (23:9–12)

The opening phrase, *concerning the prophets*, is a heading for all the sections that follow, not the cause of the feelings Jeremiah immediately expresses. That is, the profound physical and emotional disturbance that Jeremiah goes through is linked to him being the spokesman for *the LORD and his holy words* (not just to his reaction to the false prophets). We have seen the evidence for this repeatedly throughout the book. Speaking God's truth cost Jeremiah dearly at every level of his humanity. By contrast (as he will say later), the other prophets thrived on popularity with their easy and pain-free messages.

Verses 10–11 are a terse summary of so much that Jeremiah has preached before. The sin of the nation is a form of spiritual adultery, and the effects of it can be felt even in the physical environment.[3] Meanwhile the religious leaders rush headlong down an evil course, using their power for wrong ends, and corrupting even the place where God was thought to be most present – *even in my temple*. The toxic combination of corrupt priests and prophets, serving together in the temple machinery that provided religious cover for social and political evil, has been the target of Jeremiah's rebuke several times already.[4] God's judgement is certain (12).

---

[2] There are similar passages condemning false prophets and corrupt priests in other prophetic books. It would be instructive (though doubtless depressing also) to read the following texts alongside our study of Jer. 23: Jer. 6:13–15; Isa. 28:7; Ezek. 13; Mic. 2:6–11; 3:5–12.

[3] The connection between the moral order of human society and the creational order of our physical environment is a strong theme in Jeremiah. Disorder in the first is reflected in disorder in the second. Cf. 3:2–3; 4:23–28; 9:10; 12:4, 10–11; 14:1–6. Conversely, restoration in the first will bring blessing in the second. Cf. 31:5, 12.

[4] E.g. 5:31; 6:13.

2. Leaders who reinforce the wicked (23:13–15)

Everybody knew what had happened to Samaria, capital of the northern kingdom of Israel. More than a century earlier it had been wiped off the map by the Assyrians. And everybody knew what had happened to Sodom and Gomorrah. They had been wiped off the face of the earth for their wickedness.[5] So to compare Jerusalem unfavourably with both, almost in the same breath, was both a stinging insult and also a stark warning of what lay ahead. Jerusalem faced the fate of Samaria and Sodom and for the same reason – unchecked wickedness. The very same double comparison would be developed with much greater lurid detail by the younger prophet Ezekiel among the exiles themselves, as he battled to explain to them the reason for the calamity that had befallen them.[6]

The sin of the northern prophets is described as a *repulsive thing* ('a disgusting thing', NRSV). It consisted of leading the people astray into the worship of Baal, which, as we read in Hosea, included ritualized sex in the fertility cults. The sin of the prophets in Jerusalem in Jeremiah's own day is described using a stronger word, *something horrible* ('a more shocking thing', NRSV). It consisted of the same spiritual *adultery* of the northern apostasy (going after other gods),[7] but was compounded by deceiving themselves and others – they *live a lie*, lit. 'walking in falsehood' (*šeqer*). Their whole way of life and behaviour is built upon a fabricated falsehood, a national self-deception, that all was well. This is the same message as we heard in the temple sermon in chapter 7. Truth can do nothing other than repeatedly expose lies and deceit. It's what prophets are for.

But what makes the accusation far worse is not just that these religious leaders were living in a cosy bubble of self-deception, but that they were dragging others into the same dangerous place. The accusation is deadly serious. *They strengthen the hands of evildoers so that none of them turn from their wickedness.* It is comparable to what Jesus said about sin against the Holy Spirit. When those whose job it should be to warn the wicked and call them to repentance, actually confirm them in their wrongdoing and their non-repentance, they put people into the greatest danger of all. For if you close the door on repentance, you close the only door to the grace of forgiveness. It is a warning to all pastors and preachers: be careful not to

[5] 2 Kgs 17:1–23; Gen. 18:16 – 19:28.
[6] Ezek. 16:44–52.
[7] It is possible, of course, that the *adultery* Jeremiah speaks of was also literal and physical. The allegation of sexual immorality among the religious leaders would tally with what was happening in the rest of society. The rot was as much at the centre as the periphery (v. 15b).

approve what the Bible condemns, or to be silent about the repentance that the Bible demands.

The Jerusalem prophets had effectively become chaplains to the
corrupt, greedy, oppressive and violent ruling elite – described in
chapter 22 (and in Ezek. 22 in greater detail). The national religion
had been co-opted into a tool of arrogant nationalism for the benefit
of the rich and powerful. Meanwhile, the needs of the poor and needy
went unheeded. It is a small step to the comprehensive condemnation
that Ezekiel poured out on Sodom, and by implication on Jerusalem
whom he described as even worse than Sodom or Samaria (Ezek.
16:49–52).

For such a lamentable state of affairs, who was most to blame?
Those who should have been speaking the truth in God's name, those
who called themselves prophets. Where today does this accusation
bite? Is it possible that in countries around the world today some of
those who are seen as leaders and spokespersons for the Christian
church, rather than being the salt and light that fight corruption and
dispel darkness, are themselves a source of *ungodliness* that has
spread throughout the land (15)?

3. Preachers of prosperity (23:16–17)

If the answer to the question just asked is, 'In some places, probably,
yes', then in the next two verses Jeremiah puts his finger on a major
reason why. It is far more attractive to be a preacher of peace and
prosperity than to confront people with *the stubbornness of their
hearts*.

There are two main accusations, one in each verse.

First (16), these prophets bring no word *from the mouth of the
LORD*. Rather, all their preaching and predicting comes *from their
own minds*. So whatever *hopes* they hold out to the people are *false*.
The people of Judah were being deceived with a totally spurious hope
of a rosy future ahead when the reality they faced was unspeakable
calamity. For the eager consumers of the outpourings of contemporary so-called Prosperity Gospel preachers, the scale of deception
is almost as great, even if the results are not so dramatic.

Second (17), there is a total contradiction between the lives and
actions of the people who consult these false prophets and the
messages that they hear from them. When people give evidence that
they *despise* God (by their lives or words or both), when they
persist in following *the stubbornness of their hearts*, then what
they ought to hear from any person claiming to be speaking from
the living God should be words of challenge and rebuke, coupled
with an appeal to turn back to God in repentance and obedience.

Far from any such confrontation, however, these false preachers merely confirm the ungodly and unrepentant in their lethal complacency, promising them peace and prosperity (*you will have peace – šālôm*) and immunity from pain (*no harm will come to you*). 'They are no longer the conscience of Israel, but are co-conspirators in evil.'[8]

4. No message, no mission, no mandate (23:18–22)

The camera angle swivels round from what these charlatans were saying to what they were hearing – or rather, to what they were *not* hearing. The 'bookends' of this section are the statements that they had never *stood in the council of the* LORD *to see or hear his word* (18a, 22a).[9] In verses 18–20, Jeremiah makes this accusation, and in verses 21–22 God repeats it.

'The council of the Lord' is a concept that calls to mind cabinet government. YHWH himself, of course, is the supreme ruler of creation and history, but he is surrounded by spiritual beings who do his will. It is the deliberation of this 'council' that Isaiah overhears in his temple vision, as they look for a suitable messenger and Isaiah volunteers his services (Isa. 6:1–8). So the idea is that prophets are privy to what goes on in God's government, and are thereby authorized and instructed to publish God's decisions, interpret God's mind and deliver God's messages.

But these false prophets had never been anywhere near such a place. Whatever they were *saying* had no relation to anything they had *heard* from God. And for that reason it had no similarity to the message of Jeremiah, who had heard more from God than he could bear. Verses 19–20a are probably the summarized content of *his word* in the preceding verse. It is as if we should put 19–20a in inverted commas as the substance of what the prophets *would have heard* if they had been there, and which Jeremiah *had heard* and had delivered so faithfully and at such cost. This makes the final line of verse 20b all the more poignant. The *days to come* had already come – on the exiles now languishing in Babylon. By then they would certainly realize that Jeremiah's word (19–20a) had been the truth, and that all the superficial optimism of the prosperity preachers was a tissue of lies.

And so God himself disowns these false prophets (21–22). God had not sent them, but they went anyway. God had not spoken to

---

[8] Stulman, p. 216.

[9] Derek Kidner makes the nice point that Jesus claimed to have both seen and heard all that goes on in the presence of God his Father, and thus to be fully authorized to speak on his behalf (John. 8:38, 40) (p. 92).

them, but they had plenty to say. This is probably a deliberate parody of the account of Jeremiah's call, when he was left in no doubt that he had to go where he was sent and say what he was told (1:7).

Notice that the proof that they had never stood in the council of the Lord is, once again, their cavalier attitude to sin (22). The test is not their claims to spiritual experience, but their moral behaviour.[10]Anybody who has truly encountered God and been sent by God, will seek to lead people away from evil. To claim to speak in God's name while leaving people unchallenged in *their evil ways* was as contradictory then as it still is today.

5. Dreams and delusions; hammer and fire (23:23–32)

At first sight the three rhetorical questions (23–24) may seem oddly unconnected. But we can see their relevance to the issue of religious deception in high places if we read them like this:

Question: *Am I only a God nearby, and not a God far away?*
Answer: No. God is not confined to being close at hand in the temple where he can be 'controlled' by priests and prophets who serve only the interests of the rich and powerful ruling establishment. YHWH is God with sufficient distance to be able to see and evaluate all that is going on in wider society.

Question: *Who can hide in secret places so that I cannot see them?*
Answer: Nobody. God cannot be blinded. Even the temple is not a secure hiding place, as Jeremiah had bluntly pointed out in 7:9–11. God has been watching all that goes on.

Question: *Do not I fill heaven and earth?*
Answer: Yes indeed. So with such an omnipresent God, all the deceptions of the false prophets, and the evils

[10] Some commentators complain that Jeremiah's accusation (that the other prophets had not stood in the council of God) could not be proved or disproved, for it was purely subjective and spiritual. It was a useless criterion. But v. 22 makes the criterion crystal clear and it is fundamentally moral. 'The trouble with the prophets whom Jeremiah denounces is that the character of their conduct and message shows all too clearly that what they say is self-willed and people-pleasing and does not convey the will of YHWH' (Moberly, *Prophecy and Discernment*, p. 81). Moberly points out that when Abraham and Moses stood in the presence of God, the result was clear and specific moral teaching for God's people (Gen. 18:17–19; Deut. 5:23–32).

perpetrated by those for whom they provided
religious support, will be exposed and judged.
There is nowhere they can escape.[11]

How terrifying, then, when this all-seeing God, confronts the
prophets as their triple enemy (*I am against . . . I am against . . . I am
against . . .* ; 30, 31, 32).
The focal point of the accusation in this section is the favoured
method by which the false preachers proclaim the source of their
'inspiration'. *They say, 'I had a dream! I had a dream!'* (25). One
can imagine them calling this out to the gathering crowds of impres-
sionable people, who were eager to hear what exciting new revelation
might be in store. Popular preachers know how to manipulate their
audiences with whatever mystical technique has the most convening
and convincing power.
The problem here was not the method in itself. Dreams were not
in themselves to be rejected as a way that God could speak. On the
contrary, the Bible clearly shows that God can and does speak to
people through dreams, and did so on some highly significant
occasions in both Testaments. So neither God nor Jeremiah is protesting against the whole idea of claiming to have heard God's word
in a dream, but rather against the lies and deceit that these people
were then peddling under the guise of their alleged dreams. That is
the emphasis throughout. Notice: *prophesy lies* (25); *lying prophets*
(26); *delusions of their own minds* (26); *false dreams . . . their reckless
lies* (32). The issue is the *content* of their message, not the *means*
by which they claimed to have received it. And that content was
fundamentally deceitful and ultimately destructive.
It is bad enough to ignore the word of God. It is far worse to
distort it, or to claim its authority while undermining its truth, or
to quote it accurately but in such a way as to effectively deny it. All
of these things still happen today, in church pulpits and university
classrooms. And if anything is worse than rubbish claiming to be
truth it is second-hand rubbish. These false prophets lack not only
integrity but also originality. They *steal from one another words
supposedly from me* (30). Actually, the Hebrew reads, 'who steal my

---

[11] The fact that the world is 'filled with God', so to speak, is here a matter of fear,
for there is nowhere for evildoers to escape from his presence. But generally in the
Old Testament, the fact that God fills the entire universe is a matter of amazement,
gratitude and security. The love of God fills the whole earth (Pss 33:5; 119:64), as does
the glory of God (Isa. 6:3; Hab. 3:3). Such thoughts were a great comfort to the
composer of Ps. 139. 'The claim that God "fills heaven and earth" is a claim that God's
relationship with the world is comprehensive in its scope. God is a part of the map
of reality ... wherever there is world, there is God' (Fretheim, p. 342).

words from one another'. That is, even if from time to time one of them spoke a word that actually did come from God, it got syndicated and cloned by the whole gang. They were not delivering words personally received from God by standing in his council, but peddling words stolen from one another.

All such false teaching stands in complete contrast to the genuine word of God spoken with integrity. The metaphors are vigorous and unmistakeable in their meaning. False teaching is *straw*; God's word is *grain* – nourishing. False teaching soothes the complacent; God's word is *like fire . . . and like a hammer* (28–29).

In the final verdict (32), all these popular preachers with their deceptive messages are rejected on three counts: (1) they lead people astray; (2) they have not been sent or appointed by God; and (3) *they do not benefit these people in the least*. The same charge, for the same three reasons, must be brought against false teachers in the contemporary church, including the purveyors of the Prosperity Gospel.

6. Who is the real burden? (23:33–40)

The main point of the chapter has been made and the verdict delivered. This final section is a somewhat odd appendix, with some teasing play on the Hebrew word *maśśā'*. It can mean literally something that is lifted up and carried – a burden. But it can also mean an oracle – a message given by God that is a burden to be carried and delivered. (We still sometimes speak of a preacher being 'burdened' with the message God has given them to preach).

So how one reads the whole passage depends on whether one emphasizes the meaning *message* (which is what people were asking for – a message from God), or the pun on the meaning 'burden'. The NIV sticks with *message* throughout, but several other translations capture the probable pun in verse 33. The NRSV, for example, has: '*When this people, or a prophet, or a priest asks you, "What is the burden of the LORD?" you shall say to them, "You are the burden, and I will cast you off, says the LORD."*'

The basic point of the passage seems to be that God is wearied by people asking the prophets for a message from God, when they have never listened to anything he has said to them for generations. Furthermore, all the prophetic messages that are being delivered are nothing more than the fabrications of every individual's imagination (36). Verse 36, in fact, is a brilliantly succinct definition of what we have come to know as individualistic relativism: (lit.) 'the message becomes every man's own word'. Everybody treats their personal opinion as if it were a message from God. But in the process we *distort the words of the living God, the LORD Almighty, our God* (36).

That triple description of God is emphatic and shows the fatuous stupidity of such a futile exchange – one man's private opinion as against the revelation of the Creator of all humanity and the covenant God of his people. Yet that is precisely the exchange that multitudes in our cultures (including some Christians) seem happy to make. It is worth asking whether we give more time and attention to blogs and comments, and comments on the comments on the blogs, than to studying the Bible.

Theological and expository reflections

There seem to be three fundamental accusations against such false preachers and teachers, all of which deserve serious reflection and application today. Elsewhere I summarized them (from Jeremiah and other prophets) as follows:[12]

Lack of personal moral integrity

The lives of these people who claimed so much were actually sensual and ill-disciplined. By the standards of God's law they were not even good Israelites, let alone good prophets. For example, they were guilty of:

- *Drunkenness* (Isa. 28:7; cf. Mic. 2:11).
- *Sexual immorality* (Jer. 23:14). They made public pronouncements, but lived in private sin.
- *Greed* (Mic. 3:11; cf. Jer. 6:13). They were prepared to sell their clever words to the highest bidder. They claimed to have the word of God, and yet they had no shame in offering to 'sell' it, like street-vendors, or prostitutes.

So they lacked personal moral integrity. How then could they dare to speak on behalf of the God of all truth and integrity? How could they live in immorality and dare to represent the Holy One of Israel? How could they live in grasping greed, and have any contact with the heart of the God who cared for the poor and needy?

'By their fruit you will recognise them', said Jesus.[13] We also need to be watchful and discerning regarding those who claim to have, or are paraded as having, great 'prophetic ministries'. We are right to enquire whether there is personal moral integrity along with the great public persona. We are right to be suspicious if there are hints

[12] The paragraphs that follow are an abbreviated extract from Wright, *Knowing the Holy Spirit*, pp. 66–75.
[13] Matt. 7:16.

of questionable behaviour, the whiff of fraud or corruption, or evidence of a greedy, opulent life-style. The Holy Spirit is not at all honoured by, or even present in, those who use his name to feed their own lusts or line their own pockets.

Lack of public moral courage

These prophets caught the mood of the public at any given time, and then simply reflected it, echoing it back to willing listeners who were only too pleased to have their opinions endorsed by apparent spokesmen for the Almighty. They never challenged or rebuked that public mood, or that dominant social consensus, even when it was clearly in breach of the known laws and will of God.

We too live in a society that turns moral values upside down. Certainly that is true of contemporary Western society. It has become a society where basic human goodness is mocked, and God's standards for family and community life are attacked and vilified. It is a society where all kinds of practice that is contrary to God's best will for human life and human relationship is advocated and encouraged. It is a society that manages to live in obscene wealth and luxury while fully conscious of the poverty and suffering of the majority of the human race. It is a society in bondage to massive public idolatries to the false gods of mammon (consumerism), military hopes for security, and national pride.

Lack of any prophetic mandate from God

There is a gaping credibility gap in relation to these prophets, between the claims and the truth, between the charade and the reality. They claim to have come from God, but God has never seen them in his presence. They announce that they speak in God's name, but God has never sent them. They wear the prophetic mantle, but they have no prophetic mandate (Jer. 23:18, 21–22; Ezek. 13:6–7).

We should remember the sobering warning of Jesus that not all who claim his name are what they seem.

> Not everyone who says to me, 'Lord, Lord', will enter the kingdom of heaven, but only the one who does the will of my Father who is in heaven. Many will say to me on that day, 'Lord, Lord, did we not prophesy in your name, and in your name drive out demons and perform many miracles?' Then I will tell them plainly, 'I never knew you. Away from me, you evildoers![14]

[14] Matt. 7:21–23.

I find this one of the most sobering, even frightening, parts of the Bible.

- Jesus says, it is possible to have a great prophetic ministry, so-called, ostensibly in the name of Christ, and yet not belong to the kingdom of God.
- Jesus says, it is possible to have a great deliverance ministry, and yet not be owned by Jesus.
- Jesus says, it is possible to do great miracles, and yet not be doing the will of our Father in heaven.
- Jesus says, it is possible to claim to be doing ministry in the name of Jesus, and yet to be disowned and dismissed by him as an evildoer.

What does this call for? It means we simply must be discerning about all ministry claims, and the alleged statistics that so often go along with them. We should ask: Where is the fruit? Where are the changed lives? Where is the evidence of the work of the *Holy* Spirit? Where are the people who are now more like Jesus, more committed to the love, compassion, justice and integrity of God and God's kingdom? And of course, it means that we must also be ruthlessly honest with our own motives and ambitions in ministry. There is a rather old-fashioned saying that talks about someone being 'mightily used by God for his glory'. Well, it can be wonderfully true. But there are times when I look at some great and prominent people for whom this claim is made, and I wonder just who is being used by whom – and for whose glory.

Jeremiah 24:1 – 25:38
18. The good, the bad, and the ugly

'Consider the kindness and sternness of God,'[1] said Paul, when he contemplated the mysterious way that God's judgment on some of his fellow-Jews had opened the door to Gentiles coming to taste the saving mercy of God. No two chapters of the Old Testament could better capture both words than Jeremiah 24 and 25. The first speaks words of the most amazing and unexpected grace while the second speaks words of appalling and inescapable judgment. We must marvel at one and shudder at the other, and somehow wrestle with the task of holding both together in our understanding of the biblical text and (more importantly) in our understanding of the living God who speaks through it.

Each of the chapters from 24 to 29 begins with a date. These chapters give us glimpses of the life and struggles of Jeremiah during the pivotal years in Jerusalem that began in 605 BC, when Nebuchadnezzar established the power of Babylon over the whole region, and lasted until the fall of Jerusalem in 587. It is the period that includes the reigns of Jehoiakim, Jehoiachin and Zedekiah. All three kings feature in these five chapters. The chapters have not been arranged chronologically however. Rather, they begin (in ch. 24) and end (in ch. 29) with words of encouragement for the exiles, written at the time of the First Deportation in 597 BC. This reminds us that we need to read the whole book of Jeremiah from the perspective not only of those who first heard the living voice of Jeremiah in Jerusalem, but also of those who read the scroll later in exile, after Jeremiah's prophecies had come true.

God chooses to 'have regard for the exiles for good' (24:5), and tells them that he has 'plans' to give them a hope and a future (29:11). Sandwiched in between those two poles of future hope, however,

---

[1] Rom. 11:22.

are messages that describe the horrors of the judgment that was about to engulf the people and indeed all nations. The section (24 – 29) thus functions both to summarize all that the book of Jeremiah has said so far and also to prepare for the immediately following section (30 – 33) in which we are at last able to rejoice with relief that there is hope beyond judgment – hope that rests in God alone.

1. God's grace creates a future (24:1–10)

The year was 597 BC. The new king, eighteen year-old Jehoiachin (otherwise known as Coniah, or in the Hebrew here as Jeconiah), was facing the advancing Babylonian army, intent on quelling a rebellion that had been started by his late (possibly murdered) father Jehoiakim. Read the story in 2 Kings 24. Nebuchadnezzar besieged Jerusalem. Jehoiachin, either in a fit of panic, or in a flash of wisdom uncharacteristic of his royal line, surrendered the city to the invader. By doing so, he saved his life and his city – the first for the rest of his days (in Babylonian exile), but the second only for another ten years till his uncle Zedekiah reverted to the catastrophic folly that led to Jerusalem's final destruction in 587 BC.

Nebuchadnezzar was not going to be placated by a mere surrender, however. He was in a punishing mood. So although he spared the city, he imposed a very heavy fine (the treasures and gold of the temple), and impounded some very high profile hostages (the king and royal family, the bulk of Judah's armed forces, and the skilled work force). Ten thousand of the elite citizens of Judah went into exile in Babylon. Ezekiel and his young wife were among them. Five years later at the age of thirty, God would call him to be his prophet among the exiles, while Jeremiah was still suffering for God's word in Jerusalem. The First Deportation had begun.

And it was a disaster. Or was it?

Confusion reigned in Jerusalem in the immediate aftermath of Nebuchadnzzar's punitive raid and deportation in 597. How should it be interpreted? What would happen next?

Some people thought they had a simple answer: it was nothing but a short sharp shock, a slap on the wrist by Nebuchadnezzar (and God?), and so it would soon be all over. The king and the exiles would return and all the stolen treasures of the temple would be put back in place. That was the popular (and prophetic) optimism (see ch. 28).

But another way of interpreting events must have seemed even more plausible. Jeremiah had been predicting an act of God's judgment for years. At last it had indeed happened – 'foe from the North' and all. And although it was rather tough on the king and the rest of those taken hostage, it was surely not as bad as Jeremiah had made it sound (they had no inkling yet of the horrors to come in 587). No blood had been shed (yet). The city and the temple were still standing – defended by God as they always had been. The people left behind in Judah could carry on under God's protection. The ones who had been carted off into exile were the leader class. They were the ones most to blame for the nation's woes (as Jeremiah kept saying). They were the ones God had now tossed out onto the rubbish heap of history in exile. Let them rot there. They had no further inheritance in the land. Indeed, God had judged them by ejecting them out of the land. It would be the ones God had spared – God's people in God's land – who would inherit the future.

Did Jeremiah share this view? It would be understandable if he had. Had God decided to be merciful and to spare the people the worst of all that Jeremiah had foreseen? But if such a thought crossed the prophet's mind, God quickly banished it in chapter 24. The future was far more bleak for those left behind, and far more hopeful for those now in exile, than either of them could ever have imagined in 597.

The LORD showed me two baskets of figs placed in front of the temple of the LORD. This may have been in a vision, but of course it is also perfectly possible that Jeremiah simply spotted something – a basket of good figs fit for selling, and a basket of rotten ones on its way to the rubbish dump. God asks Jeremiah what he is looking at (as in 1:11). Jeremiah replies with the simple facts, and God provides a prophetic meaning to the visual metaphor.

And the message turns the popular assumptions upside down. If the people thought that those who had been carried off to exile were the ones who were headed for extinction like rotten fruit, while those who remained were in for a happier future, they were dead wrong. Once again Jeremiah's God shakes the certainties and shocks the secure. The basket of good figs represents – the exiles!

Verses 5–7 are astonishing – not merely as a contradiction of popular assumption, but as an affirmation of God's sovereign grace. God simply chooses, without any supporting reasons (for there were none at a human level), to regard the exiles *like these good figs*. Most English translations of verse 5 could lead to a misunderstanding however. Most of them read that God intends to *regard as good the exiles from Judah*. This may sound as though God has changed his earlier condemnation into moral approval; as though God now regards them as good and so deserving of a better future. But the Hebrew is more subtle than that and leaves no room for imagining that the exiles had passed from condemnation to commendation. Literally it says: 'Like these good figs, thus will I regard the exiles of Judah, whom I sent away from this place to the land of Babylon, *for good.*' In other words, it is not the exiles who have suddenly become good, but God's intentions for them that are, surprisingly, 'for good'.[2]

Sovereign grace is the essence of this vision.

God's sovereignty is clear in the way every verb in Jeremiah 24:5–7 has God as its subject, except for what the people must do (*they will return to me*). God himself will act in restoration and renewal of the covenant: *I will ... I will ... I will ... I will.* Even Nebuchadnezzar's punitive raid and cruel deportation is presented as a missional act of God (*the exiles ... whom I sent away*).[3] So if God was sovereign over the beginning of exile, he remained sovereign over its long-term outcome. God would continue his purpose for Israel and the world through those he had 'sent' in to exile.

[The exiles'] goodness does not rest in themselves, but in the sovereign assertions of Yahweh, who announces them to be good (cf. Deut. 9:6). The freedom of Yahweh in making such a dramatic assertion parallels that of Gen. 15:6, in which Yahweh 'reckons' Abraham to be righteous. This is one of the most stunning theological claims in Jeremiah. The community in exile is the wave of God's future ... this God is now allied, by free choice, precisely with the community that the world thought had been rejected. It is indeed an act of free grace which creates a quite new historical possibility.[4]

God's grace is clear in two ways. First, who is it that God chooses to 'regard for good'? These are the people whom Jeremiah had condemned unremittingly for chapter after chapter, year after year. There is no hope inherent in the moral capacity of these people themselves. Even in exile we will find that Ezekiel battles against almost unbelievable hostility from these people, along with their self-excusing refusal to repent. And indeed, in case 24:5–7 might mislead anybody into thinking that Jeremiah had changed his view of those he had been hitherto condemning, chapter 25 makes it very clear that God's just punishment had fallen on *all the people of Judah* (21:1), with no exception. So any word of hope was by definition a word of undeserved grace.

And secondly, *God's grace will give what God's covenant required* – that God's people should know him, with all that such knowledge of God implied. Verse 7 expresses the most profound theological

---

[2] 'I will look out for their good', Allen, p. 274.
[3] The same double perspective is clear in Jeremiah's letter to the exiles, 29:1 and 4.
[4] Brueggemann (1988), p. 210.

antinomy[5] that lies at the heart of the Bible's teaching on God's sovereign redeeming grace and human repentant and obedient response:

> *I will give them* a heart to know me, that I am the LORD. They will be my people, and I will be their God, for they will return to me with all their heart.

Jeremiah has made it clear that the human heart is incapable of curing itself (17:9). He has also made it clear that the people's only hope lies in a true turning back to God.[6] But how can people who *cannot* turn, actually turn? Only if God gives them the heart to do so. But that is exactly what God says now that he *will* do. God will give the new heart with which 'they will turn back to me with their whole heart'. God's sovereign grace will create a new reality that breaks out of the prison of human failure and inability. It is an act of new creation that points towards Paul's reflection on how the gospel of Christ overcomes the blinding paralysis that Satan inflicts.[7]

Jeremiah 24:7 captures in a single verse the very similar antinomy that we find in Deuteronomy 30:1–10, which is worth reading alongside these verses. That chapter anticipates the judgment of exile, but holds out hope even after it. In Deuteronomy 30:2 and 10, the people are told that they must turn back to the Lord and obey him with all their heart. That is the condition for them to be restored. But at the centre of the passage, in verse 6, God promises to do for the people what they had been commanded to do for themselves (but could not) – namely to circumcise their hearts '*so that* you may love him with all your heart and with all your soul, and live'. To love God that way was the fundamental command and demand of the law (Deut. 6:4–5). But here, in Deuteronomy 30:6, *God's grace promises what God's law demanded.* God would give them the ability to turn to God, to love and obey him. Law and gospel are intertwined in this remarkable passage (no wonder it has an evangelistic ending:

---

[5] 'Antinomy' is the word used for an *apparent* contradiction between two truths that the Bible affirms with equal strength. Our human logic sometimes finds it impossible to hold together simultaneously affirmations that seem to have mutually exclusive consequences. So: if God is sovereign in all he does, says, gives, etc., then how can human action (such as repentance, prayer, etc.) affect his control of events? But equally, if such human actions truly do 'count' and can effect real change, then does that not compromise God's sovereignty? We struggle to combine the two, but the Bible certainly affirms both: human beings make free choices, decisions and actions for which they are held responsible; yet God remains in ultimate sovereign control of history.

[6] He has used the verb *šûb*, 'turn', in just about every possible way it can be.

[7] 2 Cor. 4:3–6.

Deut. 30:19–20). The same paradoxical combination of gift and requirement breathes through Jeremiah 24:7, and points towards the new covenant promises of 31:31–34. All that remained was for Ezekiel to expand the idea of heart-surgery to include the cleansing and filling of the Spirit of God (Ezek. 36:26–28).

If that was God's plan for the *good figs* – those who had gone into exile, who then are represented by the basket of *bad figs*, good for nothing but the compost heap (8–10)? None other than those who were doubtless relieved that they had been left behind – *Zedekiah king of Judah, his officials and the survivors from Jerusalem.* Their fate is spelled out in the rhetorical language of the curses of Deuteronomy 28. They will face the full force of all that Jeremiah had been predicting for years. Ten more years would pass before Zedekiah would bring the wrath of Nebuchadnezzar crashing down once more on the country, and with it the wrath of God. But when that happened, then these *survivors* of the First Deportation would be *destroyed from the land*.[8] The future – for land and people alike – lay elsewhere.

2. God's patience laments the past (25:1–14)

Our editors now take us back about eight years to *the fourth year of Jehoiakim* (the father of Jehoiachin in ch. 24). That ominous year was 605 BC. From the start of Jehoiakim's reign there was no love lost between him and Jeremiah, as we saw in chapter 22. In fact, it seems (from ch. 36, which comes from this same year), that even by this early stage of Jehoiakim's reign Jeremiah was a marked man who could not freely move around the city for fear of arrest or worse. Chapter 36 describes how Jeremiah got Baruch to write a scroll of all his prophecies from the start of his ministry. It is quite possible that some of what we read here in 25:1–14 may have been part of that scroll – perhaps an introduction or conclusion. Perhaps the words *this book* (13) may refer to Baruch's scroll. If so, then Baruch's original scroll might have been roughly equivalent to what we now have as chapters 1 – 25. Some scholars, however, think that verse 13 more likely refers to the contents of the oracles against the nations that we now have in chapters 46 – 51.[9]

---

[8] Of course, in the event, some of those left behind at the First Deportation in 597 BC were taken off in the Second Deportation in 587 BC to join the exiles in Babylon. In that sense, under the flexible sovereignty of God, they were transferred from the basket of bad figs to the basket of good ones. Again, we stress, this did not mean they suddenly became morally good and deserving; rather it simply means that they joined the community of those through whom God would continue his ultimately good purpose for Israel, and through Israel, for the world.

[9] This is partly because of the positioning of the oracles against the nations in the LXX. See Introduction, p. 23.

The significance of the date, however, lay not just in who was on the throne in Jerusalem, but who had just taken the throne of Babylon. 605 BC was also *the first year of Nebuchadnezzar king of Babylon* (1). In that same year he had decisively thrashed Egypt at the battle of Carchemish and established the dominance of resurgent Babylon over the whole region that had been ruled by the Assyrian empire for 150 years.[10] And for that reason – the beginning of the power of Babylon and Nebuchadnezzar – it was a year that marked the beginning of the end for the kingdom of Judah. All Jeremiah had predicted ever since he saw that pot boiling over from the north at the time of his call twenty-three years earlier, would now be unleashed through this new Mesopotamian menace.

So it was an appropriate moment for Jeremiah to pause and remind the people of all he had said in the past *twenty-three years*. As it turned out, this was approximately the mid-point of his lifetime's journey as a prophet. He would go on bringing God's word to the people for almost twenty more years until the final destruction of Jerusalem and beyond.

With deliberate irony, Jeremiah contrasts the servants of God whom they had rejected (4), with the one servant of God whom they would not be able to resist (9).

a. My servants the prophets (1–7)

Twenty-three years of wilful deafness. That is Jeremiah's summary of the people's response to his own ministry (2–3). Repeated warnings had met with repeated dismissal. Three times in these verses we hear the complaint, *you have not listened* (3, 4, 7). If it was any comfort, Jeremiah's experience was the common lot of all the prophets before him. *Though the LORD has sent all his servants the prophets to you again and again, you have not listened* (4). Jeremiah claims that the warning he had brought so forcefully in his temple sermon (chs. 7, 26), was the common message of all the prophets before him – 'change your ways or leave this land'.

Three small points deserve further notice in verses 1–7.

First, there is the same antinomy[11] that we noted in chapter 7 between the apparent unconditional gift of the land to Israel's ancestors (*the land the LORD gave to you and your ancestors for ever and ever*, 5), and the condition that is clearly laid down for continued enjoyment of it – namely to turn away from evil practices and

[10] 2 Kgs 24:7.
[11] On the meaning of antinomy, see footnote 5 above.

idolatry. The territorial promise cannot be claimed without moral and social obedience. The unconditional gift comes with conditions for ongoing appropriation of it.

Second, *other gods* are described as *what your hands have made* (lit. 'the work of your hands'; 6–7). This is one of the common descriptions of idolatry in the Old Testament. And we need to understand that it is a *theological* statement, not merely an observation of the fact that idols were given physical form by being sculpted out of wood or stone. That, in a sense, is the lesser fact. The point is that whatever power or 'reality' other gods have in human communities and cultures is the product of human manufacture. There is only one living God. All other claimants to the status of 'god-ness' are in reality 'not-gods'. They are human constructs – of the imagination and will, consolidated and empowered through the generations and centuries into religions and ideologies.[12]

Third, while the consequences of social wickedness and spiritual idolatry can be described as God bringing disaster [*harm*, lit. 'evil'] upon the people (6), it can equally be described as people bringing it on themselves (7). Sin and sinners ultimately self-destruct – a point that Paul makes with great rhetorical power in Romans 1:18–32. God's judgment often takes the form of giving people up to the consequences of their own evil and folly. Nebuchadnezzar would thus be *both* the agent of divine judgment *and* the nemesis of the people's own mad choices. God's judgment would be mediated through the inevitable consequences of their own folly.

b. My servant Nebuchadnezzar (8–11)

The vivid description of what will happen when the Babylonians would eventually strike is familiar; we have heard it again and again in the earlier chapters of Jeremiah. What makes it more threatening is that *all the peoples of the north*, who had been the mysterious and ominous threat in Jeremiah's preaching for years, now have an identifiable leader – *Nebuchadnezzar king of Babylon*. He will be the one through whom God will bring about the destruction of *this whole country*.

And more shocking still, this pagan king in all his implacable imperial pretensions, is called *my servant Nebuchadnezzar* (8). To be the servant of the Lord was an honour held by few in the annals of Israel's own history. Abraham, Moses and David were called by that title. The prophets have just been called servants of God. And

---

[12] For an extended discussion of this aspect of the biblical diagnosis of idolatry, see Wright, *The Mission of God*, pp. 136–188.

of course it was a term used of Israel as a whole in the book of Isaiah. But that a foreigner and an enemy should be so described . . . !

By calling Nebuchadnezzar 'my servant', Jeremiah did not imagine, of course, that Nebuchadnezzar knew or worshipped YHWH. Rather it meant that YHWH, God of Israel, would use Nebuchadnezzar as the agent of carrying out his will and purpose. Unlike Israel, the failed servant who were frustrating God at every turn, this pagan would unwittingly do the will of God, and therefore, functionally at least, he constituted God's servant. The term must have been shocking enough when Jeremiah first used it in 605 BC, as Nebuchadnezzar rose to power. It was even more undiplomatic when he used it in an international conference some years later in chapter 27 when Nebuchadnezzar was threatening the whole region.

c. Seventy years (12–14)

Jeremiah has been shocking. Now he gets specific. Seventy years is a *long* time. But it is also a *limited* time, and both meanings are probably intended here.

Interpretations of Jeremiah's *seventy years* have varied a lot. If you try to make it a literal calculation of an exact period of years you face the difficulty that the exile itself certainly did not last that long. So two other approximations are suggested. If one takes the date of this prophecy as 605 BC, when Nebuchadnezzar came to power, then the ending of Babylon's power and the consequent ending of the exile of Judah in 538 BC came 67 years later. The seventy years is thus an approximation for the Babylonian empire itself, not the actual period of exile (which was just less than 50 years). Or, if one starts with the destruction of the temple in 587, it would be approximately 72 years until it was rebuilt in 515. That is how Zechariah 1:12 understands the period.

More likely the figure is a round number signifying a long period of time, in which at least two or three generations would pass. That was therefore the message that Jeremiah would later send to the exiles who were being misled by false prophets like Hananiah into imagining that their misfortunes would be over in two years (28:3). No, said Jeremiah, you will be there for two generations. Prepare to have children and grandchildren in Babylon (29:4–6).

The focus of verses 12–14, however, is not so much the *length* of time Judah would have to endure the tyranny of Babylon as the *limit* on the time Babylon would be able to impose that tyranny. Seventy years, no more. Babylon's time would come. All human empires, ancient and modern, run their course and collapse. We would be wise to remember this in our own turbulent times. No single great world power is ever forever.

However, it is not just that Babylon's empire will come to an end, but that God himself will intervene to bring about their downfall. *I will punish [them] for their guilt.* Literally, 'I will visit upon [them] their wrongdoing' – exactly the phraseology Jeremiah has used repeatedly for God's dealings with Israel. This raises two challenging points about God's sovereign governance of international affairs.

First, the fact that God may use one nation as the agent of his judgment against another does not make the first nation righteous. Israel was taught this lesson before they even crossed the Jordan to act as God's agent against the wickedness of the Canaanites.[13] And second, the fact that God uses human agents – individual or national – to accomplish his will does not mean that God endorses or approves all that those agents may do in exercising their own will as fallen and sinful human beings. An earlier example of this in the Old Testament itself is Jehu. Although he was used by God as the agent of God's judgment on the house of Ahab, Hosea later repudiated the blood-thirsty way Jehu went about it.[14] Likewise Assyria, whom God used as a rod with which to beat Israel in the previous century, fell under God's punitive wrath in their turn. So here, God's intention to use Nebuchanezzar and Babylon as the tool of his judgment does not absolve them from all moral responsibility. On the contrary, they will ultimately suffer God's judgment in their turn (50 – 51; cf. Isa. 47:6–7).

> This text is also testimony to the way God uses agents: God does not 'control' or micromanage their behaviours. These agents are not puppets in the divine hand; they retain the power to make decisions and execute policies. God's agents can act in ways that are contrary to God's own will for the situation.[15]

3. God's judgment engulfs the earth (25:15–38)

If Nebuchadnezzar was bad news for Israel, he was equally bad news for the whole region. None of the nations would escape unscathed. Jeremiah, remember, was called to be a 'prophet to the nations'. That is, his interpretation of events did not stop at the boundaries of Israel. That was because the rule of YHWH did not stop there either.

[13] The Israelites themselves were told not to think that way in relation to their conquest of Canaan; Deut. 9.
[14] 2 Kgs 9 – 10; Hos. 1:4–5.
[15] Fretheim, p. 357.

In a graphic vision, Jeremiah is asked by God to demand that all the surrounding nations should drink from a *cup filled with the wine of my wrath.* The image of drinking from a cup was used both of blessing[16] and of curse.[17] Here it is unmistakeably the latter. The wine has been laced with a powerful poison that will cause all who drink it to *stagger, go mad . . . get drunk and vomit, and fall down to rise no more* (16, 27). The graphic language portrays national panic, crazy policies, violent convulsions and final destruction. Such was indeed the fate of many nations in the coming years.

Once again we are confronted with the combination of divine will and human agency. For the *sword* that God will bring (16, 29, 31) will in historical fact be the sword of Babylon's armies (38). And the picture of YHWH as a *lion*, which opens and closes Jeremiah's prophecy (30, 38), is precisely the image used to describe the human enemy from the north – i.e. Nebuchadnezzar himself.[18] God's judgment would be delivered through the violence of imperial aggression.

The list of nations (17–26) is like a roll-call of the ancient Near East. It may well have functioned as a kind of 'table of contents' for the scroll that contained the more detailed oracles against the nations now found in chapters 46 – 51, since most of the names here turn up there also. The order at the beginning and end is significant. It begins with Judah, 'for it is time for judgment to begin with God's household'.[19] It then moves from Egypt, the ancient enemy, through all the other small nations that would feel the sword of Nebuchadnezzar. But then it ends, climactically and with enormous significance for the exiles: *and after all of them, the king of Sheshak[20] will drink it too* (26). That is to say, Nebuchadnezzar himself and his whole Babylonian empire would suffer the very same fate that they had inflicted on the other nations. God's judgment would be universally felt.

And why? Because YHWH the God of Israel is the God of all the earth. The God who calls Israel to account for their sins is not blind to the wickedness of other nations (29). Israel's responsibility was all the greater because they bore the name of YHWH, but if that meant God would therefore punish them all the more severely, it did not mean that God would merely overlook the guilt of the rest of humanity. The message is very similar to Amos 1:1 – 3:2.

[16] E.g. Pss 16:5; 23:5.

[17] E.g. Jer. 48:26; 49:12; 51:7; Lam. 4:21; Pss 11:6; 75:8; Ezek. 23:32; Isa. 51:17–21.

[18] Jer. 4:7; 5:6.

[19] 1 Pet. 4:17.

[20] 'Sheshak' was a cryptogram (a code-word) for 'Babel', by substitution of letters the same distance from the end of the Hebrew alphabet as the letters of the original word were from the beginning.

And so the chapter moves to its gloomy and ghastly finale (30–38). Indeed, it seems to move beyond the merely historical word of immediate judgment that was about to fall on the world of Jeremiah's own day, to a note of universal judgment. The text propels us to the third great eschatological horizon of Old Testament prophecy. The events of 587 BC were like a microcosm of the final judgment. The phrase *all who live on the earth*, even if it seems exaggerated in verse 29, becomes a solemn affirmation facing all humanity in verse 31: *to the ends of the earth . . . the nations . . . all mankind.* The highest human authorities will stand no chance in the final judgment of God. *Shepherds* (the constant Old Testament metaphor for kings and governments) will be as impotent and shattered as the people they have so badly governed (34–35).

Theological and expository reflections

- The antinomy[21] of sovereign grace expressed in 24:7 continues into the New Testament. People are commanded to repent, believe and obey. Those are all acts of the will. People must choose to take such actions, willingly and sincerely. And yet when people do, the New Testament recognizes that God's grace has been active. Repentance and faith are both portrayed as gifts of God. And the life of obedience is lived through the indwelling Spirit, who bears his fruit in the believer's life. We need to preach in a way that affirms both poles of this antinomy: the necessity of what God gives and does through his sovereign grace; and the necessity of responding in willing and active co-operation, as we 'make every effort' to 'walk by the Spirit'.[22]
- Perhaps, though, the greatest message that emerges from Jeremiah 24:5–7 (just as it does from Deut. 30 and Ezek. 36) is that there is no place so distant, no condition so awful, that the sovereign grace of God cannot bring redemption through the gift of repentance and the decision to 'turn back'. God is the God of new beginnings, of new creation, of future hope out of past or present ruin, of life out of death. And that – as Jesus graphically portrayed in his story of the Prodigal Son and the incredibly generous father – is well worth celebrating. That is gospel.
- Another paradox that needs to be faced in preaching 'the whole counsel of God' is the one in chapter 25; between the sovereignty of God in using human agents to accomplish his will,

---

[21] See footnote 5 above.
[22] 2 Pet. 1:5–7; Gal. 5:16.

while at the same time holding those agents accountable to himself for all the actions they may do in the process. How should we preach in a time of war, for example, if it appears that one nation is acting to defend itself or others against an evil and violent aggressor? We may wish to argue that God is using one nation as an agent of justice against another nation that is perpetrating injustice. Maybe so. But that does not mean God regards the first nation as morally pure in his own eyes, or beyond criticism for its own policies and actions. Even fulfilling prophecy does not grant immunity from moral accountability and criticism.

- Finally, it is important to give due weight to the terrible and terrifying reality of *the Lord's fierce anger* in the second half of Jeremiah 25. There is judgment to come and the whole Bible, including the Lord Jesus Christ himself, warns us about it. Within the wider context of the book, however, one would need to balance a word like this with the renewed call to repentance that these chapters gave to the exiles who had suffered the wrath of God in their own historical experience. We must move on to the 'gospel' words of comfort and hope that Jeremiah will soon offer in chapters 30 – 33. Judgment would not be God's final word to Israel, and it need not be his final word to us, or through us to others in our preaching, provided God's offer of grace is met by repentance and faith.

19. Half time

Chapter 25 marks the halfway point of the book in several ways. Obviously it is just about halfway through the chapters of the whole book, which may be a relief if you are working steadily through them. Clearly also the editors intend that the chapter stands as a halfway point in the historical ministry of Jeremiah, with the specific mention of twenty-three years since his call and appointment as a prophet (25:3). More importantly, the chapter marks a significant transition in the overall message of the book. So far we have been hearing words of almost unrelieved warning of horrendous judgment to come, with only a few flashes of hope. And now we have reached that ominous date, 605 BC. That was the year that Nebuchadnezzar defeated Egypt at the battle of Carchemish and asserted the rule of the new Babylonian empire over the whole region. The foe from the north was on the move. It was also the year that King Jehoiakim defied the word of God by burning the scroll of the words of Jeremiah, and set his country on a course that led to irrevocable catastrophe. Chapter 25 in that sense marks a point of no return. From here on things can only get worse.

And that is paradoxical, because from here on the book itself gets better! For the whole first half Jeremiah has been almost entirely engaged in the first part of his prophetic commission: 'to uproot and tear down, to destroy and overthrow'. He has systematically dismantled all the traditional structures of Israel's faith, all the things they put their hope it. These have included their history of election and redemption, the law, the temple, the covenant, the monarchy, the land – even their circumcision. Some of these he has even described as 'lies' – deceptions, false security. Neither their present security nor their future survival could be guaranteed on such foundations. There could be no hope for an utterly deaf and unrepentant people.

Survival depends on hope. When hope is gone, life becomes unbearable. There are only faint traces of hope in Jer 1 – 25, and these vestiges are obscured by reams of divine judgments. Instead of inspiring hope, the first half of Jeremiah dismantles configurations of hope that are based on a building and on a king; on a land and on political autonomy. Jeremiah attacks a temple theology that had become an idolatrous system (Jer 7). He employs he covenant to curse rather than to bless (Jer 11). Jeremiah assaults the community's privileged position (Jer 18) and its seemingly inviolable dynastic rights (Jer 21). He even subverts ancient land claims by insisting that the land must be abandoned before the inception of new era. The prophet demolishes these long-held understandings of reality allied with the old preexilic world, insisting that they stand under the 'wrath of love.' . . . Hence, nothing remains to support the toppling world. The few islands of hope in Jer 1 – 25 have been submerged in an ocean of death.[1]

But that did not mean there could be no hope at all. Tentatively at first, and then with increasing volume, the chapters in the second half of the book will open up to a future that only God could create anew through his sovereign grace, a future filled with hope, restoration, life and joy. Jeremiah, the man and the book, move into the other dimensions of his prophetic calling, 'to build and to plant'. We still have to endure the worst years of Jeremiah's life – the decade before the final fall of Jerusalem. We must witness his struggles with royal and religious opposition, hatred and violence. But in the midst of all that the prophet looks beyond the catastrophe and the exile with eyes of faith and hope. He sees a new reality, which first of all gave hope to the exiles themselves of a physical return to their land. But Jeremiah's vision pointed even beyond that to a transformation of the relationship between God and his people that only the gospel of the cross and resurrection of Christ would ultimately accomplish, and indeed to a transformation of the whole creation at the furthest horizon of prophetic vision that leads us finally to Revelation 21 – 22.

The central section of this second half of the book is the so-called 'Book of Consolation' (chs. 30 – 33). Alongside those soaring visions, we will also see Jeremiah putting his faith into action in symbolic actions that cost him real money. And we shall meet a few representative individuals who actually believe and respond to the message he brought, and thereby relieve the loneliness that so colours the first half of the book – men like Baruch, Ebed-Melek, and the family of Shaphan. The life of Jeremiah did not get any easier, but he proves

[1] Stulman, p. 233.

God true to his promise to protect him even the most dire distress. And although he ends up disappearing from the pages of history among the doomed remnant of Judah that dragged him with them to Egypt, his book was preserved, perhaps thank to Baruch, and has been thoughtfully and intentionally edited into the shape we now have it. So let us move on to witness the continued suffering of this man of God, but with increasingly sure and certain hope of the grace-filled future that lies beyond judgment.

Jeremiah 26:1 – 28:17
20. Dramatic public encounters

It was not yet the end. But it was the beginning of the end. Nebuchadnezzar's invasion and the deportation of king Jehoiachin and 10,000 of the elite classes of Judah in 597 BC was just a rehearsal for a far bloodier denouement ten years later. But of course, they didn't know that at the time. Most of the second half of the book of Jeremiah portrays the turbulent years between 597 and the final destruction of the city in 587. There are more biographical narratives in this section than in chapters 1 – 25, depicting the increasing isolation and deprivation of Jeremiah as the years went by. Yet out of that time of appalling national and personal suffering came the words of comfort and hope, words indeed of gospel affirmation for those who would at last pay heed to them in exile, which are structurally central to this part of the book (chs. 30 – 33). These chapters (26 – 28) begin the transformation of Jeremiah into a prophet of hope, fulfilling the final pair of his commissioning, 'to build and to plant'.[1]

1. Before the religious and political authorities in Jerusalem (26:1–24)

The series of events begins, however, with a flashback to the occasion when God sent Jeremiah to preach to the people in the temple itself. The extended record of the sermon is in Jeremiah 7, but here we are given the date, *early in the reign of Jehoiakim*, i.e. about 609 BC. 'The association with Jehoiakim is more than a mere historical reference: . . . Jehoiakim, who is a prototype of infidelity and disobedience, functions as a code word for cosmic crumbling and the collapse of moral courage.'[2]

---

[1] McConville, *Judgment and Promise*, pp. 86–91.
[2] Stulman, p. 237.

Why did our editors choose to record this event twice? Probably because, in its earlier place in chapter 7, it serves to sum up, clarify and reinforce the major themes and implications of the wild poetry of Jeremiah's oracles in chapters 2 – 6, providing a significant change of pace and tone.[3] Here in chapter 26, at the start of the second half of the book, it provides both a reminder and a summary of the core of Jeremiah's whole message in chapters 1 – 25. Also, by telling us what happened immediately after he preached the sermon the editors introduce us to the public and dangerous conflict that would surround Jeremiah for the rest of his life. Chapter 26 thus both looks back and points forward.

Another reason for placing the chapter here at the start of the second half of the book is that it reminds us of the themes with which chapter 1 introduced the whole book. Jeremiah is instructed to deliver God's word, in any place and to any audience, even the most hostile (1:7–8). As a result he will face terrifying opposition from the officials, priests and people of the land (1:18) – precisely the groups we meet in this encounter in the temple. But he is not to be afraid of them, for God will be at hand to rescue him and provide protection (1:8, 19), which is exactly what happens in 26:16, 24.

a. A sermon revisited (1–6)

We've heard the sermon before, of course, but this summary of it has some subtle emphases to note.

First, it moves more quickly to the punchline in verse 6 (which was quite delayed in ch. 7). God threatens to turn the city of Jerusalem and its temple into ruins, just *like Shiloh* – the place where YHWH's tent and ark had once stood in the days of Samuel. Jeremiah's preaching was an unthinkable attack on the very place where he was standing. Only Jesus knew the kind of courage it took to say such things in such a place. The sense of threat is even more stark and explicit than chapter 7. There the issue was put in potentially positive terms ('reform your ways and your actions, and I will let you live in this place'); here we find it bluntly negative: *If you do not listen to me . . . then I will make this house like Shiloh.* Since the people had never listened to a word God had said (25:3–7), what was left but for that threat to be fulfilled?

Secondly, the summary here brings *the law* and *the prophets* into close combination, in a way that points to the scriptural authority of both. In chapter 7 the word *tôrâ* is not used but there is clear reference to the Decalogue in 7:9, while the expression 'my servants

[3] See ch. 6, pp. 106–107.

the prophets' comes later in 7:25. Here, however, the law and the prophets are put side by side (4–5), emphasizing the importance that Jeremiah placed on both.[4] Rejection of God's word in its most authoritative form was the rejection of God himself and could lead to only one place – judgment and destruction. Jesus finished his parable of the rich man and the beggar with searing words that sound just like Jeremiah, 'If they do not listen to Moses and the prophets' ... then not even a resurrection would convince them.[5] And Stephen, the first Christian martyr who spoke like Jeremiah but suffered like Uriah, likewise accused his accusers of failing to heed their own scriptures, the law and the prophets.[6]

Thirdly, however, the threat of destruction was something God longed *not* to have to carry out. Chapter 26 starts with a private word to Jeremiah that is not recorded in chapter 7. *Perhaps,* says God (3). It is an astonishing word of divine wistfulness, suggesting that even God cannot close down the future too quickly, even at such a late stage. *Perhaps* the people just might do now what they have never done before – listen and repent. Just maybe. And with even such a glimmer of possibility, God would not have to go through with the appalling judgment that was hanging over them. Verse 3 states again the principle Jeremiah had learned in the potter's shop (18:7–8). There had been no hope of a change of heart among the people then and there will be none this time either. And yet, and yet ... God's heart aches for such a response, because he longs to put aside his anger and spare his people the consequences of their own *evil*. The words of judgment that Jeremiah must preach (4–6) were prefaced with longings of love and grace (3). Terence Fretheim reflects helpfully on the 'circumstantial will of God' (which had to be judgment), and the long-term 'absolute will of God' (for blessing).

> This mediation of sin's consequences might be termed the circum-stantial will of God: it is God's will only in view of specific circumstances that have developed. That disaster is not the primary will of God for Israel is made clear by God's commission to Jeremiah: God desires the people's repentance so that God can change God's mind regarding the intention to bring disaster. This reveals God's absolute will for the people: God prefers Israel's life to Israel's death; blessing instead of curse; salvation instead of judgment ... God's circumstantial will for judgment will in fact come to fruition, but it is not God's final word for Israel. God's

[4] On the broken Torah of the covenant, cf. 6:16–19; 9:13; 11:1–8; 16:11; 44:10, 23. On failure to listen to the prophets, cf. 7:25; 25:4–7; 29:19; 35:15; 44:4.
[5] Luke 16:31.
[6] Acts 7:51–53.

absolute will for Israel's life and salvation persists through the fires of judgment and . . . emerges on the far side of the disaster with the offer of new life and blessing.[7]

b. Sentence of death demanded (7–11)

But if that was what God longed for through Jeremiah's message, it was not what the people heard in it. All they heard, with gathering rage, was someone who claimed to be a prophet of YHWH threatening YHWH's house and YHWH's city with destruction. It was self-evidently contradictory. Worse, it was treason and blasphemy. And the law (which they otherwise ignored) told them what to do with those who prophesied lies in God's name.[8] *'You must die!'* (8).

The key players in this accusation were *the priests* and *the prophets* – that is, the religious establishment. The priests served the temple; the prophets served the state by providing oracular approval for the government's policies. These were the factions who were most obviously threatened by Jeremiah's attack, and they conspired to silence him.

Indeed, since we know there had been people out to kill Jeremiah for a long time (cf. 11:21; 18:23), it seems they are here seizing an opportune moment. The prophet stood condemned out of his own mouth. Just as the climax of murderous intent against Jesus came to a head when he spoke against the temple, so the same fate seems to be imminent for Jeremiah. Ironic, though, that it was *in the house of the LORD* that the people wanted to silence the very voice of the Lord by having Jeremiah executed. 'What is at stake at this juncture of the book is more than another instance of the community rejecting the word of the Lord. Chapter 26 presents leading sectors of the nation attempting *ritually and legally* to silence the voice of God.'[9]

The officials suspended government business at the palace and hurried to the temple, and set up an instant court. The priests and prophets repeat to these political authorities the same charge on which they had arrested Jeremiah (10–11).

The role of *all the people* in the narrative is breathtakingly fickle (as it would be, in reverse, between Palm Sunday and Good Friday). First they support the priests and prophets against Jeremiah (7–8). Later they swing to support the opposite verdict and take Jeremiah's side (16). But they are still a volatile danger from which Jeremiah needs protection (24).

---

[7] Fretheim, p. 376.
[8] Deut. 13:1–11; 18:20.
[9] Stulman, p. 238; emphasis original.

c. Self-defence and warning (12–15)

The accused is given leave to speak. Jeremiah's speech begins by restating his commission from YHWH, moves on to repeat the message (a neat opportunity to give the sermon's main points again under protection of the court), and finishes by showing that he was as competent in the law of Deuteronomy as his accusers. They had him at their mercy, but were they prepared to take the risk of executing an innocent man and thereby bring dangerous blood-guilt on themselves (not that the law had restrained them from such behaviour up to now, but could they do it in open court and in the temple)?[10]

Verse 13 expresses publicly what God had told Jeremiah privately. God could change the plan, but only in response to genuine repentance and change among the people. Exiles reading the book would know the opportunity they had squandered. What had happened to them did not have to have happened. Repentance could have averted it. But that was the one thing they refused to do back then. Would they turn in repentance even now, in exile? That would be the message, and the life's work, of Ezekiel.

d. Sentence repealed, with historical precedent (16–19)

Jeremiah's clever ploy about the risk of blood-guilt manages to isolate *the priests and the prophets* from *all the people,* who now (perhaps with their anger turning to fear) side with *the officials* in reversing the original verdict.

At this point we encounter another interesting group who appear to be sympathetic to Jeremiah – *the elders of the land.* These would be leaders of village communities, heads of local families – men who were not intimidated by the royal party and its ideology, and probably not terribly impressed with the temple establishment either. And they know their scriptures, too. By quoting from the prophet Micah they show us that there must have been written collections of the words of the prophets of the previous century.

The precedent they quote is fascinating. Micah had predicted the complete razing of Jerusalem.[11] But it hadn't happened. Why not? Because good king Hezekiah had prayed and God had averted the predicted disaster (another example of the potter scenario in action). And Micah certainly wasn't executed for his prediction, even though it had not come to pass.

[10] Deut. 19:10.
[11] Mic. 3:12.

Their words, however, are dripping with ironies.

- They seem to think that Micah, though a false prophet in their eyes (since his prediction had not come true), had not been put to death because Hezekiah's prayer averted it, when in fact Micah's prediction (though delayed) was about to come just as true as Jeremiah's would. They thought that because Micah's prediction had not come true, Jeremiah's would not either. Both prophets were simply (though sincerely) wrong, they thought. It was all just a big mistake – not a stoning offence.
- They seem to think that by not executing Jeremiah they will have done all they need to do in order to avert what they imagine would happen if they did (*we are about to bring a terrible disaster on ourselves*), when in fact the disaster was about to fall on them anyway. Killing Jeremiah would be only a final nail in a coffin already well constructed by the nation's neglect of all the prophets God had sent.
- They speak as if the only issue is, 'Will we, or will we not, kill this prophet?', when the far greater issue was, 'Will we, or will we not, obey the word of God and change our ways?'
- They are arguing over the guilt of an individual in a human court when they themselves have been found guilty as a nation in God's court.
- Furthermore, though they have decided not to kill the prophet, there is no indication that they will actually do as he urged them to do in verse 13. So they explicitly accept that he has indeed *spoken to us in the name of the LORD our God* (16), yet they are deafeningly silent about what he had actually just said they needed to do! They acknowledge the truth and reject the demands of the truth in the same breath.

And finally, the story is told to highlight the contrast between the response of Hezekiah to an unwelcome word from a prophet with that of Jehoiakim. Hezekiah spared the prophet and sought the Lord (19). Jehoiakim killed a prophet and hardened his heart (20–23).

e. Sequel: danger and protection (20–24)

So the narrative concludes by telling the story of Uriah – otherwise unknown, but a martyr who could have been included in Hebrews 11. It is a fascinating insight into how ruthlessly the government of Judah dealt with its critics, and how miraculous it was that Jeremiah's life was spared throughout this dark, violent and repressive reign. We can see just how real was the threat against Jeremiah, and how much he needed the protection of God exercised through the few friends he had, like *Ahikam son of Shaphan*.[12]

Verse 23 is usually translated as *King Jehoiakim . . . had him struck down with a sword*. While that is certainly possible, the verb in its Hebrew form is used routinely to describe someone taking that action themselves – i.e. striking somebody down with a sword. It would be another indicator of the character of Jehoiakim (cf. 22:17), if he did the bloody deed himself when Uriah was dragged into his presence (cf. NRSV). A man who could stab and burn the word of God would hardly flinch from stabbing a prophet who delivered it. No wonder Jeremiah went into hiding (36:26).

2. On the stage of international diplomacy (27:1–22)

We fast-forward about fifteen years from that defining moment in the reign of Jehoiakim, and return to the period after the First Deportation of 597 BC, which we had reached in chapter 24. Zedekiah is on the throne, having been placed there as a puppet king by Nebuchadnezzar. He was expected to behave himself and keep his kingdom subservient to Babylon and out of trouble. But rebellion is again in the air. The date of the events in this chapter is made clear when 28:1 speaks of *that same year, the fourth year* of the reign of Zedekiah – i.e. 593 BC. It seems that the political establishment in Jerusalem was divided as to whether to continue in submission to the rule of Babylon, or to unite with other nations in a regional rebellion. Into that fraught atmosphere steps Jeremiah with a word from the God of Israel. Unusually, he tells the story himself in the first person (2, 12, 16).

a. A word to the nations (1–11)

An international diplomatic conference was taking place in Jerusalem. It may have been called by Zedekiah, and it was certainly hosted by him. Ambassadors turned up from all the little states to the north, east and south of Judah. What was on the agenda? We are not told directly, but almost certainly (in view of Jeremiah's message), the conference was seeking to establish a unified front of resistance against Babylon – an alliance in rebellion.

---

[12] Shaphan was personal secretary to King Josiah. He had taken the rediscovered book of the law and read it to the king – which led to a reformation (2 Kgs 22). Another of his sons, Gemariah, was present when a very different reading took place before a king, with a very different result (see ch. 36). This influential family's support for Jeremiah shows a degree of internal opposition to government policies among the ruling classes. There were at least some in their midst who paid more attention to Jeremiah's words than their royal masters.

We can be sure Jeremiah was not on the invitation list, but he gate-crashed the party anyway. And 'gatecrashing' is not too strong a word for the entrance he must have made. For this was one of his acted prophecies, combining symbolic action and divine word. At God's instruction he made *a yoke* for himself, such as was commonly seen hitched on the necks of two oxen, with a transverse pole and ropes connected to the cart or the plough at the back. Presumably wearing one half over his own shoulders and holding up the other half, he heads for the conference hall and somehow bursts his way in.

If Jeremiah's entrance was decidedly undiplomatic, his speech was even more so. Those present were not merely ambassadors of different kings; they represented countries with different gods. Countries, kings and gods were all of a piece in their worldview. But Jeremiah claims that *the LORD Almighty, the God of Israel* demands the attention of all the kings represented round the table (4). Before they could protest at this breach of religious protocol, Jeremiah tumbles on in a breathtaking series of affirmations and a clear political conclusion.

1. YHWH the God of Israel is the creator of all the earth, and therefore of the lands of all their nations – not just of the land of Israel. Lands, peoples and even animals all lie under the sovereign power of YHWH (5a).
2. YHWH the God of Israel is the controller of all that happens among nations on the earth: *I give it to anyone I please.* This is a general and universal truth (5b).
3. The particular truth for the present moment is that YHWH has given their lands into the power of Nebuchadnezzar (6). So for now, Nebuchadnezzar has YHWH as his boss (*my servant Nebuchadnezzar*). All Nebuchadnezzar's authority and accomplishment come from the God of Israel (!).
4. But Nebuchadnezzar's power will be temporary (7) – for a period of three generations,[13] *until the time for his land comes.* Then YHWH will raise up other nations to do to Babylon what Babylon had done to others.
5. The most sensible political policy, therefore, for these small nations to adopt is to submit to the rule of Babylon until it comes to an end. Rebellion would bring even worse disaster (8).

---

[13] The reference to *his son and his grandson* probably means a period of time roughly equivalent to three generations. As it turned out, Nebuchadnezzar was succeeded first by his son Evil-merodach, then his son-in-law Neriglissar, then his grandson Labashi-Marduk. But Babylonian rule came to an end under a usurper Nabonidus and his son Belshazzar (Dan. 5:2 speaks of Belshazzar's father Nebuchadnezzar, but this is in the sense of predecessor on the throne, not biological ancestry).

In short, Jeremiah urges a policy of non-violent acceptance of their current submission, arguing that violent resistance will only produce an even more violent and destructive reaction.

6. Whatever their own religious authorities are telling them in the name of their so-called gods is nothing but dangerous lies and should not be trusted (9–10).

7. Rebellion against Nebuchadnezzar thus constitutes rebellion against the God of Israel (*I will punish . . . I will banish you*), while submission to Nebuchadnezzar is submission to the will of YHWH, and therefore the best guarantee of security for any nation (*I will let that nation remain in its own land to till it and to live there*, 11).

We can imagine the scene (perhaps Jeremiah went around the ambassadors, inviting them to share the other half of his yoke and submit to YHWH, before he was roughly bundled out of the room by the security guards). But we should marvel even more at the sheer scale of what his words affirm.

This is Old Testament monotheism in three-dimensional, practical outworking. It is deeply rooted in the great confessions of Israel's faith: 'To the LORD your God belong the heavens, even the highest heavens, the earth and everything in it . . . For the LORD your God is God of gods and Lord of lords, the great God, mighty and awesome.'[14] But this was not merely an abstract religious truth that was unconnected with human affairs in history. YHWH who created the earth also governs the histories of all nations upon it.[15]

Indeed, Jeremiah is simply repeating what had been said before Israel even entered the Promised Land – namely that these surrounding nations had been given their lands by the sovereign hand of YHWH in the movements of peoples around the region long before Israel came on the scene. This is the significance of the claims made in the otherwise obscure geography lessons of Deuteronomy 2.[16] It was the same God, the same lands, the same peoples, and the same sovereign government in control. Nebuchadnezzar was nothing more than a blip on the radar screen that would move into focus, fulfil God's purpose, and disappear.

It is not easy for us to handle and apply these Old Testament affirmations about God's sovereignty within international history – particularly because we tend to understand and interpret our faith primarily in individualistic terms. Yet the fact remains that God's dealings with the nations – in history and in eschatological expectation

[14] Deut. 10:14–17; cf. Deut. 4:35, 39.
[15] Ps. 33:6–11.
[16] See especially Deut. 2:4–5, 9–12, 19, 20–23.

– is one of the most prominent themes of the Old Testament, and forms part of the foundation for the missional theology and practice of the New Testament church. It needs to be an essential theme also for our own biblical understanding of mission. Indeed, it is contained within the opening affirmation of the Great Commission, in those words of Jesus that deliberately echo Deuteronomy 4:39: 'All authority in heaven and on earth has been given to me.'[17]

b. A word for the government at home (12–15)

We don't know the exact sequence of events, of course, but whether he was arrested at the conference and taken to king Zedekiah, or arranged to meet him later, Jeremiah gained audience with the king – who was less murderously tyrannical than Jehoiakim and more willing to consult Jeremiah (though never courageous enough to heed his words).

Before *Zedekiah king of Judah* Jeremiah *gave the same message*, but with some additional appeal. For the ambassadors, the message had been a simple statement of YHWH's sovereignty being exercised through Nebuchadnezzar with an accompanying warning and promise. But with Zedekiah Jeremiah was addressing the leader of his own people, people whose fate hung on the king's decision. If he chose the path of rebellion, he would condemn his people to all the horrors of invasion and siege (*the sword, famine and plague*). And Jeremiah could not bear that thought – having struggled with the visions of it for years. Could it be averted even now? So he appeals to the king with a desperate rhetorical *why?* (13, cf. 17).

Why will you and your people die . . . ? It is a question that echoes the fundamental choice that Deuteronomy had set before the people.

> This day I call the heavens and the earth as witnesses against you that I have set before you life and death, blessings and curses. Now choose life, so that you and your children may live and that you may love the LORD your God, listen to his voice, and hold fast to him. For the LORD is your life, and he will give you many years in the land he swore to give to your fathers, Abraham, Isaac and Jacob.[18]

It is a question that would be echoed again in an even more passionate evangelistic appeal by Ezekiel to those who ended up in exile because Zedekiah refused to heed Jeremiah's plea.

[17] Matt. 28:18. I have explored the missional significance of the nations in both Testaments in much greater depth in Wright, *The Mission of God*, pp. 454–530.
[18] Deut. 30:19–20.

Repent! Turn away from all your offenses; then sin will not be your downfall. Rid yourselves of all the offenses you have committed, and get a new heart and a new spirit. Why will you die, people of Israel? For I take no pleasure in the death of anyone, declares the Sovereign LORD. Repent and live! [19]

c. A word for the people (16–22)

After the king, Jeremiah goes on to address the religious leaders and the people themselves. As we saw in 21:8–10 (with its similarity to Deut. 30:19–20), Jeremiah could distinguish between the policies of the government that were leading the nation down the road to catastrophic ruin, and the ordinary population who, though by no means innocent, might be able to avoid the worst of the calamity by surrendering to Babylon rather than staying in the city until the horrors of the siege imprisoned them. So here Jeremiah urges them not to believe the prophets of peace and hope – and certain death. The only way to save their lives (which is what he longed they should do), was by submission to Nebuchadnezzar. So he urges that policy, with another impassioned 'Why?' *Serve the king of Babylon, and you will live. Why should this city become a ruin?* (17).

The fate of the people seemed bound up with the temple and its artefacts and vessels. Jeremiah contradicted those who were predicting that the items that had been taken away would soon be returned, while those that were still intact in Jerusalem would be safe. Jeremiah says that everything that had been left would soon be taken to Babylon – and would stay there until God himself went to fetch them (22).[20]

3. In the clash of prophetic words and actions (28:1–17)

a. Hananiah: 'Home in two years!' (1–4)

Jerusalem was obviously awash with prophets, most of them giving their spurious promises of peace and the imminent return of the rightful king (Jehoiachin) from exile and all the temple vessels with him. We know what Jeremiah thought of them from chapter 23, and they are there in the background in chapter 27. But now one of them steps into the light of named history, as Hananiah confronts Jeremiah in public.

[19] Ezek. 18:30–32.
[20] For the fulfilment of verses 19–22a, see 52:17–23 and 2 Kgs 25:13–17. For the fulfilment of verse 22, see Ezra 1:7–11.

Hananiah (whose name means 'YHWH is gracious') is introduced like any other prophet, with the names of his father and town, and he speaks in the way any prophet should: *This is what the LORD Almighty, the God of Israel says* – the precise words of Jeremiah himself in 27:4. And they are spoken directly to Jeremiah in the same public arena that Jeremiah had preached, *in the house of the LORD in the presence of the priests and all the people*. It seems a deliberate confrontation set up by Hananiah. Having picked his spot and his target, Hananiah then picks up (only to contradict) the imagery of *the yoke* that Jeremiah had used. From verse 10 we learn that Jeremiah was still wandering about with that ox yoke over his neck (being a prophet was uncomfortable even when it wasn't dangerous). So the words of Hananiah (2) had a particularly sarcastic sting.

Hananiah's straightforward prediction was that Nebuchadnezzar's reign would be over in two more years, and then king Jehoiachin, the temple vessels and the exiles would all return home and all live happily ever after. In other words, since this prediction was made about four years after the First Deportation, Hananiah was saying that the exile would last six or seven years – nothing like the seventy that Jeremiah had predicted.

b. Jeremiah: 'I wish! But . . .' (5–9)

Jeremiah's instant reaction is to agree with the sentiment embedded in the prediction – *Amen! May the LORD do so!* That's what everybody wanted, and Jeremiah could happily imagine it. But he knew better. He hadn't spent more than thirty years agonizing over the dire visions God had shown him of a far more terrible future counted in generations not years, to have it all cheerfully dissolved in a burst of false optimism.[21] But he remains initially polite in the public debate and requests that the audience take something else into consideration. The majority of Israel's historic prophets had prophesied judgment, so the burden of proof lay on the exceptions (like Hananiah) who predicted peace. The people ought not to be so easily deceived by Hananiah's message, for history was against him. Hananiah, in fact (and ch. 28 as a whole), is a dramatic example of what Jeremiah had described in chapter 27 – prophets who were leading people to 'trust in lies'. Jeremiah knew that, and the people should have known it. But in the end, 'We'll have to wait and see, won't we?' (Deut. 18:21–22).

---

[21] Jeremiah's words were not a sudden change in his message, or a sign of uncertainty over whether he or Hananiah were right. 'The real point of Jeremiah's words is simple: it is a reminder that the fact that one would *like* something to be the case is no guarantee that it actually *will be* the case' (Moberly, *Prophecy and Discernment*, p. 107).

c. Hananiah: 'The yoke will be broken' (10–11)

Hananiah was not so polite, however. His dramatic grab and smash raid on Jeremiah's symbolic yoke must have drawn gasps of astonishment. The symbolism of that yoke and its message from Jeremiah was so strong and well-known by now, that the contrary symbolism must have carried a strong counter-message: 'The word of Jeremiah is broken and replaced by this word. Believe me, not him.'

Remarkably, Jeremiah offers no word or action to counter Hananiah.[22] Clearly he had not received any immediate word from God to address this direct challenge, and he had the wisdom not to try to argue in his own strength. So he simply turns around and walks away, leaving the crowds probably thinking that Hananiah had won the argument. Hananiah no doubt exploited that popular opinion for all it was worth and for as long as it lasted – which wasn't long.

d. Jeremiah: 'You will be broken first, for your lies' (12–17)

Back comes Jeremiah some days later, having been instructed by God to reinforce the truth of his own prediction and deny Hananiah's. Whether he actually produced *a yoke of iron* to replace his broken *wooden* one seems unlikely, but all he needed was the verbal imagery now. The yoke of Nebuchadnezzar would be unbreakable – by any of the human nations he would subjugate.

Furthermore, no longer restrained by public politeness, Jeremiah declares Hananiah to be a false prophet in the terms of Deuteronomy 18:20. No human court in Jerusalem in the current climate would charge him on such grounds (since they had spared Jeremiah they would hardly execute Hananiah), but God himself would take action. Lying in general is a sinful breach of the ninth commandment. But when religious leaders lead people who stand under God's judgment, with repentance as their only hope of salvation, to *trust in lies* (15), then their own judgment is doubly severe. As Jesus said, better to be thrown in the sea tied to a millstone.[23]

---

[22] 'This is not because Jeremiah is uncertain what is going on or of what to say, but because he has already made his position clear and there is no point in saying anything further' (Moberly, *Prophecy*, p. 108). Moberly argues that the story of Hananiah is not (as commonly assumed) about prophetic discernment, but a further illustration of the kind of opposition Jeremiah faced for the message unambiguously declared in chs. 26 – 27.

[23] Luke 17:1–2. 'This sad story is a warning to the many people who claim to be prophets today. We hear many prophecies these days, all put out by people who claim to be speaking for the Lord. The story of Hananiah shows that those who take the name of the Lord in vain will suffer the consequences. It is better to remain silent if we have not received anything from God than to lie and bring the Lord's judgment on ourselves' (Coulibaly, p. 888).

And so the chapter ends on the sobering note that the man who usurped the name of the Lord to prophesy falsely that the exile would be over in two years was dead within two months (17). It is a narrative that one might call 'signal' – in the sense that it points out the seriousness of 'using' God for deception and self-interest. By God's grace not all who do so suffer such immediate retribution. But stories like this, or of the sons of Aaron (Lev. 10), or indeed of Ananias (ironically the same name as Hananiah) and Sapphira (Acts 5), are serious biblical warnings not to treat God with contempt.

Theological and expository reflections

- It is impossible to read chapter 26 with its account of Jeremiah on trial for his life because of his preaching in the temple without thinking of Jesus and how he walked the same road. We know that people compared Jesus to Jeremiah. One reason for that may be that, like Jeremiah, he stood out against popular consensus (anti-Babylonian, anti-Roman violent attitudes), and certainly criticized both people and government for their ways. Furthermore, Jesus' symbolic action in the temple was interpreted, like Jeremiah's preaching, as a direct threat, and that was a key element in the charge brought against him soon afterwards, leading to his execution. How can we exercise the kind of prophetic voice that engages political realities – resisting especially the political pressures that lead to violence, war and oppression? Do we consider that to be a valid biblical element in the mission of the church?

- The little story of Uriah raises the perennial issue of why it is that some servants of God suffer while others are spared. It may well have occurred to Jeremiah to wonder the same, when he wasn't wallowing in his own woes. As far as we know, Uriah was as much faithful a messenger of God's word as Jeremiah was. Yet God permitted the sword for him but safety for Jeremiah. One wonders what John the brother of James thought when God decreed the sword for James, but a rescuing angel for Peter (Acts 12). Certainly, such narratives expose the lie of the 'prosperity gospel', that faith guarantees health, wealth and success. For all of these people lived in faith and faithfulness, yet their experiences differed diametrically. The lesson is as clear as Hebrews 11:32–39. *Some* lived in rampant victory. *Others* died in terrible martyrdoms. But 'these were *all* commended for their faith'.

- We do not have the inspired and infallible prophetic insight of a Jeremiah, whose words carry the canonical truth of God's word, when we seek to interpret contemporary history and the

287

ebb and flow of current affairs – still less, perhaps, when we seek to discern the future – as he did in the political arena of chapter 27. But we are still committed to the biblical affirmation that the living God is sovereign over the affairs of all nations, and that his kingdom rules over all. In what ways can we discern the presence of God's sovereign governance? How can we build up the faith of God's people to see God's hand in past events, for the sake of the gospel, and to trust in God's sovereign providence in future events, and thus live in faith and hope and not in fear and anxiety? That will be a major theme of the next chapter.

Jeremiah 29:1–32
21. Letter to the exiles

How can we live as the people of God in the midst of a society and culture that dismisses or despises us at best, and may hate and persecute us at worst? That is a question we find ourselves asking in the contemporary world, but it is far from modern. Jews and Christians have faced it all through their history. For the people of Judah who found themselves in exile in Babylon it was agonizingly real. Indeed, forget most of that opening sentence; 'How can we live at all?' was what many of them felt.

But the biggest question that faced the exiles was, 'Where is the Lord? Where is YHWH the God of Israel, the God of the exodus, the God of the conquest, the God of David and all the promises made to him? Where is our God in the midst of such catastrophe?' Did God have anything to say to his defeated, disgraced, dislocated and despairing people?

To answer such questions, Jeremiah wrote them a letter. In fact he wrote several, and this chapter witnesses to some extended correspondence between Jerusalem and Babylon in the years between 597 and 587 BC. The key text, however, is the first letter: 29:1–23. And within that, the key message is conveyed in verses 1–14. Originally, of course, this letter was addressed to the first group of exiles with Jehoiachin, but its message became all the more relevant and hope-filled after the fall of Jerusalem as it was read and reflected upon by all the exiles who now faced their bleak future in Babylon. It was a letter that spoke into the trauma and desperation of a people whose world had fallen apart. It was a letter in which Jeremiah begins the transformation of his message from uprooting and tearing down to building and planting, from judgment to hope.[1]

---

[1] On the subtle hints of this transformation between chs. 26 – 29, see McConville, *Judgment and Promise*, pp. 86–91.

1. A surprising perspective: from refugees to residents (1–6)

Who was responsible for the Israelites being in exile in a foreign land? These verses give us two answers. On the one hand the narrative introduction speaks about all *the people **Nebuchadnezzar** had carried into exile from Jerusalem to Babylon* (1). But in the text of the letter we read God's own account: *all those whom **I** carried into exile from Jerusalem to Babylon* (4). And this is repeated in verses 7 and 14.

So who did it? Nebuchadnezzar or God? The answer of course is both.

At the level of human history, what any observer would have seen was the army of Nebuchadnezzar carrying out his orders. There was terrible violence, suffering, cruelty, destruction, death and loss – all the work of evil men doing evil deeds for which they themselves bore responsibility. Nebuchadnezzar did it.

But at another level, what the eye of the prophet saw (as he had seen and told for years) was the hand of God behind the hammer of Nebuchadnezzar. It was God who had brought the Babylonians as agents of his judgment upon his recalcitrant people – as he had done in previous centuries through other imperial armies. God did it, or rather, to use Jeremiah's terms: Nebuchadnezzar did it, but functioning as YHWH's servant.

This was something many Israelites could not accept, no matter how long Jeremiah had prepared them for it. A more plausible explanation seemed to be that YHWH had simply deserted them (e.g. Isa. 40:27), or that YHWH had grown old and tired and had met his match at last – the gods of Babylon had defeated him. Perhaps they would be better off choosing other gods – as their wives had urged for years (see ch. 44). But no, Jeremiah insists. *Israel* had been defeated and *Jerusalem* had been destroyed, but YHWH, the sovereign Lord God of all creation (ch. 27), was not defeated. On the contrary YHWH was as fully in control of events – even such shattering events – as he ever had been in their long history.

History is one thing. It would have been as easy for the Israelites as it is for us to look back to great events in centuries past and affirm them as 'the mighty acts of the LORD'. Their psalms were full of that kind of celebration. But the present is something else. It is far harder to perceive and affirm the sovereignty of God in current events, when you are right close up to the puzzle and panic of them.

And it is especially puzzling when God seems to be undoing all he has been doing hitherto. The repeated phrase *from Jerusalem to Babylon* (1, 4) has an ominous feeling that makes it more than mere geography. The whole history of the Old Testament had gone in the opposite direction: from the land of Babel (Gen. 11) to Jerusalem;

from God calling Abraham out of the land of Babylon to God establishing his people in the land of Jerusalem, and putting his name and his temple there. That was the flow of sacred history. But now it seems that the whole plot is unravelling. God has pressed the rewind button and history is going backwards. How can God reverse his plans? Did he no longer care about his promise to Abraham, or his promise to bless all nations through the people of Abraham? How could that mission continue if God had hurled the people back to square one, back indeed to the very land Abraham had left behind?

Israel did indeed have a continuing Abrahamic mission, even in exile, as we shall see in a moment. But before they could even begin to contemplate that, they needed to accept that it was by God's own sovereign will that they were now where they were. And if that was a surprising perspective, they needed to get over the surprise and settle down. What had happened was under God's control and it was not about to end soon. With this prophetic perspective, Jeremiah tells the exiles to settle down in Babylon for a stay that will last several generations (5–6). The language of these verses works in two ways.

First, such a perspective turns refugees into residents. The exiles were being told that they were to accept where they were, and be there with God who had put them there. They should not entertain the hopes or wild prophecies of an early return, which would keep them forever unsettled. They needed to settle into Babylon as their new home. Babylon would not be the nation's *permanent* home. But it was their *present* home where the next few generations would be resident. Prepare for it. Get on with the normality of building homes, farms and families. Life goes on.

Secondly, the language of planting, eating, marrying, having children and grandchildren, and especially the instruction to *increase in number* (5–6), resonates strongly with Genesis. It is the language both of creation and of Abrahamic promise. For Israel in exile, there was the opportunity of a fresh creational start. And the God who blessed creation with fruitfulness and growth had promised the same to Abraham.[2] The language of increase also echoes Exodus 1:7, with the implication that if the people continued to grow (after the decimation of 587 BC) even in a foreign land, God's redemption from this latter-day bondage lay ahead in a new exodus.

God's work in creation is the basis for God's work in redemption. God's work in redemption will fulfil God's work in creation (and hence the powerful creation language of Isa. 40 – 55 as well as Jeremiah, e.g., 31:35–37; 33:14–26). The effect of God's redemptive

---

[2] Gen. 1:26–28; 12:1–3; 17:3–6; 22:17.

work, finally, is a new creation (see Isa. 65:17–25; 2 Cor. 5:17; Rev. 21 – 22).[3]

So the exiles must settle down, adapt and adjust to life in Babylon, and yet remain the people of YHWH. One group who took this advice seriously was Daniel and his three friends. They were among the earliest of the exiles, taken probably when they were boys. There is no way of knowing if they ever heard the letter of Jeremiah being read out, though it is perfectly possible that they did. At any rate, they behaved in a manner consistent with its advice. In Daniel 1 we see them accepting three aspects of Babylonian life and culture (Babylonian names, education and jobs) before they draw a line and refuse to accept table dependence on the king (probably symbolizing total 'covenant' loyalty). They accepted and adapted to where God had put them, but remained faithful to God if an irreconcilable conflict of loyalties arose.

2. A surprising mission: from mourners to missionaries (7)

Spare a thought for the person who had to read out this letter publicly to the exiled community – especially when he reached verse 7, which is sensationally unexpected: *Also, seek the peace and prosperity of the city to which I have carried you into exile. Pray to the LORD for it, because if it prospers, you too will prosper.*[4]

Imagine the angry response to such words among people in the early throes of being captives of war in a foreign, enemy land. 'Surely', they may have protested, 'this letter has been intercepted by the Babylonian censor and altered. We know which city we should be praying for, and it certainly isn't Babylon. "Pray for the peace of *Jerusalem*!"[5] And we know what we want for Babylon, and it certainly isn't peace':

> Daughter Babylon, doomed to destruction,
>   happy is the one who repays you
>   according to what you have done to us.
> Happy is the one who seizes your infants
>   and dashes them against the rocks
>   – just as you did to ours![6]

Psalm 137 shows the wretched ugliness of the mood of the exiles on first arriving in Babylon, with their longings for home and their

[3] Fretheim, p. 409.
[4] Jer. 29:7.
[5] Ps. 122:6.
[6] Ps. 137:8–9.

understandable desire for vengeance on their enemies. And here is this insufferable prophet from Jerusalem telling them to seek the welfare of Babylon and pray for it! What an insult to their situation.

It was probably hard enough for the exiles to imagine that they could pray to YHWH *in* Babylon, let alone that they should pray to him *for* Babylon. It must have seemed impossible, theologically, emotionally and politically. But Jeremiah insists that this is the task before them. Once they could accept the perspective and the advice of verses 4–6 and had settled down as residents in Babylon, then they had an ongoing mission there. It was the Abrahamic mission of being the model and means of blessing to the nations. Such a responsibility turned mourners into missionaries. They should seek the *šālôm* of their neighbours in Babylon, care for their welfare, be agents of constructive peace and wellbeing in the communities in which they settled.

'But they are our enemies! They destroyed our city, slaughtered members of our families, and dragged us a thousand miles away to this pagan land.'

'Pray for them', insists Jeremiah. 'Seek their welfare.' This word of Jeremiah to the exiles is possibly the closest we come in the Old Testament to the words of Jesus, spoken to people who felt like exiles in their own land under the heel of Roman occupation: 'I tell you, love your enemies and pray for those who persecute you.'[7]

One might interpret the second phrase (*because if it prospers, you too will prosper*) as self-interested. But it is no more so than one of the reasons Paul gives when he instructs Christians to pray for pagan authorities.[8] Jeremiah believed in the power of prayer (or rather in the power of the God who hears prayer). It is somewhat ironic that this prophet who had been forbidden to pray for his own people in their own land here instructs those same people to pray for their enemies in a foreign land.

Jeremiah's instruction makes several significant assumptions:

- that God could hear and answer prayer anywhere on earth;
- that God would hear prayer on behalf of those who were not his own people (cf. Solomon's prayer for a similar thought);[9]
- that God could and would act for the blessing and welfare of the Babylonians if the Israelites would pray for them;
- that even in captivity God's people could exercise a ministry that moves the muscles of God's providence in the world.

---

[7] Matt. 5:44.
[8] 1 Tim. 2:1–2.
[9] 1 Kgs 8:41–43.

293

These are profoundly missional assumptions that should undergird our own sense of responsibility for the people around us, wherever we find ourselves, willingly or otherwise. Prayer is a missional responsibility – always.

Once again, one wonders if Daniel was among those who heard this command and heeded it throughout his life's work. We know he prayed three times a day.[10] Was Nebuchadnezzar top of his prayer list? If so, it would help explain Daniel's surprising reaction to Nebuchadnezzar's second dream, about the great tree that was chopped down and the man who would eat grass like an ox (Dan. 4). Suddenly Daniel realized that the dream was about Nebuchadnezzar himself. This man, who had destroyed Daniel's city and torn him from his home in childhood, was finally for the chop! Should Daniel not have rejoiced that he had lived to see the day of his enemy's downfall? Surprisingly not. He was so upset he could not speak, and when eventually the king insisted on hearing the interpretation, Daniel offered him some advice about how to avoid the impending judgment. One gets the distinct impression that Daniel had come to have respect and affection for his Babylonian monarch. Was that not the natural result of praying for him and seeking his welfare, as Jeremiah instructed?

It's hard to go on hating someone when you pray for them every day.

Jeremiah's instructions here form part of a wider biblical tradition that God's people can serve God by serving wider society in various occupations. The stories of Joseph, Daniel, Nehemiah and even Esther are Old Testament examples. Erastus is one such in the New Testament.[11] All forms of legitimate service can be ways of 'seeking the welfare of the city'. Paul would have included them in what he generalized as 'doing good' – a concept that did not merely mean being nice, but included concrete social benefaction, contributing to the public good of all citizens. It is a part of biblical teaching that is sadly neglected in many churches.[12]

Could it be that Jeremiah gave the instruction of verse 7 because he had a rose-tinted view of Babylon? Did he imagine that Babylon itself had somehow become God's favourite spot on earth, so that the Israelites could enjoy living there forever? Not at all. We know exactly what Jeremiah thought of Babylon. In another diplomatic postbag Jeremiah sent the massive oracle against Babylon that we now have

[10] Dan. 6:10.
[11] See Rom. 16:23.
[12] I have discussed more fully the Bible's teaching on what it means for God's people to exercise their mission in the public square of the 'secular' world, in *The Mission of God's People*, ch. 13, pp. 222–243.

in chapters 51 – 52. Jeremiah was under no illusions. Babylon itself stood under God's judgment and its time would come. But that was true of all nations and all the earth, *and it still is*. The role of God's people in the midst of such reality is still to pray for and seek the welfare of the people they live among, even when we are aware that people in every nation and culture stand under God's judgment.

3. A surprising future: from victims to visionaries (8–14)

The immediate future must be faced, and it was not what *the prophets and diviners* among the exiles were telling them (8–9). Their *dreams* of a swift return were nothing but *lies*, and they were no more sent by God than Hananiah was. Their ending would be even worse than his (20–23). No, the exiles were in Babylon for the long haul, commensurate with the long-term sins for which they were now suffering judgment. Such words about the present reality from Jeremiah bore no surprise at all. It's what he had been saying for decades.

So his next words about the future are truly and gloriously unexpected and surprising beyond belief. It would not be quick but it would be certain. Babylon their oppressor, Babylon the seemingly supreme and unrivalled greatest power in the world, Babylon about which Nebuchadnezzar boasted, 'Is not this the great Babylon I have built as the royal residence, by my mighty power and for the glory of my majesty?'[13] – Babylon's time would come, and within *seventy years* Babylon would be past history. Such is the fate of all human empires – ancient and contemporary.

And then what? Then God would (lit.) 'establish upon you my *good* word' (10). The future was 'good', for God said so. And verse 11 goes on to spell out just how good it would be. It was not merely that God would eventually bring the people back to their land, but that his overall *plans* for them were now plans of *šālôm* and not 'evil' (*rāʿâ*), to give them *hope and a future* (the reversal of 18:11). And all this is underlined by the emphatic *I know*. This is not some remote possibility, but something securely determined in and by the mind of God.

Jeremiah 29:11 probably ranks as one of the most quoted and most claimed promises of the Bible. It is found in countless text calendars, pretty pictures and sacred ornaments. It is rightly trusted as a very precious word of assurance from God. But do we take note of its context? This is a *surprising* word of hope to a people who stood under God's judgment. It is not a glib happy feeling: 'God's going to be nice to us all, me especially' (we should note that the 'you' is

[13] Dan. 4:30.

plural, not individual – this is primarily a promise to the people as a whole). It is rather the robust affirmation that even in and through the fires of judgment there can be hope in the grace and goodness of God. That is God's ultimate plan and purpose. The promise stands firm, but it does not preclude or neutralize judgment. Rather it presupposes but transcends judgment.

What then should be the response to such a surprising word of amazing grace? Not gleeful celebration. Not mere relief: 'Well that's all right then; everything will turn out fine. Let's have a party!' Rather, the people are called to respond to the restoring grace of God with renewed prayer and seeking him (12–14). The language here is taken straight from Deuteronomy 4:29–31, which had anticipated just such a return to YHWH in the wake of the judgment of exile, and had promised that when Israel would thus return with all their heart and soul they would run into the arms of the God of forgiving grace. 'For the LORD your God is a merciful God; he will not abandon or destroy you or forget the covenant with your ancestors, which he confirmed to them by oath.'[14]

We should notice the gospel of these verses, contained in the indicative verbs: *then you will . . . and I will.* The movement of the people's heart to seek God is itself a gift of God's grace,[15] even while it is at the same time the necessary condition in which they can receive his grace. God's grace gives what God demands. Similarly here, the statements *you will seek me and find me* and *I will be found by you,* are both promissory statements. They tell us that it is God's supreme will to be found and known, and that is the only source of his people's life and blessing. Their hope lies in God's willingness to be found, not in Israel's ability to search.

And this time we know that Daniel was aware of Jeremiah's words. Daniel tells us that, at some point in his study of Jeremiah's prophecies,[16] he understood that the 'seventy years' for Babylon must be coming to an end soon. And what was his reaction? Not to call in his friends for celebration, but to respond exactly as Jeremiah 29:12–14 portrayed, by seeking God in prayer and confession, appealing to God to act in forgiving and restoring grace, as God had said he would.[17]

Here then was a surprising hope for the future that turned victims into visionaries. It enabled the exiles to look up and look forward

---

[14] Deut 4:31.

[15] This is the same as God's interpretation of the 'good figs' (24:6–7, to which this passage is closely linked).

[16] This indicates that there was indeed some edited text of Jeremiah's words among the exiles in Babylon, even though Jeremiah himself ended up in Egypt.

[17] Dan. 9:1–19.

and believe. They were not going to get the instant quick fix their prophets were dreaming of. But they could trust that God would be true to his promise and that there was a future for the coming generations of God's people which (as we now know) would eventually be a future and hope for the nations.

The message of the whole letter could turn refugees, mourners and victims into resident missionary visionaries. And on such a foundation, the immediately following chapters will build an even richer tapestry of hope. The challenge is, which of those descriptions would fit the way we live as Christians in the unbelieving world that surrounds us today?

4. Postscripts (15–32)

The rest of the chapter consists of two further sections in the original letter, followed by a somewhat fragmentary account of the ensuing correspondence that Jeremiah's letter sparked.

a. About those left behind (15–19)

These verses repeat most of what had been said in Jeremiah's parable of the two baskets of figs (ch. 24) about those left behind in Jerusalem after the First Deportation, from the installed king, Zedekiah, downward. The future lies with the ones now in exile, while those left behind will endure the full weight of God's judgment when it falls (as it did in 587 BC).

However, the last line of verse 19 makes it very clear that the exiles were as guilty as those left behind, and therefore it was entirely owing to the pure and undeserved grace of God that they were now being regarded by God as 'good figs' with a hope and a future, The big question that faced the exiles reading this letter after the finality of 587 BC was, would they listen now?

b. About those false prophets (20–23)

Two prophets who were predicting the same optimistic future among the exiles in Babylon as Hananiah did in Jerusalem are named and shamed – Ahab and Zedekiah. If the fate of Hananiah was already known, then the prediction in these verses must have been chilling indeed. It seems these men were not only encouraging the exiles to believe in a rapid return, but were advocating possibly violent resistance against Babylon. Nebuchadnezzar took a dim view of such insubordination and would deal with them as he would later attempt to deal with Shadrach, Meshach and Abednego (Dan. 3). Their fate would be the due penalty of Babylonian law, just as Hananiah's had been consistent with Deuteronomic law. Their immoral lifestyle was further proof that they had no divine mandate.[18]

c. Some further correspondence on file (24–32)

The remainder of the chapter seems to refer to at least three additional letters:

1. From Shemaiah (from Babylon) to Zephaniah the priest in Jerusalem (26–28), complaining that he had not dealt with Jeremiah as any serious religious authority ought to, given that Jeremiah was such an obvious charlatan – *a maniac . . . who poses as a prophet*. Shemaiah was not a man to mince words. Lock the fellow up!
2. From Jeremiah replying to Shemaiah and referring to his letter (25), after Zephaniah had shown Shemaiah's letter to Jeremiah (29). We are not told of any action Zephaniah took on it – apparently none, perhaps not wishing to get the same answer that Pashur got.[19]
3. From Jeremiah to *all the exiles* denouncing Shemaiah in familiar terms as a false prophet who will have no future among the 'good figs' (29–32).

Theological and expository reflections

- I remember as a child the shock and horror of adults talking about how the Chinese Communist Party had expelled all foreign missionaries in 1954. It was hard to believe why God allowed it. Some thought it would be the end of the church and Christian mission in that country. Sixty years later, there are more Christians in church every Sunday in China than in all of Western Europe, including Britain. Sometimes we can only see God's sovereignty looking back. The challenge, as it was for the exiles, is to discern it in the midst of the confusion of the present.
- Another memory from my youth – singing 'This world is not my home, I'm just a-passin' through', and feeling uncomfortable with the sentiment. I used to think, 'this world in its present sinful state is not my final home, but it is my present home, where God has put me, and I want to live for him here, not just "pass through" on my way to somewhere else'. Jeremiah's

---

[18] v. 23, cf. 23:14.
[19] 20:1–6.

advice to the exiles (5–6) seems like an antidote to an unhealthy and unworldly dose of 'pilgrim mentality'. Live for God where you are.

- Is there enough emphasis in Christian churches, especially in their preaching, on the Bible's teaching on good citizenship? Jeremiah told the exiles to 'seek the peace and prosperity of the city' where they lived (7). Paul tells Christian believers not only to pay their taxes but also to be 'doing good', a word which was commonly used for public benefactors, people who contributed to society. How can we give greater value and incentive to one another to be a blessing to the wider community in practical ways?

Jeremiah 30:1 – 31:1
22. The surprises of grace

1. Introduction: 'hope springs eternal'[1] (30:1–4)

Jeremiah is writing again. In the last chapter he wrote a letter to the exiles; in this chapter he is to *write in a book* the fuller message that God has for them. That letter (29:1–14) had continued the subtle transformation of Jeremiah into a prophet of hope and salvation, after the predominant message of judgment in chapters 1 – 25. Jeremiah specifies that when Babylon's supremacy has run its course for seventy years, God would 'bring you back from captivity' (29:10–14). So we are already prepared to hear such words of hope, to catch glimpses of the sunshine of God's promises. But nothing quite prepares us for the bursts of sound and light, of joy and celebration, that suddenly dominate the book for the next four chapters, 30 – 33.

These chapters are usually called the Book of Consolation (cf. 30:2), since their primary purpose is to bring comfort and hope to the despairing exiles, urging them to trust in what God had promised in 29:14, to know that he had plans for their good, plans for a future that lay through and beyond the judgment they were now suffering.

Two introductory points are worth considering before plunging into the startling texts ahead.

a. The great turn-around

It is far more than just a change of mood and tone that we have in these chapters. It is a radical reversal. A whole new reality is being announced which will not change the *facts* (the fall of Jerusalem and captivity of the people), but will change the way they respond to

---

[1] Alexander Pope, 'An Essay on Man'. However, whereas Pope's line goes on 'in the human breast', Jeremiah's hope in the following chapters springs not from merely human longings, but from the eternal covenant faithfulness of God.

those facts and learn to imagine a future that seemed humanly impossible. God is turning things around!

That is almost literally the meaning of a phrase in verse 3 that occurs repeatedly in these chapters. It occurs first in 29:14, translated 'I will bring you back from captivity'. The Hebrew phrase is 'I will turn your captivity' – using the verb *šûb* that is so dominant throughout the book of Jeremiah (to turn away, turn around, turn back, repent, etc.). The two-word phrase (*šûb šebût*) seems to have become proverbial, meaning not just the specific ending of actual captivity, but the idea of reversal of fortune in general – when things 'take a turn for the better', as we say.

This phrase occurs seven times in Jeremiah 30 – 33.[2] Unfortunately the NIV varies its translation between 'bring back from captivity' and 'restore the fortunes of' (with footnotes indicating these as alternatives), so that the prominence of the phrase and the theme it presents is lost. This repeated phrase reflects the strong influence of the theology of Deuteronomy. The phrase stands first in the list of promises beginning at Deuteronomy 30:3. In fact, the whole of the Book of Consolation can be viewed as a prophetic expansion in full poetic colour of the expectation and promise expounded in Deuteronomy 30:1–10. It would be well worth pausing to read that chapter before embarking on Jeremiah's rendition of the same script and score.

But the great turnaround presented in these chapters goes way beyond a single repeated phrase. Chapters 30 – 33 contain constant echoes of sayings of Jeremiah in chapters 1 – 25. Sometimes a rhetorical question in the earlier prophecies (expecting a negative answer) receives a positive answer here. Sometimes a strong note of judgment is simply replaced with the promise of salvation. Sometimes a wistful longing receives a reassurance of being fulfilled. But always there is a sense of something new that transcends the past. So it is not that an old word is merely cancelled out, but that it is surpassed by a new reality made possible by the power of God's promise. God's past words were true and necessary at that time. But God himself was not bound to the past. New words for new reality! Here are some examples. It will take a moment to check through them, but it will be well worth the effort to grasp the huge reversal in these chapters.

- 30:8 echoes the prediction of Hananiah in 28:4, 11. Hananiah got the timing wrong, but even though Jeremiah predicted an iron yoke (unbreakable by any human force), God would ultimately break the yoke of Israel's oppressors.

---

[2] 30:3, 18; 31:23; 32:44; 33:7, 11, 26.

- 30:9 reverses the ending of the line of Davidic kings in 22:30, promising a new David (as also in 23:5–6, repeated in 33:15–16).
- 30:11 answers the hope and prayer of 10:24, that God would discipline, but not completely destroy.
- 30:12–17 answers the cry of the wounded at 8:22 and 15:18, while 30:17 answers the question at 15:5.
- 30:18 promises a rebuilding that reverses 9:19, while 30:19–20 reverses the depopulation of 9:21–22 and 10:20.
- 31:3–4 answers the nostalgic bittersweet honeymoon memory of YHWH in 2:2 with the promise of a fresh wooing of his bride ('you' is feminine singular).
- 31:6 answers the forlorn question at 8:19 and 14:19, as to whether the Lord would be present in Zion.
- 31:8 transforms *the land of the north* from a source of impending invasion (1:14–15, etc.), into the source of coming restoration.
- 31:9 anticipates people praying to the God who now listens, who had earlier refused to do so in 11:14.
- 31:12–13 transforms the ending of all social joy in 16:9 into a new celebration.
- 31:18–19 answers at last God's own question in 8:4–7 as to why his people never turn to him in repentance with the promise that they will.
- 31:31–34 promises a new covenant that will transcend the broken one of 11:1–8.

What needs to be stressed again, however, is that these new words from God do not cancel out the earlier words of Jeremiah's preaching (as if to say 'God didn't really mean it'). Nor do they ignore the historical and theological fact of divine judgment on the rebellious house of Israel. In the terms of Deuteronomy 30, the nation had indeed chosen death rather than life. But as that same chapter promised, God could bring life out of death and a glorious future out of a dismal past.

b. Prediction, promise, and three horizons

And that brings us to a third important point in our understanding and interpretation of these chapters (and others like them in the book of the prophets). At one level these chapters contain straightforward prediction – namely that the people of Israel would return from exile in Babylon within a span of approximately two or three generations, that life in their land would be re-established, the city of Jerusalem would be rebuilt, and normal agricultural cycles and social pleasures would be resumed. And those things did take place. Predictions were indeed fulfilled.

But the message of these chapters goes way beyond simple prediction, in at least two ways. First, the subject almost all the way through is God himself, speaking in the first person. All that will happen will be because God planned it, wills it, announces it, causes it and guides it. This transforms the whole discourse from mere 'third-party' prediction to self-involving promise. A promise is when someone, speaking for himself or herself ('I'), makes a specific commitment, binding upon themselves, to act in a certain way in relation to another person who is addressed in the second person ('you'). And that is the predominant form of speech in these chapters. Even when Israel is spoken of as 'they', it is clear that God is speaking to them as well as about them. This is all about the restoration of a relationship, not just about a return to the land. And secondly, the promises of God flowing through these chapters are repeatedly grounded in the character of God: his covenant faithfulness, his saving power, his eternal love, his parental tenderness, his compassionate memory, his healing touch, his surprising – oh so surprising! – grace.

Promise has the capacity to go on being fulfilled in ever-changing ways according to new circumstances, whereas prediction either comes true or it doesn't. Promise has elasticity and longevity. The simple promises made at a wedding ceremony do not have to be revised and rewritten every few years as the life-stages of a marriage roll along. They are phrased and intended to cover all eventualities and to sustain a lifelong mutual commitment that will find practical expression in myriad ways – most of them unforeseen and unforeseeable on the day they are spoken.

So here. God makes a promise to the exiles that goes beyond (though it includes) the prediction of a physical return, and grants a range of assurances, envisages a scale of blessings, anticipates an intensity and purity of relationship between God and his people – all of which transcend the boundaries of 'what actually happened in history'. And that is what we should expect, since the promise comes from God and God himself transcends the bounds of what seems historically possible or actual. The exiles were being summoned not just to look forward to a prediction coming true, but to re-imagine their relationship with God in a way that opened up the future to fresh possibilities only God could create.

As the promissory text embodies God's self-commitment, so the promissory text lingers in the exilic and postexilic community as an anchor for faith and hope in a context of fickleness and despair.

303

That is, the text is not a prediction, but it is a promise to which Israel clings because of Israel's confidence in the promise-maker. The promissory text is not 'used up' or exhausted in any fulfilment or partial fulfilment, but continues to stand, in situation after situation, in generation after generation, as a witness and testimony to what God intends that has not yet come to fruition.[3]

In other words, there is gospel here. There is good news that takes us past the return of the exiles in 538 BC and on to the gospel summons of John the Baptist and Jesus Christ as they called God's people home in repentance and faith and into new covenant relationship in Christ's blood, and then takes us further still to the ultimate future of God's new creation when some of the most exalted poetry and promise of these chapters will find fulfilment.

Once we grasp this promissory, rather than merely predictive, dimension of texts like these, then we can see that we must interpret them on three horizons. That is to say, we need to understand that the same text may find fulfilment at different points, or horizons, along the great biblical story line.

- *Horizon 1* is the horizon of the prophet's own world, or the Old Testament era itself. And so we need to take note of the ways in which the future anticipated in the prophetic word was indeed realized in the remainder of Old Testament history. In the case of these chapters, Horizon 1 is clearly the actual return of exiles from Babylon, in several waves starting with the decree of Cyrus of Persia in 538 BC. God did gather back his scattered people and their life continued in the post-exilic era.
- *Horizon 2* is the horizon of the New Testament. There are dimensions of God's promise here that Christians necessarily interpret in relation to Jesus Christ – such as the promise of a new king David, and a new covenant that ensures eternal forgiveness of sin. The good news preached to the exiles finds its deepest fulfilment in the gospel preached by Jesus and accomplished by his life, death and resurrection.
- *Horizon 3* is the eschatological horizon of the return of Christ and the new creation. There are soaring visions in such chapters of a relationship between God and God's people and God's creation – a relationship of perfect love, obedience, unity and harmony that we do not yet see or enjoy, but which will be realities in the new creation, according to the promises of God that flow right up to Revelation 21 – 22.

[3] Brueggemann (1991), p. 42.

2. Salvation from fearsome enemies (30:5–11)

The Book of Consolation begins in devastation. There would be no minimizing the horror of the events of 587 BC – still to come when Jeremiah first spoke these words, but a searing memory for the exiles who read them in Babylon. In fact verses 5–7 (apart from the last line of verse 7) could as easily have come somewhere in chapters 1 – 25, for it is exactly the message we have heard so often. The disaster would induce terror and panic among the population (5b) and paralyzed fear among the army (6). The imagery of labour pains for the suffering to come is familiar from 4:31, 6:24 and 13:21. Here, in a typical twist of the metaphor, Jeremiah pictures the burly warriors of Israel's army clutching their stomachs like a labouring woman, but in *deathly* fear not living hope, as they faced the terrorizing and over-whelming brutality of Nebuchadnezzar's forces.

But the familiar language of judgment is suddenly and inexplicably reversed in the unexpected closing line of verse 7 – *but he will be saved out of it.* Judgment will fall, but beyond it, salvation beckons (contrast 2:27).

Verses 8–9 shift our gaze from the paralyzed army at the time of Jerusalem's collapse to the humiliated people whose enslavement immediately followed. For them the message of the exodus liberation rings forth. They could not save themselves (any more than the Hebrews in Egypt could). Nor could their stomach-churning army save them. But God bursts in with the majestic and repeated *I will surely save you* (10). God alone will act, as he did in the exodus.

The triple promise of salvation (7, 10, 11), along with the encouragement not to be afraid because God was with them, echoes the original promise that God had made to Jeremiah at his call (1:8, 19) and extends that promise now to the whole people. *I am with you* are the words they badly needed to hear after all the years Jeremiah had told them, 'I am against you' (21:4–5, 13). The God who had carried out the covenant threats, will now revert to the covenant promises. Judgment would be terrible but not total. There would be discipline but not complete destruction of the people. 'There is punishment, but it is not ultimate. There is rescue, but it is not cheap. God is sovereign and will not be mocked; God is caring and not to be doubted.'[4]

In this way, the hope that had been expressed in 4:27 and 5:10, where it had seemed almost beyond hope, will be realized. But it will be grounded, not in some grim ability of Israel to 'survive against

[4] Brueggemann (1991), p. 51.

the odds', but in the character of God himself. The last line of verse
11, *I will not let you go entirely unpunished* comes from Exodus
34:6–7. That is the earliest and clearest definition of God's character
and ways, given to Moses in the context of the appalling sin of that
first generation of the exodus. God's faithfulness and love would
win the day, but he could not let sin and guilt remain unpunished.
It is a paradox that we do not see resolved till we stand at the foot
of the cross and see the saving forgiveness of God outpoured through
God bearing the guilt of our sin in his own self in the person of
his Son.

There are strong links throughout these chapters with the prophesies of Hosea, with which Jeremiah was undoubtedly familiar.
Verse 9 is the first of many. Hosea, though primarily sent to the
northern kingdom of Israel in the previous century, had words of
hope for Judah as well. He prophesied a restoration of *David their
king*.[5] Significantly, however, for both Hosea and Jeremiah, who
paraphrases Hosea 3:5 in 30:9, this was not just a restoration of the
kind of ungodly and apostate government that had characterized
the generations of kings in the line of David before the exile. Rather
it would be primarily a return to 'seek the LORD their God' (Hosea),
or to *serve the LORD their God* (Jeremiah). Only in that state of
repentance and obedience would they know the benign rule of a
true *David their king*, issuing in 'his blessings in the last days'
(Hosea). Here we have a case of a prophecy which is not fulfilled
at Horizon 1 (there was no restored Davidic monarchy after the
exile), but points us to Horizon 2 (Jesus, 'great David's greater Son'),
and ultimately to Horizon 3 (when 'the Root and the Offspring
of David' comes[6]). 'As for the coming of *David their king* (9), it
would have to wait for the coming – indeed the coming in glory – of
David's Lord.'[7]

3. Healing for self-inflicted wounds (30:12–17)

If in verses 5–11 we saw the panic of people who had no hope of being
rescued, in verses 12–17 we hear the cries of people who had no hope
of being healed. The scene is initially just as bleak and horrific. We
have phrases for this kind of thing. We talk about 'grievous bodily
harm', 'life-threatening injuries', 'incurable cancer', being 'fatally
wounded', or 'terminally ill'. That is the condition of the people in
verses 12–13 and it is clearly a portrait of a nation in exile, physically
emaciated by the months of siege, decimated to a fragment by the

[5] Hos. 3:5.
[6] Rev. 22:16.
[7] Kidner, p. 104. See also 23:5–6, repeated in the Book of Consolation at 33:14–16.

slaughter that happened when the city fell, emotionally traumatized, and spiritually denying the possibility of recovery. Nothing was left but dry bones and the grave.

Once again we find that a theme found in the earlier part of the book here finds an utterly astonishing reversal. For if we were to read only verses 12–15 we would think we were hearing simply the repetition of all Jeremiah's earlier preaching: Israel's sin has produced a terrible national sickness; they are like someone suffering from terrible injuries and wounds (as Jeremiah had felt himself to be, 8:22, 15:18). But the tragedy is that, although these are the wounds of God's judgment, they have actually inflicted them upon themselves by their persistent sin (cf. 13:22). Their guilt has made punishment necessary and unavoidable. The End.

Except that it wasn't.

For in the most astonishing *non sequitur*,[8] God intervenes in verses 16–17 and simply announces that he will inflict reciprocal suffering on those who had so demolished Israel, and will heal and restore the wounded victims of their violence. God will cure the incurable. No explanation is given. God simply promises this reversal as his own will and decision – the grace of God in speech and act, as surprising as it is sovereign.

The poetic power of these verses strikes even more forcefully when we see their artistic structure. The whole saying is shaped in the concentric form frequently found in Hebrew poetry. That is where two or three points are made in order, followed by a central point, and then the earlier points are repeated but in reverse order. This can be seen in the following form.

A   12–14a: Israel's incurable wound; nobody cares
  B   14b: God struck Israel as if an enemy (using their
         enemies as his weapon)
    C   14c: The explanation: Israel's guilt and sin
      D   15a: The central question: 'Why do you cry out?'

---

[8] The *non sequitur* is even more stark in the Hebrew. A *non sequitur* is something that does *not* logically follow from what has just been affirmed. Yet, although the NIV and many English translations render the first word of v. 16 as 'but' – to bring out the contrast with 12–15 – in fact it is emphatically the Hebrew word 'therefore' (ESV). But this seems impossible to our human logic! Surely the statement in v. 15 about Israel's sin and guilt should be followed with a 'therefore' of divine wrath and judgment? In earlier chapters it would have been. But here we are moving in the realm of divine logic, and indeed of the divine 'plan' – *the purposes of his heart* (24). God has willed that after judgment will come the grace of healing and restoration – 'therefore', he can present that as the logic of his own sovereign action in dealing with human sin, overcoming it, and moving forward into the realm of saving grace.

C' 15b: The explanation: Israel's guilt and sin
  B' 16: God will destroy Israel's enemies[9]
A' 17: Israel's wounds healed; though nobody cared for them
      (except the Lord).

In this instance of concentric form, the reversal of the textual order reflects and amplifies the reversal of Israel's fortunes – from incurable sickness to wholeness and health.

If we start at the centre, the key rhetorical question of verse 15a points both backwards and forwards – with opposite effect. That is to say: how we 'feel' verse 15a depends on whether we read it as the conclusion of verse 12–14, or as the rhetorical opening of the hope that climaxes in verse 17. The brilliance of the poetic structure is that it actually functions as both.

Question: *Why do you cry out over your wound,*
your pain that has no cure?

Answer looking back: From what has gone immediately before (12–14), the answer is stonily negative. They have sinned themselves into the terrible judgment of God, mediated through their implacable enemies, and there is *no remedy for your sore, no healing for you.* And worse, nobody cares. Nobody will champion your case. So if your pain has no cure, why are you crying out? Crying is futile, other than as an act of agony and remorse. That was doubtless the traumatized mood among many exiles.

Answer looking forward: But when you look in the other direction from that central question to the end of the poem – what a transformation! If God promises healing and restoration (17), then *Why do you cry out over your wound?* You say your pain has no cure –

---

[9] This note of God first using other nations as agents of his judgment on Israel, and then turning later to punish those nations for the excesses of their action in doing so, is found elsewhere in the prophets (e.g. Isaiah makes the same point about the Assyrians [Isa. 10:5–19] and about the Babylonians [Isa. 47:6–7]). Its roots lie in the mysterious 'turn around' that happens in that poetic anticipation of Israel's history, the Song of Moses in Deut. 32. After the sudden pause in Deut. 32:27, it seems certain that the nations referred to in the immediately following verses are the foreign nations whom God had used as agents of judgment in vv. 21–26. Which makes it all the more remarkable that at the end of the Song, the nations are invited to praise God along with Israel (32:43)! It was a mystery that Paul eventually built into his theology of mission in Romans.

but it has! No cure that *you* can produce. No cure
that anybody else can produce because nobody
else cares. But the sovereign God, the one who
after the exodus declared, 'I am the LORD, your
healer',[10] can cure the incurable and promises to do
so. The simple *I will restore . . . and heal* is God's
answer to the question of verse 15 and reverses the
apparent irreversibility of verse 12.

What gospel grace is embedded in these verses! The fulfilment that
we know took place at Horizon 1, as the exiles returned and their
society was restored with some measure of healing,[11] is surpassed
by the fulfilment that we see in the healing power of Christ (in all
its senses) at Horizon 2, and will be ultimately swallowed up at
Horizon 3 in the healing of all nations and all creation when the city
of God is our dwelling place (Rev. 22:1–4).

It is important not to be reductionistic in thinking about God's
healing of Israel. God's healing is as comprehensive as is God's salvation: it is individual and communal; present and future; spiritual
and psychical/bodily; religious and social/economic/political.
Healing would include both forgiveness of sins and deliverance
from the effects of sins – both the sins of Israel and the sins of others.
Indeed, the healing of all creation is in view.[12]

4. Restoration for broken community (30:18–21)

After two poems filled with potent metaphors (men trembling like
women in labour, people bowed low like oxen under a yoke, incurable injuries), this poem paints with simple realism. It describes the
restoration of Israel's society including: the rebuilding of homes
(18a), and of the city and palace (18b); the growth of population once
again (19b) as family life returns to normal (20a); protection from
external enemies (20b); and an indigenous ruler who will lead the
restoration of Israel's relationship with their God (21).

All these things had been extinguished in the dark hour of God's
judgment, when all joy and thanksgiving had been swamped in
unutterable grief and bereavement (7:34; 9:17–22; 16:9). So this
prophecy of simple reversal found its fulfilment at Horizon 1, when
the returning exiles doubtless rejoiced in their restoration. But there

[10] Exod. 15:26.
[11] The post-exilic narratives of Nehemiah and Ezra and post-exilic prophets,
Zechariah, Haggai and Malachi, however, show that it was far from perfectly healthy.
[12] Fretheim, p. 425.

are resonances in the lines that point even further back and further forward in the overarching purposes of God.

First, the promise that they would increase in numbers, not decrease (19a, picking up also on 23:3 and Jeremiah's instruction in his letter, 29:6), is an echo of the promise to Abraham. This indicates that what is in the mind of God and the mouth of the prophet is more than just a physical return to the land and the reconstruction of Israel as a nation. The re-affirmation of the Abrahamic covenant means that God's purposes for Israel and through Israel for all nations would continue. The restoration after exile was not just the beginning of a new phase of the history of Old Testament Israel; it was also the next step in the mission of God for the world. That is the reason why the event is put in such global perspective in the rhetoric of Isaiah 40 – 55, though such universal vistas are not in the camera frame here in Jeremiah. The underlying theology of the promise, however, points in that direction, as we have already seen at 4:1–2 and 12:14–17. The destiny of *nations* is bound up with the future of *Israel*. And so once again we see how the text opens up to several horizons. Naturally, at Horizon 1, the land would host a growing population once more. But at Horizon 2, Luke will see the fulfilment of Abrahamic promise in the coming of the Messiah – the one whom Simeon would celebrate as 'a light for revelation to the Gentiles [nations] and the glory of your people Israel'.[13] And at Horizon 3 the increase of Abraham's children will include the redeemed from 'every nation, tribe, people and language' who will inhabit the new heaven and new earth.[14] The promise to Israel is a promise to the nations and ultimately a promise to the whole creation.

Second, the promise of a *leader* (21) echoes the promise of a new King David in verse 9 (though the word king is not used here), with a criterion drawn from Deuteronomy 17:15 – he will be a native-born ruler, not one imposed from outside. But the second half of verse 21 anticipates a privilege for this promised leader of God's people that was not enjoyed by Israel's historical kings – namely the priestly right of access into God's presence. Uzziah in his pride towards the end of his reign presumed to do so, against the warnings of his priests, and paid a heavy penalty.[15] So who then would dare to take upon himself the risk of approaching God in that way? Only one whom God himself would choose and cause to do so.[16] Such indeed is our

[13] Luke 1:68–75; 2:32.
[14] Rev. 7:9.
[15] 2 Chr. 26:16–21.
[16] The NIV's translation of the difficult second half of verse 21 seems rather unlikely. Most other translations render the rhetorical question as 'for who would otherwise dare to approach me?'.

appointed kingly High Priest, the Lord Jesus Christ. Yet again we find Horizon 1 shading over to Horizon 2. Or as Kidner eloquently puts it:

> . . . something new: a ruler . . . who will be what no king had ever been allowed to be: their mediator and priest (21). It is one of the boldest but least-known messianic prophecies (for this ruler is clearly the 'David' of v. 9) . . . Once again God is lifting their eyes beyond the return from Babylon . . . to the promised priest-king whom David had foreseen, and whose benefits we now enjoy (Ps. 110:4; Heb. 5:7–10; 7:11–28).[17]

5. Conclusion: judgment wrapped up in blessing (30:22 – 31:1)

This chapter of stunning reversals accomplished by God's surprising grace ends with one more – using yet another poetic technique, the juxtaposition of apparent opposites. The last two verses of the chapter (30:23–24), if we read them in isolation, sound harsh and jarring after what we have just been reading throughout the chapter. Not only that, but they are in fact a repetition of what we heard before at 23:19–20, when God was condemning the false prophets for their messages of peace when in fact the terrible storm of God's wrath was about to break over their heads. Why is that past oracle of doom repeated here? For the purpose of wrapping it in the smothering embrace of the core covenant promise that Israel had known from their origins.

Look how 30:22 and 31:1 take the great Sinai covenant phrases – *you will be my people, and I will be your God; . . . I will be the God of all the families of Israel, and they will be my people* – and place them, neatly in reverse order, on either side of the earlier oracle of woe. This has the effect of creating a new prophecy of covenant grace and hope that will continue to operate through and beyond the judgment embodied in that earlier oracle. Wrath will be swallowed up in mercy. Covenant threats will be carried out, but beyond them – as Deuteronomy 30 had so forcefully and evangelistically declared – covenant grace remains. God will not abandon God's people. God's people will forever be his. Such are *the purposes of his heart.* And it would indeed take *days to come* for the full significance of such theological paradoxes to be made clear, when at the cross *the fierce anger of the LORD*, borne by God himself in his Son, would be the simultaneous outpouring of the grace of God on behalf of all those from all nations whom he would, through Christ, call 'my people'.

---

[17] Kidner, p. 105.

And so, in this first chapter of Jeremiah's Book of Consolation, we have seen the great traditions of Israel's historical faith mobilized for a new era: God's covenants with Abraham, with Israel through Moses at Sinai, and with David, and God's great act of redemption at the exodus – all of these are harnessed to drive the promissory momentum of these poems. All of these great scriptural truths gave reassurance to the exiles of a future that became a literal reality for the generation that experienced the return from exile at Horizon 1. But all of them also point further forward to gospel realities and eschatological hopes that lie at Horizons 2 and 3.

Theological and expository reflections

It is not difficult to imagine how one could preach the gospel of God's grace from these wonderful chapters. As we do so, we should pay attention to two things:

- Remember that this is surprising and sovereign grace that follows only the logic of God's own character and will. It is grace that does not deny or remove the reality of God's judgment on sin, but promises forgiveness and restoration. Ultimately we need to see both in the light of the cross and resurrection of Christ.
- Remember also the three horizons discussed above. We need to sit with the exiles and hear words of hope for their literal future in the return to the land, and recognize the fulfilment of these prophecies at that level in the ending of the exile. But we also need to hear the fuller biblical interpretation of these texts as being fulfilled in the person and work of Christ, and ultimately in the new creation when Christ returns.

Jeremiah 31:2–30
23. The strengths of love

We learn love early. Within the bonds and rounds of family life we see and hear, we receive and offer love – the love of husband and wife, of parents and children. So even when God makes an infinite statement about his own love (3b), it is immediately 'coloured in' with all the imagery of ordinary family life in Israelite village communities. The 'consolation' continues in this chapter by evoking for the exiles the familiarity of home and the eager longing for joyous home-coming. Home! to the restored life of the farming communities with their weddings, festivals and celebrations.

In our last chapter we mentioned some of the artistic poetic features that enhance the meaning and power of these chapters of Jeremiah. Here is another. There is an alternating pattern running through chapters 30 – 31 between addressing Israel as you or they (masculine) and you (feminine).[1] Six sections alternate in this way as follows:

30:5–11	masculine;
30:12–17	feminine;
30:18 – 31:1	masculine;
31:2–6	feminine;
31:7–14	masculine;
31:15–22	feminine-masculine-feminine.

Why does this grammatical effect matter? It reflects the way the relationship between YHWH and Israel is portrayed as both father-son and husband-wife. In other words, Israel, in relationship to God, can be portrayed in masculine (son) or feminine (wife) roles and addressed as such even in the grammatical form of words used. These

[1] See Bozak, *Life 'Anew'*, as referenced in Keown, Scalise and Smothers, pp. 86–87.

primary family metaphors for the covenant relationship between God and people go along with the restoration of normal joyful family life back in the land.

But of course they signify much more than that. For Israel was a son who had chosen the path of disobedience and rebellion. Israel was a wife who had been grossly unfaithful and adulterous. The relationship with God had been shattered by Israel's persistent and unrepentant sin over many generations. So the measure of God's infinite grace and *everlasting love* is seen in the way he still yearns for his wayward son and can still speak of his wanton wife as a virgin bride.

> In these poems the two most devastating and demeaning images for Israel's sinfulness, both of which had been drawn from the intimate life of the family, are redeemed and transformed. The rebellious son becomes the beloved child, and the adulterous wife becomes a virgin, a bride, and a mother of many children.[2]

The chapter opens with two of the most beautiful phrases in the Bible: *favour [grace] in the wilderness* (2), and *loved with everlasting love* (3) – the second providing the opening line of George Wade Robinson's much loved hymn. *The wilderness* (2) does double duty. It portrays initially the terror and danger of the exile, the fate of those who would *survive the sword* of Nebuchadnezzar's final bloody destruction of Jerusalem only to be driven off into the wastelands of captivity. Wilderness was bad news. But the word immediately also recalls, of course, that the wilderness followed the exodus – in which Israel had experienced God's favour and protection on the journey to the land of promise. So the return from exile is here presented, as elsewhere, using the imagery of a new exodus experience, leading to a protected journey through the wilderness and joyful entry into the land and all the blessings promised therein.

Here and throughout this chapter, Jeremiah is strongly influenced by the imagery of Hosea. Indeed, it would be worth pausing right now to read Hosea 2:14–23 and 14:4–7, to savour the language of love and longing that Jeremiah so richly embroiders.

Jeremiah goes on to portray the *everlasting love* of God through several dynamic metaphors of love in action. God loves like a lover wooing his bride, like a father caring for his family, like a shepherd watching over his flock, like a mother mourning her lost children. Around these images, the language flows back and forth between poetic hyperbole and expectations of literal reality. And so we need to similarly move back and forth between Horizons 1, 2 and 3.

[2] Keown, Scalise and Smothers, p. 87.

1. God woos like a lover (3–6)

Verse 3 takes us right back to the first recorded prophetic words of
Jeremiah in 2:2–3. There we heard God longing nostalgically for the
love and devotion that Israel had shown to him in their honeymoon
days – the original exodus and wilderness period. Here, using exactly
the same two Hebrew words (*'ahăbâ* and *ḥesed*), God speaks of his
own *everlasting love* and *unfailing kindness*, which will prove
infinitely more durable than Israel's had been.[3] With the adjective
everlasting Jeremiah expresses the fullest meaning of the 'thousand
generations' ascribed to the love of God in Deuteronomy 7:9 (a
length of time longer than all recorded human history, and therefore
more or less equivalent to 'everlasting'). While the Bible certainly
speaks powerfully of the reciprocal nature of the love between God
and God's people (God loves us; we are to love God and one
another),[4] it is God's love that initiates, redeems, restores and
sustains the relationship into eternity – 'love to the loveless shown,
that they might lovely be'.[5]

Not only is God's love enduring, it is also transforming and recon-
stituting. For it takes the adulterous, self-prostituting wife that Israel
had become and addresses her again as *Virgin Israel*, his beloved
bride (repeated in v. 21). There will again be the joys of music and
dance on a wedding day and the fulfilments of building a home[6] and
planting a farm (4–5). That imagery takes us back also to the definitive shape of Jeremiah's ministry given at his calling in 1:10. After
the years in which the first four terms of his commission had been
exercised to the full – 'to uproot and tear down, to destroy and
overthrow' – Jeremiah now at last releases the energy of the last two
– 'to build and to plant'. The terms would be literal reality for the
returning exiles as they took up life in the land again. But they
describe also the rebuilding of their faith, hopes, theology and
mission. Jeremiah had torn down the falsehoods and sham assurances
that had so fatally infected the body of Israel's faith (election,
covenant, land, temple). But having done that necessary destructive
work, it was time to build and plant that faith again, but on foundations of divine truth and power. 'This restoration reverses at least six

[3] The NIV rendering of the last line of v. 3, *I have drawn you with unfailing kindness*,
is most probably the right way to understand the clause, rather than 'I have extended,
or continued, my faithfulness to you' (cf. ESV). The imagery of Hosea 11:4 is probably
in Jeremiah's mind.
[4] E.g. Deut. 7:7–9; 6:5; 10:15; 11:1; Isa. 63:9; 1 John 4:7–21.
[5] From Samuel Crossman's hymn, 'My song is love unknown', 1664.
[6] 'A woman "built" a family or household by bearing children (Ruth 4:11) and was
herself "built" by becoming a mother (Gen. 16:2; 30:3)' (Keown, Scalise and Smothers,
p. 109).

aspects of the judgment suffered by Israel and Judah: no resting place in exile, a nation torn down, celebrations silenced, vines and plants uprooted, watchmen announcing the invading conqueror, and the temple destroyed.'[7]

There would be not only building and planting, but healing also. The term 'Virgin Israel' recalls Amos's lament for the demise of the northern kingdom of Israel,[8] while the references to Samaria and Ephraim clearly also indicate that part of the divided kingdom. There had been nothing but enmity between Israel and Judah since the fracture after Solomon and by Jeremiah's day the kingdom of Israel had been non-existent for over a century. Not only were no northern Israelites going *up to Zion* (6) any more, even the people of Judah in exile were wondering if God could ever be found there again (8:19).

But in the restored community of God's people, all division would be overcome and a unified people would gather to worship *the LORD our God* (thus incidentally predicting the rebuilding of the temple as well). God's love unifies as it redeems. This is a note that is expressed more prosaically in verses 27–28, and in the combination of *people of Israel* and *people of Judah* in verse 31.

Once again we have to move to Horizon 2 for the fulfilment of such a vision of united worship. There was never a historical reconstitution of the twelve tribes on the land, binding the old kingdoms of Judah and Israel together again in a political unity. But the prophets looked forward to a unified people of God,[9] a unity that would overcome far more than the division of Israel's tribes. It would be a unity that would eventually embrace Jews and Gentiles and people from every tribe and language and nation within the one new humanity, who have been reconciled to God and one another through the cross and resurrection of the Messiah, who have already 'come to Mount Zion' by the new covenant, and who are being built together into the temple of God's dwelling place.[10]

2. God cares like a father (7–9)

The joy continues as the metaphor shifts from the feminine of the previous section to the masculine that runs from here to verse 14. God the father of Israel the son will do even more than the father of the prodigal son – not waiting for the son to return, but going out to lead him home.

[7] Keown, Scalise and Smothers, pp. 109–110.
[8] Amos 5:2.
[9] Ezek. 37:15–28.
[10] Eph. 2:11 – 3:6; Heb. 12:22–24.

The ironies and reversals in these few verses are striking. Here are some:

- *Jacob* is called *foremost of the nations* (7) – a term that speaks not of imperial dominance (what a cruel travesty that would be, given Israel's situation in captivity), but of their election from among the nations into a unique identity and mission in the plans of God. Yet this *foremost* people has been reduced to *the remnant of Israel*, a leftover fragment crying out for salvation.
- When the people in the past had cried to YHWH, 'Come and save us', it was in cynical hypocrisy as they spent their worship and treasure on other gods – a contradiction that God turned back on their heads (2:27–28). But now, when they cry out LORD, *save your people*, God promises to do just that (11).
- In all the earlier prophecies of Jeremiah, *the land of the north* was the place of imminent danger. Indeed, even as he spoke or wrote these lines it is probable that that final outpouring of the pot boiling over from the north (1:13–16) had not yet engulfed the city. But the message now is that that same *land of the north* from which the armies of Babylon had fallen on them would now send forth a very different army of returning Israelites – *the blind and the lame, expectant mothers and women in labour* (8). God's redemption would reach to the least and lowest and most vulnerable in the community – just as a father would give special help to a disabled child or pregnant wife. Such vulnerable people would have suffered most in the conflagration.[11] Now they will be the most visible demonstration of the redeeming love and power of God in the restoration and return.
- There had been weeping in the past, but it seems to have been rejected by God as a false repentance, not accompanied by an actual change of behaviour.[12] But now *they will come with weeping* (9) on a journey that was as much a true returning of hearts to God as it was a return to their homeland. And whereas before Jeremiah had repeatedly emphasized that God would not listen to their prayers (since they had persistently failed to listen to God),[13] now the channel of prayer is open again, for *they will pray as I bring them back*.
- Israel's appeal to God as father had in the past been rejected by God as utterly inconsistent with the way they lived in disobedience,[14] while God's own longing to act as a loving and

[11] Jer. 4:31; 5:17; 6:11–12; 9:17–21.
[12] 3:21 – 4:2; cf. 3:4–5.
[13] E.g. 11:9–14.
[14] 3:4–5.

proud father of privileged children had been reduced to a wistful longing by their rejection and unfaithfulness.[15] Now however Jeremiah follows Hosea in affirming God's fatherhood and Israel's sonship as the underlying reality that motivates God's compassion and redemptive love – just as it had motivated God's original redeeming action on their behalf at the exodus when this relationship was so strongly affirmed.[16]

3. God protects like a shepherd (10–14)

Did Jeremiah know and sing the Twenty-third Psalm? Perhaps it was the idea of the returning exiles being led *beside streams of water, on a level path where they will not stumble* (9, cf. Ps. 23:2–3), that called to mind the familiar imagery of the divine shepherd and expands it from the personal testimony of the psalmist to the collective anticipation of the nation. It is a picture that we find in Isaiah also for God's care and provision for the returning exiles, in words immortalized in music in Handel's *Messiah*.[17] And in his typical way, Ezekiel later takes this image drawn from Jeremiah and extends it with graphic detail, both as a way of condemning Israel's human kings (shepherds) and promising the contrasting care and leadership of the divine shepherd. And like Jeremiah, Ezekiel follows up his portrayal of God shepherding his people with pictures of joyful abundance in nature.[18]

Like Isaiah, Jeremiah sees this historical event of the return of Israelite exiles from Babylon as something to be proclaimed among the *nations* (10a),[19] since ultimately it will be part of the great story of salvation that will be for their benefit. The nations that had been called to witness Israel's judgment (6:18) will witness their liberation. God's dealings with his people take place on the public stage, not in vacuum-sealed isolation from the rest of the world. God's mission is universal and will be ultimately visible to all.

God's promises trip over one another – *he will gather them*[20] ... *watch over them* ... *deliver* ... *and redeem them* (10–11). No wonder these resounding verbs of salvation are echoed by resounding verbs

---

[15] Jer. 3:19–20.
[16] Hos. 11:1; Exod. 4:22.
[17] Isa. 40:11.
[18] Ezek. 34:11–16, 25–31.
[19] Cf. Isa. 40:5; 49:1–6
[20] Significantly in v. 10b the God who will gather Israel is the same God who first scattered them. The verse is proclaiming salvation, but not ignoring judgment. God's hand was equally active in both. In this way it is clear that there is no conflict or contradiction between these words of hope and blessing on the lips of Jeremiah and his earlier words of judgment.

of rejoicing (12–13). This is the joy of the gospel taking hold of a whole community. It turns *mourning into gladness*, the same as Isaiah depicts (Isa. 35:10; 55:12–13).

Once again we should see the fulfilment of these verses on two horizons. There was, of course, a measure of fulfilment at Horizon 1, when the exiles did return to the land and re-established their farms and families, doubtless with great joy. But there are hints here of an unalloyed abundance and joy that will only be reality at Horizon 3, in the new creation. *They will be like a well-watered garden* surely echoes the pre-fall creational blessing of Eden, while the word translated *bounty of the LORD* (12) and *my bounty* (14) is in fact the simple word *ṭôb*, 'good', which was the refrain of Genesis 1 that proclaims the goodness of God's creation – in its origin and its destiny. This kind of prophetic vision is the source of the categorical 'no more' and 'no longer' of Revelation 21:4 and 22:3.

4. God weeps like a mother (15–22)

But what have we here? From the shouts and revels of harvest joy we are suddenly jolted by the sepulchral weeping of a bereaved mother. The contrast is enormous and clearly intentional as the poetry swings back to the feminine form again. The weeping mother is Rachel, personified here as the mother of the whole nation (though of course in the historical record she was the mother only of Joseph and Benjamin). Ramah was not far from the traditional site of Rachel's burial (just on the other side of Jerusalem). Rachel had wept in giving birth to Benjamin, which had issued in her own death.[21] But here she is pictured as crying out for the loss of *all* her children – meaning those slain in the fall of Jerusalem, and those exiles who would have trudged quite close to her grave as they were shoved and prodded north out of the city by the Babylonian soldiers. Her mourning was seemingly as inconsolable as her husband Jacob's had been – *refusing to be comforted* – when he was deceived into thinking Joseph was dead.[22] Likewise Rachel thinks her children *are no more* – a phrase of agonizing empty finality. Rachel's tears were the tincture of extinction. Israel in exile was Israel in oblivion.

But when all human helpers fail and comforts flee, the voice of God speaks the rousing command of verses 16–17. The weeping could stop, for the 'dead' would *return from the land of the enemy. So there is hope . . .*

[21] Gen. 35:18.
[22] Gen. 37:35.

319

That hope was, of course, realized at Horizon 1 within a couple of generations. Rachel's descendants would return to the land that she and her family had laid claim to only by faith and burial rights. But Matthew sees another level of fulfilment at Horizon 2. The birth of Jesus the Messiah had produced searing grief among the mothers of Bethlehem because of Herod's slaughter of their children. So in Matthew 2:16–18 he quotes Jeremiah 31:15 to express their grief. But surely Matthew wants the reader's mind to move on to the promise of verses 16–17. For in the coming of the Messiah lay also the true redemption, restoration and 'return' of Israel from exile. Mourning would be turned to joy after all.

God's voice, however, continues at verse 18 and seems to echo the broken-hearted yearning of Rachel. We have noted often already how the tears of Jeremiah mingle indistinguishably with the tears of God. Here, God seems to weep with Rachel like a mother. For although Israel is a wayward son (18–20), and then once more a faithless wife (22), God's voice trembles with powerful emotion (20). The God who is Ephraim's father feels the pain of Ephraim's grandmother. The parental heart of God swings from *delight* to yearning, from remembering to *great compassion*. God will remember those the world had forgotten and have compassion on those nobody else cared for (30:14, 17). 'This is a family matter and God will not let outsiders ridicule God's beloved wife.'[23] Nor will God let his own frustration quench the yearning for God's beloved son.

But what is the cause of such divine emotion? No longer the stubborn rebellion and blatant betrayals of God's son/wife – that had so often stirred God's grief and anger before. Now God is deeply moved because Israel is at last *moaning* in genuine shame, remorse and repentance. Now at last they recognize their suffering for what it was – the *discipline* of God's justice. Now at last they plead with God to give them the ability to repent and return. The last line of verse 18 is even more stark in Hebrew. Literally it reads: 'Cause me to turn and I will turn.' Even repentance is the gift of God (as the apostles realized).[24]

Jeremiah has drunk deep from the well of Hosea's portrayal of the agonizingly bitter-sweet relationship between God and his people. Pause again to read Hosea 10:11 right through to 11:8. Feel there the pain of God and the costliness of parental compassion. Then read Hosea 14:1–9 to hear the language of genuine repentance, of healing outpoured, of love freely given and anger turned away. Now turn

---

[23] Stulman, p. 265, commenting on 30:16–17.
[24] Acts 11:18.

back and read again Jeremiah 31:18–20. Can't you hear the rich echoes of the music of Hosea?[25]

Repentance moves the heart of God. When the prodigal son turned back home, the father ran to welcome him.[26] One could imagine the father in Jesus' parable sighing with tears the lines of Jeremiah 31:20 every day, just as one could hear the lines of verse 19 on the lips of the prodigal as he travelled homewards. No wonder there is joy in heaven over one sinner who repents, for repentance is the only gateway to salvation, the only road back into the arms of God.

And that road is well marked, says verse 21, as the text swings back to the feminine again. This time it is the wandering wife who is coming home, by a route marked out probably by the ancient *signs* and *guideposts* of Israel's *tôrâ* – the route that Jeremiah had urged his people to find again in 6:16 (without success). Amazingly, miraculously, in a way impossible for man or woman, the *unfaithful Daughter Israel* – the self-prostituting wife – will return to God as his *Virgin Israel* – a bride without spot or blemish.

The sheer shock of such a transformation is probably what we need to read into the otherwise puzzling final lines of verse 22. *The woman will return to the man* is a possible but not very helpful rendering, since the verb is actually 'will surround, or encircle'. Possibly this was a proverbial saying for something utterly unlikely and unimagineable (similar to our exclamation about some totally unrealistic prediction – 'Yes, and pigs will fly!'). The transformation of a rebel people into a beautiful bride could only be contemplated as the work of the sovereign creator God, nothing less than a new creation: *the LORD will create a new thing on the earth*. And it is only at Horizons 2 and 3 that we can see, with the apostles Paul and John, how God has created a new humanity, how in Christ there is new creation, how God will make all things new, and how his sinful, failing people (still) will one day be the spotless Bride of Christ.

5. Summary (23–30)

As we have seen our editors do before, the emotional lyricism of Jeremiah's poetry gives way to summarizing prose. Verses 23–25 and 27–28, simply restate the essential content of the promises made so far, with clarifying reference back to Jeremiah's call vision (1:10) – as if to say, 'All those years ago, this is what I said your ministry would be all about. Well, now it has been. God keeps his word.'

[25] And indeed one hears the same tones in Isa. 63:15–16 and Ps. 103:13.
[26] Luke 15:11–32.

321

Verse 26 is fascinating, almost amusing! Would this be the same Jeremiah who so roundly condemned the false prophets for dreaming dreams and touting them as the word of God (23:25–29)? Clearly Jeremiah too could receive visions and oracles as he slept, which, given the content we've just been surveying, would indeed have been *pleasant* to him.

Verse 29–30 introduces a theme that is also found in Lamentations 5:7, and developed into a full-length theodicy (an explanation and justification of the ways of God) by Ezekiel (chs. 18 and 33). It seems the exiles were tempted to blame previous generations for their own suffering. In one sense they were right: previous generations had been increasingly wicked (as recorded in the historical narratives of the Old Testament), but the axe, when it finally fell, had to fall somewhere, and it had fallen on that present generation. However, if they were tempted to use the proverb as a way of protesting that they did not themselves deserve the judgment (implying that they were suffering innocently for the sins of their fathers), then they were very wrong (as Ezekiel would hammer home). Jeremiah does not develop that point, but simply affirms that in the end God's judgment does deal with those who deserve it. Judgment is not meted out or borne vicariously – except in the case of the One person in history who did not *die for* his *own sins*, but bore the sins of many in his own body on the cross, so that verse 30a *need* not be the last word on sin and death for anyone.

Theological and expository reflection

It is a constant cause for wonder and reflection that although repentance is a condition of salvation and restoration, it is itself a gift of God's grace. In these chapters, God's promises of restoration do not *presuppose* Israel's repentance, but rather seem to *generate* it. The theological links with Deuteronomy 30 remain strong. And just as that chapter issues in its great evangelistic appeal ('choose life') on the basis of the preceding grace and gift of God, so our handling of these chapters should do the same. Repentance never 'earns' the grace of God. It is, rather, a grateful response to hearing the good news of God's promise and mercy (cf. Ezek. 33:10–11).

Jeremiah 31:31–40
24. New covenant

Reading Jeremiah 31:31–34 as Christians, it is impossible not to remember immediately those places in the New Testament where the phrase 'new covenant' occurs. In fact, the quotation of these verses in full by the writer to the Hebrews (8:8–12) constitutes the longest continuous quotation of any Old Testament text in the New. And every time we participate in a service of Holy Communion we will hear the words drawn from the Synoptic Gospels and the Apostle Paul, 'this cup is the *new covenant* in my blood'.[1] And if we are aware that the very term 'New Testament' is simply the Latinized form of 'new covenant', we might assume that Jeremiah's phrase was part of standard messianic expectation (whereas in fact the precise words 'new covenant' occur nowhere else than Jeremiah 31:31 in the Old Testament, though its concepts do).

This familiarity with the phrase 'new covenant', however, is exegetically dangerous since it can tempt us to read the words of Jeremiah immediately through the lens of their New Testament quotations, rather than through the eyes and ears of those who first heard them or read them in his edited book. It's as if we run a sharp knife around these verses, put the isolated text in our briefcase, and hurry off to open it and read it at Horizon 2 (the horizon of New Testament fulfilment). Now we shall have plenty to ask and answer when we do get to that Horizon, and indeed we shall see that there are dimensions of this text that will send us on to Horizon 3 as well. But it is a first principle of good exegesis always to start at Horizon 1, the world of the Old Testament itself. We must take this (and every) text in its context.

And that context has two dimensions – literary and historical.

---

[1] 1 Cor. 11:25; cf. the various accounts using similar words in Matt. 26:28; Mark 14:24; Luke 22:20.

The literary context is that these verses about a new covenant come within the flow of chapters 30 and 31. The promises to the exiles are framed in the language of the great epic of Israel's origins. There will be a new exodus, a new experience of God's grace in the wilderness, and a new entry into the land of promise. But the story of the wilderness included Sinai and the making of the covenant there. So if the return of the exiles is to be interpreted as a re-enactment of that great story, then it must include a reconstituted covenant relationship with God. The journey from Egypt to the land had included a journey into covenant relationship of promise and commitment. The return from Babylon to the land must include a return to the Lord on the same foundation. But chapters 30 – 31 so far have also made it very clear that the terrible realities of Israel's sin and God's judgment stand in the way. The past had produced an incurable present. If there is to be a future at all for these people, it can only be if God himself initiates something utterly new – even if it is modelled on his action in past history. And that indeed was the explicit promise of 31:22: 'The LORD will create a new thing on earth.' Now, with the repetition of that word 'new' in verse 31, we learn what this *new thing* will be. Nothing less than a *new covenant*.[2]

For the historical context we need to sit once more with the exiles, suffering the grief and trauma of the horrors of 587 BC, but also reading (somehow) the writings we now have collected in the book of Jeremiah. They now knew that all Jeremiah had predicted, about the invasion from the north, the wanton destruction and slaughter, and the unthinkable ruination of the city and temple, had come true. Probably it was even worse than the searing rhetoric of Jeremiah had painted it in advance. But they also now knew the reason why it had all happened – for Jeremiah had pressed the point again and again and again. It was God's judgment on their persistent rejection, their refusal to listen and obey, their history of congenital covenant-breaking unfaithfulness.

Imagine yourself in the depths of exilic depression reading Jeremiah 7:21–29 and 11:1–14. Read them again now. These are undoubtedly the bleak backdrop to the 'new covenant' text before us. Up to now, the only way Jeremiah had ever spoken of the covenant was to say that it was broken, shattered – lying in ruins as Jerusalem itself now was. What question would be uppermost in your mind? Surely it would be, 'Can there be any future for us now?

---

[2] Other links between this text and its immediate literary context include: the unifying reference to *the people of Israel* and *the people of Judah* (cf. 31:27); the tenderness of the way the exodus is described (*took them by the hand to lead them*, cf. 31:3); the reference to YHWH as *husband* (cf. 31:3–4, 21); the reciprocal covenant language of 33b (cf. 30:22; 31:1).

If the covenant has ended, surely it is the end also for Israel. If we are no longer the covenant people of YHWH, then we are no longer a people at all. We are without hope and without God in the world.'[3]

1. A broken covenant – but it's not the end (31–32)

They were right about the present, but wrong in their projection of the future. The covenant was broken, for sure. It had been broken for a long time and only God's patience had held back the outworking of the covenant sanctions until now.

But it had been broken before – and mended. That story of Israel at Mount Sinai includes the incident of the golden calf – that most serious episode of Israel's covenant-breaking apostasy that took place when the ink and blood of the covenant had scarcely dried (Exod. 32 – 34). On that occasion God had been on the point of destroying the people in his anger and was restrained only by the intercession of Moses. The tablets of the Ten Commandments were symbolically shattered. There had been a signal display of God's wrath, but after that forgiveness had been pledged as part of a definition of the very name and character of God (Exod. 34:6), and the covenant had been remade. The relationship survived and the journey continued. It would be worth pausing again to read the story in full in Exodus 32 – 34, or at least the recollection of it in Deuteronomy 9 – 10 (with its closing exhortation).

Could such a story hold out hope for the exiles? Could the covenant, broken and mended at Sinai itself, be mended again in the brokenness of exile? There was a crucial element missing, however. In Exodus 32 – 34 it was the robust intercession of Moses that stayed God's hand. Moses reminded God of his promise to Abraham,[4] appealed to the relationship that had been there even before the covenant was ratified (Israel had been 'your people', 'your inheritance' – even before the exodus),[5] and told God he needed to think about his reputation.[6] And God responded with patience and grace. But now Israel had no Moses interceding for them. Repeatedly Jeremiah had been prohibited from such a role, in the very texts that had denounced Israel for breaking the covenant.[7] Where then could hope be found?

If there was no hope from human intercession or intervention, then it must be placed in God alone. There will indeed be a *new*

---

[3] We know from Ezek. 37:11 that some of the exiles thought exactly like this.
[4] Exod. 32:13; Deut. 9:27.
[5] Exod. 32:11; Deut. 9:29.
[6] Exod. 32:12; Deut. 9:28.
[7] Jer. 7:16; 11:14.

covenant, but it will not just be a rerun of the Sinai covenant made after the exodus (32), *because they broke my covenant, though I was a husband to them.* It will be founded upon a new act of God that will be as freshly constitutive for Israel's future as the exodus and the ark of the covenant had been hitherto. That is the thrust of 16:14–15, 23:7–8 and 3:16.The return from exile, which will be God's sovereign reversal of history, will constitute a new redemptive beginning for Israel, and a new covenant will mark it.

But if they did not have Moses as an intercessor, they certainly had Moses as a preacher. Alongside the narrative of Exodus 32 – 34, we must place Deuteronomy 30. Already we have seen that it was hugely influential on the Book of Consolation, and nowhere more than here. For that chapter anticipates exactly what the exiles now face. The curses of a broken covenant have fallen on them in shattering, scattering devastation. But into that reality God, through Moses, had spoken a greater reality – God's own *gift* of repentance and obedience, to enable a renewed relationship of love and life: 'The Lord your God will circumcise your hearts and the hearts of your descendants, so that you may love him with all your heart and with all your soul, and live.' The logic of Deuteronomy 30:6 is astonishing in the way it turns the requirements of verses 2 and 10 into the gifts of God's grace. God will do what Israel could not do for themselves. God's grace will give what God's law demands.

And that same dynamic, drawn from Deuteronomy 30, is at work here in the new covenant vision of Jeremiah. In fact Jeremiah 31:31–34 is simply the outworking of the promise God made concerning the 'good figs' in 24:7, which is covenantal in content, even if the word is not used: 'I will give them a heart to know me, that I am the LORD. They will be my people, and I will be their God, for they will return to me with all their heart.' God himself will initiate a new covenant out of the wreckage of the old. The broken covenant did not spell the end for God's people, God's 'house', God's 'wife'. There was a future and a hope for Israel, not because of who they were, but because of *whose* they were.

2. A new covenant – but it's not entirely different (33–34)

Immediately, we hit an apparent contradiction. God announces *a new covenant* that *will not be like* the covenant made at Sinai after the exodus (32). And yet in each of the four aspects that follow, it is decidedly like that covenant! Responding from the heart to God's law, entering a reciprocally possessive relationship with God (*their God . . . my people*), knowing God, and receiving God's forgiveness – all of these were present in the earlier texts about God's covenant with Israel. All of them feature in the covenantal texts of Exodus and Deuteronomy. So we are prepared for continuity and discontinuity. There is continuity of core dimensions that were intrinsic to God's relationship with Israel from the start, along with radical newness in how those dimensions would henceforth be experienced or practised.

a. Internalized obedience to God (33a)

The heart, in Hebrew, is not so much the seat of the emotions, but rather of the will. The heart is where you do your thinking, choosing and deciding. It is the inner organ that shapes the outer direction and intentions of your life. Jeremiah has had a lot to say about the heart in all these senses.[8] And that, says God, is where he will put his law.

Now we should not think that this is unprecedented. We should not imagine that up to now Israel had only been required to give mechanical obedience to an external code of law carved in stone, whereas suddenly God announces that they need to have a change of attitude as well. On the contrary, the idea that God's law should be 'on the heart' was already emphasized by Deuteronomy. 'These commandments that I give you today are to be on your hearts.'[9] So involving the heart in obeying God's law was not new.

What seems to be new in Jeremiah 31:33a is that God not only asks for obedience from the heart (as in Deut. 6:6), but promises that *he himself will implant it there*. The two verbs are emphatic, *I will put . . . I will write.* And whereas Deuteronomy 6:6 simply asked that the law should be 'upon your hearts', God promises here to put his law 'within them' (translated by NIV as *in their minds*). It seems that a genuine internalizing of the law is envisaged. It is no longer merely that Israel should wholeheartedly obey the law when they read or hear it (Deuteronomy clearly called for that), but that they should live by an inner impulse coming from within, from God's law written on their own hearts. In other words, their whole inclination and habitual action would be to live according to God's standards and ways.

This reverses and transforms what Jeremiah had earlier described as engraved on Israel's hearts – namely, their sin (17:1). So, just as they had sinned because of the unrepentant and incorrigible inscriptions of their hearts, now they would be obedient because God

---

[8] 'The heart stands for the mind, the organ of memory (Jer. 3:16), of understanding (Deut 29:3 [Eng 4]), of ideas (Jer. 23:16), and, especially, of conscious decisions of the will (Jer. 3:10; 29:13). Only God is able to discern what is in an individual's heart (Jer. 17:9–10)' (Keown, Scalise and Smothers, p. 134).

[9] Deut. 6:6. See also Deut. 10:16; 11:18; 30:2, 6, 10, 14.

would have transformed their hearts. They would be acting from a new script, one that would be written within them by God himself. It is significant that God does *not* promise to give a 'new law'. Rather what is promised is a new ability, from within, to live in accordance with the essence of the law God has given.

Jeremiah's promise may have inspired Ezekiel's characteristically more verbose portrayal of God's radical heart surgery, replacing Israel's heart of stone with a heart of flesh, so that they would/could live in willing obedience to God, empowered by God's Spirit.[10] Undoubtedly both Jeremiah and Ezekiel believed that the community of Israel that returned to the land after the exile would indeed show a more conscientious adherence to God's law, but their words already point us beyond that post-exilic era (Horizon 1) to the newness that came through Jesus Christ (at Horizon 2). For Paul explains that in Christ God has not given us a new law (a whole new set of requirements), but rather through the indwelling Spirit has given us the power to live in a way that pleases God. Because of Christ's sacrifice we no longer stand under condemnation but have been set free so that 'the righteous requirements of the law might be fully met in us, who do not live according to the flesh but according to the Spirit'.[11]

b. Reciprocal relationship with God (33b)

There is nothing new here! *I will be their God and they will be my people* is the beating heart of God's covenant relationship with his people, as it was in the beginning, is now, and ever shall be, world without end. This was the promise of God to Abraham (Gen. 17:7), repeated before the exodus (Exod. 6:7), ratified at Sinai (Exod. 19:5–6; Lev. 26:12), renewed in Moab (Deut. 26:17–18), repeated as Israel's enduring identity and security by prophets like Jeremiah,[12] quoted by Paul as applying to Christian believers (2 Cor. 6:16), and ultimately proclaimed with a loud voice from the throne of God as the very constitution of the new creation (Rev. 21:3).

It is, in other words, a covenantal relationship that was true for the Israelites of the Old Testament at Horizon 1, that has been extended through the gospel of Jesus Christ to believing Jews and Gentiles from all nations, at Horizon 2, and will one day be the universal status of the entire redeemed human race from every tribe, language and nation, at Horizon 3. From Genesis to Revelation, God is creating a people for himself.

[10] Ezek. 36:26–27.
[11] Rom. 8:1–4.
[12] It is a favourite phrase of Jeremiah: 7:23; 11:4; 24:7; 30:22; 31:1; 32:38. Cf. Ezek. 11:20; 14:11; 34:30–31; 36:28; 37:23, 27; Zech. 8:8.

What an incredible span of history past and eternity future is contained in a mere seven Hebrew words.

c. Universal knowledge of God (34a)

'Knowing God' was never something merely cognitive – just mental recognition of the name of God, or knowing a set of affirmations about God. To know God, or more correctly, to know YHWH as the true living God, meant being committed to relating to him in love, loyalty and obedience. Knowing God was a matter of life and practice, of character and behaviour, of reflecting the character of YHWH in human relationships as well as in faith and worship.[13] In that sense, it had been Jeremiah's complaint for years that Israel simply did not know God. Whatever their protestations and proclamations, their lives were a denial of it all. So the accusation of Hosea, 'there is no acknowledgment of God in the land',[14] was echoed and amplified by Jeremiah.[15] Israel, in their pre-exilic rebellion, idolatry and social evils, simply did not know YHWH.

So this new covenant promise includes a reversal of that lamentable living ignorance. Israel – repentant, restored and returned – would know God.

Two further points need to be noted.

First, although Jeremiah speaks of individuals not needing to teach one another to know YHWH, *because they will all know me,* we should not interpret this as implying merely private spirituality. Jeremiah 31:34 has been read and preached in Christian circles (I know for I have done so), as referring to that personal relationship with God, that intimacy of access to God's presence, which we have through Christ. Here at least, we want to say, is one place where the new covenant transcends the old. We can all know God individually for ourselves, in some way that we assume was not available for the old covenant Israelites (in spite of a whole bookful of psalms written by individuals who seem to have known God rather intimately).

Now of course, personal knowledge of God through Christ is a precious dimension of Christian experience, much emphasized for example in 1 John. But Jeremiah's language points to a much more social and collective dimension of the knowledge of God than personal piety. He has used the phrase, *from the least of them to the greatest,* twice before, and in both cases it was his way of characterizing the whole community, from top to bottom. In 6:13 and 8:10

---

[13] I have explored some of the depths and variety of what 'knowing God' meant in Wright, *Knowing God the Father.*

[14] Hos. 4:1.

[15] Jer. 2:8; 4:22; 5:4–5; 9:3.

Jeremiah castigated every rung of society. The whole national culture was infected with greed, deceit and self-deception. By contrast, when the nation is reconstituted under a new covenant, the *whole community* will be characterized by the knowledge of God. It is not merely that individuals will enjoy a new personal relationship with God (though that is wonderfully true), but that the whole community of God's people will at last demonstrate in their corporate life and practice that they know and reflect the character of the God they worship. *God's new covenant is for God's new society.*

Secondly, and following naturally from that point, when Jeremiah says *they will all know me*, he cannot have meant the phrase in a purely spiritual or vertical sense. Indeed, if we were able to ask Jeremiah, 'What do you mean by "knowing the Lord"?', he might well answer impatiently, 'Have you not been listening? I have told you twice already'. For indeed, as we have seen, in 9:23–24 and 22:16 Jeremiah has given us his definition of what it means to 'know God', and in both cases it is strongly ethical and social. It means to value what God delights in: 'kindness, justice and righteousness'. It means to do what is right and just and to defend the poor and needy: 'is that not what it means to know me?'[16]

Putting these points together, Jeremiah's vision of the new covenant is not merely of a collection of individuals who all have personal access to God in worship. Rather he envisages a whole community that is collectively committed to knowing God through the practice of the covenant values that God delights in – social compassion and justice. It is a vision not merely of a new spirituality, but of a new society.

d. Total forgiveness from God (34b)

What stood in the way of the shattered community of exiles entering into these great promised blessings under a new covenant initiated by God? Undoubtedly, their guilt. For those who understood the reason for their dire situation, there would have been one main question and another one sneaking in behind that. First, unless the guilt of their accumulated generations of covenant-breaking could be dealt with, what hope could there be of a future ongoing covenant relationship with God? Could the God who had declared that he had no alternative but to punish his people for their sin (5:1, 7, 29) now turn and forgive them? With the precedent of Exodus 32 – 34 in their memory and in God's, and using the same word for 'forgive' as in Exodus 34:9, that is exactly what God promises here. The sin

[16] See the discussion of these challenging texts in chs. 7 (pp. 132–133) and 16 (pp. 240–241) above.

and guilt of the past will be forgiven, and remembered *no more*. When God remembers, it means he will act. If he chooses not to remember, then no further action will be taken. Case dismissed.

But behind that question with its happy answer, lurked another one, well articulated by R. E. Clements. 'If Israel's sins in the past brought such fearful judgment upon the nation so that it came close to total annihilation, what assurance can there be that after a future restoration has taken place the same fate will not befall Israel again?' Clements answers in terms of the first element in the new covenant promise (33a): 'The theologically conceived response to this is that God will, by the very creative power of his love, write the law of the covenant upon the hearts of the men and women who make up Israel.'[17] That indeed would be a key assurance. But it in turn is founded on this concluding element – the full and permanent forgiveness of God. The opening word of verse 34b – *for* – indicates that everything above this bottom line stands upon it as a foundation. 'All the newness is possible *because* Yahweh has forgiven . . . God has broken the vicious cycle of sin and punishment; it is this broken cycle that permits Israel to begin again at a different place with new possibility.'[18]

> Finally [referring to verse 34b], the new covenant offers unqualified forgiveness to broken people who can no longer bear the burden of their guilt. Interestingly, absolution of sins comes with no strings attached or without reference to the temple or sacrifice. Yahweh merely declares it so . . . The syntax of verse 34 suggests that forgiveness is more than a characteristic of the new covenant; *it is the very basis of the astonishing workings of God. Divine forgiveness makes possible inner transformation, intimacy with God, and an inclusive community that delights in faithful living.*[19]

But if God and his people are to live in a new covenant that will never fail, like the old one had, then not only must the sins of the past be forgiven, but there must be an assurance of ongoing forgiveness – assuming that the people would not suddenly be entirely without sin. It is hard to know whether or how Jeremiah and his hearers may have understood or even conceptualized such a quality of forgiveness that could deal not only with past sin but all future sin, so that there would be a 'no more', a 'never again', to the judgment of God. But merely asking the question points us towards Horizon 2 and the logic of the book of Hebrews. As Kidner puts it with his classic evocative simplicity, 'What would only come to light

[17] Clements, p. 190.
[18] Brueggemann (1991), p. 72.
[19] Stulman, p. 274, my italics.

when Jesus inaugurated this new covenant (Mt. 26:28), was the fact that each of these divine gifts was a costly *self*-giving. Forgiveness would be through his own blood, and it would be not only the law but its Author who would indwell the believer (Jn. 14:17, 23).'[20]

3. A new guarantee – but it's as ancient as creation (35–37)

The Book of Consolation, in support of its panorama of promises, has drawn heavily from the great redemptive narrative of Israel's faith: exodus, Sinai, wilderness, land-gift. Now Jeremiah swings to that other foundational pillar of their faith – creation itself. For YHWH was God of both creation and redemption, and either could be used to inspire hope and faith.

What is more certain than that the stars will shine in the night sky and the sun will rise tomorrow? That's how much you can be sure that God will preserve Israel (35–36). What is more unimaginable than measuring the height of the sky or the depth of the earth? That's how unthinkable it is that God could reject 'the seed of Israel' (37).

If the exiles had fears that they would die out in Babylon, God here refutes such fear in the strongest possible terms. The people of Israel would survive. Generations of Israelites had indeed rejected God, to the point where he had declared the present generation 'rejected': 'for the LORD has rejected and abandoned this generation that is under his wrath' (7:29). But this did not constitute a rejection of all their posterity. It is noticeable that the phrase 'seed of Israel' is used in both verses 36 and 37 (though NIV omits it in verse 36, while translating it *descendants of Israel* in verse 37). These are long-term promises for ongoing generations. The sin of present and past generations would not condemn all future generations to oblivion (this is partly the implication also of vv. 29–30). God's purpose for Israel will continue, in faithfulness to his promise to Abraham. Though Abraham is not named here, God's promise to him may be hinted at in the mention of the stars combined with reference to the 'seed of Israel'.[21] Indeed, God's covenant with Noah is probably even more clearly in mind, as it is explicitly in the very similar motifs of Isaiah 54.[22] Israel's future is as guaranteed as the future of earth itself.

And so, God decisively answers the plaintive anxiety of the question posed in 14:19, 'Have you rejected Judah completely?' Answer:

[20] Kidner, pp. 110–111.
[21] Gen. 15:5.
[22] Gen. 8:21 – 9:17.

In this generation? Yes.

Forever? No.

The double metaphors in verses 35–37 encompass the whole creation from top to bottom, as it were. Verse 35 points to the sky and the sea; verse 37 points to the sky and the earth and beneath the earth. They affirm the sovereign governance of God not only over the orderly regularity of the heavenly bodies (*sun . . . moon and stars*), but also over the apparent chaos of the rowdy sea. The silence of the skies and the noise of the oceans – all obey the Lord of the universe. The metaphors also affirm that all that happens in creation and all that happens in human history *both* take place in the presence of God. The phrases, *from my sight* (creation) and *before me* (Israel), are identical – 'before my face'. All natural processes and all human actions are observed by God (cf. Ps. 33). As Isaiah and Jesus further affirm, we can read something of the character of God, and especially his dependability, from observing the works of his hands.[23]

So did Israel lack confidence in their future? Let them look above, around and beneath them. God their redeemer would prove as dependable as God the creator.

4. A new Jerusalem – but it's to be holy to the Lord (38–40)

A new exodus, a new covenant, a new experience of grace in the wilderness, a new entry to the land of promise. The original story had then led on past the era of the judges to the establishment of Jerusalem by David as the city where God had caused his name to dwell. What, then, has to come next in this sequence drawn from the great narrative of redemption? A new Jerusalem! With a sense of inevitability, therefore, we reach the end of these two chapters of astonishing promises with a vision of exactly that.

Jerusalem will be rebuilt. For the exiles who survived and remembered its destruction under the Babylonian brutality, that in itself was a word of immense comfort. We need not seek to trace the geographical details of the vision, except to say that they do indeed envisage a literal rebuilding – a fulfilment of the promise at Horizon 1. But the language goes beyond wood and stone in two ways.

First, this was the city that YHWH had not only rejected but had actively destroyed as an act of divine wrath executed through human agency (as is clear from chs. 7 and 26). Yet now God says he will once again put his stamp of ownership upon it. Twice God specifies that the rebuilding of the city will be *for the Lord* – not just for the returning exiles, not even for a reinstated king in the line of David

[23] Isa. 40:12–26; Matt. 6:25–34.

who had first made the city his own. The first time is in verse 38, which reads (lit.), 'the city will be built for (or unto) YHWH'. And in verse 40, the cleansing even of the unclean place of burial (that had been defiled by human sacrifice, see ch. 19), will make the whole city *holy to the Lord.* God is reclaiming not only his people, but his city. Interestingly no mention is made here of the rebuilding of the temple, though it would probably have been assumed. But the key thing is that the future of the exiles was not to languish in exile forever. God would return with his people and the city where YHWH had put his name would once again belong to him in holiness.

Secondly, there is the remarkable promise of the very last line of verse 40: *the city will never again be uprooted or demolished.* The language of permanence here carries forward the same note that we have heard already. There is the *no longer* of verse 34a – speaking of the knowledge of God that will so pervade the future community that they will not need to teach one another. There is the *no more* of verse 34b – speaking of the totality of God's forgiveness. So here, there is the *never again* of verse 40 – speaking of God's commitment to protect the new Jerusalem from any repetition of what befell it in 587 BC.

But, but . . . (we cannot avoid interjecting), that may have been a strongly comforting word to the exiles, and to those who would within a couple of generations return and rebuild the city. But what are we to say, reading such an unequivocal promise in the light of our knowledge of what befell Jerusalem in AD 70? For in that terrible year the city was indeed *uprooted and demolished* by Roman armies with burning and slaughtering that re-enacted the barbarism of Babylon's final battery. That leads us to consider our whole text once more in terms of its fulfilment at all three horizons.

Theological reflection – at three horizons

a. Horizon 1

I trust we have sat with the exiles and heard Jeremiah addressing them with words of hope, and have been able to appreciate the terms and concepts of the new covenant text within their literary context in these chapters and their historical context of exile and after. There was indeed a future beyond the cataclysm of 587 BC. The expectations and hopes of Jeremiah's Book of Consolation, along with similar oracles in Hosea, Isaiah and Ezekiel, were indeed realized. From 538 BC onward groups of exiles returned to Judah and rebuilt the country and their city. It was a chastened community but, from what we read in Ezra and Nehemiah, a community that sought to rebuild themselves on the foundation of renewed commitment to their God and to God's law. The great covenant-renewal occasion, including the reading of the law, recorded in Nehemiah 8 – 10, bears witness to this.

We know of course that this determination to keep the law of God could lead in an unhealthily zealous direction that ended up, however fine the motivation, in the burdens imposed by Phariseeism or the fanaticism adopted by Saul of Tarsus. But we should not for that reason underestimate the new thing that God did in taking the exiles back to Judah, in renewing his covenant with them, in enabling the rebuilding of the temple with prophetic encouragement, and in giving the nation a hope and a future throughout the centuries to come. These great prophecies did indeed have a measure of fulfilment at Horizon 1 in the restored community of Judah. The return from exile was a key redemptive moment in the Old Testament story, even if the imperfections of the post-exilic community, and the later cycles of external oppression, generated the feeling that the exile had not truly ended. The people still needed to return to their God, like the prodigal son to his father. There was a need still for repentance and forgiveness. God must come and establish his reign in all its fullness. Even before we reach the Gospels, we hear these notes from the post-exilic prophets, Haggai, Zechariah, and especially Malachi. And that means we must look on to Horizon 2.

b. Horizon 2

Some commentators reject and denounce any attempt to read the new covenant text of Jeremiah 31 with Christian significance. They brand such reading as 'supersessionist', i.e. the presumed belief that the Christian church has simply replaced the Jews, who are said to have been rejected from God's purposes.[24] Such commentators

---

[24] 'Supersessionism' or 'replacement theology', as it is sometimes also called, is a view that I certainly do not hold. It flies in the face of the great biblical trajectory of the continuity of God's people. As I have argued elsewhere, the Bible nowhere says that 'Christians have replaced the Jews'. Rather it affirms very strongly that God's purpose always was that *Israel* would be *expanded* to include the Gentiles. The New Testament affirms that this happened when, first, the Messiah, Jesus of Nazareth, representatively accomplished through his death and resurrection the restoration/redemption of Israel (e.g. Luke 24:13–27; Acts 13:32–33), and second, when God through his Holy Spirit initiated the eschatological ingathering of the Gentile nations into that restored people (Acts 15:13–18), creating a new united people in Christ (Eph. 2:11 – 3:6). There is an organic spiritual continuity between Old Testament Israel and the multinational community of believing Jews and Gentiles who are united in the Messiah Jesus. The Bible does not portray Israel being 'replaced' by the church, but rather (and very emphatically in both Testaments) of Israel expanding to include the Gentiles. When I, as a Gentile, became a believer in Jesus, I did not *replace* anybody. I *joined* God's people and became a child of Abraham, as Paul told the Galatians.

therefore wish to confine the relevance and the promise of these verses to ethnic Old Testament Israel and contemporary Jewish people alone, and regard Christian appropriation of them as 'pre-emptive', and distorting.[25] However, it seems to me that it is as wrong to *exclude* a Christian reading of these texts at Horizon 2 (in relation to the New Testament's understanding of fulfilment in Christ), as it is to jump immediately to that horizon and interpret the text *exclusively* in Christian terms. But having done all we can to hear and interpret the text at Horizon 1, it is surely necessary for any reading of the text that claims to be *Christian* to reflect on how it is further and ultimately fulfilled through Jesus Christ. That is certainly what the New Testament does.

The earliest written tradition to use the term 'new covenant' is 1 Corinthians 11:23–26, where Paul quotes what he says he himself received. In other words, this is very early Christian tradition that pre-dates the written Gospels. The recollected words of Jesus are: 'This cup is the new covenant in my blood.' Jesus was bringing together the Passover context of 'this cup', with the Jeremiah prophecy (the only text in the Old Testament to use precisely those words – 'new covenant'), and linking them to his own self-offering as a blood sacrifice. The Synoptic Gospel narratives fill out the occasion and the words of Jesus.[26] There are slight variations which, in my view, do not indicate the busy embellishing hands of the writers, but rather the probability that Jesus did not merely intone set words like a liturgy, but explained and scripturally interpreted the reason why he had so surprisingly injected words about his own imminent death into the Passover liturgy they were accustomed to.

Matthew gives us the fullest version of the words of Jesus: 'This is my blood of the covenant, which is poured out for many for the forgiveness of sins.' Three Old Testament texts are bound together by Jesus in this interpretation of his own death:

- 'blood of the covenant' comes from Exodus 24:8, the great occasion when the Sinai covenant was ratified by the sprinkling of 'the blood of the covenant' on the altar and on the people. Jesus interprets his own death as the sacrifice that ratifies a greater covenant, having achieved an even greater exodus-redemption;
- 'poured out for many' comes from Isaiah 53:12, the climax of the account of the mysterious Servant of the Lord, whose vicarious self-sacrificial death would bear the sins of many;

[25] That is Brueggemann's assessment of the use of Jer. 31 by the writer to the Hebrews (1991), p. 73.
[26] Matt. 26:26–28; Mark 14:22–24; Luke 22:19–20.

- 'for the forgiveness of sins' is an echo of Jeremiah 31:34, making it clear that this would indeed be the foundation of, and the greatest benefit conferred by, the new covenant now being enacted through the death of Christ.

It seems unquestionable then, that the earliest Christian understanding of Jeremiah 31:31–34 in relation to Christ was to see that, whatever level of fulfilment the text had had at Horizon 1 in the reconstitution of the nation of Israel in the land of Judah after the exile, the promise of a new covenant had now been inaugurated in messianic fulfilment through the death and resurrection of Jesus of Nazareth.

Significantly, writing to Jewish believers, whose attachment to the great realities of Old Testament faith were strong, the author of Hebrews makes the total and permanent forgiveness of sins under the new covenant the primary point of focus in his extensive discussion of it in Hebrews 8:1 – 10:18.

c. Horizon 3

Returning to the text of Jeremiah, there are depths and dimensions of the new covenant promise that seem to point not only beyond Horizon 1 but also beyond Horizon 2. Even with the spiritual reality of the life of the Spirit and the indwelling Christ, it cannot be said that Christians living within the new covenant live in perfect obedience. Even with the knowledge of God that is freely ours in Christ, and the creation of a community that seeks to know God in the practice of love and justice, it cannot be said that we no longer need teachers.[27] On the contrary, Paul stresses the need for teaching and teachers within the new community. And even though we have the promise of forgiveness, we are far from the condition where the need for forgiveness will be a thing of the past.

In such respects, we are pointed forward to Horizon 3 when, in the new creation, the redeemed people of God will live with God in perfect intimacy, free from sorrow, free from sin, and the relational heart of the covenant will beat for all eternity (Rev. 21:3).

What then are we to make of the promises to 'the seed of Israel' and of a new and indestructible Jerusalem (31:35–40)? Verse 37 is the strongest possible affirmation that God would never reject the seed of Israel. In Romans 11 Paul faces the horrifying question that God might be thought to have done exactly that because some of his

---

[27] John rhetorically says that we don't (1 John 2:27), but he means that we don't need external teaching to give us the inner assurance of the truth that comes from the Spirit of God.

fellow Jews had persisted in disobedience and rejected Jesus as their Messiah. But he answers with a resounding negative: 'I ask then: did God reject his people? By no means! I am an Israelite myself, a descendant of Abraham, from the tribe of Benjamin. God did not reject his people, whom he foreknew.'[28]

Paul then defines who he means by 'Israel', in two ways.

First he picks up the 'remnant' language from the Old Testament. Paul sees that faithful remnant of Israel embodied in himself and fellow Jews who had believed in Jesus and were saved by God's grace. Such believing Jews are then joined by the incoming Gentile believers, who are being saved by God's grace in exactly the same way, through repentance and faith in Jesus. Israel has been expanded, just as so many Old Testament texts anticipated, to include believing Jews and Gentiles. In this way Paul follows through the distinction he has already made within 'Israel' – again in order to protect the trustworthiness of God's promise – between physical descent alone and the children of the promise received by faith. 'Not all who are descended from Israel are Israel.'[29] 'Israel', in Paul's mind is thus at the same time a *smaller* concept than the whole nation of ethnic Israelites sharing the physical DNA of Abraham (as we might say), for it is the remnant who have put their faith in the Messiah Jesus; and a *larger* concept than the ethnic Jewish people, because Israel has now come to include Gentiles who have come to Christ and are being 'grafted in', and who now share the same spiritual DNA (as he explains to the Gentile believers of Galatia and Ephesus).

But secondly Paul still thinks of the rest of ethnic Israel, Jews who had not yet come to believe in Jesus, who were still 'hardened', 'persisting in unbelief'. They had behaved as 'enemies' in relation to the gospel and the missional inclusion of the Gentiles (and how much Paul had experienced of that hostility). But, with great emphasis and scriptural support, Paul insists that 'as far as election is concerned, they are loved on account of the patriarchs, for God's gifts and his call are irrevocable'.[30] And Paul's longing is to see that love of God for the Jewish people ultimately leading them to be grafted back into their own olive tree, through the mercy of God and the obedience of faith. That is, he does not imagine a distinct or second covenant arrangement for Jews independent of what God has done through Christ, but longs to see them entering into the promise of the new covenant that was originally given to them, and doing so through faith in Jesus the Messiah.

[28] Rom. 11:1–2.
[29] Rom. 9:6.
[30] Rom. 11:28–29.

Accordingly, it seems to me we can interpret Jeremiah 31:35–37 in terms of God's commitment to the 'seed of Israel', first in relation to the continuance of the Jewish people and God's continuing love for them. There are those among them who have rejected him, but as a people they are *not* rejected by him – as Jeremiah promised and Paul re-affirmed. But also, secondly, in relation to the eternal security of those whom the New Testament sees as the 'seed of Abraham' through faith in the Messiah Jesus – both Jews and Gentiles. For they, as Paul puts it, are sons of God (as Israel was), 'Abraham's seed, and heirs according to the promise'.[31] The ultimate horizon of Jeremiah 35 – 37, with its affirmation that nothing (not even their past sins) could separate God's people from the God who created the heavens and the earth, lies in the overwhelming assurance of Paul that nothing in all creation, physical or spiritual, will be able to separate us from the love of God that is in Christ Jesus our Lord.[32]

Finally, what about Jeremiah 31:40? We might take it (at Horizon 1) as a rhetorical flourish intended to give immediate hope to the returning exiles. When they would rebuild Jerusalem, it would not be immediately *uprooted and demolished* by their enemies. They had a secure long-term lease, so to speak. But once we have lived past the destruction of Jerusalem in AD 70, it seems we have only two options. Either we say that Jeremiah was simply mistaken in his bold 'never again'. It *did* happen again. This is a failed prophecy. Or we see the ultimate fulfilment of this prophecy as something reserved for Horizon 3. And that certainly is the way Revelation 21 – 22 handles it. For the city of God, the New Jerusalem, will never pass away. It will need no temple (as Jeremiah's prophecy had mentioned none) for God's presence will pervade the whole new creation as his temple. And it will be eternally 'holy to the Lord', for there will be no more death, no more sin, no more curse.

Amen. Come Lord Jesus.

---

[31] Gal. 3:26–29.
[32] Rom. 8:38–39.

Jeremiah 32:1 – 33:26
25. Field of dreams

'If you build it, he will come.' The mysterious voice that Ray Kinsella hears in the iconic movie *Field of Dreams* urges him to build a baseball stadium in his prairie cornfield in Iowa. The dream, however, amounts to nothing more than the ghosts of legendary baseball stars from the past coming to play again in the moonlight.

'If you buy it, they will come back,' might be the voice of the Lord that Jeremiah heard, speaking about a different field. And who's to say it wasn't in his dreams (cf. 31:26)? But the field in question was totally real and the vision of its future was nothing to do with returning ghosts, but returning generations of former exiles. Not the ghosts of a glorious past, but the reality of a guaranteed future.

1. The obedience of faith (32:1–15)

There was nothing glorious, however, about Jeremiah's present location. Imagine zooming in from high above the earth to find him. You make out the shape of the small kingdom of Judah. Getting closer, some of its towns show signs of destruction and a pall of smoke lies over patches of farmland, vineyards and olive groves. Zooming closer, we see the city of Jerusalem surrounded on all sides by the armies of Babylon, with siege works battering at the walls. Closer still we may see the grand edifice of the royal palace, built by Solomon and enhanced by Jehoiakim, and within that we will see the military quarters full of armed soldiers. A cramped courtyard used by the soldiers is open to the sky and our satellite camera, and zooming in to ground level, that is where we'll find Jeremiah – under arrest by order of the king (2–3). Since everybody in the besieged city would have been suffering the deprivations of prolonged siege, the life of a political prisoner in a military garrison must have been uncomfortable (to say the least).

The prophet was imprisoned, but the word of God was not. Even (especially) in those terrible final days before the fall of Jerusalem in 587 BC, when the city hung like a punch bag between *Zedekiah king of Judah* and *Nebuchadnezzar . . . king of Babylon* (1–2), God was looking to a very different future. God's word would be delivered through a bizarre exercise of legal land purchase according to ancient custom that must have seemed totally absurd in the circumstances. And Jeremiah's message of hope must have seemed as unbelievable in the present terrible crisis engulfing the city, as his prediction of that very crisis had seemed so unbelievable when he began to preach it in the days of his youth. Jeremiah seemed out of step with the mood of the moment either way. He was mocked when he preached doom in a thriving society, and he was probably mocked when he preached hope in a dying one.

But first our text explains why Jeremiah *was confined in the courtyard of the guard in the royal palace of Judah.* And it does so with brilliant irony, by placing the word of God through the words of Jeremiah in the mouth of King Zedekiah (3–5). The irony is that Zedekiah, who had imprisoned Jeremiah to silence the word of God, here becomes the mouthpiece of God by repeating Jeremiah's words himself! The narrator lets us hear from the mouth of Zedekiah the words that Zedekiah did not wish to hear or to be heard.

This is the first time we are told of a direct encounter between the prophet and this last king of Judah. But it was not the only one. In fact, altogether we read of seven such interactions – sometimes by messengers, sometimes in private or even secret conversation.[1] Every time Jeremiah gave him the same basic message – 'this city is doomed, and so are you' – until Zedekiah could repeat the prophet's words from memory. But if he *knew* the words of Jeremiah by heart, he certainly did not *take* them to heart as the word of God. All he could mutter was, *why* (3)?

As if he didn't know why! As if Jeremiah had not spent years telling him and the whole nation why. As if he had no idea of the rhetoric and rationale that had filled the public ministry of Jeremiah and filled a whole scroll of his warnings. Sometimes it is right to ask, 'Why?' Sometimes it is profoundly understandable to ask why. But here it is pathetically inexcusable – not only to ask the question but even to lock up the only person who had already given him the answer to his 'why?'. 'If the king had listened closely enough to quote the prophet as he does, the king might have listened closely enough to know the answer to his question.'[2] And if he had listened,

[1] Jer. 21:1–7; 27:12–15; 32:1–5; 34:1–7; 37:1–10; 37:17–21; 38:14–28.
[2] Brueggemann (1991), p. 79.

if he had had the courage to take Jeremiah's advice and surrender the city, then its fate at the hands of Nebuchadnezzar (which had now become inexorable) might have at least spared the population the worst horrors of prolonged siege and massive loss of life.[3] If only.

But Zedekiah was stuck in his royal deafness.

And Jeremiah was stuck with his royal guards.

If sleep in such conditions were ever 'pleasant' (31:26), it might well have been in his dreams that Jeremiah was released from the sweating city to walk once again in his imagination through the fields of his home village at Anathoth. And in that familiar landscape where once God had spoken to him through a blossoming almond tree, God spoke again about the field of a relative, warning him to expect an unexpected visitor and an unexpected request (6–7).

Enter *cousin Hanamel* (8).

'Was there ever a more insensitive prison-visitor?'[4] The text does not explain how preposterous Hanamel's demand was, but Israelites familiar with their own laws of land tenure and redemption would have been appalled at Hanamel's self-serving and manipulative proposal. Only God's advance information prevented Jeremiah (and Baruch probably) from telling Hanamel to take his request and push off. Conversely, Hanamel was probably amazed that Jeremiah agreed so readily without some robust negotiation. What was going on?

According to Israel's ancient land laws, agricultural land belonged to the extended families living on it, to be passed down by inheritance through the generations. It was not to be bought and sold simply as a commercial commodity, for profit or speculation.[5] Not even a king could legitimately set aside the inalienability of an Israelite family's land.[6] However, if an Israelite fell into debt and needed to sell or mortgage some of his land to survive, there was a strong moral requirement that any such land should be bought (by pre-emption) or redeemed by someone within the kinship network of extended families (the *mišpāḥâ*, or 'clan'). It should not be 'sold permanently', but kept within the wider family. It was this *right and duty* that Hanamel demands that his cousin Jeremiah should exercise over a piece of land near their village of Anathoth.

Now, even in normal times such an act of kinship-redemption was a costly and potentially risky thing to do. That is why Boaz is so

---

[3] Cf. 21:8–10; 27:12–15.

[4] Kidner, p. 112.

[5] Lev. 25:23.

[6] As Ahab discovered (and must have known) when he made his offer to Naboth. It was his Canaanite wife Jezebel who overturned Israelite practice by maliciously corrupt use of Israel's own laws, in order to confiscate Naboth's land for the royal estate (1 Kgs 21).

commended for exercising it, when a nearer kinsman declined.[7] But to undertake such a purchase at this moment was plain stupid. Consider:

- Jeremiah was imprisoned with little prospect of release to enjoy the delights of rural husbandry. For all he knew, he might never live to see the field he was being asked to buy.
- He had no wife or sons of his own, no posterity to whom the land could belong in future. Indeed, Jeremiah, who had been isolated from his family by God's instruction (ch. 16), now has a family responsibility thrust upon him, at further personal cost.
- The field in question was at that moment most probably being trampled by the occupying forces of Nebuchadnezzar. Any vineyards or olive trees would have been burned to the ground.
- Jeremiah knew that the prospect for the city and its surrounding villages was utter devastation, and for the people of the land exile for at least two generations.

And your cousin wants you to buy his field at such a time? Or to be more accurate, God wants you to?

In Hanamel's case, the motivation would have been as clear to Jeremiah as to *all the Jews sitting in the courtyard of the guard* (12), who were watching with amused disbelief the fastidious legal ceremony that followed: Hanamel was converting a worthless asset into ready cash by cynical manipulation of his ageing relative. But what was God's purpose in asking Jeremiah to go along with the unscrupulous deal? We are left wondering as the story proceeds.

Enter *Baruch son of Neriah* (12).

We have not met this gentleman before but we shall encounter him increasingly, and hear a personal word from God to him in chapter 45. He comes from a family of high standing in the royal circle, and yet has devoted himself to the service of Jeremiah, particularly in matters secretarial and, in this case, legal. Was it an excruciatingly prolonged embarrassment for him to attend to all the legal formalities described in such detail in verses 9–12? *Seventeen shekels* was a paltry sum for a piece of land. Why, a millennium earlier Abraham paid four hundred shekels for a burial plot, while David paid fifty shekels for a threshing floor.[8] Perhaps seventeen shekels was all Jeremiah possessed, and it was in any case better than worthless turf to Hanamel. Nevertheless, the deal was done, the deeds were written, copied, signed, witnessed and sealed. And for

---

[7] Ruth 4.
[8] Gen. 23; 2 Sam. 24:18–25.

all we know the clay jar in which they were stored to last a long time may be still awaiting discovery.[9] But in fact, of course, the record of the event in Scripture was even more important than the storing of the deeds in pottery. 'The safe place in which Baruch deposited the evidence, even after the "earthenware vessel" (32:14), is the biblical text itself. That is the only place in which the evidence of the land deal has remained. That evidence, however, is sufficient for Israel's long-term hope.'[10] And, as we shall see, for ours.

And only when the whole procedure is finished does Jeremiah declare *what the LORD Almighty, the God of Israel, says: Houses, fields and vineyards will again be bought in this land* (15). There is a tantalizing suspense at work in the narrative. We are left wondering whether God told Jeremiah what the meaning of his purchase was going to be when he alerted him in advance to Hanamel's visit and request (we are not told in vv. 6–7). If so, that message, finally delivered in startling brevity in verse 15, would have sustained him through what must have seemed to all observers a cynical charade – the exploitation of an old bachelor's naivety. But if not . . . or if Jeremiah only had the more general hope that a restoration of the people on their land would come at some time in the future, then his action was an exercise of remarkable faith – faith in a future he would never personally see or enjoy. His was the obedience of faith. He quite literally put his money where his mouth was. All seventeen shekels of it. Possibly all the money he possessed. Faith – 'the substance of things hoped for'.[11] 'Seventeen shekels of silver were surely never better spent.'[12]

2. The prayer of faith (32:16–25)

Alone again, naturally (except probably for the company of faithful Baruch), Jeremiah's faith wrestles with Jeremiah's doubts – or at least with his questions. He had agreed to Hanamel's exploitative proposition. He had probably endured the ridicule of the crowded courtyard. He could expect to be the butt of scornful pity for days to come. Yet he had created a public, written, verified, enduring prophetic signpost, pointing to a future beyond the immediate catastrophe. He had delivered the word of the Lord that was a greater guarantee than deeds in a clay jar: *houses, fields and vineyards will again be bought in this land* (15).

And yet, and yet . . .

[9] The Dead Sea Scrolls survived in their clay jars for more than 2,000 years.
[10] Brueggemann (1991), p. 81.
[11] Heb. 11:1 (KJV).
[12] Kidner, p. 114.

Jeremiah's prayer ends with an unspoken 'why?' (25) that echoes the spoken 'why?' of Zedekiah (3), but from a very different heart and motive. Zedekiah's 'why?' was his surly protest at the approach of God's judgment. Jeremiah's implied 'why?' was his amazement at the possibility of God's renewed favour, and at the absurdity of acting now in the hope of it, when God's judgment was at that very moment battering down the walls of the city. 'For the moment, Jeremiah is captive not only to the palace guards but also to his own qualms about God's ability to create a future beyond the present chaos and disarray.'[13]

But how different is this prayer from the angry and tortured explosions of earlier years! How far Jeremiah has travelled from the wild accusation, 'You deceived me, LORD, and I was deceived; you overpowered me and prevailed' (20:7). This prayer is a sustained affirmation of God's sovereign freedom, justice and mercy, and the question that is burning in Jeremiah's heart is kept to the very end, and even then is only implied, rather than stated outright.

Jeremiah's prayer begins with an affirmation of God's sovereign omnipotence as the creator of the universe (17). But we are left wondering – what exactly is the point of the little extra observation, *nothing is too hard for you*. There is a kind of dogged assurance in it, but assurance of what? When God himself repeats it in the form of rhetorical question in verse 27, it is immediately followed by God's determination to hand over the city to the Babylonians. Is that what Jeremiah wonders (hopes, perhaps) might be *too hard* for God? For all the threats God has issued, might it just be that at the last moment God could not bring himself to do the unthinkable – destroy his own city and people? It would simply be *too hard* for him to do? But if that kind of secret hope were implied in the phrase, then it is disappointed. God's mysterious sovereignty over all creation operates also over his own people. He could, and he would, act in judgment. It would be hard, but not *too hard*.

Or might it be that Jeremiah is wrestling with the word he had just uttered in verse 15 – that God would bring about a restoration of normal agricultural and economic life, even though utter devastation of both was facing the nation? Surely that would be *too hard* even for God? But if that kind of secret fear is implied in the phrase, then it is quickly overcome. God could and would act in love and mercy, which was as true to his character as was his judgment on the wicked.

Jeremiah's prayer then goes on to explore another paradox. On the one hand it repeats very familiar lines about God's love (*you*

---

[13] Stulman, p. 278.

show love to thousands, drawn from Exod. 34:6–7 and Deut. 7:9). But on the other hand, it affirms the core principle of God's justice, that *you reward each person according to their conduct and as their deeds deserve* (19). Israel's history had demonstrated and exemplified both principles. God's undeserved love is evident in the great redemptive narrative of exodus and land-gift (20–22). But God's love had been met with disobedience (23), leading to the inevitable judgment that is now at the very gates – as God could see for himself! There is touching familiarity as Jeremiah asks God to take a look at what his words have produced – only a few yards away from where he sat praying (24). God's thousand-generation love spurned, God's inescapable judgment outpoured.

And yet, and yet . . .

God has told Jeremiah to buy a field! At such a time as this? At the very moment when the guilty past has crashed into an inescapable present, God asks Jeremiah to invest in an almost inconceivable future. Is the final denouement to be the wrath of God through the armies of Babylon, or the love of God in a new act of redemption? The suspense for Jeremiah at that moment must have been unbearable. But in fact, the answer was that it would be both, for only in exercising both wrath *and* redemption would the Judge of all the earth, for whom nothing was too hard, do right.[14]

As so often, it is only when we place these paradoxes in the light of the cross and resurrection of Christ that we begin to fathom their depth. For there indeed the wrath of God was exercised (and borne by God's own self in the person of God's Son) through the violent wickedness of human enemies (and soldiers), but the love of God was simultaneously poured out in redemptive triumph. And through the resurrection God would bring about not merely a restoration of agriculture in one ancient land, but the firstfruits of a whole new creation.

3. The horizons of faith (32:26 – 33:26)

God's answer to Jeremiah's prayer (32:26–44) tackled the question that Jeremiah had left hanging in the air, but at the same time stretched his faith imagination beyond the limits of logic, beyond the bounds of possibility and beyond the horizon of the foreseeable future. Chapter 33 then records a further *word of the LORD* coming *a second time* to Jeremiah in the same location. Most of it, we shall see, repeats messages already heard in chapters 31 – 32, with one significant addition regarding the line of Davidic kings and the line of Levitical priests.

[14] Gen. 18:14 and 25. There are strong echoes of these texts in Jeremiah's prayer.

a. Beyond logic

Two men had asked 'why?' – one in angry rebellion, one in puzzled reverence.

Zedekiah asked why Jeremiah was announcing the certainty of the fall of Jerusalem to Nebuchadnezzar (32:3–5). God's answer to him had already been given many times, and Jeremiah had repeated the well-worn history lesson in his prayer (32:23). Now, God confirms that Jeremiah had got it exactly right. The litany of condemnation in 32:30–35 summarizes with stunning severity what we have heard through the whole first half of the book. Israel's history had been *nothing but evil* for the whole of its duration – *from their youth* (30).[15] Jerusalem as a city had been making God angry *from the day it was built until now* (31). The whole society from the palace to the street was riddled with evil, *their kings and officials, their priests and prophets, the people of Judah and those living in Jerusalem* (32). They had ignored God's repeated teaching and discipline (33). They had reached the depths of depravity in the abomination of child sacrifice (34–35). The logic was inexorable – *this city has so aroused my anger and wrath that I must remove it from my sight* (31). The real question was not so much why it was about to happen now, as why it had not happened long ago.

Jeremiah asked (more or less) why God had instructed him to buy a field when the destruction of the whole country was so imminent (32:25). The answer had been given in the course of the purchase in verse 15, but since Jeremiah was still struggling to comprehend what he had at least had the faith to obey, God spells it out in expansive detail in verses 36–44.

And this is where divine logic parts company with human logic. Indeed, what God says begins with what seems so much of a logical non sequitur that some translations adjust it to something more sensible.

Look at verse 36. It begins (in the NIV) with God quoting the words of Jeremiah's prayer in verse 24, which were, after all, only what God himself had said would happen. Indeed Jeremiah stresses that point (*what you [God] said has happened;* 24). The present judgment, decreed by God, is about to fall. Yet, remarkably, God quotes Jeremiah as if to say, 'That's what *you* are saying, but I have something different to declare now. Keep up, Jeremiah.'

---

[15] The language of this verse echoes strongly the assessment of the human condition in Gen. 6:5 and especially 8:21. Israel was a microcosm of fallen humanity. The judgment that befell them signals the judgment of all (just as the promises of their redemption spells hope for the whole world).

The second half of the verse (in the NIV) then goes on, *but this is what the LORD, the God of Israel says*. However, in Hebrew it is not 'but' at all. It is 'Now, *therefore*', and in fact these words stand at the head of the verse in Hebrew, not half-way through (cf. ESV, NRSV). '*Therefore*' introduces something that logically follows on from whatever goes before. But this piece of divine 'logic' – this *therefore* in verse 36 – transcends all that has just gone before with a completely new beginning. It is a non sequitur. It just does not follow. Rather it launches a *new* redemptive reality that is generated in the heart and mind of God, not in the chain of historical causation. Judgment is the logical outcome of principles of God's own moral government (32:18–19). But beyond judgment there will be the abiding reality of God's redeeming, restoring, re-creating love.

To Zedekiah's 'Why?' (why judgment?), God answers, 'Because of your sin.'

To Jeremiah's 'Why?' (why future hope?), God answers, 'Because of my grace.'

b. Beyond possibility

God's answer echoes Jeremiah's prayer in another way. God picks up Jeremiah's creedal affirmation that *nothing is too hard for you* (32:17), and turns it into a rhetorical question: *I am the LORD, the God of all mankind. Is anything too hard for me?* (27). What is going on here? The text seems to be throwing out a challenge, a challenge to what people think is impossible for God. Even for those whose creed contains the truth of God's omnipotence, there are some things, surely, that even God could not or would not do.

There were those who had fondly believed that it was unthinkable that God would destroy his own city and temple (chs. 7 and 26). Surely that would be too hard for God to contemplate? But he could and he would, and it was only a matter of weeks now, as Jeremiah sat praying in the courtyard of the guard, before he actually did.

But there were also those who would be reading these words in the scroll of Jeremiah in the throes of exile. Their memories were seared by the fires that finally consumed Jerusalem and the *famine, sword and plague* that carried off so many of their loved ones. For some of them it must have seemed unthinkable that God could 'restore their fortunes', that the future could conceivably contain a return of the people, a rebuilding of city and temple. Surely that would be too hard for God, the God who rewards *each person according to their conduct and as their deeds deserve* (19)? Did not their deeds deserve all that had happened? Their past seemed to foreclose any possible future with God. Except that God was not bound by possibilities emerging from the past. Nothing was too hard for him, including the creation of a new future generated from his own sovereign and redemptive will.

> They [the exiles] have endured war, amputated hopes, splintered families, and the travail of a shattered world. Now, by the power of the word, God empowers these broken and shipwrecked people to imagine a future when none seemed possible.
> The Book of Comfort sees all expressions of hope as grounded in God's mercy, love, and sovereignty. Hope is not the result of human virtue, human ingenuity, human grit, or human imagination. Nor does it derive from success, military might, technological prowess, or even the elimination of scars and memories of loss. Hope is God's gracious gift to suffering people who are at their breaking point. It is the promise of life when none is expected.[16]

And yet, of course, although 'God's new thing' would be just that – a radically new beginning – there was a very important continuity also. The city that would be rebuilt was the city that had been destroyed. The people who would return to celebrate God's salvation would be the descendants of those who had gone into exile for their sins. A future still within history, but bearing a power and an intervention from beyond the mere cause-and-effect possibilities of history.

There are ways that this also finds its ultimate fulfilment in the cross and resurrection of Christ. For was the risen Jesus the same as the crucified Jesus? Yes and no. Clearly the continuity was there: God raised Jesus bodily from the tomb; he was recognized by his disciples; his body bore the marks of what had been done to him before death. Yet equally clearly there was a discontinuity, a newness, a transcendent dimension to his new life that was assuredly not less than physical ('a ghost does not have flesh and bones, as you see I have'),[17] but certainly more than the physicality we experience. The risen Jesus was the firstfruits of the new creation.

And similarly also, both the cross and resurrection confounded the limits of what some people thought possible. It was surely unthinkable (wasn't it, Peter?) that God's Messiah should die on a cross. But he did. It was surely unthinkable (wasn't it, Sadducees and Sanhedrin?) that God could raise him from the dead. But he did.

And so the wrath and judgment of God visited on Jerusalem in 587 BC, *and* the grace and redemption of God that raised the people

---

[16] Stulman, pp. 283 and 285.
[17] Luke 24:39.

to new life again,[18] both found their ultimate expression and saving power when Jesus 'died for our sins in accordance with the Scriptures . . . and was raised on the third day in accordance with the Scriptures'.[19]

c. Beyond the horizon

'Look at me!' (*hinnēnî*, lit. 'behold, I'), says God in the arresting opening of verse 37. '*You* have been saying what you have been saying, Jeremiah, but this is *me*, and here is what I, and I alone, am going to do.'

At one level, of course, God simply expands the curt prediction of verse 15, a prediction that had given meaning to the purchase of a field in a country on the brink of extinction. *Houses, fields and vineyards will again be bought in this land*, because people will come back and get on with doing those things (37). *Calamity* will be replaced by *prosperity* (42). What Jeremiah had done in lonely faith will become the routine practice in a repopulated countryside (43–44). All these things came to pass at Horizon 1. They were fulfilled in the return of exiles under the decree of Cyrus. Once more the people of Israel would know themselves to be God's people in God's land in a renewed covenant relationship (38).

But verses 39–41 lift our eyes to a different level, to a horizon glowing with ultimate and infinite perfections. It seems impossible to read these verses without being transported by them to Horizon 3.[20] Now of course, it is fair to say that we can also read them as rhetorical hyperbole – simply rejoicing in the joys of the people of Judah who came home to their own land under God's blessing, described in an understandably exaggerated kind of way. We may pay all due respect to the post-exilic community. We can see the returning exiles, no doubt, as a chastened people, determined to live in such a way that the calamity that had driven their forebears into exile should never happen again, and that the sins that had caused the calamity should not be named among them. We can draw powerful lessons from the laudable efforts in that direction in the memoirs of Ezra and Nehemiah and the prophecies of Haggai – great

[18] Ezek. 37 portrays the restoration of Israel in the language of resurrection from the dead.

[19] 1 Cor. 15:3–4. I have explored more fully how the Old Testament narrative of exile and return helps our understanding of the central redemptive narrative of the Bible – the cross and resurrection of Christ – and forms a part of what Paul meant by speaking of both as 'in accordance with the scripture', in Wright, *The God I Don't Understand*, pp. 143–157.

[20] For an explanation of what I mean by Horizons 1, 2 and 3, see the concluding section of ch. 24, pp. 334–339.

moments of rebuilding walls, of reading, understanding and obeying God's word, of renewal of covenant commitments, and of rebuilding the temple. Yet even from those books we hear of recurrent oppression and exploitation, of the temptations of foreign gods, of disobedience to God's law. And if we had only the book of Malachi to go by, we would know for certain that the soaring superlatives of Jeremiah 32:39–40 could not be applied to the people Malachi addressed less than a century after the return. People who were showing contempt for God's name, wearying God, robbing God and speaking against God,[21] could hardly be identified as those who with *singleness of heart and action* would *always fear* God and *never turn away from* him.

And so, it seems we are driven by the divine energy of the phrases in verses 39–41 to the eschatological Horizon 3, and to the vision of the new creation, when God will indeed dwell with those whom he will have planted to dwell with him there forever (41), when the inhabitants of the city of God will have 'one heart and one way' (39, lit.), and when the destruction of all that is evil will herald an eternity of the original '*good*' of creation – in doing good and receiving good.

Why not take a moment to read Revelation 21:1–5, followed by Revelation 21:22 – 22:5, and then immediately come back and read again Jeremiah 32:38–41? And having done so, do we not say with Peter, 'This is that which was spoken by the prophet'? And must we not also echo the awe of the psalmist, 'This is (will be, and can only be) the LORD's doing, and it is (will be) marvellous in our eyes'[22]?

So as we sit with Jeremiah in the double imprisonment of a military garrison in a besieged city, let us hear, as he did, the threatening noise of the enemy at the gate, agents of the righteous judgment of God on Israel's embodiment of the sin of fallen humanity including our own. But let also see, with his eyes of faith, the vision of an ultimate future beyond even the final judgment, the vision of an *everlasting covenant*, of a people enjoying the undiluted goodness of God, a people pardoned, purified and planted by God. That is the future promised by the God and Father of our Lord Jesus Christ, accomplished by the cross and resurrection of his Son, guaranteed by the Holy Spirit. That is the future that is ours to contemplate now by the faith that is 'the substance of things hoped for, the evidence of things not seen'.[23] That is the future, the 'real estate', to which God holds the title deeds. That is the 'land' purchased with a price infinitely more than Jeremiah paid, a security more eternally durable than even Baruch's clay jar.

[21] Mal. 1:6; 2:17; 3:8; 3:13–14.
[22] Ps. 118:23.
[23] Heb. 11:1 (KJV).

d. Promises renewed and extended (33:1–26)

Jeremiah 33 is largely a repetition of promises already expressed in chapters 30 – 31, but with one major addition in 33:17–26.

- 33:1–5 repeats the words of impending doom from 32:28–29, as the siege of Jerusalem reached its murderous climax.
- 33:6–9 repeats the words of a hope-filled future from 32:36–44. 33:8 also echoes some of the content of the new covenant promises of 31:34, while 33:9 turns the language of nostalgic wistfulness of the past in 13:11 into a promise of the future.[24]
- 33:10–13 repeats in shorter form the expansive promises of restored agricultural and social life after the return, which filled 31:1–14.
- 33:14–16 repeats the messianic prophecy of 23:5–6.

In 33:17–26 we have an expansion of the immediately preceding prophecy about a coming son of David who would rule in righteousness. God promises that *David will never fail to have a man to sit on the throne of the house of Israel.* In other words, the kingship of Israel will forever be Davidic. This is immediately followed by a matching promise to the tribe of Levi, that they will always provide priests to offer the sacrifices before God. These promises are then placed on the same permanent foundations as the orders of creation (33:20–21), echoing the same kind of comparison in 31:35–37. Finally, the promise to both the descendants of David and the Levites is linked to the language of the covenant with Abraham, saying that they will be *as countless as the stars of the sky and as measureless as the sand on the seashore* (22).

How are we to understand such promises? We could treat them as poetic and rhetorical hyperbole. With such exaggerated language, we may say, Jeremiah was simply pointing to a restored Davidic leadership of Israel and a restored sacrificial priesthood functioning in a rebuilt temple. We may indeed see those realities at Horizon 1 in the post-exilic period. But it stretches the imagination to think of the post-exilic governors (not kings) of Judah (a tiny province of the Persian empire) as sitting *on the throne of the house of Israel . . .* ruling over *the descendants of Abraham, Isaac and Jacob,* or to speak of them along with the priests and Levites as *countless as the stars in the sky and as measureless as the sand on the seashore.*

---

[24] The words *renown, joy, praise* and *honour* echo (with the addition of *joy*) the triplet that is found not only in Jer. 13:11, but comes originally from the covenantal promises of Deut. 26:19.

It seems once again that we are driven forward to Horizons 2 and 3. For certainly the New Testament affirms that the eternal nature of both the throne of David and the Levitical priesthood was taken up and fulfilled by Jesus Christ. The angel declared the former (Luke 1:32–33); Hebrews declares the latter (Heb. 8 – 10). Kingship (David) and priesthood (Levites) are two of the great realities of Old Testament Israel's life and faith that were explicitly declared to be 'forever' – just as 'forever' as God's covenant with creation itself. But we are taught very clearly in the New Testament that their 'forever-ness' is taken up and fulfilled by the kingly and priestly work of Christ. Christ embodies the eternal reality that was promised under the form of existing Old Testament realities – kingship and priesthood. This should help us when it comes to that more vexing issue of the land of Israel. For that too was promised 'forever' to the children of Abraham – a promise that is then used to justify the claim to the whole land of Palestine made by some in the modern Israeli state and supported by many Christians. But the New Testament makes it clear that Old Testament 'forevers' are consolidated and guaranteed within the eternal nature of the person and work of Christ and the new age of God's kingdom that he inaugurated for all those who are in him.

And Horizon 3? The Abrahamic language of verse 22 should alert us to the eschatological dimension. The mission of God through Israel had always been that they would be the 'first-born son' of a very large family, the nation through whom God would bring blessing to all nations on earth. And so, just as Israel's calling had been to reflect the kingly and priestly role entrusted to humanity within creation, as 'a kingdom of priests',[25] so that identity is now shared by the great multi-national community of believers. And they will indeed ultimately become 'a great multitude that no one could count, from every nation, tribe, people and language', 'a kingdom and priests to serve our God, and they will reign on the earth'.[26]

Theological and expository reflections

- Jeremiah 32 is a classic example of faith being exercised in practical obedience, even in circumstances that seem to make the act of obedience pointless. It is an event that could easily be included among the examples of faith in action in Hebrews 11.
- Both chapters also illustrate the importance of reading Old Testament prophecies at the three horizons. We need to see the

[25] Exod. 19:4–6.
[26] Rev. 7:9; 5:10.

levels of fulfilment that happened in the Old Testament itself, in and through Jesus Christ, and ultimately in the new creation.

- Finally, Jeremiah 32 is one of many great prayers in the Bible from which we can learn so much. It is a fine example of the way to pray in a desperate situation: concentrating first on the creative power (17) and perfect fidelity and justice (18–19) of God; remembering next his great redemptive acts (20–23a; to which the Christian can now add the greatest of them all); and then with this background, laying before God the guilt of the past (23b), the hard facts of the present (24) and the riddle of the future (25).[27]

[27] Kidner, p.113.

Jeremiah 34:1 – 35:19
26. Promise-breakers and promise-keepers[1]

'Legalism is yesterday's obedience.' That is an aphorism that I owe to Chris Sugden.[2] The point it makes is that there are times when God's people respond to particular evils or temptations within their surrounding culture by insisting upon certain behavioural choices. For them at that time, that may be how their obedience to the gospel finds practical expression. However, cultures change, while resolutions and rules tend to solidify. So what may have been a form of living obedience at one time can later become a rather needless legalism in a very different world.

Perhaps the Rekabites (ch. 35) might be a case in point. They were rigidly following a pattern of behaviour mandated 250 years earlier by their ancestor – somewhat characteristic of counter-cultural sects. Eccentric? Antiquated? Perhaps. But their unswerving loyalty to their founder's instructions becomes an object lesson in the hands of Jeremiah.

In stark contrast, 'yesterday's obedience' for the leaders of Judah was nothing more than exactly that – yesterday's. Yesterday they made a promise to obey God's law. Today they have broken it already (ch. 34).

So our editors have pulled together in the text two incidents that are actually ten years apart in time, with the clear intention of contrasting the one with the other. In chapter 34 we have an incident during the final siege of Jerusalem (588 BC) that illustrates the congenital disobedience of Judah – in spite of a short-lived spurt of good

---

[1] I owe the title for these two chapters to Derek Kidner, p. 116.

[2] 'Obedience is not legalism. Legalism is a static concern with forms of obedience which may have been important once but are now irrelevant or trivial ... Legalism is yesterday's obedience: it blinds us to the crucial issues of today' (Christopher Sugden, *Radical Discipleship* [London: Marshall Morgan and Scott, 1981], pp. 78–79).

resolution. In chapter 35 we have an incident during Nebuchadnezzar's earlier attack on the country (598 BC) that contrasts the disobedience of Jerusalem's urban elite with the long-term fidelity of a clan of country cousins.

We can see from a number of other features that the two chapters ought to be read (and preached) together. They are enclosed between two declarations by God about what is about to happen to the city and nation (34:1–7; 35:17–19), but in each case the words of engulfing judgment are combined with a positive alternative future (potentially for Zedekiah and actually for the Rekabites). Both stories are about covenants or commands made by a leader (Zedekiah, 34:8; Jehonadab, 35:6), though the response of their respective followers is very different. Both stories involve something that happened in the temple (Zedekiah's covenant, 34:15; Jeremiah's drinks party, 35:2–5). Both stories highlight repeatedly the theme of listening (or not) to the word of God and choosing to obey (or disobey) what God has commanded (the Hebrew word *šāma'* – 'to hear, to obey' – occurs multiple times through both chapters). Both stories climax with words of judgment beginning with the ominous *therefore* (34:17; 35:17).

1. Two verdicts anticipated (34:1–7)

It's back-to-reality time. For four chapters we have relished the 'Book of Consolation' and its soaring promises of a future for Israel beyond judgment and indeed a future for the world that still lies ahead of us. But now we are jolted back to the imploding present – the besieged city of Jerusalem.

The situation was desperate. Nebuchadnezzar had invaded and systematically destroyed the land of Judah. Apart from Jerusalem only two fortified cities still held out – Lachish and Azekah – and they would soon be reduced to mounds of rubble. From inside the city, it felt like the whole world was ranged against them – for that indeed is how verse 1 rhetorically describes Nebuchadnezzar's forces. The Hebrew literally says, *Nebuchadrezzar, king of Babylon, and all his army and all the kingdoms of the earth within the rule of his hand and all the peoples were making war against Jerusalem*. And that was not the worst of it. The God of all the earth was against them as well. Indeed the armies of Nebuchadnezzar were merely the agents of God. The language 'imagines the assault on Jerusalem as a massive cosmic battle'.[3]

Jeremiah's message to the king was hardly new. We know from 32:3–5 that it had become Jeremiah's settled conviction that the fate

[3] Stulman, p. 287.

of the city was now sealed. And so was the fate of King Zedekiah – up to a point. Verse 3 repeats Jeremiah's prediction that Zedekiah would not escape capture but would have a personal face-to-face encounter with Nebuchadnezzar prior to being taken to Babylon. But what fate would await him there? That is where our text seems ambiguous.

If we take verses 4 and 5 as a straight predictive *promise* (that Zedekiah's life and death in Babylon would be 'in peace'), they stand in tension with what we read elsewhere – namely that he witnessed the execution of his sons, before being blinded and shackled, and died later in a Babylonian prison (39:5–7; 52:8–11). For that reason, some prefer to read these verses as a *conditional* promise (with an implied 'if' at the start of verse 4), describing an alternative *possible* future if only Zedekiah would listen to God's word through Jeremiah.

From the beginning of Zedekiah's reign, Jeremiah had made it unmistakeably clear (and visible through the yoke he carried around, ch. 27) that Nebuchadnezzar was carrying out God's purposes and that the best possible policy for Zedekiah was to submit to Nebuchadnezzar (and thereby submit to God). Even when the siege had begun it was not too late to do so, since to surrender the city would have spared it the worst horrors to come. And, we assume, would have spared Zedekiah the treatment he actually got for having held out in rebellion to the bitter end.

If that is the message that is assumed in the abbreviated report of 34:2–3, then the beginning of verse 4 is an emphatic and contrasting piece of advice. 'But, yet' (the opening word is emphatic), 'listen to the word of YHWH, Zedekiah . . .' The word *promise* (NIV) is an interpretation (and a commonly acceptable one) of the simple 'word' (*dābār*). The flow of thought then becomes, 'If you will listen to the word of the Lord (as Jeremiah has been telling you) and surrender the city (as he has advised), then *you will not die by the sword; you will die peacefully*'.[4] In the event, however, Zedekiah did not listen, and so he lost the chance of a less painful personal outcome.

2. A promise quickly broken (34:8–22)

a. The king's covenant (8–11)

Zedekiah had an idea. He would get the agreement of the wealthier

---

[4] An imperative followed by a future tense may be a simple instruction: 'Turn left at the bottom of this street and you will come to the church.' But it can also be an implied conditional, usually either a warning or a desired outcome: 'Eat all that and you'll be sick.' 'Take this medicine and you'll get better.' The implied 'If . . .' at the beginning then also becomes an implied 'But if not . . . then not'. The reading adopted above takes Jeremiah's word to Zedekiah in as such an implied conditional.

citizens to put into practice the ancient law about releasing debt-slaves. The language used in verses 8 and 14 makes use of a mixture of phrases drawn from Exodus 21:1–11, Leviticus 25:8–12 and Deuteronomy 15:12–18. The phrase *proclaim freedom* (*dĕrôr*) precisely echoes Leviticus 25:10 (the jubilee), but the reference to *Hebrew* slaves and the *seventh year* (14), is closer to Exodus and Deuteronomy. Whatever the precise scriptural warrant, Zedekiah wants it done. So he *made a covenant*, ratified in the temple, no less (15), and everybody *agreed* (10; literally, 'they listened', which was more than they had ever done for God, 35:14–15).

We are not told why Zedekiah came up with this plan. Speculations abound, none of them very convincing. Was it economic – fewer mouths to feed at a time of siege? But apart from relieving the owners of the responsibility of feeding their own slaves, releasing them would not increase the stock of food available for the whole community. Was it military – to get more men into the army? But why could they not be enlisted to fight as slaves, and why emphasize the release of *female slaves* also? Was it religious – an act of pious compliance with ancient laws to cajole God into rescuing them?[5] But why such economically radical measures when some special time of fasting, prayer and sacrifices would be the usual prescription (unless fasting in a time of siege might seem less than voluntary piety)? Or was Zedekiah sincerely trying to emulate his father Josiah, in contrast to his brother Jehoiakim, by doing what was right and just (22:15–16)? If so, his good intentions escaped the notice of the historian (2 Kgs 24:19).

But if we don't know the reason behind it, we certainly know the sequel that followed it, and that is all that matters for the point of the story. With blunt simplicity we read, *but afterwards they changed their minds and took back the slaves they had freed and enslaved them again* (11; the language is strong – they 'forced them back', as in v. 16). Perhaps this happened when the Babylonian army withdrew from the city (21; 37:4–5) and the danger seemed past. But the Babylonian retreat would turn out to be as temporary as the freedom of the slaves had been.

And so Zedekiah's little foray into covenant obedience and social justice was short-lived. Whatever the king thought about the sudden abandonment by the wealthy and powerful of their solemn and binding agreement (and he was clearly too weak to enforce it), we can only imagine the anger, disappointment and sense of betrayal that the slaves felt. They would not be the first or the last generation

[5] 'Foxhole religion', as Brueggemann (1991) calls it (p. 107): 'Dear God, get me out of this danger and I promise to . . . (whatever)'.

of the world's poor and marginalized to feel the sting of a government's broken promises and U-turns.

b. God's covenant (12–16)

Anger, disappointment, betrayal. Transfer the slaves' feelings to God and multiply by infinity. God speaks, not out of the sting of a single broken promise but out of countless generations of covenant-breaking going back to the exodus.

Verse 13 echoes verse 8. Zedekiah *made a covenant with all the people in Jerusalem* – a royal decree in a national emergency. God himself (the word 'I' is emphatic) *made a covenant with your ancestors when I brought them out of Egypt, out of* 'the house of slaves' (13).[6] Zedekiah had arranged for the release of slaves in the besieged capital of a shattered rebel state. God had brought a whole nation out of slavery in the most powerful empire of the region. So whatever binding power the king's covenant might have been thought to possess (and it obviously wasn't much), was vastly surpassed by the binding power that should have attended their Lord's covenant – the God who had redeemed them from cruel oppression and state-sponsored genocide.

And on the basis of that great redeeming, liberating act (the exodus), the *very first law* God had given to his people (after the Ten Commandments themselves) significantly instructed them to release slaves after six-year 'contracts' (14, cf. Exod. 21:1–11). The link between God's release of Israel from Egypt and Israel's own slave-release law is quite explicit in the re-promulgation of the law in Deuteronomy. 'Remember that you were slaves in Egypt and the LORD your God redeemed you. That is why I give you this command today.'[7]

The Old Testament's laws on slave release are complex, but the very fact that there are two editions of the sabbatical (seventh) year regulations (in Exod. 21 and Deut. 15), along with the additional procedures for the redemption of land and slaves, and the capstone of jubilee release and restoration (in Lev. 25), all this shows a strong commitment to principles of justice, humane treatment, and respecting the human dignity of debt-slaves.[8] And it was all explicitly and

---

[6] The emphatic 'I' and the double phrase 'out of the land of Egypt, out of the house of slaves' is a clear echo of the opening declaration of the Decalogue (Exod. 20:1). God's law was founded upon God's redeeming grace. Even the book of Exodus itself presents this crucial theological truth in the structure of the book. We have eighteen chapters of salvation before a single chapter of law. Grace comes first. Obedience is response.

[7] Deut. 15:15.

[8] Debt was the commonest reason for entering into such bondage. Either the debtor or one of his dependents would work off the debt. On the economic laws of the Old Testament in relation to debt and slavery and their theological foundations, see Wright, *God's People in God's Land*, and Wright, *Old Testament Ethics*, pp. 146–181.

repeatedly based on reminders of God's own generosity in the redemption of Israel from slavery at the founding moment of their nationhood.

So it was not unreasonable, was it, for God to demand of his nation of released slaves that they should provide for the periodic release of those in their midst whom impoverishment had driven into slavery, along with the remission of any remaining debts owed? *Your ancestors, however, did not listen to me or pay attention to me* (14b). Which implies that the sabbatical legislation on debt cancellation and slave release had gone unheeded during the centuries of increasing economic polarization that followed the reign of Solomon. The growth of a greedy, land-accumulating elite at the expense of an impoverished, debt-ridden underclass had gone on unchecked by the requirements of the law or the rhetoric of the prophets.

Until Zedekiah and his sudden decree. Even God was pleased (and a little surprised?). *But you, this day, you turned around and did the upright thing in my sight, by proclaiming release, each man to his neighbour, and you made a covenant in my presence in the house that bears my name* (15, my own translation).

But then comes the shock, the betrayal. The action of the slave-owners was not only a breach of faith with their king but also an even worse (and utterly characteristic) breach of faith with their God. *But you turned around again[9] and profaned my name[10] and each one of you caused to turn back your male and female slaves, whom you had let go free according to **their** desires, and you forced them to be for **your** benefit slaves, male and female* (16, my translation).

Commercial self-interest trumped covenant obligation. It usually does. It's the economy, you see. It's the market. And it's wartime. You can't go indulging in this humanitarian sentimentality just to please a desperate king, or even a God whose antique instructions are unworkable in contemporary economic conditions. A token gesture, that's all, then back to the way things were.

Except that very soon nothing would ever again be the way things were.

---

[9] The repeated use of *šûb* is typical of Jeremiah. Exactly the same form of the verb 'You turned' means repentance (turning away) from evil ways in v. 15, and then turning back to those evil ways in v. 16.

[10] They had profaned God's name because they had made their covenant in the temple that bore the name of YHWH and the ceremony would have included swearing an oath in the name of YHWH. So when they went back on their commitment, they not only broke their oath, and broke the law of slave release, they also broke the third commandment against such treacherous use of the divine name.

c. Covenant consequences (17–22)

Therefore – the word introduces the classic court verdict of the covenant Lord. His speech repeats the same implacable message that Jeremiah had given to Zedekiah (the doom of the city, at the hands of the Babylonian army, summoned by God himself, 21–22). But it includes a few words specific to the immediate breach of faith.

- The behaviour of the slave-owners was not just reneging on a promise to the king, but constituted classic covenant disobedience to God: *you have not obeyed me* (17; lit. 'listened to me'). This is the thrust of both chapters 34 and 35, as it has been, of course, in so many chapters before. Judah's mortal illness was their deafness to God's voice. People who will not listen to God will not listen to the claims of their own conscience or the claims of the poor or the claims of covenant love and justice. They are deaf to God and the world, insulated in self-interest, insistent on self-rule. The idolatries of autonomous individualism and consumerism are not very distant from the cynical behaviour of the wealthy and powerful in Jeremiah's Jerusalem.
- The terms God uses to describe the victims of this treachery are very telling. Their social and economic status was 'male slaves and female slaves'. But their human dignity was that they were 'brothers and neighbours' (*own people*, NIV, dilutes the force of the terms). Not only are such terms redolent of mutual covenantal responsibilities that are woven through the Torah (e.g., 'love your neighbour as yourself'[11]), the text also makes them deeply personal and relational. Literally verse 17 reads, 'You did not listen to me to proclaim release, each man to his brother and each man to his neighbour.' God sees more than macroeconomic conditions. God sees more than units of production, more than commodities to be bought and sold, more even than that oddly impersonal concept 'human resources'. God sees local, personal and family obligations, and God condemns failure to treat other people for what they are in God's sight – kinsfolk and neighbours to whom we owe duties of love, compassion and justice.
- The punishment would match the crime, or to be more precise, the punishment would be exactly what the slave-owners had invoked upon themselves by the symbolism of their oath-taking. The Hebrew for making a covenant was 'to cut a covenant', reflecting the practice of cutting a sacrificial animal

[11] Lev. 19:18.

in two and walking between the pieces. The implied message was, 'May I be like this animal if I fail to keep my oath.'[12] Very well, says God, you have, so you will. The terms of your oath will be the terms of your judgment (19–20).

So then, this depressing tale of the betrayal of the poor by the wealthy stands in our text at one level simply as an illustration from Jeremiah's day of the people's failure to listen and obey. They could not even do that for their human king, how much less for their covenant Lord. But at another level, it illustrates the people's failure to live up to the core standards and ideals of what the redeemed covenant community was supposed to be like. Verse 18 tellingly combines both the immediate *covenant they made before me* (i.e. Zedekiah's), with *my covenant* (i.e. God's). What Zedekiah asked the people to do was simply what God had expected of his people all along. The sabbatical law itself had made the point very clearly: 'Do not be hard-hearted or tight-fisted toward [your poor brothers]. Rather, be open-handed and freely lend them whatever they need.'[13]

This singling out of a particular act of disobedience to one specific law is seen to be illustrative of transgressing the covenant as a whole. In that respect it is very similar to Deuteronomy 26. There the Israelite farmer brings the firstfruits of his harvest to the Lord at the sanctuary and makes a double declaration. First (and necessarily prior) he recounts God's redeeming grace in the nation's history (Deut. 26:1–11). Then (and only then) he declares his own committed obedience to all God's law in response (14). But the law that is singled out as *proof* of such obedience is that he has given the triennial tithe that was specifically set aside for the landless, the homeless and the family-less (12–13; cf. Deut. 14:28–29). God's law had not been kept if the poor had not been cared for – a challenge the rich young ruler stumbled at, the rich fool forgot, and the rich man in Jesus' parable ignored and went to hell for.[14] Rather, when you have fulfilled covenant responsibility to the needy, you can speak of obedience to covenant law, anticipate covenant blessing and renew covenant commitment (Deut. 26:14–19).

So here, only negatively. The slave-owners' despicable abuse of their slaves was a slap in the face to God. To break faith with the poorest in society was to break the whole covenant with YHWH.

[12] Gen. 15:9–21 provides a startling example of this custom. In the darkness of his dream Abraham sees a firepot and torch (doubtless representing God) pass between such severed animal pieces. God himself was swearing his oath to Abraham on God's own life.
[13] Deut. 15:7–8.
[14] Matt. 19:21–22; Luke 12:13–21; 16:19–31.

'Whoever oppresses the poor shows contempt for their Maker, but whoever is kind to the needy honours God.' 'Whatever you did not do for one of the least of these, you did not do for me.'[15] But we live in a society that will not listen to Jeremiah or Jesus and the betrayal of the poor goes on and on.

3. A promise resolutely kept (35:1–16)

So we move to a contrasting story. While the governing urban elite could not keep their promise to the king for more than a few weeks, come and look at a community that had been keeping their promise to their founding ancestor for more than two centuries. After the lesson in treachery (ch. 34), we now get a *lesson* (35:13) in fidelity.

a. A tempting invitation (1–5)

Of all Jeremiah's 'acted prophecies', this one grabs the imagination most vividly. A scruffy bunch of 'alternative lifestyle' folk from the very edges of society, being offered free drinks by God's prophet (when everybody knew they were strictly teetotal), and it's all happening in church! It's as if the dean of St Paul's Cathedral in London had invited the whole community of tent-dwellers in the Occupy protest (in the winter of 2011–12) to come down to the crypt for mulled wine and mince pies (maybe he should have done).

So who were these *Rekabites*? Actually we know very little more than they themselves tell us here. They may have been linked to the Kenites, a somewhat marginal group who settled in Israel.[16] But this particular group traced their ancestry to *Jehonadab son of Rekab* (6), who was an ally of Jehu during Jehu's purge of the house of Ahab in the ninth century BC. The story is in 2 Kings 9 – 10 and Jehonadab turns up at 10:15. It was a very violent revolution in which Jehu and supporters like Jehonadab massacred the family of Ahab, including his Phoenician wife Jezebel, and then exterminated all the prophets and priests of Baal – all in the name of re-establishing the worship of YHWH. It was effective, but its excessive bloodiness was later condemned by Hosea (1:4–5). At any rate, it was all a very long time ago. The time between Jehonadab's life and his family living in Jerusalem in the reign of Jehoiakim is about the same as between John Wesley and twenty-first century Methodists.

From what their descendants tell Jeremiah, it seems that Jehonadab had then taken his brand of Yahwism to mean a rejection of a settled

---

[15] Prov. 14:31; Matt. 25:45.
[16] 1 Chr. 2:55; cf. Judg. 1:16; 4:17; 1 Sam. 15:6.

life in the land. Perhaps it seemed to him that such a life only fostered the temptation to comfortable affluence and falling into the kind of 'health, wealth and sex' culture of Baalism – since Baal was the god of fertility (of land, crops, herds and women), and the god of business and money and everything that seemed to matter to landed people. By contrast, Jehonadab seems to have thought, the life of the wilderness, living in tents, living off the direct provision of God – that was the true calling of faithful followers of YHWH. So he and his family stayed outside the settled communities of Israel's farming villages and fortified towns, rejected mainline culture and lived an austere nomadic lifestyle, forbidding not only the planting of vines but also the enjoyment of their fruits. They seem to fall somewhere between the Bedouin (without the camels) and the Amish (without the pacifism – judging by the story of Jehonadab himself).

But it's hard to live like that if you can't roam the land freely. So Nebuchadnezzar's invasion of Judah had driven the Rekabites to find refuge in Jerusalem – a place they must have found intolerably cramped, distasteful, and compromising of all their principles. Where do you pitch your tents in a city? Perhaps they felt able to live temporarily in houses, so long as they hadn't built them (7).

'Go and find them,' God tells Jeremiah, 'invite them to the temple and *give them wine to drink*' (2).

Again we are left to wonder about the details. Where did Jeremiah get quantities of wine (*bowls full*), and how did he pay for it? How did he get permission for his little piece of entertainment in a temple side room? The narrator leaves our curiosity to our imagination, and we watch a shuffling little cluster of misfits and outsiders, doubtless awed and shocked by the size and splendour of the temple courts they had just been led through, wondering what they had been invited for, cramming into a side room under the glare of some tutting officials (4), staring in disbelief at the tables laden with pitchers of wine and cups for everybody, meeting the notorious prophet from Anathoth, who smiles (for once) and starts offering drinks all round: 'Aw go on. You'll love it. Temple's best vintage, you know. You must be parched in the heat out there. Just one, surely? What about you, sir?'

b. A principled refusal (6–11)

But they refuse whatever Jeremiah may have done to persuade them. And as Kidner points out, it was a subtle but severe test.

> In this test of their conservatism everything was arranged to maximize the pressure on them. The gathering of the whole

clan (3), the exalted meeting place (4), and the hospitable provision (5) which it would seem churlish to refuse, all contributed to the persuasiveness of so special an occasion. Added to this was doubtless the family's consciousness of having already accepted one compromise by moving into the safety of Jerusalem (11). Not the least of these pressures, perhaps, was the spiritual prestige of Jeremiah their host.[17]

But they go on refusing, and cite in justification the commands of their distant ancestor (6–7). They seem to have it as a little creed, a 'pentalogue' as Brueggemann calls it. Here is their recipe to ensure they would *live a long time in the land* (as indeed they had, so far).

- You shall not drink wine.
- You shall not build a house.
- You shall not sow seed.
- You shall not plant a vineyard.
- You shall live in tents.

'This pentalogue seems designed to warn against accommodation to the values of the dominant society. Thus the Rechabites are something of a "sect" whose identity entails resistance to the comfortable accommodations of settled, urban society.'[18]

c. An unwelcome lesson (12–16)

So what is Jeremiah's point, as the proud Rekabites turn on their heels and make their sober way back out through the temple courts, while Jeremiah is left with a bill for the wine they wouldn't drink?

There is no comment at all on the rights or wrongs of the Rekabites' way of life. It is neither commended nor denounced in itself. The text is not written to set the Rekabites before us as a model to emulate – either in their rejection of cities and agriculture or in their refusal to drink wine (though there have been sects in ancient and modern times who have understood it in that way and even adopted the name). The lesson lies solely in the contrast between their unflinching commitment to obedience to the rule laid down by their human ancestor, and Judah's casual and careless disobedience to the covenant established by their God. For that reason, if the Rekabites are a model of anything, it is to point us to the prime calling to live in obedience *to God* (which is the point Jeremiah explicitly makes), not

[17] Kidner, p. 118.
[18] Brueggemann (1991), p. 113.

365

to treat *human* ancestors in the faith as infallible in all the teachings they laid down for their followers.

The key issue is one of 'listening', in the sense of heeding and obeying. The verb *šāmaʿ* occurs no fewer than seven times in 35:8–16. That is the *lesson* that Jeremiah immediately brings from the incident in verse 13: *Will you not learn a lesson and obey my words?* Around that central question, we are reminded three times (8, 10, 14a) that the Rekabites *had* obeyed the instructions of their human ancestor. This is in stark contrast to the people of Israel who, we are again told three times (14b, 15b, 16b), have refused all attempts to get them to obey *the LORD Almighty, the God of Israel.* A tiny, marginal, self-excluded 'community of intense obedience'[19] who could all fit in one room, has put to shame those who like to think of themselves as the covenant people of God but who are in fact a community of unremitting rebellion.

Promise-breakers, exposed by promise-keepers.

4. Two verdicts confirmed (35:17–19)

So the tale of two events in the same city comes to its conclusion. And just as it began, there is a word of judgment and a word of hope.

For the people of Judah and Jerusalem, the doom was writ (17). God had spoken, again and again, but *they did not listen*. God had called, *but they did not answer*. The conversation was over. At least it was for the people listening to Jeremiah the prophet in Jerusalem. But for the people in exile reading Jeremiah the scroll, those on whom the doom had by now fallen, the words of *all my servants the prophets* called out yet again: *turn from your wicked ways . . . then you will live* (16). Repentance was still the gateway to life and restoration. Chapters 34 – 35 provide the same indisputable justification as the rest of the book for the fact of exile. But they still hold out, by hints and implication, the same route to restoration and hope for the future that pulsated through chapters 30 – 33.

But for the Rekabites there is a remarkable promise. Their signal obedience, understood as a model of loyalty and perseverance, even under pressure to compromise, is rewarded with the promise of survival into the future (7; as their ancestor himself had promised). Amazingly, the language of God's promise in 35:19 echoes what is said regarding the line of David and the Levitical priests in 33:17–18. At Horizon 1, i.e. within the Old Testament period itself, we do indeed hear of the descendants of Rekab again in the post-exilic era, listed in 1 Chronicles 2:55, and helping to rebuild the walls of

Jerusalem under Nehemiah – that is if 'Malkijah son of Rekab' indicates the same clan.[20] But if the literal sense of the promise is eventually lost in the flow of history, the inclusion of this group of Rekabites in the Scriptures preserves their memory for our admiration in the same way as the gospel record has fulfilled Jesus' promise to the nameless woman who anointed his head at Bethany.[21]

Theological and expository reflections

The main point of the two chapters side by side is to contrast cynical breaking of a recent promise with exemplary faithfulness to an ancient one. They are very human stories, but they are intended to illustrate contrasting attitudes to God and the obligations of those who claim to be in covenant relationship with God. So they can be applied and extended by contemporary illustrations of the same contrasting behaviours today.

At the same time, we should not overlook the specific internal content, especially of chapter 34. How we behave towards the poor and needy directly reflects how we behave towards God. Jesus reinforces that message of Jeremiah. We might therefore find it worthwhile to study the Old Testament's economic laws and institutions and reflect on the riches of wisdom God gave to ancient Israel and the tragic extent of our loss for ignoring them.

[20] Neh. 3:14.
[21] Matt. 26:6–13.

Jeremiah 36:1–32
27. God's word: in the fire but not consumed

The end is rushing towards us. The final destruction of Jerusalem will be described in chapter 39. But our editors want us to see something more of the plight of Jeremiah during those final days before the catastrophe, especially his imprisonment by Zedekiah. First, though, they step back yet again to the previous reign of Jehoiakim and to a date that was ominous in every way. *The fourth year of Jehoiakim* (1) was 605 BC. It was also the first year of the new king of resurgent Babylon, Nebuchadnezzar (25:1). That in itself was ominous, since Jeremiah would describe him as the servant of YHWH who would carry out God's judgement on Israel (ch. 27). The foe from the north is on the scene. And in that same year Nebuchadnezzar won the decisive battle of Carchemish, defeating Egypt, the only other major power, and thereby signalling his imperial intentions over the whole region. Babylon rules, OK.

It was also in that year that God had told Jeremiah to summarize all that he had been preaching for the past twenty-three years (25:1–3). Chapter 36 turns the messages referred to in chapter 25 into a written scroll (which may possibly be the 'book' referred to in 25:13).

Chapter 36 describes an event which, even though it happened eighteen years before the fall of Jerusalem, made that fall finally unavoidable. God's final appeal for a change of heart not only went unheeded, but was stunningly rejected in the most brazen way. Jehoiakim's action on that cold December day set a course that led his people inexorably to the edge of the cliff and hurled them over it. And Zedekiah, who presided over the last ten years of that course, did nothing to avert the crash – in spite of Jeremiah's repeated warnings, as we shall see in chapters 37 and 38. The fire that consumed the scroll would be nothing compared to the fire that would consume Jerusalem.

1. God's word written and read (1–10)

God tells Jeremiah to produce a written scroll of all his prophecies. For us, the idea of writing stuff down seems so normal (and necessary) that we could easily overlook the significance of this moment, at various levels. About this scroll, consider the following:

a. Who wrote it?

Enter Baruch again (4). Actually this is the first time (chronologically) that Baruch appears in Jeremiah's story. We met him doing the legal necessities for Jeremiah's land purchase in chapter 32, but that event took place later during the siege in the reign of Zedekiah. Here in chapter 36 we find him already aligned with Jeremiah early in the reign of Jehoiakim. And in chapter 45 we hear a word from God directly for Baruch, given at the time of the events of chapter 36. So some scholars speak of the whole section (chs. 36 – 45) as 'the Baruch Scroll' – that is, material directly edited by Baruch himself, who participated in the events described (the years immediately before and after the fall of Jerusalem). That does not mean that those chapters (36 – 45) were the content of the scroll Baruch wrote at Jeremiah's dictation – for they describe events that took place *after* Jehoiakim's scroll-burning day. Most probably the content of the scroll that Jehoiakim burnt and Baruch rewrote, was substantially what we now call Jeremiah 1 – 25.

Baruch belonged to a family that was high in the king's service. He was the brother of Seraiah, a staff officer of the royal family (51:59). For that reason he had access to the kind of inner government circles that had rooms in the temple complex (10) and in the royal palace (12–15). He was also an educated man and a professional scribe, trained for the kind of work described here and in chapter 32. And he had chosen to serve Jeremiah – a decision that was politically dangerous. We shall think about the personal cost to Baruch when we come to chapter 45. For the moment the main point to notice is what Jeremiah's request set in motion, namely the production of a part of what we now know as the scriptures contained in our Bible. This is a rare insight into the earliest processes that led to us having a Bible at all. Here is scripture in the making. Even kings and bonfires cannot stop it.

Baruch joins a company of writers that includes Tertius (who wrote Paul's letter to the church in Rome) and Silas (who wrote Peter's letter),[1] most of whom remain unnamed – the people who

---

[1] Rom. 16:22; 1 Pet. 5:12.

first wrote down the texts through which God continues to speak. If 'The Bible Speaks Today', we owe part of it at least to Baruch. It is very possible that we owe the whole book of Jeremiah as we now have it to the editorial work of Baruch, but the complexity of variant texts (especially the Greek version)[2] and their uncertain history makes that only a conjecture (though a nice one).

b. Whose idea was it?

Jeremiah had been bringing God's word to the people of Israel for twenty-three years. Did he suddenly think, 'I'd better get all this down in writing before I forget, or go the way of Uriah' (26:20–23)? No, the idea was not Jeremiah's but God's. Jeremiah lived in a culture that was literate but oral – that is to say, significant messages were fully and accurately remembered whether they were written down or not (in fact, they were remembered all the better precisely because they were not necessarily written down). Jeremiah and his contemporaries would have had no difficulty remembering all he had ever said. But God was thinking longer term. How would the word of God through Jeremiah reach those whom Jeremiah in person could never address? How would those born in exile hear his words? How would future generations of God's people have access to words spoken by a living human voice centuries, millennia, earlier?

So *God* says, 'Get it written down.' The message of Jeremiah's words, and its authority as God's word, will not depend on the living presence of the human spokesperson, but will be transferred and carried by the written word, the scriptures – written, copied, translated and read within the community of faith. The Bible is God's idea – not just the human construct of religious people preserving their sacred writings for posterity.

c. Whose words were written down?

Well, Jeremiah's of course. But God's instructions tell him to write down *all the words I have spoken to you* (2). God had told Jeremiah at his call, 'I will put my words in your mouth' (1:9). So the words would be God's words, spoken by Jeremiah. And that is exactly the double truth about this scroll. Note how its content can be referred to as *the words of the LORD* (6, 8, 11), and at the same time *the words of Jeremiah* (10, and cf. 18). This single scroll embodies the dual authorship which is true for all the

[2] See the Introduction, pp. 24–26.

scriptures.[3] It was simultaneously a fully human document (dictated by one man to another,[4] written in pen and ink on a papyrus scroll), and also a fully divine word, the word of God expressed through human words first spoken and then written.

Through the act of writing, divine words take up residence on paper, and by means of their inscribed presence amongst us can be proclaimed again and again, venturing forth into the world to do their job of tearing down and building up . . . Written words enable the word to be heard into the future, and, more than this, enable the word to shine more brightly than ever it did by preserving it until it can be illuminated by its eventual fulfilment.[5]

Because it is word of God, it shares the capacity of the living God to address God's people in any generation: the Bible speaks today. But because it is also the words of a human being who lived in a very particular slice of history and culture, and experienced all the uniquely personal, emotional, spiritual, social and physical cost of bringing that word (and says so!), we must pay attention (as we have done all through our exposition) to the man and his times. It is *as the words of Jeremiah* that it comes to us as the word of God.

d. What was the purpose?

Writing a scroll was laborious work for one man (nine months seem to have elapsed between the command to write it and the reading of it, 9). Producing the whole Bible was infinitely more so, requiring an army of writers over more than a thousand years. What justifies such time and effort in either case? Verse 3 gives God's reason, which Jeremiah repeats in verse 7. The words were (predominantly) words

[3] The same double affirmation is made about the scrolls of the Torah, read by Ezra in the great ceremony described in Neh. 8. They are referred to as 'the Book of the Law of Moses' (the human authority behind the text), with the immediate ascription 'which the Lord had commanded' (the divine source of the law; Neh. 8:1, 8, 14).

[4] The fact that the words were dictated by Jeremiah to Baruch does not mean that they had been simply dictated also by God to Jeremiah. The doctrine of biblical inspiration does not imply mechanical dictation by God in a way that ignored or overrode the humanity, rationality, emotions and culture of the human speaker/ writer. It is very clear that all the biblical authors thought and wrote out of their own personality with all the individual gifts and powers of their own minds and creativity. But in the mystery of God's providence the words that Jeremiah personally thought and spoke were at the same time words that he received from God. What he then, secondarily, dictated to Baruch could properly be described both as words of Jeremiah and words of God. Not partly one and partly the other, but wholly both.

[5] Shead, *A Mouth Full of Fire*, p. 243, in a rich and stimulating chapter – 'Word and permanence'.

of judgment, but the motive was salvation. In warning the people in such stark and repeated terms about the danger that lay ahead (as we saw all through chs. 1 – 25), God's primary desire was that they should heed the warning, change their ways, and avoid it. God's word was *anger and wrath* (7), but God's longing was repentance and forgiveness – *perhaps . . . they will each turn from their wicked ways; then I will forgive their wickedness and their sin* (3).

God's word in the whole Bible is directed at the same goal. It tells the whole story: of God's good creation; of human wickedness and sin; of God's accomplishment of salvation through Christ; of the final judgment to come and the new creation beyond that. And it calls people to turn from their own ways to God, to receive God's forgiveness, and become part of that story and its eternal future. For the people of Judah who would hear the message of Jeremiah's scroll in 605 BC, any such hope had now become a very slender, though repeated, *perhaps*. By the end of that December day Jehoiakim would have snuffed out even that possibility. But for all those who hear the message of the Bible and respond in repentance, faith and obedience, that 'perhaps' is swallowed up in the assured promise of the gospel.

e. Who was it intended for?

Ultimately, of course, it would reach the king, but Baruch was sent first to the temple on a day when *a time of fasting before the* LORD *was proclaimed for all the people in Jerusalem and those who had come in from the towns of Judah* (9). The city and temple courts would have been packed. We are not told why *a time of fasting* had been proclaimed, but if the people gathered to find out, they got a lot more than they expected when they heard the public reading of much of what we now call Jeremiah 1 – 25. God wanted *all the people* (10) to have a second chance to hear what some of them at least would have heard on various occasions over the past two decades. Only now it was coming at them not from the familiar voice of Jeremiah himself, but from a member of the governing class, Baruch son of Neraiah. Old words in a fresh accent. The words of Jeremiah in a place where Jeremiah could no longer be heard in person (5). Ironic, is it not, that God had to use such methods just to get a word in, right in his own house! But he went to such lengths because he wanted everybody to hear the message – again. This was Jeremiah for everybody. Just like the Bible as a whole.[6]

So this event, in which a tiny fraction of the Bible got written, contains truths and principles that apply to the rest of the scriptures.

---

[6] Note the universality of passages like Deut. 30:11–14; 31:10–13; Neh. 8:1–2.

The whole Bible, like Baruch's scroll, was written by human beings in very particular circumstances; was written at God's initiative and instruction; contains words that must be read and interpreted as simultaneously human words and the word of God; was written in order to lead people to repentance, forgiveness and salvation; and was written for all to hear and heed.

So, then, Baruch goes off on his risky mission on a cold December day in 604 BC (8–10). He goes where he knows he is among friends (at least for the moment), and the scroll has its first reading.

2. God's word read and feared (11–19)

The men whose cabinet meeting in *the secretary's room in the royal palace where all the officials were sitting* (12) was rudely interrupted by young Micaiah (hotfoot from the temple courts), were an interesting group. The most significant was possibly Micaiah's own father Gemariah. He was one of several sons of Shaphan, and it was Shaphan who had played a significant part in the great reformation of Josiah some twenty years earlier.[7] His family seem to have stood on the reforming side, represented by Jeremiah. It was another of Shaphan's sons, Ahikam, who had protected Jeremiah when he was almost lynched after his temple sermon just a couple of years before this event (26:24). We know less about Elishama, Delaiah, Elnathan and Zedekiah (not the king), except that it was Elnathan son of Akbor who had done some dirty work for King Jehoiakim in bringing the prophet Uriah back from Egypt to face execution (26:22). Of course, he may not have approved of what he was required to do by the king.

At any rate, their response to the second reading of the scroll by the hastily summoned Baruch (13–15), suggests that they represented a faction within the governing class in Jerusalem who favoured the policy being advocated by Jeremiah – namely that the wisest course was to submit to Babylon (ch. 27) and spare the country and city all the foreseeable consequences of rebellion (invasion, conquest, devastation, siege). That, of course, was not the policy of the king and presumably of those who held the reins of power at the court. We need to remember that the life and words of Jeremiah and Baruch were embroiled in a whirlpool of political factions jostling to sway the policy of the king this way or that.

The position of this group can be judged from the mixture of fear, political opportunism and prudence that we can see in their words and actions.

---

[7] 2 Kgs 22. His son Ahikam was also involved in that reforming event, as was Acbor, father of Elnathan.

They looked at each other in fear (16); not surprising, really, if you had just listened to all of Jeremiah 1 – 25. Who wouldn't be afraid if the terrifying scenarios painted in some of those chapters, with all the inexpressible grief and mourning attached, were just around the corner? If these men were among the few who believed that Jeremiah (not Hananiah) was telling the truth, then they had everything to fear and so did the whole country.

But could there be one final chance to swing *the king* to their side? Surely if only the king could hear what they had just listened to, he might switch sides and agree to a change of heart and of national policy. That consideration is probably why they say, *we must report all these words to the king*. Why *must*? Because, they thought, if anything might change his mind, this scroll could do it.

But they knew their king. If the murder of Uriah had already happened, they knew what might happen to Jeremiah. They would not be able to protect him any longer. So they give brilliant advice. They tell Baruch to get Jeremiah and himself hidden – but not to let anybody (even this group) know where (19). They could not risk a traitor even in their own midst. If none of them knew, none of them could tell. Nor could they be accused by the king of harbouring his enemies. Their human wisdom was confirmed by God, who kept his servants safe (26).

3. God's word read and burnt (20–26)[8]

It's Jehudi I feel most sorry for. Imagine the shame and embarrass-ment he endured. He was just the runner, who had been sent once to fetch Baruch, and then sent again to fetch the scroll. Now he's the reader too. There he is standing in front of His Majesty, King Jehoiakim, in the royal courtyard, getting his breath back, not needing the nearby fire to warm up, clearing his throat as the official reader on behalf of his political lords and masters, even if it was a speech somewhat on behalf of His Majesty's Opposition.

A scroll is a large and awkward thing to handle; you need both hands to unroll it from left to right, rolling the part you've just read on to the spindle in your right hand. And you can unroll about enough at a time to read *three or four columns* (23). Jehudi has just

---

[8] Jehoiakim's action has had many ancient and modern counterparts. 'Book burning (also biblioclasm or libricide) is the practice of destroying, often ceremoniously, books or other written material . . . Book burning . . . is usually carried out in public, and is generally motivated by moral, religious or political objections to the material . . . Book burning can be emblematic of a harsh and oppressive regime which is seeking to censor or silence an aspect of a nation's culture' (Wikipedia <http://en.wikipedia.org/wiki/Book_burning>).

finished those first few columns and is about to roll them on and expose the next section. But as he pauses for breath, he staggers back in shock as the king whips out a knife and slices through the scroll, grabs the part Jehudi had just read, and tosses it into the fire-pit that is keeping him warm on this frosty winter day.

Listen to the shocked gasps of everybody, followed by a mixture of laughter by *the king and all his attendants,* and the protests of *Elnathan, Delaiah and Gemariah* who *urged the king not to burn the scroll* (25). 'Your Majesty! Please don't! Do you not fear YHWH?'

What happens next is even worse. If Jehoiakim had simply grabbed the whole scroll and thrown it in the fire, it could have gone down as an act of impulsive rage. But no. He sarcastically orders Jehudi to carry on. Picture the poor fellow struggling to recover the flapping torn end of the scroll, finding his place, reading on for the painful minutes that another few columns would take – then the swiping knife again, and again, and again, until I imagine him almost holding the final columns out for the ritual severing and burning. Jehudi himself must have been cut to the core by the mockery and laughter of the king and his court.

Jehoiakim's act was cold, systematic, repeated, and intentionally cruel to the reader. How much more painful to the prophet and his scribe when they heard what happened at court. Column by column, the scroll so laboriously written had been consumed in the fire.

Jehoiakim knew, of course, that this was more than wanton waste of papyrus. It was the word itself he was rejecting – the word of Jeremiah, claiming to be the word of YHWH, God of Israel. But not content with saying, 'I will not listen to any of that', he *insisted on listening to every word* and then publicly repudiated every word he heard. Jehoiakim's rejection of the word of God was not a hasty mistake. It was the most deliberate act of defiance of the spoken and written word of God recorded in the Bible – 'an awesome attempt to eliminate the concrete, sovereign word and will of God'.[9]

Undoubtedly the story highlights the contrast between Josiah who, when he heard the Book of the Law read to him, tore his clothes in anguished fear and repentance, and Jehoiakim who, hearing the word of God *showed no fear* and refused to *tear his clothes* (24), but instead tore the word of God and burned it (the word *cut* in v. 23 is the same Hebrew word as *tear* in v. 24).

4. God's word – scroll on (27–32)

Jehoiakim's act was as futile as all such attempts to destroy the word of God by destroying the paper it is written on have always been.

---

[9] Brueggemann (1991), p. 137.

THE MESSAGE OF JEREMIAH

The God who was speaking through Jeremiah's living voice and who would continue to speak through the written record of Jeremiah's words, would not be silenced by a knife and brazier.

Jeremiah responds with a message to Jehoiakim of unmistakeable doom. He would die unloved, unmourned and unburied (29–31). He had sealed not only his own fate, but that of his nation. The finality of verse 31 cancels out the possibility still lurking in the *perhaps* of verses 3 and 7. But there is almost a touch of bleak humour in what happens next. Jeremiah says to Baruch, 'OK, we'll do it again. Or rather, you will!', and Baruch ruefully adds the last line of the chapter, that the second scroll was even longer than the first!

The king is dead. Long live the scroll.

And now Baruch's scroll is embedded within our Bibles and translated into thousands of languages across all the earth.

> God is indomitable. God is not deterred in the least by the king's refusal. God is a scroll-maker and will continue to make scrolls. Any particular scroll from the God of Israel can be dismissed as was this first one; but it will promptly and boldly be reiterated ... It is clear in this dramatic narrative that scroll-making (i.e. Bible production) is a daring, dangerous human enterprise. It is equally clear that this scroll-making is paradigmatic of the way in which God counters human pretension and resistance. God will not leave the king scroll-less, even if the king wants no scroll.[10]

God's voice will be heard. God is not mocked, and God's word will endure. 'Chapter 36 thus makes a faith-filled claim that the word will accomplish all that God intends (cf. Isa. 55:10–13), and that God, not human cunning or royal power, is in charge of the destinies of nations.'[11]

Theological and expository reflections

- Jeremiah 36 was intended by the compilers of the final book of Jeremiah as a revealing insight into how the words of the prophet spoken by his living voice became the written words of Scripture, and how the living word of God stands behind both. There is an unbroken chain of transmission: the words of God are given to the prophet, who speaks those words as word of God; the spoken words are later dictated to Baruch the scribe so that the scroll now contains the words of Jeremiah,

[10] Brueggemann (1991), pp. 137–138.
[11] Stulman, p. 301.

constituting the word of God. Baruch then becomes the living voice of Jeremiah by proxy, as he reads the words of the scroll, and in that action, they become, for the listeners, the word of God to them. By extension, this process in a variety of ways over many centuries is the means by which the text we have in our Bible is simultaneously the words of human speakers, writers and scribes, and the word the God wants us to have from himself. It is worth telling and preaching the story in such a way as to make this point, and its relevance to the nature and authority of Scripture, clear.

- The story shocks us with the brazenness of Jehoiakim's action, but it should also compel us to reflect on the ways in which people continue to reject God's word, perhaps more politely, but no less defiantly.

Jeremiah 37:1 – 38:28
28. God's prophet: in the pit but not silenced

Jeremiah's *via dolorosa* – is how some commentators describe the prolonged suffering of his final years in Jerusalem. The comparisons with the passion of Christ are notable: there is unjustified arrest, false accusation, the malice of leaders who felt threatened, the collusion of the one man with authority to release God's servant, the steadfast refusal to speak other than God's truth, the prospect of a slow and horrible death. One major difference is that Jesus, having won the battle in prayer with his Father in Gethsemane, at no point asked his human captors or executioners to release him or ease his suffering, as Jeremiah understandably did. For Jeremiah, however, it was his attempt to help others save their lives (38:2) that led to him losing, if not his own life, certainly his freedom and security – what Kidner calls 'this faint foreshadowing of his Master's suffering, of whom it would be said, "He saved others; himself he cannot save."'[1]

1. New king, same old story (37:1–10)

From the end of chapter 36 we jump forward seven years, from King Jehoiakim to his brother King Zedekiah, who was imposed on Judah by Nebuchadnezzar as a puppet king, after deposing the true heir, Jehoiachin, and taking him off to Babylon.[2] The rest of the story will revolve around Zedekiah's ten-year vacillation between loyalty to Babylon who had installed him, and those who were urging him to rebel again and look to Egypt for support. In the midst of this political cauldron, Zedekiah was also vacillating whether or not to heed what Jeremiah kept telling him. The whole fate of his

[1] Kidner, p. 123.
[2] See 2 Kgs 24 for the details of this transition.

kingdom and nation hung in the balance, suspended by the 'will he or won't he?' indecision of this king. The verdict is anticipated for us in verse 2. This king will finally be no different from Jehoiakim, in that *neither he nor his attendants paid any attention to the words the LORD had spoken through Jeremiah the prophet.* New king, same old problem – royal deafness.

Both kings *heard* Jeremiah's words, loud and clear. The difference was that Jehoiakim *chose* to listen in detail with the deliberate intention of rejecting every word he heard. Zedekiah, on the other hand, actually *asked* to listen with what appears to be an open mind, prepared at least to believe that Jeremiah did have access to the mind of God. In the end, of course, it made no difference to the outcome since Zedekiah's ultimate refusal to act on Jeremiah's advice amounted to a rejection of God's word to him, as verse 2 summarily states. So we know how it will all end, but the narrator does not spare us the ignominious journey.

The first indirect encounter between Jeremiah and Zedekiah is recorded in 37:4–10. The final siege of Jerusalem had begun (in 588 BC). But Egyptian forces under Pharaoh Hophra were on their way to help Judah. So the Babylonians withdrew from Jerusalem to deal with that threat (this was the interval mentioned in 34:21–22). Zedekiah sends officials to ask Jeremiah, *please pray to the LORD our God for us.* It's hard to know if the request was sincere, with any acknowledgment of the national sin that had led to this situation, or (more likely), if it was a vain hope that God might change his mind or Jeremiah change his message. It smacks of the same hypocrisy of an earlier request (21:1–2) that hoped God might work another miracle such as the one that saved Hezekiah from Sennacherib – overlooking the godliness and penitence that had marked that king's reign. And as before, Jeremiah gives the same message: 'Sorry, but the city is now doomed. Egypt is useless. Babylon will be back. You could not even fight your way out of your fate' (6–10).

2. Arrested, accused, condemned (37:11–16; 38:1–6)

At this point we hit some ambiguity. As the text stands from here (37:11) to the end of chapter 38, we appear to have a continuous account of two arrests, two accusations, two imprisonments (with one remarkable rescue) and two secret conversations with King Zedekiah. It is perfectly possible that that is exactly the sequence of events in those tumultuous final months. However it is also possible, as several commentators suggest, that we have here two complementary accounts of a single series of events, in which

Jeremiah was arrested, accused, imprisoned, rescued, summoned for secret talks with the king, and finally deposited in the courtyard of the guard (where later the purchase of the field in ch. 32 would take place). In other words, 37:11–21 and 38 might be complementary in the same way as chapters 7 and 26 give us complementary accounts of the temple sermon and its aftermath. Consider that in both accounts:

- it is the royal officials who get Jeremiah authoritatively arrested (37:14–15; 38:1–4);
- the accusation is that he was pro-Babylonian, which was treacherous and demoralizing (37:13; 38:1–4);
- he is lethally incarcerated in a dungeon that was in a 'cistern-house' (37:16[3]), or an actual cistern (38:6);
- he is summoned secretly by the king who asked for a word from God (37:17; 38:14);
- there is a request not to be returned to his underground imprisonment (37:20; 38:26);
- he ends up being sent back to *the courtyard of the guard* (37:21; 38:28).

The main difference, then, would be that 37:11–14 provides the *occasion for his arrest*, while 38:7–13 provides the *means of his escape* from what would have been fatal imprisonment.

We will comment on the two strands, then, as though referring to a single series of events, but not with any certainty; it is perfectly possible that Jeremiah went through a devastatingly repeated cycle of arrests and imprisonments. Many of God's faithful servants know exactly what that is like, from the Apostle Paul[4] to the present time.

The temporary Babylonian withdrawal gave people opportunity to leave the city, which Jeremiah took, intending to settle some business with his family's land (37:11–12). Since he never got there, it was cousin Hanamel who later came to Jeremiah to sort it out (to his own advantage), as we saw in chapter 32 (which comes chronologically after the events of 37 – 38).

The assumption of the soldier who arrested him (37:13) was not entirely unreasonable; that Jeremiah was simply doing what he had been urging others to do – defecting to the Babylonians (38:2). The royal officials decide that this gives pretext enough to have him charged with treason (not true, he was advocating surrender for the

---

[3] The translation *vaulted cell in a dungeon* obscures the fact that the description is literally 'the house of a cistern'. The word *bôr*, for a pit or a cistern, occurs in both 37:16 and 38:6.

[4] 2 Cor. 11:23–25.

good of the city and nation), and with demoralizing the troops and inhabitants (undoubtedly very true). The king acquiesces with their demand in a way that shows his terrible weakness (38:5) – 'perhaps the most abject surrender in biblical history until the moment when Pilate washed his hands before the multitude (Mt. 27:24)'.[5]

What the officials requested was that *this man should be put to death* (38:4). But they were not willing to have his blood on their own hands, possibly remembering the scary warning of 26:14–15. So in an eerie re-enactment of what Joseph's brothers did to him and probably for the same reason,[6] they put Jeremiah in a place where he was bound to die, but they could always deny blood-guilt and say they hadn't laid a finger on him. Cautiously they even *lowered Jeremiah by ropes*, lest the more satisfying act of just tossing him in headlong might directly break his neck.

And Jeremiah sank down into the mud (38:6). 'Mud' is too polite a word for the stinking, slimy, infested ooze that would have settled at the bottom of an urban cistern. Even if he might not sink completely underneath, it would be impossible to lie down and sleep. Without food and water, he faced the horror of a slow death in the darkness by starvation, dehydration or drowning.

3. 'He lifted me out of the slimy pit'[7] (38:7–13)

What now of God's promises? What now of Jeremiah's prayers? Had he come from the God-ordained womb to perish in this God-forsaken tomb? Had he praised God as a spring of living water only to end his life in a broken cistern? Did he think of the prayer of sinking Jonah?

> To the roots of the mountains I sank down
>   the earth beneath me barred me in forever.
> But you, LORD my God,
>   brought my life up from the pit.[8]

But cisterns don't vomit out their captives . . .

Did he pray with those psalmists whose experience of false accusers and lethal attackers felt like being sunk in the bottomless mire of a pit? For Jeremiah it was no metaphor but an engulfing

---

[5] Kidner, p. 124.

[6] See Gen. 37:21–24. The same word, *bôr*, is used there to describe the deep pits for collecting water in the desert and here for the vaulted cisterns that were carved out for water storage in cities.

[7] Ps. 40:2.

[8] Jon. 2:6.

literal horror. Psalm 88 could have had no more urgent recital than Jeremiah might have given it.[9]

Whether or whatever Jeremiah prayed, God remembered his promise, 'I am with you to deliver you'. God's deliverance came from an unexpected source, from someone in the very palace itself. *Enter Ebed-Melek.*

This man, who is more or less nameless since the words just mean 'servant of the king', joins the company of distinguished rescuers of God's servants, some of them also nameless like the widow of Zarephath who saved Elijah's life.[10] He was a black African from Cush,[11] an important kingdom and nation to the south of Egypt that played a significant role at various times of biblical history. He is remarkable in several ways: for his singular righteous indignation at what the other officials had done (not for the first time a foreigner gives a lesson in justice to people who should have known better[12]); for his courage in approaching the king in a public place and making an appeal on behalf of a prophet who, as everybody knew, was regarded as a public enemy (38:7–9); for his resourcefulness in rescuing Jeremiah (incurring the wrath of those who had imprisoned him). He accomplishes Jeremiah' ascent in the same manner as his descent, only with the thoughtful touch of a few *old rags* for cushioning (38:11–13). The detail of the narrative is delightful!

4. 'Is there a word from the Lord?' (37:17–21; 38:14–28)

As noted above, we may have in these two passages the accounts of two separate conversations between Jeremiah and Zedekiah, with Jeremiah hauled from two different prisons to the palace. Or it may be that 37:17–21 is a shorter summary account of a single conversation, with 38:14–28 the more extended version of what passed between them, ending with its reference back to something Jeremiah had requested in the shorter account.

The brevity of 37:17 is almost comic. Jeremiah says it all in five short words. To the king's question, *Is there a word from the LORD?*,

---

[9] Stulman (p. 315), makes the fascinating connection between Jeremiah's experience and a number of psalms of lament where 'the pit' (the same word, *bôr*, as here for 'cistern') is the graphic image of terrible danger from which the only way out is by God's rescue. It is well worth reading the following passages and thinking of Jeremiah: Pss 28:1; 30:1–3; 69:1–2; and especially the whole of Ps. 88.

[10] 1 Kgs 17:7–24. And e.g. Joseph's cup-bearer friend (Gen. 41:9–13), Moses' sister Miriam (Exod. 2:1–10), David's friend Jonathan (1 Sam. 20), Paul's friends in Ephesus and his nephew in Jerusalem (Acts 19:23–41; 23:12–22).

[11] Cush is often translated as 'Ethiopia', but it was rather what we would now call northern Sudan, or Nubia, rather than the modern country of Ethiopia.

[12] Gen. 12:18–19; 20:8–10.

Jeremiah first grunts, *Yes*.[13] Then four single Hebrew words that spell Zedekiah's fate: 'Into-the-hand / of-the-king / of-Babylon / you-will-be-given.' However, what exactly would happen to Zedekiah 'in the hands' of Nebuchadnezzar was not 'fated'. It need not be as horrendous as it sounded – but that depended on choices Zedekiah must make (38:17–18).

But before getting to that, Jeremiah the prophet speaks as Jeremiah the human being. He has two rhetorical questions and a request. The first question (18) is a plea of innocence, which makes his imprisonment unjust and illegal. The second question (19) is a plea of vindication; if he was in fact the only prophet whose prediction of exactly what was now happening had come true, why was he being treated in this way? Sadly, although he was entirely justified in both questions, politics is rarely kind to those who get proven right in the end. His request (20) is expressed with a politeness that he never showed to Jehoiakim. Zedekiah, as his next action showed (21), was a more malleable monarch.[14]

The longer version of the conversation in 38:14–26 is an intense dialogue which, as dialogues do, reveals a lot about both characters.

Listen to Jeremiah. These are his last words to the king before the fall of the city. He is a prisoner, aware of the possibility of execution at any moment (38:15), or a return to the slimy darkness of the pit, yet he speaks clearly, uncompromisingly and urgently, seeking the best interests of the king who had allowed such treatment to happen in the first place. Could the king's fulsome oaths and promises (16) be trusted? Why speak truth to power if a) it gets you killed and b) power won't listen anyway (15)? Jeremiah's bluntness is courageous. Presumably he felt there was nothing he could lose; nothing worse could happen than he already faced.

The king and the kingdom face their very last chance. Nothing could prevent the city falling to the Babylonians, but there was every difference in the world between the fate of a city that surrendered in advance and one that held out in futile rebellion to the bitter end. Jeremiah spells out the alternatives with crystal clarity (38:17–18). The *if . . . but if . . . not* of these verses show the essentially conditional nature of all that Jeremiah had been prophesying. He had repeatedly painted the horrific picture of a city in the terrible wasting

---

[13] The Hebrew is the mono-syllable *yēš* (meaning, 'there is', but pronounced not very differently from the blunt English 'Yes').

[14] '*Or I will die there*' is a hint that the imprisonment referred to at *the house of Jonathan* (which was a 'cistern house', 16), was in fact the deadly cistern described in 38:6 – even though that is called *the cistern of Malkijah*. We do not know enough about either place to exclude the possibility that these might have been different names for the same complex of buildings including a home, an office and a cistern.

diseases and famine of prolonged siege, ending in slaughter, rape and pillage, and ferocious burning. *But it did not have to be that way.* Zedekiah had a choice and Jeremiah urges him for the last time to make the right one, the choice that God and Jeremiah were pressing on him (20), the choice that could lessen the loss of life and especially spare the lives of Zedekiah's own family.[15]

Listen, on the other hand, to Zedekiah. He seems a tragically indecisive figure, knowing that Jeremiah is the one who brings the true word of the Lord, yet unwilling to act upon it. He swings between protecting Jeremiah and throwing him to the wolves. He swears an oath, on the life of the God who gives life, not to have Jeremiah handed over to death, when he had done exactly that at the time of his arrest (38:4–5). Was Jeremiah to believe his words in private or his record in public?

Zedekiah is faced with a stark alternative for himself, his family, his city, his nation – a life or death alternative (38:17–18). But all he can think of is the illogical possibility that the handful of citizens who had defected to the Babylonians might hand him over (19; why would that matter if he had surrendered to Nebuchadnezzar anyway?). What does it say about this king that he is more afraid of his own people than the Babylonians?

'To see what hung on the king's yes or no, we have only to read the next chapter for the horror awaiting him and his sons, or to read Lamentations 4 for the living skeletons and cannibals of the city's last days. With suffering on this scale in the balance, the king's reply in verse 19 is unbelievably trifling.'[16]

Jeremiah hauls Zedekiah back to the realities confronting his closest family. Surely the awful fate awaiting his own wives and daughters, not to mention *all the women left in the palace* would convince him to make a decision that could save them? He had sons too. Would he not think about *all your wives and children* ['sons'] being paraded before the victorious Babylonians, then suffering a fate he would not wish to contemplate (but would be forced to)?

Astonishingly, Zedekiah responds to all this urging to make a decision with . . . no decision at all (which amounted, of course, to a default decision to carry on with the present disastrous policy). All he can do is lamely end the conversation with even more self-serving secrecy, dressed up as concern for Jeremiah's life (24–26), but surely designed to spare himself more humiliation from his officials.

---

[15] If the condition and choice so clearly summarized in these verses was the consistent message of Jeremiah to Zedekiah all through his reign, then it further supports the view expressed in our comments on 34:4–5, interpreting them as a conditional promise – conditional, that is, on Zedekiah obeying God's command through Jeremiah.

[16] Kidner, p. 125.

For they are the ones who seem in control of events (38:27). The king is powerless. The prophet is silenced, except in secret conversations. The word of the Lord is heard but not heeded. The political leaders have set their course. The 'true patriots' have wrapped themselves in the flag. No truck with surrender monkeys like Jeremiah. The end is coming. *The day* is at hand (38:28).

Theological and expository reflections

- The clash of idolatrous patriotism with the prophetic word resonates still today. We still suffer the global effects of those who identify the interests of their own country with the will of God and resist the voice of any other perspective or any alternative wisdom.
- And what would Jeremiah say today to those who resort so easily to the suicidal folly of war, except to lament the fact that those who do resort to war these days can afford the luxury of waging it in far off places, inflicting 'collateral damage' on people who don't really count? Do we have to wait until the enemy is at the gate before we renounce the reflex of violence?
- And what might he make of the irony that people whose culture has systematically excluded God and refused to listen to his radical scriptural word can still turn to prayer in moments of crisis. 'God, we don't really believe you exist; we don't like the rules you ask us to live by; but now would be a good time to help us, if you can.'

Jeremiah 39:1 – 41:18
29. The fall of Jerusalem

The end had come. Or had it? Certainly it was the end of the road for the whole Jerusalem political establishment that had led the mad folly of resistance to Babylon. It was the end for the long dynasty of the house of David, in terms of a king on the throne in Jerusalem. It was the end for a whole culture and ideology that had blindly trusted in the great traditions of Israel's past (land, covenant, temple, election, law), but refused to listen in obedience to the God who had addressed them persistently through this prophet and many before him.

But those in exile in Babylon, who would later read these tragic chapters, could know it was not the end. For our editors have carefully made sure that we've read chapters 30 – 33 before we hit the crunch in chapter 39. Future hope lay ahead, but first the fiery horror.

1. Double catastrophe (39:1–10)

The fate of both the city and the king is narrated here with terse factual reporting, abbreviated from the more detailed accounts in chapter 52 and 2 Kings 25. The facts speak for themselves.

The siege began in January 588 BC and lasted eighteen months until July 587 BC. By that time food had run out and starvation stalked the streets (52:6). With the walls finally breached, the Babylonian top brass take centre-stage control (3), while Judah's king, court and army flee by night, stumbling down the eastern mountainsides to the Jordan valley (4). The Babylonians capture the king, the army melts away (52:8), and Zedekiah is hauled to Riblah, miles away to the far north (5). There he meets Nebuchadnezzar face to face, as Jeremiah had predicted (34:3).

Zedekiah meets the kind of fate specially reserved for rebels – which is what he was. He had been personally placed on the throne of Judah by Nebuchadnezzar. He had sworn an oath to keep his tiny kingdom loyal to the empire (2 Chr. 36:13). But he had spent a decade in sporadic rebellion, had failed to suppress the nationalist faction at court, and had forced Nebuchadnezzar into months of costly siege warfare. He paid a high price, worse even than Jeremiah had warned. The last thing he would see on earth, apart from Nebuchadnezzar's face, was the execution of his sons, before being dragged, blinded and in chains, to Babylon (6–7). And along with him perished *all the nobles of Judah*, the elite governing class that had urged him on his suicidal course.

A month later (52:12), *Nebuzaradan, commander of the imperial guard* (and clearly Nebuchadnezzar's senior officer) arrives to oversee the sequel to the siege. That requires the punitive destruction and burning of the rebel city (including its royal palace, its defences and houses, and the looting of the temple [52:17–23]; 8), the arrangements for deporting the leading citizens to Babylon (9), and the reconstruction of Judah as a vassal province of the Babylonian empire (10). Job done.

It is a cold factual account indeed, and we cannot help but notice what is missing. Where is the prophetic passion? Where is the theological rationale? Where is the listing of sins that brought all this about (such as 2 Chr. 36:11–21 provides)? Where, indeed, is God? And the short answer is, they are all there in the rest of the book we've just read through.

To the first three questions Jeremiah might say that he has given us about all we could bear in terms of passion, rationale and sins. When we have read texts such as 6:1–8, 22–26; 9:17–22; 13:18–27; 14:18; 15:1–9 and 19:7–9, we need nothing more for our imagination to picture what the siege and fall of the city involved for those who endured it. And as for the theological rationale and the sins that precipitated the catastrophe – what else has Jeremiah's whole ministry been about since his earliest preaching in chapter 2, with its combination of lawsuit accusation and kaleidoscopic imagery depicting Israel's unfaithfulness? No more explanation need be given than had already been said.

To the fourth question, 'where is God in chapter 39?' the answer must be, 'conspicuous by his absence' – at least his absence from this text. From the rest of the book we know that the rod of Babylon, like the rod of Assyria,[1] was in the hand of the sovereign Lord God. The message of 25:8–11 is unambiguously clear on that point. The divine judgment operated through human agency, and human beings would face their full accountability for all that was done in the process.

[1] Cf. Isa. 10:5–6.

THE MESSAGE OF JEREMIAH

And yet . . . when the moment comes, the account is given in a way that noticeably shifts from God's conspicuous presence in earlier texts predicting his judgment, to his conspicuous absence in the description of the execution of it. Is this a hint that God, as one might say, could scarcely bear to look? That the moment of final abandonment of the city and the people who bore his name – whom he had planted and built, whom he had loved as husband and father – the abandonment of *these* people to their self-inflicted desecration, decimation and destruction was simply too painful for God to participate in? There is more than a hint of this, actually, in God's words to Baruch in 45:2–4, as we shall see. The wrath of God was at work. But the eyes of the God who takes 'no pleasure in the death of the wicked',[2] the God who 'does not willingly bring affliction or grief',[3] were brimming and blinded with the tears of rejected love that his prophet had shed so abundantly on his behalf. God turns his face away.

Abandonment. God mysteriously absent. God turning his face away as his judgment was outpoured through the hands of wicked men. If this was so when the object of such divine-human wrath was a people who had persisted in rebellion against their divine covenant Lord and had needlessly goaded a human emperor into vengeance on their treaty violations, how much more awesome, mysterious and profound was the silence of abandonment when the sinless Son of God cried out, 'My God, my God, why have you forsaken me?' Why indeed, in both cases. In Jerusalem's case, the answer was: 'for their own sins'.[4] In Jesus' case, the answer equally clearly is: 'for ours'.

There is a double irony in the contrast between the fate of Zedekiah (5–7) and the treatment of *the poor people who owned nothing* (8–10). At one level there is the simple reversal of fortunes – reminiscent of Mary's song, the *Magnificat*.

> He has brought down rulers from their thrones
>   but has lifted up the humble.
> He has filled the hungry with good things
>   but has sent the rich away empty.[5]

Zedekiah and the whole wealthy, powerful and oppressive Jerusalem elite had been humbled in the dust of death, while the poorest in the land, the truly destitute, had been given resources and assets that would help them build viable lives for themselves and their families.

[2] Ezek. 33:11.
[3] Lam. 3:33.
[4] The question is asked and answered very clearly in Lam. 3:38–42.
[5] Luke 1:52–53.

But the other irony is: who accomplished this inversion? Answer: a foreigner. This was the very thing that God had instructed *Israel* – and especially Israel's political leaders – to attend to, namely, economic fairness and provision for the needy. But it was one of several major covenant requirements that they had not only neglected but trampled upon. Deuteronomy had held up the ideal that 'there need be no poor people among you'.[6] It was a pagan governor who gave at least some provisional and doubtless temporary reality to that ideal, in the midst of the tragedy that engulfed the state as a whole. Ironic, that as the covenant people sank into two generations of exile under God's judgment, some of the neediest among them (the neglect of whom was part of the reason for the judgment) received (or received back) at last a share in that most tangible token of covenant blessing – land. And received it from their conqueror!

2. Double deliverance (39:11 – 40:6)

An even greater contrast immediately follows. Jeremiah 39:1–10 has succinctly described the greatest single catastrophe to happen in the Old Testament history of Israel. The story of the fall of Jerusalem and the exile stands alongside narratives like the flood, or Sodom and Gomorrah, or the perishing in the wilderness of the whole exodus generation, or even the conquest of Canaan – as signal moments of God's outpoured wrath on human disobedience and rebellion. But in the flood God remembered and rescued Noah and his family. Out of Sodom God remembered and rescued Lot and his family. Of the wilderness generation, Joshua and Caleb were spared to enter the Promised Land. And the first Canaanite whom we meet in the book of Joshua is a converted one who gets saved – Rahab along with her family. For in wrath God remembers mercy, and even in the great acts of God's judgment there are trophies of saving grace. So it is here. In the very midst of the engulfing storm two people are saved by God and (in one case) protected by a pagan officer. Judgment is penetrated by salvation.

The story of the release of Jeremiah is split in two, in a way that seems confusing, but probably with the deliberate intent of sandwiching the promise to Ebed-Melek. Thus, Jeremiah, God's prophet, is given his freedom and protection by a foreigner, while Ebed-Melek, a foreigner himself, is promised that his life will be saved by the God of Israel.

At first reading, it might seem that Jeremiah was initially liberated from the courtyard of the guard at the time of the conquest of the

---

[6] Deut. 15:4.

city (39:11–14), but somehow got arrested and put in chains along with others destined for exile, and had to be liberated a second time from the 'holding pen' at Ramah (40:1). Now it is quite possible that in the confusion of the times, such a sequence could easily have happened. On the other hand, it may be that the first account is a brief summary (Jeremiah was taken from the courtyard of the guard, along with others who were taken prisoner at that time, but eventually handed over to Gedaliah and given freedom to go home and live with the people left behind). Then the second account (40:1–6) is the expanded version of what transpired between his initial release from the courtyard of the guard and his final release into the care of Gedaliah. This may be a more natural reading since 39:14b is equivalent to 40:6, suggesting that they constitute the same ending to a single story.

The promise of salvation to Ebed-Melek is out of place chronologically (Jeremiah made the promise during the siege, not after the fall of the city), but placed here for its theological impact. This faithful African brother had saved the life of Jeremiah. In return his own life would be saved. In fact, the vocabulary of salvation granted to him (39:17–18) echoes the same words first promised to Jeremiah himself at his call (1:8, 19; 15:20–21).

However, it is interesting that God's final word to Ebed-Melek is not that God will save him because he saved Jeremiah, but rather *because you trust in me* (39:18). Here is a foreigner who was doing what the Israelite leaders were refusing to do – trusting in God. The faith of a foreigner is contrasted with the hardened unbelief of Israel. At the same time, of course, it was precisely because he was profoundly willing to trust God that he took courageous action. His faith was demonstrated in word and deed. Long before the New Testament presents us with God-fearing Gentiles who surprised Jesus and the apostles with the strength of their faith (in contrast to Israel's lack of it), here is a trusting foreigner prepared to act on his faith. Hebrews might well have included him in its hall of faith ('By faith Ebed-Melek rescued Jeremiah with old clothes'). James would certainly have included him beside Rahab as one who was 'considered righteous for what she did',[7] in saving the lives of the Israelite spies. Like her, Ebed-Melek was saved by faith, but it was faith that proved itself in works.

We asked above, 'Where is God in this story?' And here we have another irony. The only appearances of God in the whole of chapters 39 – 41 are when he speaks – twice. The first time it is to address a foreigner (39:16–18), and the second time it is to speak through the

[7] Jas 2:25.

mouth of a foreigner (40:2–3). It is as if God and Israel have nothing more to say to each other, so much so that even what God does have to say can be spoken by a foreigner on his behalf. This will not remain so permanently, of course – the next chapters will show that, not to mention the continuing prophetic ministry of Ezekiel in exile. But for the moment, reality is too painful for words.

The encounter between Jeremiah and Nebuzaradan is fascinating. It presents this Babylonian governor in a remarkably positive, humane, discerning, and even generous, light. It also shows, of course, that Nebuchadnezzar had a robust intelligence service, with detailed information about the so-called 'pro-Babylonian' party in Jerusalem during Zedekiah's reign, and Jeremiah's alleged favouring of that policy (39:11). To get such preferential treatment from the Babylonians would have done nothing for Jeremiah's popularity among his fellow-countrymen, but then he'd had a lifetime to get used to that so it was hardly his major concern.

It's hard to read what Nebuzaradan says to Jeremiah in 40:2–3 without a wry smile. We can imagine Jeremiah thinking to himself as Nebuzaradan made his speech, 'Tell me about it. I've been saying that for the past forty years. Nice of you to agree.' The rest of Nebuzaradan's speech (4–5) shows amazing magnanimity. And it all finishes with another Deuteronomic note. Not only did this pagan governor unwittingly fulfil an ideal of Deuteronomy 15 in giving land to the poor (39:10), he also fulfilled the law about providing a generous gift to someone being released from slavery (40:5b).[8] Here is another Gentile unwittingly obeying the law the Israelites so neglected (cf. ch. 34).

3. A fresh start and a tragic ending (40:7–16)

Enter *Gedaliah*.

He was the man of the moment. Sadly he was also a man of not much more than a moment. His very promising prospect of leadership was cut short within a few months. Who was he? Repeatedly his ancestry is given: *the son of Ahikam, the son of Shaphan*, in order to stress that he belonged to that illustrious family that had supported the reform movement of Josiah, had protected Jeremiah from lynching, and had hoped that the publication of his scroll might achieve a change of government policy during the reign of Jehoiakim.

Now that the policy of his faction had been vindicated, Gedaliah rises to a kind of internal leadership. But that is then reinforced through his official appointment by the Babylonians. Effectively,

[8] Deut. 15:13–14.

Gedaliah became the indigenous governor of an occupied territory in the process of being reconstructed as a province of the new Babylonian empire.

To be put in such a position is to be asked to walk a tightrope. You belong to the occupied people, yet you will incur their anger and hatred for serving the occupying enemy. You serve the imperial overlord, yet you will always be under suspicion as a potential traitor. Gedaliah's position resembles that of James Dorr, native inhabitant of Jersey and leader of its puppet government under German occupation during the Second World War in the (fictional) TV series, *Island at War*. It seems impossible to please both sides.

And yet, remarkably, Gedaliah seems to win the trust of both sides, perhaps most surprisingly, of the various remnants of the Judean population left in the land and those scattered to surrounding countries during the crisis. They rally to him (7–8). Various armed groups submit to him. He makes a speech (9–10), which is a model of wisdom, aimed at satisfying both sides of his tightrope (and in the process echoing exactly what Jeremiah told the exiles in Babylon in his letter in ch. 29). He insists that he is one of them in relation to the Babylonians, not a Babylonian imposed on them (10a). And he urges a return to productive farming in the land, which is met with the kind of success that spoke of God's gracious blessing (12b).

And where is Jeremiah in all this? He had chosen (6) to join the motley bunch of refugees in their own land now settling around Mizpah, picking up the shreds of their lives as the ruins of Jerusalem smouldered over the horizon. Though offered the choice of going to Babylon under royal protection and with royal provision, he had declined, even though theologically he knew that the future lay with that portion of God's people – the 'good figs' of chapter 24. True to the way his whole life embodied his faithfulness of his calling, he *stayed among the people* (39:14; 40:6). He would serve them still, and he would bring God's word to them still, even if (as he later found) they were as little inclined to listen to him now as they ever had been before.

We know nothing of Jeremiah's ministry during those autumn days with the people at Mizpah, whether he found encouragement and vindication there or continuing hostility. It seems rather far-fetched to imagine, with John Skinner, 'that these short weeks spent at Mizpah were the happiest period of Jeremiah's long life',[9] but to say the least, living in the open and fruitful land in the midst of a good harvest must have been infinitely better than his suffocating

[9] Skinner, *Prophecy and Religion*, p. 279.

imprisonment in the city under siege. Sadly, whatever the condition of his time there, it was to be short-lived.

Gedaliah seems to have been a tragic combination of personal integrity and generosity, with a fatal naivety and misplaced trust. The story from 40:13 onwards leaves the reader grieving over the death of a good man, wondering what might have happened to that small group of surviving Judeans if the first promising leader they had had for years had not met such a treacherous end.

4. Murder, massacre and mayhem (41:1–18)

Enter *Ishmael son of Nethaniah*.

We know almost nothing about him except that *he was of royal blood and had been one of the king's officers* (1). Disgruntled, then. Devastated and angry by the failure of his king's resistance to the enemy. Embittered by the Babylonians' execution of the royal family at Riblah. Resentful, no doubt, that Gedaliah, from the family that had been such a constant critic of his king's policy, was now in leadership and serving the hated Babylonians. An angry young man, leader of other angry young men. Angry enough to spill the blood of their own, as if enough had not been spilt already by the Babylonians.

The depressing account of the murder of Gedaliah, followed by the appalling slaughter of many others who were simply 'in the wrong place at the wrong time', takes one back in memory to the worst days of the book of Judges. Or to the bloodbath that Jehu unleashed on the house of Ahab and Jezebel. The story tells itself and needs little comment.

Pity most the poor people who had huddled in Mizpah hoping for a future that might soften the trauma of the past eighteen months. Freed by the Babylonians, they had not only survived the siege of Jerusalem, but also escaped the fate of those they had last seen trudging north in chains, leaving the land behind forever. For some of them at least, the future was brightened by the gift of some portions of land by that oddly generous Nebuzaradan. But now, in the midst of fresh and horrible bloodshed, they are taken hostage at the point of the sword (swords they had seen were only too readily used). First they are yanked off to the east (10), towards exile in the land of the Ammonites across the Jordan valley – where Ishmael had ingratiated himself with King Baalis (doubtless intent on profiting to the maximum from Judah's collapse and chaos). Then, suddenly and to their great relief, they are rescued by *Johanan son of Kareah,* though Ishmael and his gang escape to Ammon anyway (11–15).

But now where to go? The scared little crowd of homeless refugees in their own homeland – scared of internal enemies, scared of the Ammonites to the east and scared of the Babylonians to the north (who would want reprisal for the murder of Gedaliah) – turns in despair to the only other direction they know: south (16–18).

South to Egypt.

South to a destiny that would spell the end for Judah for the following two generations. Egypt held no future. The only future hope for Israel now lay with those farthest away – the exiles in Babylon.

Theological and expository reflections

The chapter offers a number of themes and models worth exploring in relation to other scriptures:

- The fall of Jerusalem in 587 BC is a disaster comparable to other signal acts of judgment in the Bible, and as such it prefigures both the cross (as divine judgment accomplished through human hands) and the final judgment. Is this in part what Paul may have meant in saying that 'Christ died for our sins in accordance with the scriptures'?
- Ebed-Melek stands as a model of faith in action, noticed and rewarded by God. Yet Gedaliah, who seems to have been a man of wisdom and integrity, is unjustly murdered. Is there an anticipation of both sides of the story reflected in Hebrews 11?
- How do we reflect on the sovereignty of God, and his ability to act and speak through pagans who do not belong to his people, in the light of what we read here of Nebuzaradan, the Babylonian officer?

Jeremiah 42:1 – 44:30
30. Death on the Nile

Pathos, irony and tragedy. Such are the ingredients of these closing scenes of Jeremiah's life. *Pathos*, because the last we see of this faithful servant of the Lord is him being carried off, against his advice, to Egypt. There, with Baruch alone as his trusty friend, he would live and die among an increasingly unfaithful people who, as they had done all his life, refused to listen to him. *Irony*, because though the people deliberately and emphatically shut their ears to the word of the Lord, they still took Jeremiah with them and so could not escape that word of God that he embodied in their midst. The word followed them and would finally destroy them, for it would be God's word, not theirs, that would stand (44:28). And *tragedy* because there was an alternative. The possible future that had seemed so promising when first offered by Gedaliah (40:7–12), but had been so bloodily cut short, is offered yet again by God himself as a choice backed by God's own rich promises (42:10–12). The tragedy was that, in bluntly refusing that offer, the portion of *the remnant of Judah* that chose to go to Egypt instead effectively wrote and signed their own suicide note. Chapter 44 will snuff out all hope for that self-exiled group in Egypt,[1] whereas chapter 52 will end with a sign of hope for those who had been carried off to Babylon.

1. Jeremiah's last words in Judah (42:1 – 43:7)

Chapter 41 ended with the ragged company of traumatized refugees

---

[1] That is to say, it was the end of them as a community that would participate in the return to the land and the re-establishing of God's covenant people there. Communities of Jews did survive in Egypt, and among them would eventually be found those who would translate the Hebrew scriptures into Greek in Alexandria, those who gave refuge to Joseph and Mary and their baby when they fled from Herod, and indeed that remarkable cross-cultural teacher of the early church, Apollos (Acts 18:24–28).

heading south towards Egypt. But somewhere near Bethlehem, before the route leads them irrevocably out of the land, they pause. Shouldn't somebody pray about this? Shouldn't we get God's confirmation on our plans? Even though we read later that they were pretty determined to follow their own plan, we may read their request to Jeremiah at face value as a genuine seeking of guidance from God. God (who has been absent since ch. 38) and Jeremiah (who was last seen silent among the settlers in Mizpah, 40:6), are back in action.[2]

a. God's word requested (42:1–6)

It was not God or Jeremiah, however, who took the initiative to reopen communication. It was emphatically and unanimously requested by the whole community (*all the people from the least to the greatest*). They start off very politely – recognizing Jeremiah as a true prophet of YHWH – *the LORD your God*. They plead with him to take up the authentic prophetic role of praying for them and seeking God's guidance. The fact that Jeremiah agrees to do so shows that the earlier prohibition on him praying for the people has been lifted. That ban had been in place when the judgment on Jerusalem was still future but inevitable. Now it has fallen and this little remnant of survivors can rightly be prayed for.

Their lament – *we were once many, now only a few are left* – is a pathetic reversal of the Abrahamic promise. It is also deeply ironic inasmuch as they are planning to go to Egypt, the land where the few had grown to be many in the first place.[3] This is one among many hints of 'exodus-reversed' in these chapters (see below).

Jeremiah agrees to intercede for them (4), and the people respond with a fulsome affirmation of their willingness to comply with whatever God might say. Indeed their words constitute an oath, or a vow, promising unconditional obedience to *act in accordance with everything the LORD your God sends you to tell us . . . we will obey . . . we will obey . . .* (5–6). Literally the repeated promise is: 'to the voice of the LORD our God (notice it is now *our* God again) we will listen . . . we will listen to the voice of the LORD our God.' But would they even listen to themselves?

---

[2] Stulman, p. 331, draws attention to the many ways in which the narrative to follow echoes moments in the story of Israel from the exodus, through the wilderness, to the borders of the promised land (in Exodus and Numbers); the requests for intercession; the promises to obey whatever God says, only to renege on the promise very quickly; the perverse longing to go (back) to Egypt; the persistent worship of other gods; the judgment that they would not enter (or come back to) the promised land.

[3] Exod. 1:1–6; Deut. 1:10; 10:22.

With raised eyebrows we call to mind two previous occasions, under Moses and under Joshua,[4] when such promises had been made – neither of which give us confidence that this one, for all its verbal sincerity, will be any more honoured in the outcome. Still, the request has been lodged and the promise made. We wait in suspense.

b. God's word received (42:7–22)

And indeed, they all waited in suspense – for *ten days*. For refugees terrified that at any moment Nebuchadnezzar's soldiers would appear on the horizon to take revenge for the murder of his appointed governor, this must have been agonizing. All they wanted to do was hit the road south as soon as possible. But Jeremiah knew better than to speak too soon.

Ten days later the answer came. It occupies the rest of chapter 42, but by the end of Jeremiah's reported speech, it seems that a response has already been made, which is then built into his final words. There is a certain telescoping of the dialogue, such that the people's intentions are anticipated and built into the word of God through the words of Jeremiah.

God's response to the people's question is unambiguously clear. Using a classic double 'if . . . then' structure, it sets out two alternatives with two diametrically opposite potential outcomes.

(i) First alternative – stay in the land (10–12)

It is presented as an 'option' – *if you stay in this land* – but it is of course God's imperative. It is the straight answer to their request that God should tell them *where we should go and what we should do* (3; cf. 19). But the implied command is reinforced with an amazingly rich battery of promises and encouragements. What Gedaliah had said to reassure the people at Mizpah (40:9–10) is now transformed into the word of God himself, with even stronger guarantees. The words Jeremiah had heard at his commissioning (and on other occasions since) are now deployed for the benefit of these fearful fugitives. God himself would *build* and *plant* them. Twice God addresses their very understandable fear with his personal promise of salvation and deliverance (11; cf. 1:8). Since God had changed his stance towards them (10), and since Nebuchadnezzar was simply the instrument of God's sovereignty, they need have no further fear of him. As he had been the agent of God's anger, so now he would be the agent of God's *compassion* (12). He was still, after all, *my servant* (43:10).

[4] Exod. 24:3–7; 32 – 34; Josh. 24:16–24.

The theological foundation for Jeremiah's words here is remarkable in two ways: in God's relenting (10), and in God's control of
affairs (12).

I have relented (NIV 2011) is a better translation than the NIV's
earlier *I am grieved*.[5] The verb *niḥam* can express a sense of regret
or pain at an unwelcome outcome (as in Gen. 6:6). And it could be
that here in God's first speech after the fall of Jerusalem in chapter
39 (where we observed his absence from the narrative), we hear again
the agony of God himself at the suffering of his people – even though
it was suffering brought on themselves through God's inevitable
judgment on their covenant breaking wickedness and rebellion. But
the verb more correctly expresses a change of attitude and intention
in response to new circumstances. Up until the fall of Jerusalem,
God's intention was judgment. Now that judgment had been fully
exercised, God's intention can and does change. 'You do not stay
angry forever, but delight to show mercy.'[6] The words and the
meaning here in 42:10 are thus almost exactly the same as in Jonah
3:10. In response to the repentance of the Ninevites, 'God relented
concerning the disaster (*rā'â*) he had said he would do to them and
did not do it.'[7] Both texts reflect the principle that God had declared
at the potter's house in 18:8 (using the same language). What is
remarkable here is that (in contrast to Nineveh) we have heard
nothing of the people's repentance. God is promising a change on
his part in the hope of generating a change on theirs – which would
be demonstrated in their obedience to his instruction to stay in
the land.

As for Nebuchadnezzar, he too would behave in tandem with the
mind and will of God. The one who had exercised God's wrath could
equally exercise God's compassion (12). The flow of the verse is
significant in putting God's decision first as the dynamic intention-
ality within international affairs. *I will show you compassion* **so that**
he will have compassion on you. Nebuchadnezzar, of course, would
do whatever he would choose to do in the exercise of his own considered foreign policy. He was a free agent and a head of a sovereign
state and expanding empire. But Jeremiah does not hesitate to set

---

[5] It is better also than the NRSV, 'I am sorry for'. God was not *apologising* for having
had to act in judgment, in the sense of regretting his own righteous anger and covenantal faithfulness. But that did not mean God did not feel the pain of those who
suffered in the process. The whole testimony of Jeremiah's agonized life has shown
just how much the heart of God was torn with grief. Similarly, a parent may affirm
the necessity of disciplinary punishment of a disobedient child while suffering inner
grief and pain *with* the child as that punishment is carried out.

[6] Mic. 7:18.

[7] Jon. 3:10; my translation.

such human freedoms and political policies firmly within the over-arching purposes of God.

> The statement [of v. 12] . . . witnesses to the precise convergence of *Yahweh's covenantal resolve* and *Babylon's foreign policy*. It is the mercy of Yahweh which will make Babylon a merciful over-lord, who will make living in the land a viable option. The prophet inserts a theological, covenantal dimension into the fearful realities of international politics.[8]

(ii) Second alternative – go to Egypt (13–18)

'If you insist on saying . . .' The participial form of the verb implies that the will of the people was already being expressed in a constant murmuring: 'We can't stay here. Let's get moving to Egypt.' If that was the alternative they were determined to choose, then Jeremiah spells out the consequences as starkly as he possibly could.

The people's reasons for wanting to go to Egypt are understand-able (14). Their lives had been shattered and shredded for two long years now, through the horrors of invasion, the ravages and hunger of a long siege, the death or exile of large numbers of their relatives, internal displacement as refugees in their own land, chaotic and violent civil war among rival leaders, and continuing perceived threat from 'the enemy from the north'. They longed for a place of plenty, peace and stability, free from war and want. Egypt seemed to offer all of that, even if it meant leaving their beloved homeland. It was very alluring. It was also utterly illusory.[9]

Jeremiah counters that alternative in three ways. First, it would be acting in straight disobedience to the Lord (13). And did they not have enough experience already of what that produced? Second, Egypt would disappoint all the hopes they were placing in it (as it always had in the past). It would be no safe house (16–17). Third, and worst of all, they would cut themselves off from the covenantal blessing of God and the future he still planned for his people (18). If they insisted on a reversal of the exodus, they would suffer a reversal of Abraham also. Instead of the promise to 'be a blessing', and a model of blessing that would be invoked by all nations (Gen. 12:1–3),

---

[8] Brueggemann (1991), p. 179.

[9] '. . . they fear famine. Famine leads people to do stupid things. It can drive men and women to leave their villages, their cities and their countries of origin to search for a better life elsewhere. As the proverb says, "the neighbour's vegetable garden is always better watered". Yet when we see the incredible risks that some Africans today will take in order to reach Europe or America by illegal means, we wonder if it is really worth the trouble. Salvation may be found in the very place where we are' (Coulibaly, p. 909).

they would become *an execration, a horror, a curse, and a taunt* (18b, ESV). And, in case they hoped for a short stay until things had settled down, Jeremiah cuts off all hope of return to the Promised Land. The last line of verse 18 cancels the future by nullifying the great moments of their past: the promise to Abraham, the purpose of the exodus, the longed-for destination of the wilderness pilgrimage, and the mighty acts of God through Joshua. *You will never see this place again.* Egypt would be a place of no return.

The alternatives were clear, then. Stay in the land and trust the promises of God. That way they could participate in the future God was planning – the building and planting, the destiny of the 'good figs'. That would take enormous courage and faith, in the face of very real fears. That was what God now commanded and called for. Or go to Egypt for illusory safety and defy the word of God they had requested. That way they would cut themselves off from the purposes of God, sever themselves from his covenant blessing, and exit the plot. God's story with God's people would continue, but they would not be part of it. For them, the story would end where it had begun – refugees in Egypt, but with no exodus ahead.

As Jeremiah delivers what would be his last words spoken on the soil of Judah, he ends not with an appeal (such as Moses in Deuteronomy 30:15–20), but with a weary recognition that this people have already chosen (19–22). And their choice is the one they had made all through his life and through their whole history – 'you have not listened to the voice of the LORD your God'. They had asked to hear it. They had promised to obey it. They now refused to do so. It was a *fatal mistake.* They had, in short, chosen death, not life.

c. God's word rejected (43:1–7)

'*You are lying!*' The viciousness of the people's response is breath-taking. The politeness of their request (42:2–3) has vanished. There is no hint of 'Thank you for your frank answer to our question, but after due consideration we regret to say that we take a different view. Please feel free to leave us now, with apologies for any inconvenience caused . . .' No, the first word they hurl at Jeremiah is *šeqer!* 'Lies! Deception!' – exactly the word that Jeremiah himself had used repeatedly about the false prophets. Perversely, having insisted that Jeremiah should pray to *the LORD your God* (42:2), they now insist that *the Lord our God* had not sent him at all (43:2). Having asked for the truth, they call it a lie. Having heard God's voice, they refuse to listen. Having sought God's will, they follow their own. We may detect echoes of the story of Ahab, who insisted on hearing the truth from Micaiah but deliberately and fatally chose to defy it.[10]

To their theological case (rejecting Jeremiah as a false prophet) the leaders add a political one. They repeat the accusation that had earlier cost Jeremiah his freedom – namely that he was a pro-Babylonian traitor, the pawn and mouthpiece of the pro-Babylonian party (cf. 37:11–15; 38:1–6). They see Baruch still attending Jeremiah and accuse him of manipulating Jeremiah to support his family's policy of appeasement. So they reject both the assurance of Gedaliah (40:9–10) and the reassurance of God himself (42:10–12).

And so the story comes to its dismal conclusion (4–7). The tragedy, irony and pathos continue, as we see people who had only recently returned *to* the land from earlier scattering among surrounding nations (presumably those who had fled from Nebuchadnezzar's invasion of Judah and from Jerusalem before it was finally shut up in siege), now trudging *from* the land once more in triple displacement (5). The decision and its implementation constituted for this part of the remnant, as distinct from the Babylonian exiles, 'an outrageous act of defiance that nullifies the great exodus of Israel out of Egypt. Israel has gone full swing. In returning to the place of bondage, the people of God have dealt a deathblow to the story of salvation ... The womb of Israel's birth (Egypt) now becomes the abode of death'.[11]

It is a small but very mixed crowd we see on that road south: men, women and children, old and young, from rags to royalty. And in their midst – *Jeremiah the prophet and Baruch son of Neriah* – released from captivity by the Babylonians, only to be taken into captivity by their own people, forced for the rest of their days to dwell among a disobedient people in the land from which God had delivered their ancestors (7).

2. Jeremiah's last words in Egypt (43:8 – 44:30)

a. The Pharaoh: dethroned (43:8–13)

Tahpanhes was a city in the north-eastern corner of the Nile delta close to the coast. It would have been the first place of settlement of the arriving Judeans. Doubtless they thought they were safe at last from the long arm of Babylon. Perhaps they also thought they were

---

[10] 1 Kgs 22. The word used to describe the men who respond to Jeremiah in this way is *arrogant*. It is a word (*zēdîm*) used in the Psalms for those who, with insolent absence of any fear of God and confident assumptions of impunity, falsely accuse or physically abuse God's faithful ones. Cf. Pss 86:14; 119: 21, 51, 78; Prov. 21:24.

[11] Stulman, p. 346.

free at last from the unwelcome preaching of Jeremiah. In both respects they were mistaken.

Jeremiah's last 'acted prophecy' is recorded in 43:9. He took *some large stones* and either buried them, or perhaps embedded them visibly, *in clay* in the forecourt of one of Pharaoh's palaces (possibly a provincial governor's residence). They would remain there as a tangible reminder of the words he next spoke and as a potent sign that would vindicate him as a true prophet when his prophecy was fulfilled. The same Nebuchadnezzar, from whom they thought they had finally escaped, would turn up in Egypt and put his own throne on top of Pharaoh's (metaphorically). All the religious symbols of Egypt's imperial power would prove to be humiliatingly 'combustible, portable or breakable' (12–13).[12] Again we note how the prophet describes an action that would have been Nebuchadnezzar's own military and imperial decision as being at the same time an action of God himself. Once again Nebuchadnezzar is called *my servant* (i.e. the one who carries out the will and purpose of God), and his assertion of sovereignty over Egypt is claimed by God – *I will set his throne over these stones* (10). With such a sovereign God in charge of affairs, the matter would seem, from Nebuchadnezzar's point of view, as easy as a shepherd picking lice from his cloak (12).[13]

We know from a 'fragmentary inscription',[14] as well as a prophecy of Ezekiel,[15] that Nebuchadnezzar did invade Egypt in 567 BC. It was not a full-scale conquest, but it did establish his political dominance in the region. So although Jeremiah's stereotypical imagery was not literally enacted, it truthfully symbolized the superiority of Babylon's throne over Egypt's, and proved to the exiles in Egypt that they had not escaped the reach of 'God's servant' as they had hoped.

b. The warning: delivered (44:1–14)

It ought not to be surprising that the last recorded confrontation between the aged Jeremiah and the people of Israel (albeit a fragment of the nation he had confronted in his youth), centred on the issue of idolatry. It had been the burden of Jeremiah's ministry since the day of his call. There are strong echoes of 1:16 in 44:2–8.[16] The opening chapter of the book warned that God would bring judgment

[12] Kidner, p. 132.
[13] This translation (NIV 2011) seems to have gained favour over earlier readings that picture a shepherd wrapping his cloak around himself.
[14] Thompson, p. 671.
[15] Ezek. 29:17–20.
[16] Note these phrases common to both: 'their wickedness (*rā'â*)'; 'burning incense'; 'worshipping other gods'; 'what your hands have made'.

on 'all the towns of Judah' because of this fundamental sin and all the wickedness that accompanied it[17] (1:14–16). This closing chapter of Jeremiah's ministry shows him giving the same warning to those who had suffered God's judgment in Judah, but were incurably intent on persisting in the same sin in their self-imposed exile in Egypt.

No date is assigned to this last word of Jeremiah, but it must have been some considerable time after the flight to Egypt described in chapter 43. The Jews have had time to spread out and form communities over a distance of about 400 miles from north to south, between the delta towns of *Tahpanhes* and *Midgol*, the city of *Memphis* (near modern Cairo), and 'the land of Pathros', i.e. *Upper Egypt* at Elephantine, close to the First Cataract on the Nile, modern Aswan. And in their settled geographical state, the state of their hearts, lives and worship has now become apparent. And it is sickeningly as syncretistic as it had ever been.

Jeremiah's last word is to *all the Jews* in Egypt. Whether this means there was some representative gathering that he addressed, or that he travelled and visited all the scattered communities, giving them the same message, we can only speculate. For those who have ever enjoyed a cruise on the river Nile as far as Aswan and the island of Elephantine (where there is evidence that a Jewish community survived for a long time), it is tempting to imagine one might be following the last journey of Jeremiah.

Jeremiah's final word takes classic shape: a historical review (2–6); the specific indictment (7–10); and the final verdict (11–14).

He begins by recalling the painful memory of the recent past (the fall of Jerusalem), described as *disaster* (rā'â). But, as in his early preaching, he links the recent to the longer past – the persistent *evil* (rā'â again) of generations. And to the sin of the idolatry itself, Israel had added their perennial sin of refusing to listen to/obey God. Repeated pleas from *my servants the prophets* (4) had fallen on deaf ears and hard hearts. *Wickedness* reigned (5; rā'â again). God's anger had fallen. Judah lay in *ruins* (6).

Now comes the charge against the present generation, in the form of four rapid-fire rhetorical questions:

- *Why . . . ?* (7)
- *Why . . . ?* (8a)
- Will you *destroy yourselves . . . ?* (8b)
- *Have you forgotten . . . ?* (9)

[17] The constant repetition of the word rā'â ('evil, wickedness') should prevent us imagining that this whole argument was merely about religious rituals (incense, etc.). The whole sphere of social and economic ethics and political policies is involved in the meaning of idolatry.

The rhetorical thrust of the first three questions is to warn the communities in Egypt that by repeating the sins of their fathers they were in danger of provoking the same judgment.

The point of the final question (9) is clear from the fivefold repetition of the word *rāʿâ*. Literally Jeremiah says, 'Have you forgotten the wickednesses of your fathers, and the wickednesses of the kings of Judah, and the wickednesses of their wives, and your own wickednesses, and the wickedness of your wives?' It is clear that the accusation is not one of mere religious deviance in the rituals of worship, but includes serious moral disobedience to the whole demand of the covenant law: *nor have they followed my law and the decrees I set before you and your ancestors.*

Therefore, the judgment of God on this remnant in Egypt will mirror the judgment that had already fallen on Judah (11–14). The community as a whole would perish from the story of Abrahamic blessing and instead become *a curse and an object of reproach* (12). There would be no community return by Egyptian Jews to the land (as was promised to, and experienced by, the exiles in Babylon), though a few individuals would survive and return (14b).[18]

c. The people: defiant (44:15–19)

Jeremiah had not changed his message in forty years. We are hardly surprised that the people did not change their response to it either. They had never listened before (5); they refuse to listen now (16). Defiant to the end, the whole community (15 and 20 are emphatically inclusive) makes their bluntest statement yet. Literally, they say, 'The word which you have spoken to us in the name of YHWH, there isn't one of us listening to you.' Could any congregation be more contemptuously dismissive of their preacher? Could any refusal to heed God's word be any more brazen?

The worship of *the Queen of Heaven* seems to have been a seductive combination of the Ishtar/Astarte cults of Mesopotamia and Canaan with the Isis cult of Egypt. Jeremiah had already spoken against this during the reign of Jeroboam in the 'temple sermon' in 7:16–19 (see commentary there).[19] The cult was popular with whole families, including especially the women. So Jeremiah's fresh attack on it brings a rude and robust defence from the men and their wives.

'Give it up,' says Jeremiah.

---

[18] Small communities of Jews did survive in Egypt on the margins of biblical history, and some from Egypt were among the Jews who heard the first preaching of the risen Messiah Jesus on the day of Pentecost and came to faith. Was Apollos among them? (Acts 2:10; 18:24).

[19] Pp. 114–115.

'We simply won't,' say the men.

'Motion seconded,' say the women.

'Carried unanimously,' chorus the combined forces of Adam and Eve, for once defending rather than blaming each other (19).

Their perversity, however, did not stop merely at refusing to give up their worship of the Queen of Heaven. They blame all their recent troubles on having actually done so in the past! When they had been giving her unfettered homage in the past, they were sated with prosperity and peace. But ever since they *stopped* (probably referring to the purge of such practices during Josiah's reformation which Jeremiah had supported), all the evils had befallen them. The controverted argument of verses 17–18 is breathtaking – but of course it is characteristic of those who are determined to find any evidence from their own reading of history (personal or wider) that supports their conviction that their own gods bring prosperity while the God of the Bible just brings trouble.

d. The future: determined (44:20–30)

In the face of such determined perversity, Jeremiah announces an equally determined future. His words become increasingly impatient in a crescendo of judgment.

He opens with more rhetorical questions, saying, in effect, 'Do you think YHWH was not aware of all that was going on? The evil that has befallen us is not because you *stopped* worshipping other gods, but because you refused to stop, and brought God's judgment on yourselves' (20–23).

Then he turns up the heat of irony and sarcasm. They had better go on keeping their vows then – not the one they had made to obey whatever YHWH told them (42:2–6), and then promptly broken, but rather the one they have now clearly made to the Queen of Heaven. Go on then. Just do it. But know that you will now be forsaken by the God you have chosen to forsake. God's oath in verse 26 is powerful and damning. It effectively removes God's name from these people. And without the name of the Lord, who were they? No longer his covenant people, no longer beneficiaries of his protection. 'Without YHWH's name on its lips the community forfeits its core identity as God's people. The allusion to God's name, once revealed in Egypt and now rescinded in Egypt, takes the community full circle.'[20]

Those who refuse to honour God will find themselves cut off from him. But the choice was theirs and the result was their own doing.

[20] Stulman, p. 341.

THE MESSAGE OF JEREMIAH

Such is the inevitable destiny of those who exchange the glory of the living God for the worship of idols. It is a short distance from this text to the dark analysis of the spiritual and social consequences of idolatry in Romans 1:18–32, in which Paul speaks very much in the spirit and tone of Jeremiah. 'God gave them up . . .' (ESV).

A final echo of his own call vision concludes Jeremiah's last word. Jeremiah had been the embodiment of the word of the Lord through-out his whole life from his conception. In his very first vision God had promised to 'watch over' his word, to ensure both that the word itself was fulfilled and that Jeremiah, its mouthpiece, was vindicated (1:11–12). That would be true positively for the exiles in Babylon (24:6; 31:28), but negatively for those who had disobeyed in going to Egypt and were persisting in idolatry there (27). They had been given the choice by God to remain in the land and await God's good purposes there. Instead, 'they chose a different path and shaped for themselves a different future, but that was their doing, not God's'.[21]

Few they were when they came to Egypt (42:2). *Few* they would remain, even those who might survive to return to Judah (44:28a).

At the end of the day, only one word would stand. And it would not be theirs (28b).[22]

Theological and expository reflections

- 'Egypt' stimulates many theological reflections in the Bible. The most prominent one in this text, of course, is the allurement of Egypt as the symbol of worldly security and sufficiency. Stulman captures this 'robust metaphor' well:

> Egypt symbolizes raw human strength and inexhaustible resources. It is the place of political autonomy and economic opulence. While other nations rise and fall, it exudes enormous staying power . . . [But] . . . To remember Israel's story is to call to mind that Egypt is a place of tears and death. It is a place where taskmasters exploit and brutalize. It values production over people and muscle over mercy.[23]

No wonder Israel had been severely warned never to go back there, or that, if they did, it would be a sure sign they were

[21] Fretheim, p. 569.

[22] A final sign brings Jeremiah's words to an end: Pharaoh Hophra would suffer the same fate as Zedekiah (whom he had tried to help with an ill-fated attempt to relieve the siege of Jerusalem). He would die at the hands of his enemies as Zedekiah had. It seems that in fact he did die in an internal coup in 568 BC.

[23] Stulman, pp. 343–344.

406

putting themselves into the place of God's curse, not God's blessing.[24] And yet, in spite of all the warning and the symbolism, the allure proved too powerful. A people who had schooled themselves in not trusting in God found no alternative but to trust in the embrace of a system that would ultimately swallow and digest them into itself. Do modern Christians in the great globalized economic empire of the West face the same temptation, the same syncretism, the same cultural absorption?

And yet . . . Jeremiah's was not the only word about Egypt nor was judgment God's final word about them either. Even they could be included in the universal promises of grace and Abrahamic blessing that have surfaced earlier. And Isaiah makes it explicit in one of the most breathtaking prophecies in the Bible.[25] The day would come when the blessings of salvation, 'exodus', knowledge of God and inclusion among God's people will be extended even to those in Egypt who call on his name (of whom there are now many thousands).

- Is there any similarity between the people's deliberate refusal to listen to the voice of God, even when they ask Jeremiah to bring it to them, and what Jesus calls sin against the Holy Spirit? They heard the truth and called it a lie. How dangerous can that be?
- Once again we see the connection between spiritual idolatry and moral wickedness. Jeremiah's lifelong battle against the worship of other gods (ever since 1:16) was not just a matter of religious ritual or preference. To forsake YHWH meant to forsake the ways of YHWH, and they included all that the Torah taught about justice and compassion in the social and economic realm. As we observe the gross injustice, greed and callousness of contemporary society we need to recognize the fundamental idolatry that lies behind it and that is manifested in such behaviours and the societal breakdown they lead to.

[24] Deut. 17:16; 28:68.
[25] Isa. 19:19–25.

Jeremiah 45:1–5
31. Baruch's signature

There are some very important unimportant people in the Bible. That is, there are those who have no glory in the histories of world empires, but who play a vital role in the service of God and the outworking of his kingdom purposes. We might list among them Moses' mother and sister who saved the life of Israel's greatest leader; the unnamed widow who preserved Elijah's life; the slave girl who introduced Naaman to Elisha; the women who provided for Jesus' needs; the nephew who gave Paul the tip-off about the threat to his life.[1]

And Baruch. We know very little about him. He occurs in the narrative only four times. And yet it is very possible, if not highly likely, that we owe the book of Jeremiah that we now have in our Bibles substantially to this faithful servant of God's prophet.

Structurally, chapter 45 clearly connects with chapter 36. Both are dated to the same year, both refer to the writing of the scroll of Jeremiah's words, and both involve Baruch. They function like book-ends to the chapters in between, which describe the final events in Jeremiah's life during the reign of Zedekiah, the siege and fall of Jerusalem, and the subsequent chaos and flight to Egypt. It seems likely that Baruch was with Jeremiah the whole time (43:3, 6–7). This little chapter is Baruch's way of 'signing' the record of events he has compiled.

The date was significant. It was the fourth year of the reign of Jehoiakim, 605 BC. It was the year Nebuchadnezzar stunningly defeated Egypt at the battle of Carchemish, thus paving the way for his expansion and dominance over the whole region, including Judah in due course. It was the year Jehoiakim brazenly rejected the word of God through Jeremiah and set his kingdom on a path that would

[1] Exod. 2:1–10; 1 Kgs 17:7–24; 2 Kgs 5; Luke 8:1–3; Acts 23:12–22.

lead to its final destruction. It was the beginning of the end.[2] Now that that ending has been described, Baruch takes us back to the start and gives us a glimpse of what it had meant for him.

1. Baruch the man

All we know about Baruch is what we have in the book of Jeremiah.

He belonged to the family of Neriah, a family that had connections with the government. His brother Seraiah was a staff officer of the royal family (51:59). For that reason Baruch probably had access to inner government committees meeting in the temple complex (36:10) and in the royal palace (36:12–15). He was also an educated man and a professional scribe. And he had chosen, in spite of all that, to put his skills at the service of this unpopular prophet Jeremiah. That probably means that his family was among those few who aligned themselves with the political and international policy that Jeremiah was advocating (submission to Babylon). But a deeper personal and spiritual loyalty seems to have been involved as well.

In chronological order, we first meet Baruch in chapter 36 (see the exposition there), when he wrote Jeremiah's scroll and then went to the temple to read it aloud in public. The story shows he was a model secretary – accurate, persevering, hard-working and reliable. It also shows that he had enormous courage to put himself at grave risk by publicly reading the collected sayings (twenty-three years' worth) of a banned dissident prophet. Chapter 45, as we shall see in a moment, shows something of the personal cost involved in his commitment.

We next meet him about seventeen years later in chapter 32. We discover that he is still serving Jeremiah even though the prophet is confined to the courtyard of the guard in the palace compound during the final months of the siege of Jerusalem. Faithful and meticulous as ever, Baruch does all the legal formalities connected to the purchase of the field from cousin Hanamel and ensures that the deeds are carefully stored for posterity – not that Jeremiah would ever benefit from them.

Then, as we saw in 43:3, 6–7, he was still with Jeremiah in the party that emigrated to Egypt after the chaos and mayhem of the months following the fall of Jerusalem. After that we know nothing for certain. Perhaps he died in Egypt as Jeremiah must have done. It is possible, however, that after Jeremiah died Baruch left Egypt and travelled to Babylon. His brother Seraiah was already there

---

[2] 'This date [605 BC] . . . sets in motion a series of events that would shake heaven and earth and transform Judah's character forever. This moment signifies the onslaught of exile and powerlessness, as well as fear, panic, and death' (Stulman, p. 347).

(51:59–64), and possibly others of his family. As a member of a high-ranking family who had supported a pro-Babylonian policy, he could expect a friendly reception.[3] This is pure conjecture, of course, but it might explain how the edited scroll of Jeremiah's prophecies eventually reached the exiles in Babylon.

And that's it. There are some apocryphal books that bear his name, but are the product of much later centuries.

2. Baruch's lament

Chapter 45 is one of only two passages where Jeremiah gives a word directly (and unsought) to an individual. The other is to Ebed-Melek in 39:15–18, and there are some interesting parallels. Both were individuals in their own right of course, and God's word to them was intensely personal and promissory. But they were also representative individuals, representative of those who had supported, befriended, and even risked their lives for Jeremiah.[4] By doing so they had also, of course, demonstrated their faith in God and their acceptance of the truth of God's word through Jeremiah, when the rest of the world refused to do either.

In the prolonged period of close collaboration on producing the scroll of Jeremiah's prophecies Baruch must have expressed his feelings, anxieties and frustrations – just as Jeremiah did. It is not surprising that Baruch's own lament echoes his master's.

Baruch seems to have been wrestling with two strong emotions. One is expressed by Baruch himself (3) and the other is exposed by God (5).

a. Unrelieved suffering (3)

Woe to me! The LORD has added sorrow to my pain; I am worn out with groaning and find no rest. The echoes of Jeremiah's grief are very strong (cf. 8:22 – 9:1; 15:18). And probably the cause of Baruch's pain is the same as the prophet's – contemplation of the awfulness of all that God had spoken through Jeremiah. Imagine him having not only heard Jeremiah's prophecies one at a time over the past

---

[3] At least, assuming the Babylonian authorities had not read the message concerning Babylon that Seriah had carried there (chs. 50 – 51)!

[4] Brueggemann sees a political dimension also in this affirmation of Baruch, not only as an individual person but also as 'a representative person. Mention of Baruch is a convenient way of referring to all those who stood with Jeremiah in his radical "Babylonian reading" of his time and place in God's history. This concluding oracle then is a commendation and vindication of those who have shared the faith and discernment of Jeremiah' ([1991], p. 205).

quarter century the first time round, but now also having to hear them all over again, all together, accumulating, compounding, filling his ears, his mind, his scroll – in a crescendo of doom and destruction. And alongside that, every day he was being reminded of the ugly truth about the God-defying, covenant-breaking wickedness and corruption of the people he belonged to.

Imagine. Spend a few moments skimming back through the pages of Jeremiah 1 – 25 and feeling the passion of the unrelenting message there. Then imagine having to write that all out by hand, line by line, with pen and ink, day after day. Then remember that, for Baruch, this was not some ancient scroll about a far distant time and place and people. This is here and now. This is your own people. These are your own times. This is what faces your people and your family. This is your own immediate future. This is your God. These are God's words. This is God's voice speaking through the mouth of your friend.[5] And you know it is the truth. And your job is to write it down. And then read it all out in the temple. And you know there is no escape. Could you sleep for groaning?

b. Unfulfilled ambition (5)

Should you then seek great things for yourself? God's words to Baruch express what he was thinking but had not actually spoken aloud. They expose a root of frustrated ambition, a longing for something bigger and better, a hankering after some more significant place in the corridors of power in national politics than being a prophet's word processor. Can we guess what lies behind such feelings?

Perhaps Baruch had once felt called and privileged to serve Jeremiah, just as Jeremiah had once found it a joy to 'eat' the word of the Lord and a privilege to bear his name (15:16). His master was a true prophet of God, and when God would vindicate his word through Jeremiah, Baruch would be among those who could say 'I told you so'. But now? As the years dragged on, had Baruch come to regret that decision? Was he becoming as disillusioned as Jeremiah seems to have become at times? For if Jeremiah's direst predictions came true, then what would be left of Baruch's life? He and his family might perish along with the rest of the governing class in the final conflagration. And even if they did not come true, Baruch's career was in ruins anyway. Since he had so irrevocably identified himself with the government's most hated critic they were not likely to

---

[5] The translation *dictated* (1) is literally, 'from the mouth of Jeremiah the prophet' – which recalls 1:9, 'I have put my words in your mouth'. The impact of the phrase is to reinforce that the words written in Baruch's scroll were the words of Jeremiah which constituted the word of God (1:1–2)

employ his professional skills any time soon. Any ambitions he might once have had of high office, any 'great things' he might once have sought or could still hope for, seemed increasingly futile with every line he wrote.

3. God's answer

How, then, does God address this double lament? By giving him a reference point for his pain, a rebuke for his ambitions, and a reassurance for his life.

a. God recognizes his pain (3–4)

Verse 4 seems oddly irrelevant to Baruch's complaint at first. It merely repeats what we heard at the call of Jeremiah. God is in wrecking mood. But then the connection leaps at us. What God is doing is deeply painful – *to God*. The emphasis of the sentence (as is clear from the word order in Hebrew and the double personal pronoun 'I'), is on *what I have built*, and *what I have planted'* (cf. ESV). What God is tearing down is what God himself had so carefully nurtured for so long. So if Baruch is groaning over what lies ahead, think what God is feeling.

Now of course, we all know people who, the moment you share some personal ailment, will regale you with a tale of woe of their own that surpasses yours by a mile. They are not going to be outdone in the suffering and martyrdom department. No pain you can mention but they have a worse one. And they think they are being sympathetic! Is that all God's response amounts to? Merely trumping Baruch's suffering with God's own? Well, yes, in a sense, but then that is like comparing the number 1 with infinity, or a molecule with the universe.

For these words of God condense a thousand years or more of patient 'building and planting' a people, from their improbable beginnings in the geriatric loins and womb of Abraham and Sarah, to this shattering prospect of seeing all that loving handiwork, all that investment in people and land for the sake of the nations and the earth, violently ripped to pieces and tossed on the bonfire of Babylon's vengeance. For any of us, it is a heart-breaking thing to lose what you have invested yourself in. It was a tearful wrench for my sister to move from an apartment with a garden that she had tended for forty years knowing that redevelopment of the site would mean bulldozers ripping up that garden to make way for a car park. Families in Palestine have had homes and olive groves that their families have tended for generations demolished in a few hours by bulldozers. The pain is beyond words. Multiply that pain by infinity, and imagine the heart of God watching the destruction of the 'vineyard' he had planted. Whatever suffering and pain Baruch feels (and God recognizes that he is indeed suffering), is a pinprick by comparison with God's.

As we said so often in our exposition in the earlier chapters of the book, God's anger is soaked in tears – both the tears of love that had been betrayed and rejected, and the tears of contemplating the suffering of so many people in the conflagration to come. God's wrath comes at the cost of God's pain.

Ezekiel put it so unforgettably:

Do I take any pleasure in the death of the wicked? declares the Sovereign LORD. Rather, am I not pleased when they turn from their ways and live?

I take no pleasure in the death of the wicked, but rather that they turn from their evil ways and live. Turn! Turn from your evil ways! Why will you die, people of Israel?[6]

Isaiah too reminds us that God suffered along with his own people: 'in all their distress he too was distressed'.[7]

There is a rabbinic tradition that imagines the angels wishing to sing in celebration (as the Israelites were doing) after the crossing of the sea and the destruction of the Egyptian army during the exodus. But God rebuked them with the words: 'The work of my hands is drowning, and will you sing songs?'[8] It reminds us that while we must believe the Bible's constant witness that ultimately God will judge and destroy all evil and unrepentant evildoers (and believe it with relief that evil will not triumph forever in God's moral universe), there is no pleasure in such reality. If it brings God no joy to see the wicked destroyed, if, on the contrary, it causes him intense pain and sorrow, then we need to guard our own emotions at the thought of the downfall of the wicked. We also need to remember that whatever pain and suffering may fill our hearts because of what we see in our world, it is only the very finite quantity of suffering that one pair of eyes can witness and one heart can bear. I sometimes wonder how

[6] Ezek. 18:23; 33:11.

[7] Isa. 63:9.

[8] 'Rabbi Johanan taught that God does not rejoice in the downfall of the wicked. Rabbi Johanan interpreted the words zeh 'el zeh in the phrase "And one did not come near the other all the night" in Exod. 14:20 to teach that when the Egyptians were drowning in the sea, the ministering angels wanted to sing a song of rejoicing, as Isa. 6:3 associates the words zeh 'el zeh with angelic singing. But God rebuked them: "The work of my hands is being drowned in the sea, and you want to sing songs?"' (Wikipedia <http://en.wikipedia.org/wiki/Beshalach>).

God can bear it, God who at every moment of his omniscience and omnipresence knows and feels the pain of every person on the planet. How can God bear the mountain of human suffering, let alone the voiceless suffering of his non-human creation?

So, in his word to his suffering friend, Jeremiah invites Baruch to place his own suffering in the context of the infinite suffering of God. And let that fortify him to go and declare God's word to the people, in the hope that they might yet repent and be spared (see 36:3 and 7). For even in the midst of impending historical judgment, God longs to show mercy. And even as we anticipate that ultimate and final judgment, our mission goes on.

b. God rebukes his ambition (5a)

The opening word of verse 5 (*you*) contrasts with the double personal pronoun 'I' in verse 4. 'This is what *I* have to do,' says God. 'And *you*? You are seeking for yourself great things? Don't seek them.'

We are not told what *great things* Baruch may have been seeking. There is nothing wrong with ambition, of course, when it is a godly ambition in line with the will of God. But while a desire for personal advancement for its own sake is contemptible at any time, there are times when it is not only inappropriate but absurdly futile. And such a time was this. To have personal career ambitions in Jerusalem right then was like applying for promotion to chief steward on board the *Titanic*. Nice work if you can get it, but somewhat lacking in long-term prospects. Baruch's world was falling apart in a cataclysm in which divine judgment would operate through human imperialism (recalling that Jeremiah affirmed it was the hand of God wielding the sword of Nebuchadnezzar).

The impact would be far wider than the small world of Jerusalem's petty politics. Two phrases in verses 4 and 5 portray what we might call the 'global' scale of God's work: 'the whole earth', and 'all flesh' (NIV, *throughout the earth . . . all people*). We can read this in two ways. On the one hand it is a rhetorical exaggeration in order to make the point that the whole Middle Eastern region, the whole world of Judah's existence and all the nations within it, would be impacted by the rise of the neo-Babylonian empire under Nebuchadnezzar. God's sovereign work of judgment on Israel would have 'global' effects on the surrounding nations – as indeed it did. But on the other hand, the events that Jeremiah and Baruch would witness (the fall of Jerusalem and beginning of the Babylonian exile), and those they would not witness but clearly predicted (the return of the exiles and their restoration to the land), constituted part of the much wider and truly global mission of God. For whatever God was doing in Israel – whether in judgment or salvation – God was doing as part of his sovereign redemptive plan for the whole world. This part of the story, tragic though it would be, was no less a part of the great unfolding of the promise to Abraham than the exodus or conquest. In the end, this would be God's doing, marvellous in the eyes of 'all flesh'.

Now Baruch may not be able to grasp all of that. We struggle to grasp it ourselves, even standing on this side of the cross and resurrection of Christ. But he needed to realize that God was about something far bigger than his personal career goals.

So God sets Baruch's ambitions in the context of the coming judgment and all that it signified. In the light of God's global agenda, Baruch's *great things* appeared very small indeed. There seems to be, then, a note of rebuke in God's response, somewhat similar to the way God had handled some of Jeremiah's complaints (e.g. 12:5; 15:19–21). But that does not at all mean that God was contemptuous of Baruch himself – as if *he* were too small and unimportant to count for anything in God's great plan. Quite the opposite. Baruch was an essential part of God's plan to preserve part of his word in the Bible. Baruch the man was crucially important. Baruch's personal ambitions were not.

c. God rescues his life (5b)

God's last word to Baruch may seem a somewhat niggardly concession: 'Here's the good news; you'll keep your life, but that's about all you'll keep.' However, in view of the presumed fears and anxieties that Baruch had, especially as he listened to the goriest parts of Jeremiah's visions of mayhem and slaughter in the streets of Jerusalem, to be told you would survive at all would be pretty comforting.

I will let you escape with your life is somewhat weak. God literally says, 'I will give you your life as booty' – that is, as a 'prize of war' (ESV) that soldiers take after a battle. It is a strong metaphor. It means: in the coming conflict, you will survive, but the only booty you will take with you will be your own life. Everything else may be lost, but you will get your life to hold on to like a precious trophy. Since the previous chapter had ended with the gloomy prediction of communal 'death' of the exiles in Egypt, this is a contrasting promise of life to a faithful servant of God. And in that respect it echoes the exact same promise, using the same words, made to Ebed-Melek (39:18). In the midst of the terrifying destruction that will engulf the kingdom and those who wield power within it, two people who seem marginal, small and insignificant are promised life.

There is a certain 'Magnificat' moment in this, as Stulman has observed:

> [The promise to Baruch] unmasks the illusion of power and hints at God's place among the broken of the world. The text suggests that hope exists on the margins and not at the centre. It is not found in triumphant nationalism or military might; that is, in the garb of winners . . . Instead, hope emerges among the vulnerable and wounded. It is born in those who are no longer privileged in the old ways and who no longer benefit from the insulation of a safe and reliable world. Although Baruch (and those he represents) will not receive the 'great things' that he so much desires, he will at least survive. And the promise of survival, during times of massive loss, is nothing to scoff at![9]

And so here we have a minor word to someone who was not even a minor prophet. And in it, God acknowledges Baruch's pain and his frustrated ambitions. However God says to him, in effect, 'I share your pain (more than you can ever know), but I challenge your ambitions.' *God calls Baruch to put his anxieties in the context of God's infinite suffering, and to put his ambitions in the context of God's imminent judgment.* And then, once he's done that, to bear the pain and get on with the work.

And he did.

Baruch finished the job. He went to the temple. He read the whole scroll in the presence of government ministers, risking arrest and imprisonment or worse at any moment. He went into hiding with Jeremiah, only to hear that all his work had literally gone up in smoke. Then he wrote it all out again, with even more additions (as he ruefully tells us; 36:32). And almost certainly he edited and organized most of what we now have as the book of Jeremiah. And he leaves this small signature, this tiny personal word (tiny in comparison with the rest of Jeremiah's preaching). And yet how many have ever heard of him?

For it is Jeremiah who gets the canonical glory, so to speak, while Baruch goes off into apocryphal obscurity.

But Jeremiah needed Baruch. And God still needs Baruchs – those who will be faithful, self-effacing servants of the servants of the Lord. Those who rarely ever come on stage and hear the applause, but without whom the drama would not go on.

When I was young we used to heartily sing a chorus to encourage us to stand up with bold courage before the hostile world:

[9] Stulman, p. 349.

> Dare to be a Daniel,
> Dare to stand alone!
> Dare to have a purpose firm!
> And dare to make it known.[10]

It's all very well to 'dare to be a Daniel'. The challenge is, can you bear to be a Baruch?

Theological and expository reflections

- Reflecting on the pain of God in the act of judgment ultimately takes us to the cross of Christ. And few have expressed more powerfully what it means to contemplate some of the implications of God's suffering there than John Stott. In a chapter devoted to reflections on the suffering of God in relation to the questions posed to classical theodicy by the suffering all around us in the world, he moves towards his climax in these words:

> There is good biblical evidence that God not only suffered in Christ, but that God in Christ suffers with his people still . . . But his 'sympathy' is not limited to his suffering with his covenant people. Did Jesus not say that in ministering to the hungry and thirsty, the stranger, the naked, the sick and the prisoner, we would be ministering to him, indicating that he identified himself with all needy and suffering people?
>
> I could never myself believe in God, if it were not for the cross. The only God I believe in is the One Nietsche ridiculed as 'God on the cross'. In the real world of pain, how could one worship a God who was immune to it? I have entered many Buddhist temples in different Asian countries and stood respectfully before the statue of the Buddha, his legs crossed, arms folded, eyes closed, the ghost of a smile playing round his mouth, a remote look on his face, detached from the agonies of the world. But each time after a while I have had to turn away. And in imagination I have turned instead to that lonely, twisted, tortured figure on the cross, nails through his hands and feet, back lacerated, limbs wrenched, brow bleeding from thorn-pricks, mouth dry and intolerably thirsty, plunged in God-forsaken darkness. That is the God for me! He entered our world of flesh and blood, tears and death. He suffered for us. Our sufferings become more manageable in the light of his. There is still a question mark

---

[10] Refrain of 'Standing by a purpose true', Philip Bliss, 1883.

against human suffering, but over it we boldly stamp another mark, the cross which symbolizes divine suffering. 'The cross of Christ . . . is God's only self-justification in such a world' as ours.[11]

- Baruch reminds us that the lives of ordinary and 'unimportant' people can be greatly significant for God. None of us is unimportant in the plan of God. All of us need to align our personal plans and ambitions (what we are 'seeking', great or small) with what God is doing in the world. And since 'what God is doing' is ultimately to bring both final judgment and final redemption to his whole creation, the question we need to ask is: where and how do my life, my gifts and abilities, my ambitions and dreams, find their proper place within that great agenda? In the light of the coming wrath and the coming new creation, I might wonder if my personal ambitions will count for anything at all. The marvel and miracle of God's redemption is that they do, when they are invested in seeking first the kingdom of God and his justice, knowing that if anyone is in Christ, new creation has already begun.

---

[11] Stott, *The Cross of Christ*, pp. 335–336. The quotation at the end comes from P. T. Forsyth, *The Justification of God* (Duckworth, 1916), p. 32. See also the Introduction (pp. 28–32), for reflection on how we can relate the abundant descriptions of the grief and suffering of God in Jeremiah to the traditional doctrine of God's 'impassibility'.

Jeremiah 46:1 – 49:39
32. Shaking the nations

'Today I appoint you over nations and kingdoms to uproot and tear down, to destroy and overthrow, to build and to plant.' The words God spoke to Jeremiah at his call (1:10) set him up for an international ministry wider than the tiny kingdom of Judah. Until his final journey to Egypt, however, Jeremiah never travelled (as far as we know) to any of the surrounding nations. But the scope of the word of God through him extended to the whole region. Indeed, the list of nations mentioned in these final chapters of the edited book cover every nation bordering on Judah and several others on the outer edges of the world as viewed from Jerusalem.

There is an immediate link with the context. God had said to Baruch that what he was about to do would have devastating impact 'throughout the earth' and on 'all people' (45:4–5). These chapters confirm that prediction. By being placed here at the end of the book,[1] following the account of the fall of Jerusalem in chapter 39 and its immediate sequel, these chapters widen the horizon to show that the events of 587 BC happened on a 'world stage'. In using Nebuchadnezzar as the agent of God's judgment on Israel, God necessarily drew in the whole of the region. That is the way of empires. They spill their ambitions all over the map.

So at one level, these chapters are consistent with the message of the rest of the book. We have been told, again and again, that the actions of Nebuchadnezzar would in effect be the actions of God.

---

[1] The LXX places these 'Oracles Against the Nations' (OAN), as they are called, immediately after 25:13. That is an understandable location, in view of what is said in that chapter. But the Hebrew text, by putting them at the end of the book, and especially by ending with the oracle concerning Babylon, achieves a different climax, making the book as a whole end on a note of hope for the restoration of Israel – a message the exiled readers needed to hear.

Nebuchadnezzar's military and political subjugation of Judah would constitute God's judgment on his people. But God's sovereignty extends over all nations, and the moral foundations of God's activity in the world apply to other nations as much as to Israel. Similarly, as we shall see, God's saving activity in the world applies to other nations (and all nations), not just to Israel.

The series begins with Egypt (where we last saw Jeremiah), and ends with Babylon. The climax of the whole book, therefore, combines judgment and hope: judgment on Babylon and hope for Israel's future. This is an important counterbalance to Jeremiah's alleged 'pro-Babylonian' stance in the political conflicts in Jerusalem. Jeremiah had argued that the safest policy for Judah was to surrender to Babylon and avoid the massive violence and bloodshed that did eventually happen. But that did not mean that Jeremiah idealized Babylon as the source of future salvation and blessing. Babylon, though it was the agent of God's historical judgment in the immediate present, stood under God's judgment with the rest of the nations. Their time would come. And when it did, God's future would proceed through his covenant people Israel.

As we turn to the texts we should remember that this kind of prophecy had a conventional and stereotyped form of language. Jeremiah adds a great wealth of poetic imagery of his own (as we have seen him do in his accusations of Israel), but we should not read these texts in a literalistic way, looking for precise historical fulfilment of every detail or being disappointed if none seems forthcoming in the records. There is a combination of some very local knowledge (in the multitude of place names, for example) with some very stylized descriptions of military defeat, invasion, displacement, national collapse, and so on.

1. Egypt (46:1–28)

Chapter 46 contains two prophecies concerning Egypt from different historical occasions.

The first (2–12) comes from that fateful year 605 BC, *the fourth year of Jehoiakim* (cf. chs. 26 and 36), and describes the definitive battle at *Carchemish* in that year. Nebuchadnezzar's victory in that battle destroyed all Egypt's ambitions over the region and established Babylon as the new superpower that would replace the collapsed Assyrian empire. *Pharaoh Necho* had earlier marched north in 609 BC to try to support Assyria against Babylon. King Josiah had made a rather foolhardy attempt to resist him and was killed in a battle at Megiddo.[2]

---

[2] 2 Kgs 23:29–30.

But where Josiah had failed, Nebuchadnezzar decisively succeeded. Egypt was driven back, wounded and shamed (11–12).

Jeremiah's vision portrays the heat of battle and chaos of defeat (3–6). He mocks the overweening hubris of Egypt, who had thought they could flood the world with their imperial power as the Nile flooded their own fields (8). Such pride, we will find again and again in these chapters, is a prime factor in the downfall of nations. There would be no healing for them, any more than for Israel when the judgment fell (11; cf. 8:22).

The second prophesy (13–24) comes from some period after the fall of Jerusalem and refers to an attack upon the land of Egypt itself by Nebuchadnezzar. This may connect with the prophecy delivered by Jeremiah in Egypt (43:8–13) and the brief invasion by Nebuchadnezzar in 568 BC. The cities named (14) are the ones where the Jews had settled. The prophecy takes the form of a taunt song, mocking the impotent boastfulness of *the king of Egypt* (17) contrasted with *the King whose name is the LORD Almighty* (18). Jeremiah's talent for striking imagery is evident in describing Egypt in defeat as a stung *heifer*, a herd of stampeding calves, a hissing snake slithering away from danger, and a forest being chopped down (20–23). But the theological point is made in the epilogue: God's real target is the axis of political and religious power – kings and gods – who govern the nation's policy and are responsible for its fate (25–26). It's a theme that will occur often.

The beautiful words of hope for Israel (27–28) echo almost exactly 30:10–11 and have strong resonances with Isaiah.[3] But they are preceded by words of hope for Egypt too, in the first of several places in these prophecies where foreign nations are promised a restoration comparable to Israel's. What Jeremiah confines to half a verse (26b), however, Isaiah spells out in far more breathtaking eschatological visions for the future of Egypt when they turn to the Lord and experience his exodus-style saving power.[4]

2. The Philistines (47:1–7)

The word *concerning the Philistines* does not specify any particular wickedness for which they were being judged (unlike Amos 1:6–8). Its point is simply that the judgment of God (the *sword of the Lord*, 6) that was falling on Israel through the rise of Babylon would slice through other nations in the whole region. Being so strategically placed on the major route between Egypt and the empires to the

[3] E.g. Isa. 41:8–14; 43:1–5; 44:1–2.
[4] Isa. 19:19–25. Ps. 87 also includes Egypt ('Rahab') among the future native-born citizens of Zion.

north and east, the Philistine cities could not escape the turmoil of the ebb and flow of imperial ambitions. Verse 1 describes an attack on *Gaza* by Egypt – which may have been by Pharaoh Necho during his campaign of 609 BC, or possibly one that he is known to have launched in 601 BC. Verse 2 however indicates that their real enemy will come from the north, not the south – an unmistakeable allusion to the expansion of Babylonian power.

Jeremiah brings no word of hope or restoration for the Philistines, but a remarkable prophecy of Zechariah does just that – envisaging the remnant of the Philistines being cleansed and incorporated into Israel as one of the clans of Judah.[5] Psalm 87:4 goes even further, including Philistines among the native-born citizens of Zion.

3. Moab (48:1–47)

Only the prophecy concerning Babylon is longer than this one about Moab. It is the most poignant of all these oracles, probably reflecting the close relationship between the kingdoms of Israel-Judah and Moab over many centuries. As Judah's closest neighbour (they could see each other across the Jordan rift-valley), each knew the other's people, politics and places intimately. More than twenty towns in Moab are individually named. King David's ancestor Ruth came from Moab and he sent his own family there for safety, though the small empire of David and Solomon subjugated and taxed Moab. For these reasons, Moab features prominently in the oracles of other prophets.[6]

In the face of Babylonian aggression Moab made common cause with Judah in the alliance brokered by Zedekiah in 594 BC (27:3), and chapter 48 records that they paid a heavy price for that act of rebellion. Their land would be as devastated and their people as displaced as Judah's. The suffering would be horrendous and their national pride would be shattered.

Two primary notes are sounded again and again as we travel painfully through the chapter.

First, Moab is characterized by *pride and complacency*. They trusted in themselves and their god, Chemosh (7, 13). They had settled like undecanted wine on its lees that eventually tastes and smells terrible (11). Their military boasting (14), fame (17), and national arrogance (29–30), would be humbled, and their defiance of YHWH,

---

[5] Zech. 9:6–7.
[6] Amos 2:1–3; Isa. 15 – 16 (with which Jeremiah's word has many similarities); Zeph. 2:8–11; Ezek. 25:8–11.

God of Israel (26, 42),[7] would bring them the same destruction as Judah would suffer.

But secondly, the dominant tone of the whole chapter is one of *mourning and profound lament*. There is, of course, the expected weeping and wailing of the people of Moab themselves in the grievous suffering they face (4–5; 34; 38). But alongside that, and unexpected, is the summons to others (Israelites?) to weep and mourn for the agonies of their neighbour (17, 20). And most unexpected of all, God himself weeps for Moab. Three times God speaks of his own mourning (31, 32 [using four separate words for his grief], and 36). The 'I' of these verses must be God since God is the subject of the surrounding verbs (30, 35). Of course, we have heard the sobs of God before, through the tears of Jeremiah (9:10–11). The fact that God weeps not only over the suffering of his own people Israel as he brings judgment upon *them*, but also over the comparable suffering of *other* nations, is an astonishing and very important insight into the character of the God of biblical revelation. It is not enough to affirm with Ezekiel that God takes no pleasure in the death of the wicked. We must also affirm with Jeremiah that God weeps over it. It is a divine grief that found human outlet in our weeping prophet and incarnate expression in Jesus himself.

> The Godward side of wrath and judgment is grief; for God, internal grieving always accompanies wrath and judgment . . . The net effect is that God enters into a lament that is as deep and broad as the laments of the people. As with Israel [8:18–9:1, 10, 17–19; 13:17; 14:17], so with Moab, God has entered into judgment; but once the judgment has fallen (or is anticipated) God mourns with those who mourn.[8]

The last verse of the chapter (47) is another surprise. Just as Isaiah had called for refuge to be provided for the fleeing Moabites to await a better day,[9] so Jeremiah predicts a restoration of their fortunes. Whatever that may have meant in terms of later recovery for Moab (and we hear nothing of it), the remarkable point is that, once more, Jeremiah applies to a foreign nation words that we heard again and again spoken for the comfort and benefit of Israel (29:14 and throughout chs. 30 – 31).

---

[7] This probably refers to the fact that they joined Judah in rebellion against YHWH's 'servant' Nebuchadnezzar. They would have heard the word of God that Jeremiah was telling Judah (ch. 27), but they chose to ignore it just as much as Judah did.

[8] Fretheim, p. 605.

[9] Isa. 16:4–5.

4. Five smaller prophecies (49:1–39)

a. Ammon (1–6)

Ammon was north of Moab but south of Syria, closer neighbour to the northern kingdom of Israel than to Judah. Like Moab, it had kinship ties with the Israelites,[10] but there was little love lost between them. After the fall of Jerusalem it was Baalis, king of Ammon, who had instigated the murder of Gedaliah (40:14; 41:15). Like Moab also, Ammon figures in the oracles of several other prophets.[11] It seems there were running territorial disputes between them and the tribes of Gad (49:1) and Reuben who had settled on the eastern side of the Jordan. The main points of attack in Jeremiah's oracle are similar to those concerning Moab: arrogance (4) and trust in a worthless god (3). *Molek* was notorious for the cult of child-sacrifice. But the other point Ammon has in common with Moab is the promise of restoration in identical words (6). God's sovereign gift of their lands to Moab and Ammon, which Israel had been instructed to respect,[12] is here matched with a promise comparable to Israel's.

b. Edom (7–22)

No such promise of restoration comes at the end of the prophecy concerning Edom, nor is there any note of mourning at their impending doom (though there is a note of remarkable compassion for the most vulnerable victims, 11). Edom seems to have had a perennially vicious relationship with Israel, going back to the wilderness period.[13] Consequently they come under sustained condemnation and judgment. Much of what Jeremiah says here echoes the rhetoric of Obadiah. When Jerusalem fell to Nebuchadnezzar, it seems Edom took full advantage to attack and plunder Judah at its weakest moment – true to form.[14] They were never forgiven for that.[15]

This prophecy, like the others, is locally targeted. Edom was famous for its intellectual *wisdom* (7) and its impregnable mountain fortresses (16). Both would be brought low by God's judgment. And so it happened. Edom as a separate kingdom was destroyed and nomadic Arabian tribes occupied the territory.

[10] Gen. 19:36–38.
[11] Amos 1:13–15; Zeph. 2:8–11; Ezek. 25:1–7.
[12] See the remarkable instructions, and their theological rationale, in Deut. 2:9, 16–23.
[13] Num. 20:14–21.
[14] Cf. Amos 1:11–12.
[15] Ps. 137:7; Lam. 4:21–22; Ezek. 25:12–14; 35:1–15; Isa. 34:5–15; 63:1–6.

c. Damascus/Syria (23–27)

The kingdom of Syria to the north lay right in the path of any invader from Mesopotamia heading round the fertile crescent towards Palestine. So once again, Jeremiah sees that the turmoil caused by Babylon's expansion will engulf Syria as well, and they will be as powerless to resist as *a woman in labour* (24). The judgment about to fall on them in Jeremiah's day, though much delayed, will fulfil the prophecy made more than a century earlier by Amos.[16]

Damascus was a famously beautiful city (and remains one of the oldest continuously inhabited cities in the world). Even God turned up as a tourist, it seems, from the curious note in verse 25. That God delighted in Jerusalem, the city that bore his name – and was therefore stricken with grief at its impending destruction – was well known. That God should use the very same words about a foreign city in apparent lament for its fate too, is another remarkable insight on the universality of Israel's God. God's love is far from parochial or nationalistic.

d. Kedar/Arabia (28–33)

Kedar was the name of a group of tribes in the desert regions of the Arabian peninsula to the east, lying between the Jordanian lands and Mesopotamia.[17] From Jerusalem's perspective Kedar was as far to the east as Kittim was to the west (2:10). The nomadic tribes living there would also feel the wrath of Nebuchadnezzar. The things they felt gave them security (their protection by the distances and caves of the desert itself, so that they thought they had no need of fortified cities, 30–31), would be futile against his rapacious raids.[18]

Kedar was the name of one of the sons of Ishmael, another being Nebaioth.[19] Significantly, both are envisaged as joining the nations who will be attracted to the light that will shine in Israel when the glory of God will arise in their midst.[20] Arabia was indeed among the nations present in Jerusalem on the day of Pentecost.[21] There have been believers among Arab nations since New Testament days, and we long for their number to grow within the heartlands of Arabia itself.

[16] Amos 1:4.
[17] The location of *Hazor* is unknown, but being paired with Kedar it cannot refer to the fortified city in the northern part of Israel.
[18] Cf. also Isa. 21:16–17; Ezek. 27:21.
[19] Gen. 25:13.
[20] Isa. 60:7.
[21] Acts 2:11.

e. Elam/Persia (34–39)

Elam was a small ancient kingdom at the head of what we now call the Persian Gulf (southern Iran), and was eventually assimilated into the wider Persian Empire. It is amazing that the reach of Jeremiah's prophetic vision took in nations on the far side of Babylon itself. The language used against them echoes many things that God had said he would do to arrogant Israel. It is noteworthy that every verb in these verses has God as its subject – including the final affirmation of restoration in verse 39. Residents of Elam were also among those who heard the preaching of the gospel by the apostles on the day of Pentecost.[22]

Theological and expository reflections

Themes that run through these chapters (amplified even more in 50 – 51) include the following:[23]

- The folly of human arrogance, bombast, hubris and inflated ambitions.
- The futility of trusting in false gods that turn out to be useless in the day of disaster.
- The illusion of security and complacent faith in one's own resources or natural defences – God (and the Nebuchadnezzars under his mandate) can penetrate them with ease.
- The 'rebound' effect of violence and aggression – those who violate even fallen conventions of humane behaviour find themselves facing divine and human retribution.
- The terrible suffering caused by war, and the floods of weeping and mourning – human and divine – that give voice to it.
- The interaction of judgment and hope in God's sovereign weaving of international history. Nations rise and fall and rise again. God remains constant according to principles announced in chapter 18.

Above all, what these chapters show is that God deals with all nations consistently. The book of Jeremiah has given us the most lurid details of God's impending judgment on Israel, his own covenant people. These chapters would remind the exiles that they had not been singled out for unfair treatment. All nations are accountable to God, are judged by God. 'One after another, these nations are brought

[22] Acts 2:8.
[23] For more in-depth reflection on the contemporary and missiological significance of the oracles against the nations, see Wright, *Message of Ezekiel*, pp. 229–272.

before the bar of justice, accountable to God for who they are and what they have done ... No matter how great their empires, how sophisticated their policies, how brilliant their officials, God will hold all of them accountable.'[24]

And if there is hope to be found it will be found, as much for any nation as for Israel, in God's power to redeem and restore.

[24] Fretheim, p. 579.

Jeremiah 50:1 – 51:64
33. Sinking Babylon

These two vast chapters are Jeremiah's equivalent to Isaiah 40 – 55. Their message is the same: God will bring crushing judgment upon Babylon and as a result the exiles of Judah will be able to return to their own land, forgiven and redeemed. In view of this future certainty, let the exiles put their hope and faith in God, whose invincible power in creation and history will accomplish this. And let them be ready to flee Babylon when the time comes.

But both Isaiah and Jeremiah go further and describe the judgment of Babylon and the restoration of Israel in language that takes us to a cosmic plane beyond the historical events of the fall of one nation and revival of another. Rather, the whole sequence is seen as symbolic of God's universal judgment on all that stands in arrogant and evil opposition to God, and the extension of God's salvation to include people from all nations and the joy of all creation. Ultimately the message of these chapters, echoed and amplified in the book of Revelation, is that the victory of God spells death for Babylon (and all it stands for) and life for the world.

Within the structure of the book, chapters 50 – 51 are linked to chapters 25 – 29 and match the message of the Book of Consolation in chapters 30 – 33. In chapters 25 and 26 we stepped back to the ominous fourth year of Jehoiakim, 605 BC, when Jeremiah, at the half-way point of his ministry, declared the certainty of exile. But in that year also he declared the certainty of God's eventual judgment on Babylon – and indeed on all nations in a terrible oracle of universal judgment (25:15–38). That picture is amplified in these final chapters. Chapters 27 – 29, however, took us forward to the fourth year of Zedekiah, 594 BC, when the *first* deportation had already happened. At that moment, Jeremiah urged Judah and the other nations to submit to Nebuchadnezzar and spare themselves the terrible consequences of rebellion (ch. 27). And in the same year, he wrote his letter to that first group of exiles (ch. 29), telling them to settle down in Babylon, in the confidence that a future generation ('seventy years') would return to the land. At that point in the editing of the book, we are treated to the beautiful exposition of that hope of return (chs. 30 – 33). *And it was in that same year* (594 BC), that Jeremiah sent the scroll containing chapters 50 – 51 to Babylon itself, with this awesome message of judgment on Babylon and hope for Israel. We learn that from the instructions that accompanied it (51:59–64). The dates match.[1]

We need to read these chapters, then, through the ears of those exiles of *both* deportations. They must see themselves as a people with a past full of guilt, a present full of suffering, but a future full of hope – the hope of forgiveness and new life. By contrast, Babylon is an empire with a present full of unrivalled and arrogant world dominion, but a future filled with judgment and eternal death. These mirrored reversals, this intertwining of judgment and redemption, bring the *words of Jeremiah* to their climax and close (51:64) on the resounding note of the universal sovereignty of *the King, whose name is the* LORD *Almighty* (51:57).[2]

And on that invincible purpose of God rests the gospel, the good news that all that is evil will ultimately be judged and destroyed and that God's people and God's creation will be liberated from bondage. It may not feel like it as we read through Jeremiah 50 – 51, but in this massive oracle we are already anticipating the cosmic accomplishment of the cross and resurrection of Christ and the climactic events that will accompany his return. That is why the last book of the Bible can make such extensive theological and rhetorical use of these last chapters of the book of Jeremiah to depict the destruction of evil and the victory of God.[3]

1. Six movements

It would be important to take the time to read right through both chapters. And when you finish, you may well feel exhausted and overwhelmed by the swirling imagery and recurring themes, and the disturbing juxtaposition of the most lurid and lengthy passages of utter devastation with moments of tender promise. Many scholars have despaired of finding any structure here and see the chapters as a loose collection of sayings. But some discern a pattern of 'movements' and progression of thought. The outline that follows is based on the work of Kenneth T. Aitken and is a plausible way of

[1] Compare 51:59 with 27:1, 28:1 and 29:3.
[2] Cf. 46:18 and 48:15; and the unchallengeable power of God in 50:44b.
[3] See especially Rev. 18.

structuring the material, though other ways of dividing it can be proposed.[4]

Aitken suggests that 50:1–3 and 51:54–58 form an outer framework that summarizes the essential content: the proclamation/cry that Babylon will fall beneath the judgment of God meted out through a conquering foe. Within those bookends, the remainder falls into six sections.

a. First movement (50:4–20)

The main message of this movement is carried by the matching beginning (4–5) and ending (19–20) which strongly echo the promises of restoration in chapters 30 – 31, and especially build on the new covenant promise of forgiveness by, and intimate relationship with, *the LORD their God* (4; 31:31–34). Within this outer affirmation, there is another balancing description of Israel as *lost sheep* (6), *a scattered flock* (17), who have been *devoured* by the great empires (7, 17–18). Those enemies imagined Israel was *guilty, for they sinned against the LORD* (7), and they were right. But if they thought they themselves were *not guilty*, they were very much mistaken, since God's retributive punishment was about to fall on them too (18). So the people of Israel need to be ready to *flee* and return home (8, 16b), because, as the central section expands (9–16), Babylon itself is going to be destroyed by *an alliance of great nations from the land of the north* (9). It is intentionally ironic that Babylon itself had been that great enemy from the north against Israel, and now will suffer the same fate. What they had done to others, God will visit upon their own heads (15–16). And the reason? Because in their crimes against humanity they had *sinned against the LORD* (14; cf. 24, 29). So there will be two great reversals – in the situations respectively of Israel and of Babylon. Those who stand in *everlasting covenant* with God will move from judgment to forgiveness, while those who stand in flaunted rebellion against God will move from plundering aggression to utter desolation.

All the themes that will surface again and again in the following movements have been put on the table in this opening one, the two major ones being the certainty of Babylon's ultimate collapse and the promise of Israel's restoration.

b. Second movement (50:21–32)

The single focus of this movement is on the destruction of Babylon.

---

[4] Aitken, 'The Oracles Against Babylon', pp. 25–63. Aitken's division of the material is followed by Smothers (in Scalise, Keown and Smothers, pp. 360–362), and more loosely also by Stulman, pp. 372–383.

It is portrayed as carried out by other nations but entirely under the command of the Lord. The primary motif is a list of battle orders, directed against the polluting arrogance of this evil empire (31–32).

The appalling character of the empire sharpens in this act. Babylon is no longer a nation that has merely 'sinned against God' (50:14) but is at this point the 'hammer of the whole earth' (50:23), 'a horror among the nations' (50:23), a country that has 'challenged' (50:24) and 'arrogantly defied the LORD' (50:29); indeed Babylon is the 'arrogant one', the epitome of insolence (50:31–32). The true colours of Babylon now appear. Such pride and aggression incite Yahweh to address the nation directly. 'I am against you . . .' (50:31; see also 51:25). If there were any doubts as to the appropriateness of divine judgment, they are now gone. Babylon's affront to God must be avenged.[5]

c. Third movement (50:33–46)

This movement begins, like verses 4–20, with the promise of Israel's restoration, in spite of their apparently powerless situation (33–34). Like Isaiah 40 – 55, Jeremiah draws on the exodus as the source of his language. As in Egypt, Israel in Babylon seemed to be held fast by a strong empire that was *refusing to let them go*. But YHWH *their Redeemer* is stronger still, and *will vigorously defend their cause* – as he did in Egypt.

After another section in which God's comprehensive judgment on Babylon is described (possibly using the *sword* as equivalent to the plagues on Egypt in their devastating effect; 35–38), the point is added that YHWH will be able to do all this because his power is beyond challenge. The rhetorical questions of verse 44b are very reminiscent of Isaiah 40 – 55: *Who is like me and who can challenge me? And what shepherd* (i.e. king or emperor) *can stand against me?*

d. Fourth movement (51:1–33)

The tirade against Babylon intensifies throughout this long movement. But we are emphatically reminded of the reason that lies behind it. Verse 5 begins with *for*, making it clear that God's dealings with Babylon are for the sake of his ongoing purpose through Israel. Even the word order is emphatic: (lit.) 'For **not** widowed (forsaken),

---

5 Stulman, p. 375.

Israel and Judah, from/by their God, from YHWH of Hosts.' Here is God's blunt answer to the imagination of the nations that Israel had so sinned against *the LORD, the hope of their ancestors,* that he had abandoned them (50:7). Not at all, says God. The relationship goes on, in spite of the acknowledged reality of their guilt (5b)[6] – for that will be forgiven (50:20). God's people remain *the people of his inheritance* (19).

Babylon, meanwhile, is incurably sick (8, language used before about Israel, 8:22). Like all empires it flourishes for a while, then languishes in terminal decay. The remnant of Israel in their midst may have prayerfully worked for its good, in obedience to Jeremiah's instruction to 'seek the welfare' of the city where God had sent them (29:7). But not even the presence and wishes of believers in their midst could bring ultimate healing. In the end, the only choice (as Lot faced; cf. 50:40) would be, *leave her.*

Babylon's evil grows to global scale, as the name takes on the symbolism of universal, destructive arrogance. She has poisoned *the whole earth* (7), reverted to her original sky-scraping arrogance of the tower of Babel (9), and become like a volcano that would *destroy the whole earth* (25). But her destruction is decreed because the true God of all the earth, *the Maker of all things,* is sovereign over all creation and all man-made gods and ambitions (15–19).

e. Fifth movement (51:34–44)

The exiles speak for the first time in verses 34–35. They describe the experience of 587 BC like being chewed up and *swallowed, flesh* and *blood,* by a monster *serpent.* So they call for God to act in retribution.[7] God promises exactly that, in a gory reversal that will see Babylon itself poisoned like wild beasts, then slain as in sacrifice (38–40), but not before it had been compelled to *spew out what he has swallowed* (44), a graphic way to portray the release of the exiles that hints at the 'death and resurrection' of Jonah – and a greater than Jonah. Cosmic imagery completes the picture with *the sea,* symbol of chaos, swamping Babylon like a surging tsunami, leaving behind nothing but deserted desolation (42–43). Evil will release its victims and then itself be swallowed up in its own source. God summons evil to its own self-destruction.

---

[6] *Their land is full of guilt.* Some versions understand 'their land' as referring to the Babylonians (e.g. ESV). But it seems to me that the logic of the verse is that both halves refer to Israel, and expresses the familiar paradox that God deals with the guilt and continues the relationship, through his sovereign grace and pardon.

[7] Cf. Ps. 137.

f. Sixth movement (51:45–53)

Such is no place for the people of God to linger, so the call goes out once more for the exiles to flee from Babylon, but to do so with no fear, for its destiny will not be theirs (45–46). The cosmic scale of Babylon's sin (responsible for *the slain in all the earth*, not only *Israel's slain;* 49), is matched by the cosmic scale of rejoicing when *Babylon must fall.* The celebration of *heaven and earth and all that is in them* is the joy and relief that erupts when the Lord finally brings all evil to an end (48). It is the same creational rejoicing that rings out in Psalm 96:10–13. When the Lord who is truly king (57) comes to put things right (i.e. to 'judge the earth'), then the whole creation will rejoice. For, as Paul puts it, the liberation of God's people will herald the liberation of all creation.[8]

2. Six themes

Having surveyed the six movements in linear sequence, it will be helpful to 'cut the cake' differently, noting the major themes that occur repeatedly. Please be sure to read through the list of verses in the footnotes for each of the following sections, to see how the repeated concepts flow through the two chapters.

a. The violence of Babylon will be avenged[9]

A strong retributive dimension surfaces again and again. While the book as a whole clearly affirms that God had used Babylon, in the same way that he had used Assyria, as the tool of his judgment against the sin of his own people, that did not exonerate Babylon from the wanton and excessive violence that characterized its expansion. Empires are human constructs and human beings tend towards aggression and violence, as the earliest biblical narratives make clear. But the principle articulated by Jesus applies not just to individuals but to whole systems, cultures and empires, that 'all who draw the sword will die by the sword'.[10] Violence bounces back and usually bounces higher each time. In the end God 'visits' the evil upon the evildoers such that they become the victim of their own wickedness, receiving back what they have done to others. So it will be for Babylon.

---

[8] Rom. 8:18–21.
[9] 50:11–12, 15, 28– 29; 51:6, 11, 24, 35, 49, 56.
[10] Matt. 26:52.

b. The arrogance of Babylon will be brought low[11]

Along with violence often goes arrogance, for when you are 'top nation', wielding the most powerful military force in the world, it is easy to feel at liberty to behave with self-interest and greed and simply crush opposition or dissent. Such hubris is seen in all its godless ugliness in these chapters. The trouble with such behaviour, however, is that it breeds enemies who will eventually strike back. And by that means the pendulum of God's justice swings back, through human agents who bring the boasting tyrant low.

c. The gods of Babylon will be powerless to save them[12]

False gods never fail to fail. Israel had learnt this the hard way in abandoning the Lord God for the gods of Canaan. Babylon would learn it too when the great imperial gods of their Mesopotamian pantheon would prove impotent before the power of YHWH and his agents. Jeremiah's mockery of the gods of Babylon is not as rhetorically dominant as in Isaiah 40 – 55, but just as forthright. The idolatry of Babylon, of course, like all national idolatries ancient and modern, was the glorification of their own empire, wealth, resources, arms and conquest. In trusting their gods they were trusting their own military, cultural and economic dominance (notice the list of things that constituted *a land of idols* in 50:35–38). The great statues of gods and kings proclaimed their self-made power to the terrified world – but they would be the ones terrified and powerless in the end.

d. The land of Babylon will be devastated by enemies from the north[13]

Jeremiah's commission to be the agent of God 'to uproot and tear down, to destroy and overthrow' (1:10) had been fully exercised on the people of Israel. Babylon had been the physical agent of those actions, but it was the words of Jeremiah that had systematically dismantled the whole structure of Israel's trusted traditions and institutions. Now, in classic reversal, Babylon will feel the full force of that prophetic commission on themselves. And in matching classic irony, the agent of God's wrath will be 'from the north', just as Babylon had descended on Judah from the north.

---

[11] 50:31–32, 36–37; 51:13, 41. Condemnation of the arrogance of empires is strong also in Isa. 13:19; 46 – 47; Ezek. 26 – 30; and well illustrated in Dan. 3 – 6.

[12] 50:2, 38; 51:17, 44, 47.

[13] 50:3, 9, 13, 23b, 39–41; 51:1–4, 11, 25–26, 27–29, 37, 42–43, 48b, 54–58, 64.

The language of destruction is the most prominent tone throughout these chapters and hardly needs listing. The overwhelming point is that Babylon's fall will be final and irreversible. This raises a historical and a theological point.

Historically, Babylon did not fall as a result of massive armed invasion and destruction. It was taken without resistance, it seems, when Cyrus king of Persia decided to expand his already vast conquests west and east to the south. So we need to see that there is a high degree of conventional rhetoric of conquest in the hyperbolic descriptions of enemy attack, defeat and destruction. The fact that these details were not literally fulfilled in the event does not invalidate their key affirmation: Babylon will fall, irrevocably. It did.[14]

The theological point lies in that irrevocability. Human empires by their nature replace one another. When a tyrant is toppled, rejoicing may last for a short spring and a honeymoon summer. But another tyrant may usher in an even longer winter. And so, at the historical level, the end of Babylon was but the beginning of Persia . . . and then Greece, and then Rome. . . However, the good news was, first of all for the exiles, that the fall of Babylon would genuinely spell the end of its power and the end of their captivity in that place. Those who returned home from Babylon would never be taken back. But secondly, at a deeper level, the language of permanent and irreversible destruction of the evil empire surely speaks of the final defeat of all evil, the eradication of all oppression, ultimately the death of death. These prophetic images, then, point not only to the victory of Cyrus over Babylon, but ultimately to the irreversible victory of God over all that Babylon stands for. They point us eventually to Horizon 3 and Revelation 18.

e. The fall of Babylon will signal the restoration and return of Israel[15]

The overwhelming weight of words in these chapters are words of judgment. But the underlying and far more enduring reality is the promise of redemption. Or to put it more precisely, when God acts in judgment it is to serve God's redemptive purpose. The fall of Babylon not only involves God bringing down on them the retributive consequences of their own sin, but also signals the restoration of God's people to their land, a fresh start in their covenantal

---

[14] In the same way, we know that the actual return of the exiles to Judah did not literally match up to the soaring poetic rhetoric of Isa. 40 – 55. But that does not invalidate those prophecies: the oppressor was destroyed; there was a 'new exodus'; the people did return.
[15] 50:4–5, 8, 19–20, 33–34; 51:5–6, 10, 45, 50.

435

relationship, and the first step towards the establishing of that new covenant based on God's forgiveness.

f. The fate of Babylon carries cosmic significance[16]

It is clear to see how the language describing Babylon's sin and destruction grows in scope and intensity through the movements. A historical event that was a matter between the tiny kingdom of Judah and the imperial ambitions of Nebuchadnezzar escalates into language about many or all nations and the whole earth. And matching that (and of course infinitely surpassing it) is the universal sovereignty of God as creator of the whole earth. This is Jeremiah's way of making the same point that Isaiah makes when he portrays the historical fall of Babylon and return of the exiles in terms that involve 'all flesh' and 'the ends of the earth'.

All that God was doing in and for Israel, and all that God did in the defeat of their oppressors, was, at one level, simply the out-working of the historical course of events over which God is sovereign. But this prophetic language invests those events with cosmic 'sign-ificance'. That is, they point onwards beyond their own horizon to the ultimate horizon of God's redemptive purpose for his whole creation and all nations. That redemptive purpose, as we have said, inevitably demands the final defeat and destruction of evil and all that defies God and seeks to destroy God's people. The event so dramatically portrayed in chapters 50 – 51 was the necessary prelude to the historical future for Judah that had been promised in chapters 30 – 33. And similarly, the event portrayed in Revelation 18, in language richly borrowed from Jeremiah, is the necessary prelude to the eternal future for the whole creation that we glimpse in Revelation 21 – 22.

The word has been spoken and written down. All that remained was for the exiles to hear, for the last time, the word of the Lord through the *words of Jeremiah* – which they did once more (as in ch. 29) by way of the diplomatic mailbag carried, this time, by Seraiah the brother of Baruch on a royal mission to Babylon with king Zedekiah himself (51:59). It would have been a sizeable scroll, but in view of its fate (63) we may be sure that one or both of the brothers kept a copy of it for posterity and its place in the canon of scripture.

Jeremiah's instructions to Seraiah include three significant actions: to read *aloud* the word of God through the written words of Jeremiah – effectively the reading of Scripture (61); to pray aloud words of

---

[16] 50:23, 46; 51:7, 9, 15–19, 25, 27, 41, 48, 49.

reminder to God of God's own word, thereby affirming its certainty (62); to perform a symbolic action with accompanying words, thereby demonstrating in act and word the expected future (63–64). The combination of Scripture reading, prayer and symbolic action with explanatory words, is powerful and suggestive.

Last words matter, even though Jeremiah was still years from his deathbed. And these last words (in the book if not in his life), though they are characteristically words of judgment against Babylon, are also reflexively words of hope and future salvation for Israel. Babylon would sink like a stone. Israel would rise to newness of life by the power of God's word.

The last line of chapter 51 (lit., 'up to here *the words of Jeremiah*'), uses the precise words with which the book began. And the editor would want to insist that in hearing *the words of Jeremiah* through reading their written record in the book, we have indeed been hearing 'the word of the LORD' (1:1–2).

Theological and expository reflections

How might one possibly preach a text like Jeremiah 50 – 51? Three reflections may help.

- When we contemplate texts of terror such as this, the unvarnished rhetoric of the wrath of God against his enemies, it is sobering to draw them to Horizon 2, the New Testament gospel of the death and resurrection of Christ. For then we are reminded that all of us stand with Babylon as enemies of God and deserving of his judgment. Our sins may not have scaled Babylon's arrogant heights of imperial ambition, but we cannot avoid the verdict of Paul that all of us, Jew or Gentile, share in the rebellion of our race against our creator. Nor can we forget the humbling truth that 'because of his great love for us, God, who is rich in mercy made us alive with Christ', and that 'while we were God's enemies, we were reconciled to him through the death of his Son'.[17] And above all we remember that, in that death of Christ, God bore in himself the full weight of God's uttermost wrath against all sin and evil (for which even the language of Jer. 50 – 51 is inadequate), and 'rescued us from the dominion of darkness and brought us into the kingdom of the Son he loves, in whom we have redemption, the forgiveness of sins'.[18] Contemplation, then, of this singular historical act of God's judgment drives us

[17] Eph. 2:4–5; Rom. 5:10.
[18] Col. 1:13–14.

to gratitude for the rescuing mercy and grace of God in which alone we stand, and do not sink to the depths with Babylon.

- Then, as we have hinted above, we find that the New Testament itself reads these chapters at Horizon 3, using them as a way of portraying, on the one hand the Roman empire as the 'Babylon-lookalike' of their day, and on the other hand the ultimate cosmic victory of God over all evil in all history in all the world, as the necessary precursor to the redemption and renewal of all creation. It would be very helpful at this moment to simply read through the whole of Revelation 18 and marvel at the number of direct echoes of the themes we have identified in Jeremiah 50 – 51. We notice especially how the action of 'a mighty angel' replicates the action of Seraiah (Rev. 18:21). But don't stop. Read on into Revelation 19, for there the *implied* message on which the book of Jeremiah ends (namely that the oppressor will eventually be overthrown and God's people liberated), breaks forth into the fourfold hallelujah – the rejoicing of creation in the victory of God.

  In this sense, even such chapters as Jeremiah 50 – 51 can take their place within the gospel. For it is assuredly good news that evil will not triumph for ever, that tyrants will not have the last word, that satanic pride, greed, aggression, violence and death will ultimately be destroyed. That is the invincible will of God and the ultimate realization of the kingdom of God. So when we pray, 'thy kingdom come, thy will be done, on earth as in heaven', let us remember what such prayer includes.

- But meanwhile, we live between Horizons 2 and 3, between the victory of the cross and resurrection of Christ, and the ultimate implementation and consummation of that victory at the return of Christ. We live in the fallen world of evil and oppression, but we live in hope of redemption. In that sense, our position is comparable to the exiles in Babylon. And for that reason we must listen carefully to the balance of what Jeremiah wrote to them. For in fact he wrote and sent *two scrolls*[19] in quick succession in the early years of Zedekiah – the letter we have in chapter 29, and this massive oracle in chapters 50 – 51. Their message is not contradictory but complementary.[20]

[19] The word *sēper*, 'scroll', is the same for the 'letter' of ch. 29 and the oracle of 50 – 51.

[20] Many scholars have denied the authenticity of Jer. 50 – 51 on the grounds that somebody who was so manifestly 'pro-Babylonian' in chs. 25, 27 and 29, could not have spoken or written in such an 'anti-Babylonian' tone in chs. 50 – 51. But this reduces the whole issue to a shallow and simplistic level of political alignment, as if Jeremiah was simply the pawn of one of the squabbling factions in Jerusalem. Jeremiah

In his letter (ch. 29, see exposition there)[21], Jeremiah tells the exiles to accept reality, settle down in Babylon, and live there with God and as agents of God's Abrahamic blessing by praying for, and seeking the welfare of, the city where God had put them. God's people live *in* the world and have a mission to pursue in the world, as citizens who are 'eager to do good' (Paul), as salt and light who stand against corruption and darkness (Jesus). Daniel exemplifies both. These instructions and the examples still carry authority and relevance for us today. We have a mission in and to society, even the pagan society around us.

But in chapters 50 – 51 Jeremiah shows that he knows the true colours of Babylon: an arrogant empire with an idolatrous culture held together by military aggression, violence and threat. Daniel and his friends knew all about that too. He is aware of the fingerprints of Satan on the sceptre of human power and authority. We are called to such an awareness also, to understand the ambiguity of our location *in* the world but not *of* the world. The empire surrounds us but does not own us.

And for those whose lives in this world are, still today, lived under the threat or the reality of state persecution, violence and death, the visions of Jeremiah 50 – 51 provide a vehicle of hope. God will not allow the tyranny to last forever. Louis Stulman applies their message as follows: these texts, he says,

> belong to the world of worship and not warfare, their weapons are rhetoric and imagination, not military hardware . . . The exiles dare to make a number of startling assertions. They declare

was not 'pro' or 'anti' Babylon in those terms. He saw clearly that *YHWH the God of Israel* was sovereignly using Babylon as the agent of his purpose of judgment against Judah, and therefore advised the people to submit to that *divine* will by submitting to God's (for the present time) servant, Nebuchadnezzar. Rebellion would not only be resistance to God but would make their fate much worse than it need have been (as happened). But Jeremiah saw equally clearly that Babylon, like all empires, while it might fulfil God's purposes for a season, would ultimately fall victim to its own hubris and violence. Its time would come. Its end was certain. So he advised the people to endure the reality of Babylon *present*, but to live in the hope of Babylon's *future*. Ronald Clements, even though he sees chs. 50 – 51 as later additions, affirms this compatibility in tension: 'We can understand not simply that the two positions can be held together but that they can be used to support one another. The expectation of divine eschatological judgment upon Babylon at an undefined point in the future can inculcate a political stance which enjoins acceptance of the unwelcome conditions of the present' (p. 264).

[21] Pp. 289–299.

- that the Lord reigns and is involved in the world;
- that God's purposes are realized in and through the contingencies of history;
- that the plight of suffering people is not beyond the scope of God's power and concern;
- that God neither forgets nor ignores those whose lives are full of pain and brokenness;
- that God acts on behalf of those who cannot defend themselves;
- that unjust and oppressive power structures will not endure;
- that raw power is not ultimate reality;
- that acts of callous disregard for life do not impugn divine justice;
- that God holds all people responsible for their actions regardless of military muscle and religious claims; and
- that God's salvation extends beyond the borders of any one people.[22]

Metaphorically, there is a time to settle and a time to flee, and the rhythm of the messages of Jeremiah 29 and 50–51 can be the rhythm of the believer's life. That balance preserves us from the danger of self-righteous separation from the world, on the one hand, and the danger of uncritical acceptance of, and absorption by the world, on the other. In our daily working lives we serve God in the place he has put us, seeking the welfare of the community around us. In our regular worship we 'flee from Babylon', reminding ourselves of its true colours and its ultimate future. Babylon may be our present home, the place of our calling and mission. But the future belongs to the kingdom of God and our destiny is God's new creation in which all the glory and splendour of the kingdoms of the world, purged of evil and redeemed, will be brought into the city of God.[23]

[22] Stulman, p. 385.
[23] Rev. 21:24–27.

Jeremiah 52:1–34
34. The end . . . and a small beginning

Why, we might well ask, if 'the words of Jeremiah end here' at the end of chapter 51, have we got one more chapter in the book? The editors of the final scroll of the book of Jeremiah decided to add this closing appendix (which is largely a word-for-word repetition of 2 Kgs 24:18 – 25:21, and 25:27–30), for several probable reasons. Chapter 52 achieves the following:

First, it provides *literary* closure to the structure of the book as a whole. This chapter clearly matches the book's editorial opening, by describing the events that happened 'when the people of Judah went into exile' (1:1–3).

Secondly, it completes the great *historical* sweep of the book by reference to the key dates. The book begins with the call of Jeremiah in 627 BC (1:2), reaches its first climax in 598 BC with the exile of Jehoiachin and the first group of deportees (24:1; 52:28), then its major climax in 597 BC with the destruction of Jerusalem (39; 52:29), then reports a further taking of exiles in 582 BC (52:30), and finally ends with the release of King Jehoiachin in 560 BC (52:31). So, although the ministry of Jeremiah himself lasted approximately forty years (we do not know the year of his death in Egypt), the book of Jeremiah spans approximately sixty-seven years, from 627 BC – 560 BC.

Thirdly, it rounds off and confirms the *theological* message of the whole book, while at the same time vindicating and validating the whole prophetic ministry of Jeremiah. His commission had been, in the power of God's word, 'to uproot and tear down, to destroy and overthrow, to build and to plant' (1:10). The first four have now been categorically completed. Jeremiah's preaching has systematically dismantled all the foundations of Israel's self-confident assurance (temple, election, covenant, law and monarchy), and now Nebuchadnezzar has systematically demolished the physical realities of statehood (city, temple, royal palace, military defences, and above all, land).

So we need to read the bald account of the fall of the city with all those theological resonances in mind. Sometimes that theology is explicit, as in verses 2–3, where Zedekiah's political act of rebellion is synonymous with his doing *evil in the eyes of the* LORD, and Nebuchadnezzar's taking captives into exile is synonymous with God thrusting them *from his presence.* Sometimes the theology is implied but very close to the surface, as in verses 17–23, where the painfully detailed description of the desecration of the temple by the Babylonian soldiers (who treat its holy objects as just so much loot), fulfils Jeremiah's words that God himself would abandon and destroy the house that had become a 'den of robbers' (7:12–14). That was not just a desecration of the temple but a calculated insult to the God who was presumed to live there. YHWH had become just one more on the list of defeated gods of the nations conquered by imperial Babylon.[1]

The account is concise but comprehensive: Nebuchadnezzar's army starve the city for a year and a half then breach its walls and invade (4–8); they capture, torture and enslave the king, after executing the royal household (9–11); they systematically destroy and burn the city (12–14); they take the elite of the country into exile, leaving the poorest to remain in the land (15–16); they brazenly loot the wealth and treasures of Solomon's temple before burning it (17–23, 13); they round up and ruthlessly slaughter the nation's religious, military and political leadership (24–27). King, city, people, temple, leadership – all gone. Never were four words more fully realized: 'uprooted, torn down, destroyed, overthrown'.

The word of the Lord through the words of Jeremiah has accomplished its work, in spite of the unbelief and resistance of the people. Or rather, has accomplished part of its work – the necessary first part of judgment and destruction. Can there be confidence, then, that God's word will finish its remaining task in the rebuilding and replanting of the nation? This final chapter provides two hints, as we shall see, that such hope in God will be justified and that chapters 30 – 33 will not be an idle dream.

Fourthly, therefore, this closing chapter 52 has a *pastoral* purpose. It may not have amounted to much, but those who would read this conclusion to the great scroll of the book of Jeremiah while still in exile would discern two grounds for hope in it. First, the fact that they existed at all as a surviving remnant of Israel in exile, and second

---

[1] 'The wealth of the city and the prestige of Yahweh are both forfeited in a single act. This indeed is the Good Friday of the temple!' (Brueggemann [1991], p. 289).

that King Jehoichin, the exiled king in the line of David, has his 'head lifted up' (31, literally) and is given a 'seat of honour'.

As to the first, the listing of the number of exiles over three deportations (28–30) is an insertion in the quoted text from 2 Kings 25. The numbers are very precise, and the first one (3,023 in the deportation under Jehoiachin in 598 BC) is considerably smaller than the number mentioned for that deportation in 2 Kings 24:14, where it is ten thousand. The most probable explanation is that Jeremiah 52 refers to the numbers of adult males, while 2 Kings gives a round number for the total number of people – i.e. between three and four times the number of men. So the number given in 52:30 (4,600), if that refers to adult males, implies a total exiled population of around fifteen to eighteen thousand people.

Now you could think of that number in two ways. On the one hand, it is graphic proof of the almost total (but not quite) destruction of the nation. Those left in the land were only the poorest. Those who had gone off to Egypt had walked off the stage of God's purposes. Only a few thousand remained, and those in abject captivity in a foreign land. As Amos had prophesied so long ago, Israel would survive, but 'as a shepherd saves from the lion's mouth only two leg bones or a piece of an ear, so will the Israelites . . . be rescued'.[2] But on the other hand, that number was a precious guarantee of the future. Israel would survive, not because of some national durability, but because God would rescue them from the stomach of the lion. And they would be rescued not as mere fragments of sheep bone and ears, but as his redeemed flock restored to their land and covenant fellowship, 'for I will forgive the remnant I spare' (50:17–20). The 'good figs' might be few, but their future was secure in the promises of God (24:4–7; 29:10–14).

And finally, the book ends, as does the great Deuteronomistic history (Joshua, Judges, Samuel and Kings), with an event in the midst of the exile that gave a small signal of hope, of 'grace in the end'.[3] King Jehoiachin was not exactly a success as a king. He reigned for three months in Jerusalem as an eighteen-year-old, surrendered the city to Nebuchadnezzar and then spent thirty-seven years in a Babylonian prison. Jeremiah's estimate of him is both scathing and filled with tragic pathos (22:2–30). He will end his days in exile (as he did), and he will in effect be the end of the line of David's earthly successors on the throne of the kingdom of Judah (as he was).

And yet, and yet . . . Even though that remained the ultimate verdict on him, God grants him a measure of grace and rehabilitation

[2] Amos 3:12.
[3] *Grace in the End* is the evocative title of J. Gordon McConville's book, subtitled *A Study in Deuteronomic Theology* (Grand Rapids: Zondervan, 1993).

that could be taken as a small sign. If grace could be shown to their exiled king then God had not abandoned his people. *Awel-Marduk* became king in 560 BC,[4] and his release of Jehoiachin may have been to mark his coronation with a token of generosity. It went beyond mere release, however. He (literally) 'lifted up the head' of the king of Judah,[5] treated him as a friend, elevated him above the kings of other captive nations and granted him a kind of state pension.

The release of their captive king would doubtless have been grasped by the exiles as a sign from God of the eventual release of the rest of the exiles from captivity. Exile would not be the death of the nation, for God would open their prison. God would raise them from their grave.[6]

Only a glimmer of hope, but a glimmer indeed. This last in the line of kings descended from David, though raised from prison, would still die in exile. But there is the faintest glow of light on Horizon 2, when 'great David's Greater Son', a descendant indeed of David through Jehoiachin (Matt. 1:12), would be 'appointed the Son of God in power by his resurrection from the dead, Jesus Christ our Lord'.[7]

---

[4] This is the Babylonian form of his name. Most earlier English versions give the Hebrew form of the name: 'Evil-Merodach'.

[5] As Pharaoh did for his imprisoned cup-bearer (Gen. 40:20–22).

[6] Ezek. 37.

[7] Rom. 1:3–4.

The Bible Speaks Today: Old Testament series

The Message of Genesis 1 – 11
The dawn of creation
David Atkinson

The Message of Genesis 12 – 50
From Abraham to Joseph
Joyce G. Baldwin

The Message of Exodus
The days of our pilgrimage
Alec Motyer

The Message of Leviticus
Free to be holy
Derek Tidball

The Message of Numbers
Journey to the promised land
Raymond Brown

The Message of Deuteronomy
Not by bread alone
Raymond Brown

The Message of Judges
Grace abounding
Michael Wilcock

The Message of Ruth
The wings of refuge
David Atkinson

The Message of Samuel
Personalities, potential, politics and power
Mary Evans

The Message of Kings
God is present
John W. Olley

The Message of Chronicles
One church, one faith, one Lord
Michael Wilcock

The Message of Ezra and Haggai
Building for God
Robert Fyall

The Message of Nehemiah
God's servant in a time of change
Raymond Brown

The Message of Esther
God present but unseen
David G. Firth

The Message of Job
Suffering and grace
David Atkinson

The Message of Psalms 1 – 72
Songs for the people of God
Michael Wilcock

The Message of Psalms 73 – 150
Songs for the people of God
Michael Wilcock

The Message of Proverbs
Wisdom for life
David Atkinson

The Message of Ecclesiastes
A time to mourn, and a time to dance
Derek Kidner

The Message of the Song of Songs
The lyrics of love
Tom Gledhill

The Message of Isaiah
On eagles' wings
Barry Webb

The Message of Jeremiah
Grace in the end
Christopher J. H. Wright

The Message of Ezekiel
A new heart and a new spirit
Christopher J. H. Wright

The Message of Daniel
His kingdom cannot fail
Dale Ralph Davis

The Message of Hosea
Love to the loveless
Derek Kidner

The Message of Joel, Micah and Habakkuk
Listening to the voice of God
David Prior

The Message of Amos
The day of the lion
Alec Motyer

The Message of Obadiah, Nahum and Zephaniah
The kindness and severity of God
Gordon Bridger

The Message of Jonah
Presence in the storm
Rosemary Nixon

The Message of Zechariah
Your kingdom come
Barry Webb

The Message of Malachi
'I have loved you,' says the Lord
Peter Adam

The Bible Speaks Today: New Testament series

The Message of the Sermon on the Mount (Matthew5– 7)
Christian counter-culture
John Stott

The Message of Matthew
The kingdom of heaven
Michael Green

The Message of Mark
The mystery of faith
Donald English

The Message of Luke
The Saviour of the world
Michael Wilcock

The Message of John
Here is your King!
Bruce Milne

The Message of Acts
To the ends of the earth
John Stott

The Message of Romans
God's good news for the world
John Stott

The Message of 1 Corinthians
Life in the local church
David Prior

The Message of 2 Corinthians
Power in weakness
Paul Barnett

The Message of Galatians
Only one way
John Stott

The Message of Ephesians
God's new society
John Stott

The Message of Philippians
Jesus our Joy
Alec Motyer

The Message of Colossians and Philemon
Fullness and freedom
Dick Lucas

The Message of Thessalonians
Preparing for the coming King
John Stott

The Message of 1 Timothy and Titus
The life of the local church
John Stott

The Message of 2 Timothy
Guard the gospel
John Stott

The Message of Hebrews
Christ above all
Raymond Brown

The Message of James
The tests of faith
Alec Motyer

The Message of 1 Peter
The way of the cross
Edmund Clowney

The Message of 2 Peter and Jude
The promise of his coming
Dick Lucas and Christopher Green

The Message of John's Letters
Living in the love of God
David Jackman

The Message of Revelation
I saw heaven opened
Michael Wilcock

The Bible Speaks Today: Bible Themes series

The Message of the Living God
His glory, his people, his world
Peter Lewis

The Message of the Resurrection
Christ is risen!
Paul Beasley-Murray

The Message of the Cross
Wisdom unsearchable, love indestructible
Derek Tidball

The Message of Salvation
By God's grace, for God's glory
Philip Graham Ryken

The Message of Creation
Encountering the Lord of the universe
David Wilkinson

The Message of Heaven and Hell
Grace and destiny
Bruce Milne

The Message of Mission
The glory of Christ in all time and space
Howard Peskett and Vinoth Ramachandra

The Message of Prayer
Approaching the throne of grace
Tim Chester

The Message of the Trinity
Life in God
Brian Edgar

The Message of Evil and Suffering
Light into darkness
Peter Hicks

The Message of the Holy Spirit
The Spirit of encounter
Keith Warrington

The Message of Holiness
Restoring God's masterpiece
Derek Tidball

The Message of Sonship
At home in God's household
Trevor Burke

The Message of the Word of God
The glory of God made known
Tim Meadowcroft

The Message of Women
Creation, grace and gender
Derek and Dianne Tidball

The Message of the Church
Assemble the people before me
Chris Green

The Message of the Person of Christ
The Word made flesh
Robert Letham